Oskar Maria Graf

We Are Prisoners

A Confession

Translated from the German and
introduced by Ed Walker

Originally published as

Wir sind Gefangene

Copyright 1927

Drei Masken Verlag, Munich

First English translation published 1928 by

Alfred A. Knopf Limited, New York as

Prisoners All

Translated from the German by

MARGARET GREEN

This edition published 2020 by
RedLines Press
redlinesblog.com

© Ed Walker

ISBN: 9781077383449

*The cover features Georg Schrimpf's
celebrated portrait of the author.*

CONTENTS

Oskar Maria Graf:
The Anarchist in Lederhosen

In the autumn of 1989, the last year of a divided Germany, I convinced my reluctant girlfriend to go with me on a walking holiday in Bavaria. We were to walk the King Ludwig's Way from Lake Starnberg to the Royal Castles of Neuschwanstein and Hohenschwangau. Before leaving the next morning on the main route via the Andechs brewery to Diessen in the company of a group of boozy old age pensioners from the Upper Rhineland, the evening prelude was a short outing to the village of Berg, a few miles along the shores of the lake via Kempfenhausen, and specifically, to the spot where King Ludwig II drowned in 1886.

It had been a sunny day. As we set out, the wind got up and the clatter of rigging in the many pleasure-yachts announced the imminent end of summer. At Berg, a beautiful autumnal light lit up the lake and the first spots of rain fell; we hurried back to our hotel in Starnberg and dined on white sausage, pretzels and wheat beer. It did not stop raining for the next four days. We struggled to keep up with the pensioners, sustained by the sound of Wagner's overtures on a Sony Walkman and the sight of rococo church architecture during the day, and pork knuckles or gamey meat and dumplings, washed down with lots more beer, in the evening. It was only on the last morning that we woke to the sound of cowbells and sunshine, revealing the steep, lush meadows of the foothills and the snow-capped peaks of the Alps. It was a magical moment that will live with me forever.

You will find virtually none of this in *We Are Prisoners*. The Bavaria of the travel guides and the souvenir shops is entirely absent.

Many years later I read a review of Oskar Maria Graf's work in a now defunct Trotskyist magazine, *Linksruck*. It mentioned that he was born in Berg, and on that basis, I went out and bought the book. I tried to get an English translation. But no bookseller in London had heard of the book or the author. So I persevered with the original, fascinated by Graf's story and his struggles through life, even though my German was not really up to the task. But who was this Oskar Maria Graf? And why does he remain virtually unknown in the English-speaking world? "I came into literature out of the bakehouse," he told the Soviet writer Sergei Tretyakov. On his business cards Graf called himself a "provincial writer" and a "specialist in rural affairs".

This was Graf's self-deprecating humour, but also an ironic response to the association of his regional *heimat* literature with the ideology of the National Socialist movement. He was certainly more than a provincial poet; Bertolt Brecht said he was one of the best writers to be chased out of Germany. A recent biography explicitly refutes the idea that he was, as some would claim, a Bavarian poet laureate, arguing that he was, in fact, a cosmopolitan rebel.[1]

A family group portrait circa 1902: Graf's mother and, from left to right: Maurus, Anna (Nanndl), Oskar (seated), Lorenz and Emma. Missing are Max and Theres (Resl).

[1] *Oskar Maria Graf: Rebellischer Weltbürger, kein Bayerischer Nationaldichter*, Ulrich Dittmann & Waldemar Fromm; Verlag Friedrich Puste, Regensburg

There is plenty of evidence of this in the text of *We Are Prisoners*; for example, he was sufficiently acute to turn down the offer of a job as editor of a magazine whose proprietors wanted to promote a provincial southern prejudice against northern Germany.

But his greatness lies precisely in the fact that his style is earthy; it is effortless, the voice of ordinary people. It is not "literary" in any bookish or pretentious sense of the word. Graf rarely chooses a long or unfamiliar word where a shorter or simpler one will do. His work, whether autobiographical or fictional, connects with the everyday concerns of ordinary people, whether they be honest, sturdy peasants or unreliable city bohemians forever cadging the money needed for the next round of drinks. The author is rooted in Bavarian soil, but he speaks universal truths from the perspective of the downtrodden.

For this reason, I prefer to categorize Graf as not simply a rebel, but a *proletarian* writer and would set his work alongside the greats of the English language in this tradition such as Robert Tressell, Upton Sinclair and Alan Sillitoe, as well as the German-born B. Traven.

Virtually everyone we meet in *We Are Prisoners* who arouses our sympathy, whether it is a soldier, a seamstress, a factory worker, a mental patient or even a cheap confidence trickster, is just about managing to hold his head above water through hard grind, slyness, dishonesty or acts of foolish desperation. Any of them could easily go under at any time. The characters who repel us are in positions of unmerited authority or wealth: army officers, capitalists, landladies, moralists.

There are chapters and long passages describing the humiliating and degrading nature of work ("noble gift of heaven" as Graf ironically calls it) in a flour mill, bakeries, factories and in the army. Graf hates his capitalist employers, but he reserves his greatest contempt for the grovelling toadies who refuse to stand up for themselves. Echoes of Tressell here, though Graf writes with a lighter touch.

The proletarian nature of *We Are Prisoners* also expresses itself in Graf's attitude towards well-meaning but patronizing members of the upper classes, as in his encounter with a gentleman who does charity work for the Red Cross, and has no idea what it is like to work long hours in unpleasant conditions: "I looked at him with that concealed contempt that a worker always feels when someone quizzes him about things of which he knows nothing … I said: 'Yes, of course, quite right, yes,' though secretly I was thinking: it's easy for you talk. You live off the fat of the land and lecture people who have to do hard work on empty stomachs about how fine it is to slave for others."

Graf is even more judgmental in his attitude towards the gentleman's lady wife who, despite having money, ostentatiously dresses down in a manner that we would today refer to as virtue-signalling: "She was tall and scraggy and wore a washed-out reform dress. Everything about her, from her plaited hair to her shabby sandals, had something embarrassingly neat and frugal about it. From the moment I first saw her, I took an instant dislike to her elderly, skinny face, which seemed Protestant, somehow."

Here, Graf's communistic proletarian outlook merges with the Bavarian Catholic's inbred suspicion of the protestant virtues of thrift, work ethic and self-denial.

Later in the book, as Graf enjoys his first literary successes and is welcomed into high society – and in particular, the circle of acquaintances around the rich Dutchman – his outlook is compromised (today, we would probably say he becomes "conflicted" but it is in any case the classic dilemma for the working-class intellectual who is feted by the rich). "A man must show gratitude for such abundant hospitality," Graf writes, as he is wined and dined by his rich friend, having just told him that the revolution will lead to the expropriation of his private wealth.

Yet he soon grows weary and irritated by easy living: "My God, my God, how infantile, how boring, how stupid wealth makes people, I kept thinking."

Graf grew up working in the family bakery, where, after the death of his father, he was bullied, beaten and exploited by his brother Max. So long as his father lived, and for a short time afterwards, the Graf family worked hard but enjoyed relative comfort and a harmonious existence, with several businesses doing well. But it was a large family that could not support several young adults; a series of disasters reduced them to poverty and wage labour. That is to say, they were proletarianized.

It is hardly surprising, therefore, that Graf fled to Munich at the first opportunity, and that he was so easily influenced by the city's anarchist and socialist thinkers, including Erich Mühsam and other members of the group *Tat* (Action). In particular, he met Franz Jung, Georg Schrimpf (Schorsch) and Richard Oehring, who became his closest friends and political collaborators. Nonetheless, Graf remained only on the edge of the militant group. Mühsam himself mentioned Graf just once in his diary, on 27 August 1912 when, it seems, Graf had pestered him to help with his "dilettantish poetic efforts".

Graf also soon rejected what we would today call the "alternative lifestyle" of the anarchist communes of Monte Verità and Locarno in Ticino as madness and filth with their obsessive vegetarianism, teetotal morality and wacky utopian projects (Monte Verità later comes to Munich in the form of the hippy prophet Gusto Gräser). It is the same tension that I recall from the anarchist scene in the late 1970s, between anarcho-punks and anarcho-hippies and which doubtless persists in some form today.

At any rate, already, at this early stage in the book, Graf raises themes that are familiar and unresolved today, finding expression, for example, in radical green movements. "We wanted to live," Graf wrote, "and it seemed to us, they just wanted to scheme."

The Pickelhaube *has never looked less menacing.*

Shortly before he died, Graf wrote that he hoped his autobiography had something to say to the youth of today. Indeed it does. In fact, I recognize much of my own youth in this book, which is one of the reasons why I wanted to see it once again in English and determined to translate it. Another is that it paints a picture of a lost Germany that will come as a surprise to many English-speaking readers. But most of all, I find it hard to think of any other book has made me laugh and cry quite so much as *Wir sind Gefangene*.

A proletarian odyssey

What are we to make of the title? If we are indeed prisoners, who or what is imprisoning us? Graf's first answer is that it is money – capitalism – that keeps us in shackles:

> Money, that was always the Alpha and the Omega, wherever you turned. Money was fortune and misfortune. As time went on, for me, money had really become like a demon that controlled my life. It was all nonsense, what the poets and philosophers talked about morality, ethics, strength of character, idealism and God knows

what other fine qualities. In the final analysis, these qualities were subordinate to money: money created them or annihilated them at will. Mankind had invented something to which he must, sooner or later, submit, without further resistance, body and soul. If he had no money, he was a nobody; if he possessed it or earned a good income, it was easy for him to be virtuous and humane.

There is an instinctive materialism in Graf's writing, entirely rooted in experience and love of life rather than political theory; it is a resentment of everything that is unjust and unfair in the world, expressed most poignantly in the "sullen rebelliousness" that he feels following the death of his sister from the terrible illness of tuberculosis, which killed millions of poor and working-class people even in relatively affluent countries like Germany, and which today is making a return.

But if it is money that imprisons us, *work* – the compulsion of wage labour – that is our gaoler. According to Graf, there is absolutely no dignity in the drudgery of the daily slog, and above all none in back-breaking physical labour. Capitalists and their allies in politics and the media worship "hard work" and "hardworking families" today more than ever, 100 years after Graf wrote *We Are Prisoners*. Only creative work, Graf felt, has dignity. Graf was at one with Karl Marx's son-in-law, Paul Lafargue, who wrote in his essay "The Right to Be Lazy" that laziness, along with creativity, is a motor of human progress. This too is a recurring theme in truly proletarian literature in complete contrast with the hypocritical workerist literature of every bogus "communist" state.

And yet, much as we might rebel against the oppression of capitalism and wage labour, this will only intensify our alienation if we act alone.

"At least I was not in solitary" – here, towards the end of the book is the first pointer to the true meaning of imprisonment. For (and here comes my spoiler alert), it suddenly becomes clear that Graf's story is not simply a random sequence of picaresque episodes dealing with the adventures of a rough and dishonest but appealing hero, but rather, as the critic Walter Jens wrote, "it follows a very exactly constructed composition-schema: it presents the attempt of a man to be entirely himself – an attempt which therefore leads the protagonist constantly into new ghettos, because he does not see through to the true reasons for his imprisonment and sees individual failure (or success) in what, in reality, is socially determined."

The path out of imprisonment to freedom is therefore not through acts of individual defiance; and in the course of his odyssey, Graf tries out most if not all of them – but collective action. Only solidarity with your fellow sufferers can break you out of your personal ghetto and destroy your individual demons – "the master, my landlady, hypocrisy, toadying, cant, suspicion of everybody, and calculating what was to my own best advantage, it was all the same."

Graf's worldview

A passage in *We Are Prisoners* that seems to present Graf's personal (rather than political) outlook, the view that would inform his later short stories and novels about life in rural Bavaria, is the following:

> As far as my father was concerned, anyone who occupied an official position counted more or less as a bogus layabout, who pursues a fraudulent existence at the expense of the local community or the nation by means that are beyond the reach of the law. Nothing disgusted him more than to occupy a post of honour that commands public respect; and yet, he not only valued popularity very highly, but also sought it. He was not in the least bit curmudgeonly. Nor was he spiteful, quarrelsome or malevolent. Above all, he loved cheerful, loud and completely uninhibited sociability; he could entertain and be truly charming. But whenever he encountered any official, his cheerful disposition immediately vanished. If there were any opportunity to play a trick on anyone, he was up for it. He even looked for opportunities himself, and I know of cases in which he gave us young ones and the parish labourer, Schmalzer a whole mark, or paid for the journeyman's beer, if we had got up to some mischief. He took a fiendish pleasure whenever we pulled off some prank.

When I first read this passage, I found it very English; in fact, it seemed as though Graf was in some ways describing my own grandfather, who applied the lethal knowledge he acquired as a member of the Home Guard – making bombs capable of blowing the tracks off a tank from weed-killer and sugar – for the fiendish pleasure of disrupting everyday life that would be quite unthinkable today; *épater le bourgeois*.

"Let's make a bomb," he would say to me if life got too boring. And so we did, along with a lot of other mischief-making.

It is through this lens that I understand and recognize Oskar Maria Graf's view of the world as expressed in his later writing. In their study, *Heimat – A German Dream*, two critics of German literature categorize Graf as a "critical *heimat* writer"; on the surface, there is a strong emotional attachment to his homeland, which is very narrowly defined – no more than a village.[2] It is an attachment that is highly resistant to any criticism from

---

[2] Elizabeth Boa and Rachel Palfreyman, *Heimat – A German Dream:* Regional Loyalties and National Identity in German Culture 1890-1990, (Oxford Studies in Modern European Culture), 2000.

outside; but scratch the surface and you soon uncover the social tensions and animosities that lie beneath. In *We Are Prisoners,* when Graf delivers his daughter to the care of his family, he expresses his fondness for the rural outpost ("life carries on as ever: the farmer ploughs, the corn grows, winter comes and then summer, people are born and die, everything is beautiful and peaceful") but as soon as he reflects further, he is utterly bored by it. Lake Starnberg is reassuringly familiar, but also appears "old and ugly".

Graf has been infected by the cosmopolitan life of Munich and Berlin; therefore, being an authentic and honest writer, he can only view his *heimat* in critical terms. His rural patriotism is the antithesis of both the Nazi interpretation of *heimat,* which sought to weld the various German regions to the extended family of the entire *Volk* and thus the Third Reich, and the escapist *heimat* literature and films of the 1950s, which sought to portray a rural idyll in which the "natural order" had remained entirely undisturbed by the traumatic events of the recent past.

Graf also has the proletarian's instinctive hatred of the police: a police detective is the worker's class enemy, and all is fair in the class war: lying, deceit, dissembling. This is made abundantly clear in the chapter, "The Interrogation"; it is not merely the rebelliousness of a callow youth, or the theoretical anti-authoritarianism of the anarchist, because Graf's encounter with the forces of law and order prompts a childhood memory of what his mother had once said about a well-dressed aristocrat and his mistress: they are no better than us, when they have no clothes on, they are naked like everyone else.

Despite attending meetings of the Independent Socialists, the USPD, right up to the outbreak of the November revolution Graf entertained anarchist-pacifist ideas about passive resistance. Even after the October revolution in Russia, he is still saying, "now that everything is in motion, we have to spread rumours, the wildest rumours ... The masses be roused, so much that even the stupidest philistine becomes completely sceptical ... Then comes absolute passivity ... That's all that matters! ... Don't rise up against the war, simply refuse to support it, that's all." In fact it was precisely only when the High Seas fleet mutinied, and armed soldiers' and workers' councils were established, that the military leadership realized the game was up; the "majority" still supported the "war effort".

Graf is sometimes positioned as a "democrat" for his later opposition to the Nazi dictatorship. But this is based on the assumption that dictatorship and democracy are necessarily and by nature opposites. The word democracy does not appear in the 350-odd pages of *We Are Prisoners* except in the context of a condemnation of German social democracy's betrayal of the working class in its support for the war. The word "democratic" only appears in order to poke fun at Schorsch's naive belief that people are freer in democratic Switzerland than in Imperial Germany.

Later, Graf's biographer Gerhard Bauer wrote, "Graf would only allow himself to be presented as a 'democrat' if the meaning of the word had been stripped of everything normative". By which is meant, the norms of compromise and opportunism within bourgeois democracy, the focus on formal and legal human and citizens' rights.[3] He thus opposed the idea of a popular front based on an attempt to align the irreconcilable interests of opposing classes. Fascism and war could only be overcome by ruthlessly uncovering the material needs felt by the masses, and the consequent psychological injuries, and unleashing their ferocity and aggression against the prevailing order. It was in this sense only that he sought a common working-class front to resist the Nazis.

There is a similar need to confront the banal binary opposition between pacifism and militarism. Graf is often described as a pacifist, because he opposed the war, and found militarism to be an absurdity, and because violence repelled him. Yet he clearly struggled to reconcile pacifism (in the commonly accepted meaning of the word, i.e. someone who abjures all violence) with the dilemma, how can a revolution possibly succeed without armed struggle; at many points in the book he expresses support not merely for passive resistance but for insurrection.

Graf writes that in the weeks of revolutionary upheaval, he felt as though he was shut up in a barrel, being flung this way and that. He struggled to arrive at a programmatic position on how to achieve a communist, post-capitalist society. He was still in the grip of Stirnerite individualism and Tolstoian asceticism (despite his own boozy lifestyle). Graf admits, following the farce of his public meeting to declare the "League of Free Peoples" that his politics were still immature at those critical moments in German history. Caught between personal ambition and a desire for change, he flitted from one obsession to another, relapsing into a kind of classless, humanitarian, educationalist, pacifist mush ("we need the right quality of individual etc.") at one moment and wanting to murder all newspaper publishers the next.

Although Graf moved away from individualist anarchism, in common with German left-communists in the tradition of Rosa Luxemburg (and later, the KAPD) and in complete contrast to the Stalinists who would lead the mainstream Communist Party of Germany, he believed that communism could only succeed if driven from below, by the anonymous masses. When he experiences their struggle and the agony of their defeat, he writes: *I finally knew where I belonged, and with whom.*

---

[3] Bauer, Gerhard: *Gefangenschaft und Lebenslust. Oskar Maria Graf in seiner Zeit.* Munich, 1987.

The Bavarian Soviet Republic

The fate of the Bavarian Soviet Republic provides the climax and resolution of Graf's personal story.[4]

"The Bavarian Soviet Republic," wrote Paul Frölich, "began as a farce. It ended as a tragedy. But despite that it has historical significance." When news spread that the sailors had mutinied in Kiel, hundreds of German sailors based in Austria – now in revolutionary turmoil – set off homewards and stopped off in Munich. The writer and journalist Kurt Eisner, now head of the Independent Social Democratic Party (USPD) in Bavaria, seized power when the city was gripped by strikes and demonstrations. The Majority Social Democrats had no choice but to throw in their lot with him – for the time being.

Eisner's regime was something of an anomaly in conservative Bavaria. It owed its position to the presence of a strong working class based in Munich and tens of thousands of demobilized soldiers, but also to the division between separatists and centralists in the Bavarian middle classes.

Despite its declarations in favour of workers' councils, the Eisner government organized democratic elections in which all classes participated, but which the KPD – the newly founded Communist Party of Germany – and the Revolutionary Workers' Council boycotted. On 12 January, the USPD only obtained 2.5% of the vote in these elections – probably a record low for a governing party anywhere.

After a few weeks of conflict between the newly elected assembly and the USPD-led executive, Eisner decided to submit his letter of resignation to the "people's representatives". As he was entering the assembly, however, he was assassinated by Count Arco.

In response, the central committee of the Bavarian workers' councils proclaimed a general strike and the assembly spontaneously dispersed. Eisner's funeral was the occasion for a massive demonstration. The councils implemented some dictatorial measures: they arrested 50 reactionary hostages, shut down the bourgeois press, and tried to arm the proletariat. But they promptly handed over power to the assembly, which elected an SPD-USPD government, presided over by Hoffmann (SPD).

Whereas in other regions, the *Freikorps* intervened to restore the powers seized by the councils from the local assemblies, in Bavaria the councils themselves saved them the trouble, voluntarily surrendering their power at this stage. Nevertheless, the new government was largely powerless to act, as Hoffmann himself later explained: "As I took over government on 17 March there was organized against [us] an army of 30,000 un-

---

[4] A fuller account of the Bavarian Soviet Republic can be found in *The Lost Revolution, Germany 1918 to 1923* by Chris Harman.

employed."

The Communist Leviné, recently arrived from Berlin, made a speech at a meeting organized to discuss the formation of a Council Republic by the right-wing Minister of War Schneppenhorst. He said, "A soviet republic cannot be proclaimed at a conference table. It is founded after a struggle by a victorious proletariat. The proletariat of Munich has not yet entered the struggle for power. After the first intoxication the Social Democrats will seize upon the first pretext to withdraw and thus deliberately betray the workers." In response, Schneppenhorst angrily screamed: "Punch the Jew on the nose!"

It was Gustav Landauer who then proposed, on 6-7 April, the creation of a "Soviet Republic". One part of the Bavarian government, composed of the enlightened members of the USPD, the anarchists, and even some SPD members, pompously decreed this Republic under the influence of Russia, Hungary and above all of the power of the Bavarian councils. The Communists, led by Leviné and Frölich, did not join the government of the new republic.

This "Pseudo-Soviet Republic" led by Landauer, Ernst Toller and Erich Mühsam lasted for six days of raucous and at times ridiculous confusion as well as weakness.[5] The Commissar for Foreign Affairs, Dr. Franz Lipp, famously informed Lenin and the Pope by cable that the ousted former Minister-President Hoffmann had taken the key to the ministry toilet with him, and declared war on Württemberg and Switzerland because they had not lent him 60 locomotives.

Hoffmann now formed a new government in Bamberg, a quiet city in Franconia, and began planning his next steps. He had little trouble destabilizing the Pseudo-Soviet Republic. He rallied various cities to his cause, and the peasants refused to supply the city of Munich.

The story of the short-lived Pseudo-Soviet Republic was recently recounted in *Dreamers: When the Writers Took Power, Germany 1918*, by Volker Weidermann, which draws heavily on Graf's eye-witness accounts in *We Are Prisoners*, though without the context of Graf's spiritual odyssey.[6] It received much praise in the bourgeois press: *The Telegraph, The Spectator,* even *Tatler*.

On reading this I thought it was time to reclaim OMG "for the benefit of those to whom he belongs". The German revolution was not just about "dreamers" and certainly not just about "writers".

---

[5] As attested by Graf's experience as a "censor" at the Catholic and ultra-reactionary *Bayrische Kurier*.

[6] Published in English by Pushkin Press, 2018.

Graf was highly sceptical about the intellectuals and artists of the Revolutionary Artists Council who had assumed leadership of the events in Munich. "What has all this to do with the workers?" he frequently asked the other members, and reflected: "I was one of the millions who only take action when their own interests are at stake, who struggle when they are forced to defend those interests, and who only intervene when they feel that there is a tangible meaning behind the cause, in line with their desires." The gulf between the self-appointed intellectual leadership of the revolution and the interests and motivations of the working class led him to have doubts not only in the possibility that the revolutionary movement might succeed, but also in the movement itself. Hardly surprising that he sought consolation in his drinking bouts with rich friends in Nymphenburg. But all that was to change.

The Communist Party of Germany seized control of the Bavarian Soviet Republic and replaced Ernst Toller as its head of state with Eugen Leviné on 12 April. When it came the next day, Palm Sunday, the initial reactionary assault was annihilated with a battle at the railway station lasting hours. Factory delegates created a committee led by the KPD. They proclaimed a ten-day general strike, paid for by the factory owners in order to allow the workers to prepare for combat. The Red Army, organized by Rudolf Egelhofer but barely trained, held a massive parade. Factory councils were elected. The revolutionaries took complete possession of the central railway station and other key points in the city. There remained a major challenge: Munich was isolated. The countryside and the other towns and cities of Bavaria remained hostile and starved Munich of supplies; the bourgeois and Social Democratic press portrayed the city as being subjected to a red terror.

Despite its initial military successes such as the defence of the railway station, this genuine Soviet Republic was militarily crushed during the first days of May, as described in this book. Future Nazis played their parts in the White Army: Himmler, Rudolf Hess, and Von Epp.

So, a tragedy, the full implications of which would be revealed after 1933. But Paul Frölich defended the actions of the Communist Party on the basis that there was no turning back after the defeat of the Palm Sunday putsch. It was all or nothing.

A "fine revolutionary hero"

In *We Are Prisoners* we see a young man who is struggling to reach a mature world view. Graf describes his journey with buttock-clenchingly painful honesty. There is a constant dialectic between the rooted country boy, the urban proletarian factory worker and the bohemian with literary pretensions and a half-baked left-wing philosophy that turns this way and the other.

Consequently Graf attracted criticism from the orthodox left, as was the case when a Russian foundry worker responded to a review of *We Are Prisoners* in the magazine *Linkskurve* in 1930. [7] "Odd [literary] criticism you have, when a book such as *Wir sind Gefangene* is termed left-wing. A fine revolutionary hero! One who goes boozing *sekt* with his sweetheart while letting others struggle on his behalf."

Graf was unapologetic in his response. He said that he did not write to please critics and intellectuals or even fellow writers but for his class comrades. He went on:

"So – you are completely right, my dear Russian comrade, I was indeed a 'fine revolutionary' and I did go boozing *sekt* and visiting whores while others were in struggle. On the other hand, I never claimed in my book that I was a soldier of the revolution. I was an indecisive, slightly rebellious, mindless bohemian type, no more. A quite indisputably bourgeois phenomenon, therefore. And I have presented myself in that way according to the best of my knowledge and conscience: 1) because all so-called literature disgusted me, 2) because I found it basically mendacious, and finally 3) because it was important for me to show, by my example, truthfully and ruthlessly the type of person on which the German revolution pinned its hopes, and into which category most comrades still fall today."

Graf concludes: "You, dear foundry worker, labour for the benefit of your class. Do you really believe that a man who wrote *We Are Prisoners* writes books out of vanity, or to produce something beautiful for a better class of people? No, he also writes books *for the benefit of those to whom he belongs.*"

Indeed, *We Are Prisoners* is not only full of self-deprecating humour, but also, here and there, self-disgust. Graf is not setting himself above anyone; rather he is saying, like Brecht's heroine Nanna: *Schliesslich bin ich auch ein Mensch.* He addresses profound political questions, such as the nature of revolutionary power, but he does so as an artist, not as a politician. That is to say, he poses the questions, but he can only hint at the answers.

The episode with the play, *The Dictator* illustrates how difficult it is to write political fiction or drama without making yourself utterly ridiculous. However much an author might want to be a soldier of the revolution, his words must spring from an authentic imperative. Authenticity, clarity and charm finally come together as the book reaches its climax, not

---

[7] *Linkskurve*, 1930, Vol. 1, page 36. *Linkskurve* was the publication of the *Bund proletarisch-revolutionärer Schrfitsteller* (BPRS) – the federation of proletarian-revolutionary writers, which was closely aligned with the Communist Party of Germany.

least in Graf's letter to "the girl" in Berlin; for, in the end, this is the story of a young man finding the love of his life amid momentous events. And, at the same time, given what we now know, it is even more prophetically sad and deeply depressing: *"the NCOs cannot be eradicated in Germany. They want order, and they will emerge victorious"*.

Dictatorship and exile

From 1920 Graf worked as a dramaturg (literary advisor) to the proletarian theatre, *Die neue Bühne* (The New Stage), until he achieved literary fame in 1927 with *We Are Prisoners*, allowing him to live as a freelance writer. Graf established a reputation as a "provincial novelist" and a "poet of the peasantry". Misunderstanding this as reflecting their *völkisch* ideology, the Nazis tried to recruit Graf to their cause. They saw what they wanted to see, the depiction of life in rural Bavaria, oriented as it was towards public tastes, while (being utter philistines) missing the irony and parody. In fact, though some of his characters may be dressed up in Bavarian *Tracht*, Graf dealt with universal themes such as passion, love, deceit and economic success and ruin, The Brechtian principle, *Das Volk ist nicht (volks-)tümlich* ("folk are not folksy") applies to Graf more than anyone.

Along with 400,000 other "un-Germans", many of them intellectuals, and 2,000 or so active in the arts in some way, Graf left Germany shortly after the Nazi seizure of power. His *Verbrennt mich!* (Burn me!) protest in the Viennese *Arbeiter-Zeitung*, published in 1933, demanding that his books be burned alongside others, gained worldwide attention. He wrote:

> The Third Reich banished almost all German literature of significance and disavowed all genuine German writings. It has driven the majority of our best writers into exile and made it impossible for their works to be published in Germany. The ignorance of a few, arrogant, opportunist scribes and the unrestrained vandalism of the present dictators are trying to stamp out everything of international stature in our literature and art, and to replace the concept of "German" with a narrow-minded nationalism.

In its obituary, *The New York Times* wrote that "He was one of the earliest and most outspoken opponents of the Nazis." But he was an opponent of militarism, nationalism and philistinism long before they found their ultimate expression in the Hitler regime.

Graf moved first to Austria and subsequently to Prague, where he became one of the editors of *Neue Deutsche Blätter*. He was deprived of German citizenship, along with Albert Einstein and others, in March 1934.

Oskar Maria Graf was one of the German authors who immediately grasped the appeal of National Socialism to the "apolitical" petty-bourgeoisie, the (non-Jewish) lower middle classes caught in the great clash between the bourgeoisie and the proletariat – shopkeepers and other small businessmen, the teachers, professors, students and petty officials *(Beamte)* who enjoyed special privileges not available to the workers.

These layers of society had seen their savings wiped out in the great inflation of 1923 and had been devastated by the economic crisis following the Wall Street Crash; they provided ready recruits to the SA and the Nazi Party.

The real danger sprang, in Graf's interpretation, not from the minority of ideologically motivated fanatics of the NSDAP, however, but the vast swathes of the population who passively supported the Nazis to defend their economic interests and privileges. A large part of this project, of course, was the elimination of Germany's Jews, who were perceived as a source of unwelcome competition for careers in the professions, markets and social status.

Graf's novels *Bolwieser* (1929) and, in particular, *Anton Sittinger* (1938, never yet translated into English) view the world from the "non-ideological" perspective of the petty bourgeoisie. At no point is the Post Office Inspector Anton Sittinger actively *in favour of* the NSDAP or Hitler's terror, he just longs for a peaceful existence, the return to order and prosperity, i.e. an end to the class struggle. Though he is fond of quoting "difficult philosophers" he is at heart a reactionary. His drinking pals all blame communists, Jews and the French for their personal problems. This is satire making a deadly serious point: "The Sittingers are the improbable philistines of whom twenty millions make up that class of the German population, to which we owe the Führer and his government", wrote a contemporary reviewer.[8]

In *Der Abgrund* (The Abyss, 1936), Graf had already observed a similar mentality in functionaries of the German SPD who are decent and honourable men, "but are essentially workers who have lost sight of their proletarian roots, and have settled for petty bourgeois comfort, reliance on the strength of the party machine, and of the reformist process, instead of preparing to fight the real menace which National Socialism represents."[9] Germany's "socialist" party had definitively ceased to be a party *for* the working class after it voted for War Credits on 4 August 1914; this betrayal of proletarian youth is a theme of *We Are Prisoners*.

---

[8] Balder Olden, *Die Neue Weltbühne* No. 18 (1938), pp 554-8 quoted in Ernst Loewy, *Exil – Literarische und politische Texte aus dem deutschen Exil* 1933-49 (Stuttgart, 1979) p. 65.

[9] Quoted from J.M. Ritchie, *German Literature under National Socialism*, Barnes & Noble Books (New Jersey, 1983).

The New York Stammtisch

In 1938, Graf left Europe via the Netherlands, arriving in New York City in July. "I never felt like an immigrant," he said. "Because I am a German writer and the German language is my *heimat*." But more than that, even in New York he wore his *heimat*. Literally. In 1958 he admitted, "My appearance in *lederhosen* quickly made me popular everywhere, and that is tremendously advantageous for doing business."

He finished one of his most famous works, *Das Leben meiner Mutter* (My Mother's Life) in exile in New York. With help from Thomas Mann, he had it published in English in 1940. But Graf was short of money. His beloved second wife Mirjam, a cousin of writer Nelly Sachs, covered living expenses. She worked as editorial secretary and journalist with the newspaper for German émigrés, *Der Aufbau*.

Graf said of himself, "In the bars groups of regulars, always formed around me at once." So from 1943 Graf found a new and important vocation in life, as founder of the *stammtisch* in German Town, New York. A *stammtisch* is a very German institution. If you see a wooden sign bearing the legend *stammtisch* on a table in a pub or inn it is a very bad idea indeed to intrude upon it, because it is strictly reserved for the locals, the people who "belong". Graf gave it a more expansive definition. He got a friend to make him a wooden sign for his *stammtisch*, bearing the inscription: "We are in favour of everyone and everything." It became a fixed institution in New York, though not physically, as it moved from one hostelry to another. Twelve years after Graf's death, the author Will Schwaber wrote in *Der Aufbau:* "A voice is missing. The voice that had dominated the table in the past, a voice that could laugh resoundingly, a voice could sing and thunder, that could tease and argue sharply and could make the most heartfelt declarations of sympathy. The voice of Oskar Maria Graf ... It was Schwabing in New York ... In the late hour, when the table was in a lively mood, it often experienced a special treat ... The 'other' Graf came to the fore, the tender, yearning, and infinitely humane man, who was even stronger than the Bacchant that many saw in him."

You can discover more about OMG from the Oskar Maria Graf Gesellschaft, www.oskarmariagraf.de

A note on this translation

Although this is a new translation, I have relied heavily on Margaret Green's 1928 text to check meanings and have used her own words where it made no sense to change them. Technically speaking it is a fine piece of work and without it, I know I would have made many more mistakes.

That said, I hear a rather different voice in Graf's writing. The language and tone of that first translation is, in my opinion, not entirely true to the original. Some of the robustness is lost. The word "tipsy", for instance, is not a sufficiently strong word to describe someone who is roaring drunk after a whole night on the piss. Elsewhere, the Green translation appears (perhaps unintentionally) unsympathetic to the author's perspective, which speaks the language of rebellion, and struggle, although without being in any way "earnest".

Some of the renderings in the Green translation are unintentionally comical, as when a member of the Workers' Council addresses Graf as "your servant", a mistranslation of the word "servus", which is a south German dialect word that simply means "hello" or "cheerio". Of course, it is easy to criticize; translators a century ago did not have access to the wealth of information that is now available electronically.

Although the narrative in *Wir sind Gefangene* is written in standard German, Graf sometimes uses words drawn from regional dialect. You need to reach for a specifically Bavarian dictionary now and again to look up words like *pimperlwichtig*. Moreover, Graf occasionally transliterates local accents in dialogue, which adds some colour to the book. None of this appears in the Green translation, which I thought was a shame. I have therefore, where I thought it appropriate, rendered accents into what I consider rough English equivalents, taking into account the fact that German regions are almost the reverse of English: received pronunciation is the language of the northwest, and the stronger regional dialects are in the south, while in the east, in particular Saxony you will find strong twangy accents. Therefore Swabian becomes Geordie and I have thrown a bit of Mancunian into the Munich dialogue. The Erzgebirge, a mining district, becomes south Yorkshire. The Berlin working class accent is, of course, the equivalent of London Cockney, and Swiss (and Alsatian) German is as foreign-sounding to the Germans as Glaswegian is to the English. On the other hand, the Viennese accent is nasal, so Brummie seems an appropriate equivalent.

Some of the words used in the original translation have an entirely different meaning today and are inappropriate. In general, while trying to avoid words that have only appeared or taken on new meanings in recent decades, I have endeavoured to make the language less old fashioned. This is, after all, a book dedicated to the follies and insights of youth.

Here and there I have added footnotes. They are designed to provide the background information that would have been self-evident to the contemporary German-speaking reader.

Ed Walker
Mannheim, December 2019

FOREWORD
by Oskar Maria Graf, on the first edition after 1945

This book, which now appears unchanged from the first edition published in 1927, was of fundamental significance for my entire literary existence. Up to that point, I had acquired only a certain amount of local popularity, which barely extended beyond the artistic quarter of Schwabing, through a slim volume of run-of-the-mill expressionist poems, some rough satirical peasant sketches in *Simplicissimus* and *Jugend*, and a booklet of earnest village tales, but chiefly through my wild bohemian life in Munich. What's more, I must confess quite frankly that at the time I considered my writing quite a questionable affair, an effortless occupation that consisted of nothing more than a lustful narrative talent, a great deal of vanity, a fair number of original ideas, and a very cheeky, ballsy heedlessness.

That changed entirely at a stroke with the appearance of *Wir sind Gefangene.* The book caused a tremendous sensation, was widely discussed in all circles, unanimously admired in the leading daily press and serious periodicals, and translations appeared in English, French, Spanish, and Russian in quick succession. Apart from the strongly supportive propaganda of the publisher, which had a poster with a larger-than-life-sized picture of me and the headline text "The author of the day – The book of the year" plastered on all the advertising columns in all of Germany's cities, the enthusiastic, in-depth opinions of such great minds as Romain Rolland, Maxim Gorky, Thomas and Heinrich Mann, Hugo von Hofmannsthal and other well-known authors of my generation first enabled this instant fame to have a far-reaching impact. With this, I was, so to speak, accepted into the canon of serious literature, and not only that! "In *We Are Prisoners*, the fierce scream of terror from a youth disenchanted by the war, the post-war and the failed revolution echoes for the first time and accuses us all!" says a long review by Theodor Lessing, who later emigrated to Czechoslovakia and was murdered there by Hitler agents, and I suddenly stood – unexpected and unintentionally – as the spokesman representing my young generation at the forefront of the social and intellectual conflicts of those turbulent years.

To tell the truth – and quite apart from the raging vanity that such an unexpectedly easy triumph produces – if, today, after more than thirty years, I remember my condition at the time, I must admit that all this unexpected success disturbed me immensely, yes, shocked me to the core, because in all my superficial existence, I had for a long time been engrossed with the works and teachings of my great teacher Tolstoy, and that had not failed to leave its mark on me. Now, all of a sudden, I began to think deeply about myself and my position on literature and always ended up with the oppressing question: "For what purpose, and for whom, does one write? Is the writer only there to achieve the highest level of mastery over language, to use sublime knowledge of psychology to make real-life situations of any kind understandable, and to fascinate his readership through the art of his narrative, or does his task as a writer consist far more in fighting against injustice in the world, wherever it appears, to make people receptive to and socially responsible for social and moral insights, to brand any war as a crime, and, at the risk of being misunderstood and suspected for a lifetime, always to speak out for a social order in which equal rights apply and in which the voluntary nature of participation in the whole finally becomes a moral rule?"

From then on it became clear to me that I could only be a writer in the latter sense of the word, a life-long so-called "engaged" writer whose talent was also an absolute human and social obligation. Certainly, I saw in everything of beauty, in all art something humane, but this humaneness only ever stirred and delighted, dissipated again and left no profound effect. It did not penetrate into the ambiguity of the human character, it did not destroy its inherited, thoughtlessly accepted ideas, it was unable to turn the cowardly, opinionless Joe Public into a person who could think and act for himself. Art was also rather like an "Opium for the People". It made the individual, and entire peoples, incapable of resisting the nonsensical and the evil in everyday life that we had to experience in the recent decades of horror. That could and should never again be the task of writers, artists, intellectuals! If they were to stick with their old ways, they would pile immeasurably more culpability on top of the gruesome complicity that they undeniably had in the past. And the worst of all: then all of their further work and effort would go, without any resonance, into blind nothingness and mean nothing other to subsequent generations than a curious "hobby" from grandfather's time.

But *Wir sind Gefangene* also had — as I now see it today — another quite different significance to the German public at the time, that went beyond me. The book was a forerunner for all the soon-to-appear, memorably powerful anti-war novels by Remarque, Renn, Plievier, A.M. Frey, and others, initiating an almost hectic increase in the production of similar works of all political directions, which — depending on the prevailing economic situation — became a highly lucrative business for many publishers.

But my book, written down with all the unquestioning, flickering subjectivity of a rebellious thirty-year-old, was very different from all these works that came later. *It was in no way just an anti-war protest book. It had, without my suspecting or wanting to do so, expanded, as it were in the course of its writing, into a comprehensive document of that most turbulent period from 1905 to the collapse of the 1918 German Revolution, and because one of the anonymous masses, who did not consider himself a superior prosecutor, alarmist or admonisher who positioned himself outside of his social environment, but remained within it and openly acknowledged: "I too am complicit! I too am responsible for the catastrophe!" – the youth of that time had found her unintended spokesman in this book.*

Thomas Mann was the first and only one to fully pick up the scent of *precisely this* in his review. Possibly for this reason *Wir sind Gefangene* won the hearts of my peers and contemporaries and gathered no antiquarian dust, because even today, countless letters from readers from all walks of life testify to how frankly and lucidly they find their own youth conjured up in this book, and the most peculiar thing is that since that time, not a few historians have used this subjective confession as an objective source-work on those far-off times. We therefore hope that this autobiography has something to say to the youth of today. Above all, because it shows that the youth of that time, despite all the disappointment and hopelessness it experienced, courageously acknowledged this as their era, and yet remained faithful to the future. That this future was not fulfilled as had been hoped was not the fault of this youth, which time and again staked its life in the bloody struggles for these goals. To repeat it once again: the emergence of a completely different, more terrible future was and remains largely the fault of those intellectuals who, as soon as politics necessarily descended into repugnant detail, immediately withdrew to produce flawless art.

New York, USA, Spring 1965
Oskar Maria Graf

PREFACE

The recollections that follow cover the period from the eleventh to the twenty-fifth years of my life, starting in 1905 and closing at the end of 1919. The text of the first part was concluded in April 1920, that of the second part was completed in the years 1924 to 1926.

Nothing in these pages was made up, embellished or written in support of a particular tendency.

Word followed word at the call of memory and subsequent reliving of the past. This book is intended to be nothing other than a human record of our time.

Munich, late June 1926
Oskar Maria Graf

Part One

EARLY YEARS

1.
A CHANGED LIFE

On that May afternoon, when the teacher suddenly came through the door, approached me and my sister Anna and told us we could go home because our father was very ill, I did not feel anything. On the street, we talked a little and made serious faces. Basically we were glad that we had the boring maths lesson behind us. We were good at learning and were happy to attend school, but I did not like maths. It never surprised you, it always ran in straight lines. It was a wonderfully sunny and vast day, the meadows around us were in lush greenery and flower-speckled, the apple trees bloomed to the left and right of the road.

At the edge of the village a farmer's wife met us and said, standing still: "Go home, your father is seriously ill. His number's up." We hurried on. At home it was kind of quiet. We entered the kitchen, which also served as a living room, and saw mother at the cooker, fiddling with bottles. She said, quite simply: "Go up and see your father," and broke into tears. We put down our satchels and went up. As we entered, we started to cry. We did not know why. I felt no pain, just a faint terror. There was a strong smell of medicine and sweat in the room. My brother Eugen was sitting by the bed, tirelessly watching over his father. Behind him stood Theres and Emma. Both were weeping, quite gently. Max, my oldest brother, stood against the wall and stared at us. Maurus leaned on the window, and Lorenz whispered to us: "Go in". His face was quite tear-stained

We stepped, rather hesitantly, up to the bed, saying together:

"Father!" The sick man lay motionless. He was already wheezing. His face was a macabre yellow and haggard. My younger sister snuggled up to the bed and whimpered again: "Father!" At this, he moved his head a little and stared at her in silence. We all looked at him and now began to sob loudly. Eugen wanted to lay his arm under father's neck, to help him up. At that moment, however, the dying man uttered a coughing sound, his body stretched, his face twitched, and the whites of his eyes bulged out hugely. Death had arrived. Lorenz ran to the door and as he opened it, screamed: "Mother!" We all stood sobbing at the bed and put our hands together. Only Max remained calm. Our mother entered the room and approached the bed, crossed herself, threw a pained glance to heaven, put her hands together and whispered a prayer. As she did so, tears ran down her crumpled cheeks. After a while she crossed herself again, bent over the dead man, and closed his eyes. Meanwhile, Emma and Theres lit the two candles that were still standing there from the last rites, fetched holy water and sprinkled it on the dead man. With a heavy voice our mother started to say the Lord's Prayer, and we all joined in. After that, we left the room and descended to the kitchen in silence. We discussed the burial and sent for the undertaker, a lady, and the priest. Already by six in the evening the hearse stood before the house and, amid loud wailing, the coffin was loaded and driven to the parish mortuary. We walked behind and many villagers bowed their heads and prayed a rosary. As the coffin lay in the mortuary, people came to mother and the eldest siblings and shook hands with them. They looked sympathetically down on us children and said:

"Poor kids," or similar.

The next day we were awoken by solemn bells, which rang all morning. The flag of the Veterans' Association was lowered three times into the grave; nearby, a small cannon fired its salute, as my father had taken part in the war of 1870/71.

At noon we ate in the inn. All of our family and cousins joined in the meal. All kinds of stories were told about father and what he had said at this time and that. In the afternoon the whole family and our relatives went down to the lake and drank coffee together in the restaurant. It all seemed like a Sunday and we children actually quite enjoyed it — only now and then the thought of our father came back to us, and we became fleetingly sad.

From this point on, everything changed at home. We had a flourishing bakery, a grocery store and a confectionery, about twenty acres of meadowland, some forest, four cows, a horse and usually four to five pigs in the shed. My mother came from a large farm and my father had been a baker. When they married, the house was very small but now — because of the pleasure father took in building — it had become a splendid colossus.

My grandfather, rest his soul, the rakemaker Lorenz Graf, dreamed all his life of such a house. But because he never got anywhere with his meagre work, he started to rely on sudden good fortune. He took part in a lottery they had back then with the greatest enthusiasm, thereby exhausting the very last penny of his savings, to the detriment of his many offspring. He got poorer and poorer, and when he died, his property was in hock and dilapidated.

My father's health deteriorated in the last years of his life, and after Max had been discharged from the army, he took over command, so to speak. The manner of his command was curt, brutish and harsh, provoking angry quarrels while my father was alive. Once, the old man even picked up a knife and, cursing, wanted to attack the young one. Our mother threw herself between the two of them.

After that, they never spoke to each other again, and father took to drink. He ordered *Affental* wine by the barrel, sat on the sofa all day grumbling, slowly pouring glass after glass. He ate alone in the parlour, so he did not have to see Max. The two avoided each other, where possible, and when they had to speak, again they would break into a bitter argument, causing us children to burst into tears and run away. After such events we usually found our mother broken down and weeping. Father left the house, got drunk in some pub or other, and came home late in the night.

We all hated Max. With him, something alien had entered the house. He goaded us with cutting words. Was incapable of kindness, hit out immediately. With his hand, with a dough-paddle, anything that was within reach. Eugen, the only one who matched him in strength, was in the military at that time. Lorenz, "Lenz", worked at night with the journeymen, Maurus was learning artisan confectionery in Karlsruhe, and Emma dressmaking in Munich. Theres, who came after Max in age, kept out of his way. In the mornings she drove out with the horse to deliver bread, and for the rest of the day worked elsewhere in the house. Max did not interfere, as she knew how to answer. The two of them took no interest in each other, but they were sworn enemies.

After father's death we, the younger siblings, drew ever closer to one another. Lenz read a lot of Karl May's books, secretly ordered Teschins and, while distributing bread in the morning, shot pheasants, rabbits and squirrels, put them in the breadbasket and fried them at night with the help of the journeymen. At first, I was not in on this secret. It was only when I had to go with Lenz that he pulled me into the forest, got his "carbine" out of a hole in the rock and told me everything. I was thrilled. A new Teschin was immediately ordered for me from Solingen. Such things always came cash on delivery to the village shoemaker. He received bread as hush money.[10]

After a while, this occasional poaching no longer sufficed. Everybody of our age in the village was initiated and on Sundays we stalked the woods. Everything that stood in our path was shot down. Whoever killed a game-animal with his first shot was awarded the "Hunter's Prize", which meant that the jointly bought Teschin became his sole property. The affair gradually became common knowledge. The gendarme came to our house. We lied as a matter of principle, but there arose a terrible brawl between Lenz and Max that ended with Lenz travelling into the city and looking for a job as an assistant and we heard no more about him. Later, after a really romantic waltz through Germany, he embarked in Hamburg for America.

At this time I left day-school. I now also had to help out at night. Max controlled me with a keen eye. Intimidated, for a long while I did nothing. But on Sundays we destroyed the new benches of the newly es-

---

[10] A Teschin or Tesching was a very small-calibre handgun.

tablished Village Improvement Society, for which Max was President, tore up saplings or set fire to a haystack. Something inside drove us to do such things. We literally regarded it as our task and could not keep calm. "Lenz must be avenged," I always said. Something had to be done. We hated the villagers. At the time, we were reading the Red Indian book, *The Downfall of the Seminoles*. The last lines were beautiful, unspeakably beautiful: "The last Seminole bends over the dead chief, slashes his vein, and drinks the blood that screams for eternal vengeance. Then he goes to the Sioux and takes up arms against the white man ..." There were three of us: Martin, a schoolfriend of mine, my sister Anna, and me. One day we met up in a cornfield outside the village. I proposed the plan for revenge, the other two knelt down, solemnly raised their arms and said: "On my oath!" We had agreed the one who betrayed anything should incur the worst. Then came the actions. The miller had left his iron plough standing in the middle of the field. We unscrewed it and cast the parts in all directions. The landlord on the lake built a wooden hut on the so-called Etztal hill. Over the course of four Sundays — constantly disturbed by harmless walkers — we worked it loose from the ground, then it flew crashing down the hillside. That had an immediate, gigantic effect: trees that stood in its path were broken up, the debris hurtled downwards, and the wooden colossus rolled threateningly on. Down below, people gathered, as at a fire, able to do nothing. There was a terrible noise and the whole house shattered. We had long since disappeared and were playing harmlessly at home in our yard, building a house from empty crates.

The Mayor's foals grazed on the pasture. We channelled water from the nearby stream into the meadow, made a fire in the middle, and kept the animals running over fire and water until they steamed. Then we removed the fenceposts around the meadow, and the unsettled foals ran off. It was only late at night that they were found, shaking and nervous, on a narrow rock path in the castle park.

We stole the tablecloths from the covered garden tables at the inn, and burned them, drying out and ruining the most beautiful beech and oak trees. They always said: "That's the baker's kids." But whenever people said anything to mother, she always replied: "Away with you! It's nothing of the sort! Away with you, how could such small children do that!" Curiously, Max heard little or nothing at all.

Something had to be done! The revenge was much too small. It did not hurt anyone, in our opinion.

Once again, Teschins were ordered. The hunt started all over again, except this time we simply left everything we shot lying. A journeyman was given three days in gaol owing to the business with Lenz. He wanted nothing more to do with such things and was always threatening me at night with a beating. There was no alternative to keeping everything secret. We renewed our oath every Sunday, after we had gradually sensed the dangers that were creeping up on us. The ritual became less romantic with the passing of time. I was the chief, and after my sister and Martl swore the oath, together we ate a stick of "Andreas Hofer Fig Coffee", which we had stolen from the store. It tasted terribly bitter. We got tummy trouble from it, but precisely because the stuff was so awful, for us it was a kind of sacred meal for co-conspirators. For some inexplicable reason, we called the fig coffee "Claro", as this sounded foreign and Indian, and was written on the cigar boxes in our shop. Sometimes when we met on week-days, if any of us suspected a danger, we whispered to each other: "We have to eat Claro again!" We understood and asked no further questions.

We had to work hard. I was woken up in the evening by the jour-neymen. In winter at 11, in summer at 9. We worked right through the night. At six in the morning mother counted the loaves into my basket, laid rolls on top, and filled the rucksack for Anna, who was already waiting in the kitchen, yawning sleepily. And off we went into the cool morning air until noon. Anna carried on with her rounds the whole afternoon. I had to help in the patisserie. I whisked the egg whites next to Max, mixed the Madeira cake, kneaded shortbread. At five in the evening I could go to bed. That was the daily routine. Around Easter, Whitsun and Christmas it was often much later. Besides this I had to chop wood and cut chaff. And always this scourging, threatening: "Get on with it! Come on! Quick march!" In return for this work mother gave me five marks a week in summer and in winter, three marks each Sunday. At Christmas and on my birthday, I got something in my savings account, which I could then see entered in my book. But I couldn't let Max know about it. He had his own ideas about me. When he came back from the army, he said in his offhand way: "The lad must become a cabin boy!" He carved a crossbow for me and wanted to take me shooting, but it was badly constructed, so the crossbow practice soon ended abruptly. Then I was made to learn to play the zither. The moment I got home from school, I had to practice. Always the same, first the notes and finally the melody *"Rosenstock, Holderblüh!"* But I learned nothing, even if Max was really strict. I bribed the tailor who gave me lessons on the zither with bread and beer. He bothered me no more. I began to hate the zither. It was torture. One day, as Max was going out and I was supposed to go to the tailor, I lurked behind the neighbour's fence until my brother was out of earshot. Then I opened the zither-case, filled it with sand and stones, and sank the hated instrument in the neigh-bour's fishpond. On the next day, when I was supposed to play, the zither was nowhere to be found. I lied and lied and finally got a severe beating, but I was free. From that time on I was subjected to the strictest discipline. So it was good that soon afterwards I left school and worked at night.

This went on for two years. Our Indian revenge campaign gradually came to an end. A journeyman had the book, *How to Become an Inventor*. I read it, and my life took a new turn. I ordered technical books through the same shoemaker who had always taken delivery of our rifles for us. I began to draw. I hid all my writing materials in the attic. I invented. A boothook. I sent the drawing to a Patent Agency in Kassel. By return I received an encouraging letter, which promised great things. But I would first have to send seventy-five marks. Seventy-five marks! My heart raced. With such a sum I could earn thousands, once the patent was secured. I secretly showed the letter to Therese. She was red-hot with enthusiasm. Mother was let in on the secret. I received the money and sent it off. Five weeks later, I was the owner of a German Imperial Patent. I sent printed brochures in all directions, and waited, sure of success. Every day I dropped in at the shoemaker's. Nothing but refusals.

One company requested a sample. Damn it! A sample! A sample! Another sixty marks was needed for this, and once again, mother and Theres provided it on the quiet. The sample arrived at the shoemaker's and did not work. Refusal after refusal. Theres was smiling already. I consoled myself. Even Edison did not become a millionaire overnight. You just have to tough it out. Be indefatigable.

A new scheme! An honest man in Mecklenburg wrote to me that all patent agents and lawyers were fraudsters. He could do the job for the low price of eighty marks — he set out an honest and itemized quotation — and would promise to refund the money if the invention did not sell. There are honest people in the world after all, I told myself.

I launched my second invention. I sent the drawings by registered post to Mecklenburg, and once again the patent was secured within five weeks. A cork that pulled itself from the bottle. An item that would be mass-produced and sell in the millions!

I now sent personalized letters to leading manufacturers. I wrote in a collegial style. Refusals. I wrote in an even more collegial style: "Right Honourable Director or Dear Mr. Bayer! I have an invention, which I am sure you can make a commercial success of in your factory. I shall be glad to turn over all rights to you for the small price of 1,000 marks. With best wishes or I remain, respectfully yours, Oskar Graf, Inventor." Refusal! I rephrased: "Sir, I have invented a highly saleable item. I enclose a sample. I will transfer all rights to this invention to you for 500 marks, though I shall also be happy with less. Please take it off my hands. I would even be content with 300 marks. Best wishes, Oskar Graf, Inventor." Refusal. Or no answer whatsoever. The blackguards would not even offer fifty, not even thirty marks. The world simply refused to recognize my genius.

At about this time Maurus came home from Karlsruhe. He brought books with him. A vast quantity of back copies of *Die Jugend*, Reclam editions of Stifter's books, a volume of Uhland, Lessing's dramatic masterpieces, *Napoleon's Love Affairs and Mistresses*, Ibsen's *Enemy of the People* and Viktor Scheffel's stories. He spoke High German with a slight Swabian accent, told me about a book about Kaiser Wilhelm II, entitled *He,* and recited Shakespeare to me. He did so with such passion, with such drive, that it fired up my ambition. I started to read the books. But within a week Maurus was already quarrelling with Max and gave everything up. After a bloody, tearful and braying scrap, he packed his suitcase and headed off to Bamberg.

What now?

A cow fell ill. Four pigs perished. The horse died of colic. The Mayor lent Max a book, *The Veterinarian*. I read it through the night. Slowly, a lively interest awoke in me. At the same time, I was wondering what profession I'd really like to follow. Another cow fell ill. The district vet came and gave us a lecture in the cowshed. That was the trigger. I made up my mind: I was going to be a vet.

The cow broke down. "Infection" said the district vet. Infection? What's that?

I ordered my first book for my future veterinary practice from the publisher Paul Parey in Berlin: *Diseases of the Cow.* It was a slim, elegant, dark-blue volume with fine gilt lettering. All right!

I read and read. Suddenly, I hit a snag. A word, just like the others, stood out: "Immune". But what did that mean? What did it mean?

I immediately wrote off for a glossary of veterinary terms. And I now set out to learn them by heart. From A to Z. On every delivery round, I occupied myself with reciting out loud the most outlandish words. If by chance the district vet drove past, I respectfully doffed my cap and ran some distance behind his carriage with a beating heart. For this man was some kind of God to me, whose brain must be packed with things learned off by heart.

After *Diseases of the Cow* came books on horse-breeding, diseases of the dog and various breeds of poultry, sheep mange and finally even books on breeding fish. All of my brothers and sisters were ambitious; an indefinable keenness to get ahead of the others and rise above our station drove each of us. Above all else, none of us could bear to be less able than the others. What you learn is your own, I thought, and perhaps you'll astonish your future teachers. I remember very clearly when I started reading books with Maurus. We competed with us in our reading, and for me it was a great feeling of triumph when I could say: "Ha! You haven't read that yet! ... That's something completely different."

The Agricultural College in Pfarrkirchen announced its syllabus for the semester in the newspaper. I reckoned: I will start there and finish at the Veterinary University in Munich. Veterinary school didn't suit me. That wasn't good enough. It must be something with "University" in the

34

title. On my customer rounds and before going to sleep I read my compendiums out loud and it was extraordinary how the driest material stirred my emotions. An impressive number of books lay above me under the tin roof, well-preserved and packed in a large cardboard box. Whenever I was ready for bed, I got down on the floor, listened out with beating heart to make sure no one was coming up the stairs, slowly pulled out the box, smoothed my book covers, and picked one out. It never happened that I fell asleep without first hiding the precious gem under the mattress, because if I had been found out, I would have been beaten so hard I'd have been unable to stand. For one thing, the books cost a fortune, and secondly, since failing to learn the zither, I was under strict orders to become a baker. And that was that.

The weeks came and went. It tormented me. I had to say something. At four in the morning our mother came downstairs and put the coffee pot on the kitchen hob. Time and again I repeated the same grievance. The journeymen were rough; they beat me up because I often fell asleep. On one occasion, one of them hit me over the head with a two-hundredweight sack. My whole body crumpled. There was no escape. I could not let Max hear about it. My mother always cried over my sorrows. In her irritation, she said: "If only we could have a bit of peace and quiet."

But – something had to be done! Something had to be done!

"Right then. Today I'm going to tell Max, I want to go to Pfarrkirchen. You must tell him. I just don't want to be a baker! I don't like it! The others were allowed to learn something: Eugen was sent to commercial college. Maurus went to Karlsruhe and is now a confectioner; Lenz was simply thrown out of the house, and he means to get rid of me some day," I wailed. Every day the same complaint, dogged and stubborn. It wore my mother out completely. Her face got more and more doleful and she stared at me, helpless.

"Hm... I don't know! A vet ... There's nothing in that! As a baker you can always earn a wage. And you're never short of grub," she wanted to persuade me. But it was no good. I was as stubborn as a goat. The Pfarrkirchen semester started on 15 September. It was August. I hustled and hustled, day after day without success.

"He'll just give you a right good beating, and that will be that," my mother said about Max. "I don't care if he beats me to death, I'll never change my mind," I replied stubbornly. Nevertheless, nothing happened. I had an idea. I wrote to Eugen. The ruffian could do nothing to him. There also couldn't be a punch-up or an unsettling scandal, as Eugen was away with the army in Augsburg.

I wrote: "Dear Eugen! Since nobody at home will listen, and because I believe I will show my talent if I am allowed to study, I am turning to you as only you can make this possible. Without your help I will go to the dogs at home. In short, I would like to enter the Agricultural College in Pfarrkirchen on 15 September, and then on to the Veterinary University in Munich, because I want to become a vet. But, as you well know, I can't say anything to Max. The brute would just give me a good beating. But I must become a vet, or it will be the end of me. So please help me. Just write a decent, impassioned letter to him. He is afraid of you, but he will only beat me up. But don't say in your letter that I wrote to you, otherwise I'll only get another drubbing. I'll send you something to eat, if you help me. Your loving brother Oskar."

A few weeks later — it was already 8 September — I came back from delivering bread and asked our mother quietly by the kitchen hob: "Have you seen anything? Has Eugen still not written?"

My mother said out so loud that I had to calm her down: "If only I could have a bit of peace and quiet ... Just carry on as a baker, you'll earn far more money." Max heard her. At the time he was sitting as usual at the desk in the adjoining room, and the door was open. "What's that?" he asked roughly.

"Oskar wants to be a vet, and is about to start, he says," our mother answered plaintively. My whole body trembled. I was gripped by a terrible suspense. I could hear my heart beating. I stood there in anticipation, because now something had to play out that would be decisive for my entire life. In the meantime I fleetingly imagined my time in Pfarrkirchen, almost as if I was already there, going into school every day from my lodgings in my Sunday best.

Max suddenly got up and stood in the doorway. He said: "What do you want? Stupid boy, just listen to me! ... What good would it do you? Schatzlpeter has already been studying eight years and still has nothing to show for it! ... I'll drive those daft ideas out of your head." And that was that. In the end, I was glad that this request had been so easy, without getting a drubbing or being bawled out. But my anger against Max went to my very core, and I swore the bitterest revenge.

I carried on working in the bakery by night, slaved through the day, and slowly gave up my interest in becoming a vet. It was strange, after a period of high tension my energy gave out and my keenness became dulled. A new search began. My inventions gathered dust on the attic floor, the veterinary books lost their fascination and rotted away under the tin roof.

2.
EVENTS

Time flew by. Winter overwhelmed the roofs of the village houses with snow. Christmas approached. There was a huge amount of work to do. All day long I had to roll out the shortbread alongside Max and cut out shapes, arrange them on the greased tins, and bake them. In the evening, whole baskets stood there, filled to the brim with cinnamon stars, nut rolls and marzipan cookies. At ten o'clock I could go to bed; at 12 o'clock the journeyman woke me for the night shift. As in a dream, with a thick head I plunged my naked arms into the dough and kneaded it. If I dozed off, I got jogged awake, followed by a good beating. And so it went every night. At six o'clock in the morning, I trudged through the snowy darkness with the full breadbasket and brought the bread to the distant villages. Around midday I came home, soaked to the skin. I ate, got changed and once again I had to make Christmas tree cookies with Max. And so the weeks slipped by. One night as I dozed off, I sank into the dough. The journeyman fell upon me and punched me with his bony fists. I snatched my arms out of the dough and wailed off to Max to complain. Startled out of his sleep, he tumbled out of the bed and lashed out at me blindly, so that I ran back downstairs in horror again and carried on working in tears.

"He'll tell you what's what!" scoffed the journeyman, and elbowed me on the slightest pretext, so that I carried on doggedly kneading the dough like a dumb animal. I can't go on like this, I thought each night, and plotted my escape.

On Christmas day itself work stopped. The journeyman went into the city. There was punch in the parlour, and each one of us received a small present. And we could sleep through the night.

The Christmas festivities finally came to an end after New Year. There was less work to do in the pastry shop. And less day-time work. Now I had to go into the forest with Max every afternoon to chop wood. Snow lay everywhere thick on the ground and on the trees. Max spoke little, but he climbed up in the trees and sawed off thick branches. When the opportunity arose, he took great delight in shaking the tree, so I got covered in snow. Now and again he laughed when I shook myself, shivering.

At the end of February Maurus came home from Bamberg. He took charge of making the pastries. There was little to do, and I helped him. For whatever reason, Max avoided him. The two hardly spoke to each other.

So I spent the entire day with a different boss. At first, we got on well with one another. Maurus talked to me about books again, and foreign parts, and occasionally even stooped to playing the fool with me. I grew more attached to him.

If Max was out, we worked faster, got everything done in a hurry, sat down on the bakery bench, and then Maurus read *Henry IV* to me. I had trouble understanding these verses, though he often explained the jokes clearly and in great detail, and now and again he gave me encouragement. To avoid getting a slap, I often laughed out loud, which he really liked. There was now little night-work. The other journeyman, the one who had been very grumpy, left. He had stolen too much bread. An old and grey assistant had come from the city. He was drunk most of the time. But he baked good bread, and as he seldom laid a finger on me, I was happy to work with him. Every day he came up with a new name for me and joked around in all kinds of ways. When he was inebriated, he started singing old songs from his days in the reserves. He often lay in the oven-hole and bawled out, as if speaking to a horse: "Whoa! Whoa boy! ... Easy Vogel, easy!" Then I helped him up, and he kissed me so that his sooty face left a mark on my cheeks. He stood there unsteadily and called out in a loud, hoarse voice: "Here I am! . . . Major Vogel! General Vogel! Knight of the highest order! Decorated with the Order of Max the Silly Cow! Hurrah! Hurrah! Hurrah!" The house echoed with his voice. He hugged me, all choked up, and thanked me for being so kind to him.

"Oskar!" or "Siegfried!" or "Alois!" he always said. "I will never forget you! You're a good lad!" And that touched me within. I worked like crazy and did everything that I could for Vogel. They were good nights. During mealtimes, and while the dough was fermenting, the journeyman snored away on the bench and I read Indian stories and travel books, before waking him when the time came. So when our mother came at about four in the morning, we were usually finished. The maid came down and did her work in the cowshed. We drank coffee, and at six I had to go out delivering bread with Anna.

Being together on the country road was our happiest time. On the way home we told each other stories we had made up in which we – in the leading roles – lived on a giant ship in the Pacific, surrounded by fabulous riches and luxury beyond all imagination. Sometimes these stories took a dramatic turn. There were fights with hostile pirates, whom we then overcame and punished with extraordinary cruelty. If there was someone in the village whom we hated, he was brought into the story and taken prisoner somehow or other. There then followed a terrible vengeance.

On bright Sunday afternoons, Maurus and I set out on our bikes to find an undisturbed sunny nook in the forest, where he read books to me. I got better acquainted with Ibsen's plays, Kleist's novellas and above all Shakespeare, whom we read again and again. Then there were the Russians – mainly Tolstoy – and Heine and Lessing. Maurus read with passion, and my enthusiasm to read with a competitive spirit, and the feeling of triumph over the others when I knew something that the others had not read, revived. I now persuaded Anna to read books, and our bread-rounds lasted longer and longer. This very often ended in a lashing from Max.

When we came home one day, Maurus and Max were quarrelling. We did not know why. They shouted louder and louder at each other and it ended in fisticuffs. A terrible fight began, and it was not until Maurus was with his back to the wall and bleeding profusely that Max left him, went upstairs, and got dressed, because it was Tuesday, and he had to go to choir practice. Despite this, neither had defeated the other. Anna and I went up to Maurus, looked at him meaningfully, and clenched our fists: "He shall pay for that, the brute!"

Maurus sobbed with rage, then got a grip of himself and washed in the spring. That same evening he went into the city and we heard nothing about him for ages. Max was once again the sole master; he knew how to drive troublesome siblings out of the house.

After his military service had come to an end, Eugen moved to America and my sister Theres did as Emma. She also learned dressmaking in the city.

The household had changed. Apart from our mother, Anna and I there was a maid there, the journeyman Vogel and Max, whose orders we followed almost spinelessly.

And Fate even caught up with General Vogel. One day he went into the city and got so drunk that he fell asleep in the train and travelled all the way to Tutzing. There he hired a cart late at night, arriving back at our house at two in the morning. He was in no condition to work and I could not get everything done on my own. He lay there, snoring. Every now and then he let out a wheezing cry. I had to wake up Max, and we baked the bread. The next day Vogel got the sack. He cried like a child, because he liked it with us. But things could not go on like that. Another journeyman was hired. He beat me more than any of his predecessors. I had no one to help me, no one to whom I could speak about my nightly torments. Max certainly must not be allowed to know anything about it. My mother always answered my wailing with soft and helpless sobbing. There was only one person in the whole house who sometimes understood me, and if this largely went unnoticed, I felt it. Leni, the maid.

One morning I was leaning with a blood-stained head against the kitchen dresser, crying quietly to myself. My mother simply said: "If only we could get some peace and quiet for once," and went into the shop. This upset me more than ever. Leni came in and saw me as she walked towards the cooker.

"What's up, Oskar? You're bleeding, aren't you?" she asked, moving closer.

"He beat me silly," I said. Leni went over to the cooker, shaking her head, and said with her back turned to me: "The lout!" It was just a word.

But there was something in her voice that I had never known before. Something cosy and comforting. As she was going out of the kitchen, she again stopped beside me and said, in the same tone of voice: "With us it was our father," and disappeared.

I went to the spring and washed myself. This last, short sentence had revealed someone who also suffered all her life and understood. It was as if someone had emerged out of the darkness and silence and said to me: "Look, I suffered the same!" A happiness sprang up in me, and untold consolation.

Every day when I came back from my bread-rounds I had to cut chaff with Leni. She fed the machine and I turned the flywheel. Every time we stood alone on the threshing-floor and talked together, we shared experiences in words tinged with sentiment. We were happy. We gazed into each other's eyes and then lowered them, without knowing why. One day – I don't know how – I fell helplessly onto Leni's breast and hugged her tight, moaning incessantly: "Leni! Leni!" and kissed her passionately. She by contrast resisted forcefully. She was horrified, but not really angry. I saw her red face, her breasts rising and falling. I would have liked to bury myself inside her, but she pushed me away and said: "Oskar? Why, Oskar! ... What's up with you? ... What's come over you?" I let her go, pulled myself together and stood there panting, ashamed and confused. She stroked my forehead and spoke in motherly tones: "You can't just do that." For the moment, I did not know what to do and all of a sudden, I jumped up and grabbed the handle of the threshing machine and turned the flywheel faster than ever. When we were finished, I hurriedly ran back down into the bakery without giving Leni another look. At lunch, when we were sitting opposite one another at the table, we looked down and afterwards I slipped out in haste. Nothing further happened between the two of us. We remained good friends to the last and although Leni was a woman of 30, and a hard-working, sensible and very pious creature, she knew about all of my antics and often helped me out of a tight spot when Max threatened trouble. Often, after I had been allowed to go to bed, I secretly looked out of the window for hours, as Leni was doing the washing below. That was the extent of my love.

3.
ESCAPE

Maurus had gone. He had left his books behind. I read ever deeper into them. Then he wrote asking for them, and even this pleasure was taken away from me. Anna too, or as we called her, "Nanndl", read everything I gave her. There grew in us a craving for those lost worlds. What was to be done?

We saw an advertisement for Bong's Classics in the newspaper. There was a picture of the books and they looked very impressive. We thought about it. After a few bread rounds we reached a decision. We raked money together. Nanndl her tips and I my weekly wages. Then we ordered, once again via the shoemaker, Schiller's works, followed by Lessing, Petöfi, Mörike, Lenau and Grabbe.

All of these volumes were bound in red with a gilt spine. That attracted us. But we were afraid that Max could discover our secrets, so for the time being we left the books with the shoemaker. However, his small children scrawled over them. We racked our brains trying to think of an alternative and felt wretched.

I thought of Leni. But Nanndl, who knew no more about what had happened between the two of us than anyone else in the household, was against the idea.

My inventiveness stirred. What if I made my cupboard, which stood in the journeyman's room, accessible to just the two of us?

It was an idea that would not leave me alone. I had to carry it out. It was just a matter of doing the work while nobody was looking.

On Sunday afternoon the journeyman was usually away. And Max had to visit the various customers who kept inns and have a drink with them. Our mother mostly sat knitting in the summerhouse and Leni went to church.

We set to work. We made an accurate drawing of the cupboard door, cut out the shelf and split it down the middle, so that there was a fairly wide-open space between the door and the shelf. Nearly half the depth of the cupboard. We then applied all of our craftsmanship to fashion a new door for the inner cupboard, equipped it with a lock, and attached it. After this we made a fake shelf, just like the original, and nailed it to the fake doors, so that when you opened the original cupboard doors, the interior seemed unchanged, although there was a secret compartment behind. We arranged everything in the front of the cupboard as it was before, and we stashed away our books – arranged in a neat row – at the back. The secretive cupboard stood there, just as before. The key was in the lock, as it had always been; the door could be opened and there was nothing to be seen apart from uninteresting clothes, collars on the shelf, a few ties, and my hat. The work had taken three Sunday afternoons – dangerous and exciting. We skipped at our feeling of triumph, as everything worked perfectly. Then we slipped out to the shoemaker and fetched our classics one after the other and arranged them next to each other in our secret compartment, with the golden spines gleaming outwards. Until then we usually looked glum when sent out on an extra, unexpected bread-round, but now we were willing, keen even. One of us ran quickly upstairs, furtively grabbed a book, hid it under our clothes, then we hurried out. Only as we left the village, where there was not a soul to be seen, did we start reading. As a rule we read out loud, if it was poetry. If it was prose, we separated, agreeing on a place where we could meet again. It did not matter if we understood what we were reading. What mattered was that we had read it and were familiar with it all. It was quantity that counted.

We were in raptures. The sound of the words intoxicated us. In the end I knew many poems off by heart, Schiller's "Song of the Bell" simply flowed from my lips. and one day I read the first of my own poems to Nanndl. Of course, I read it with such pathos that all other poems seemed like pitiful efforts by comparison, and that made an impression on Nanndl. She praised it to the hilt. I compared it with Uhland and Schiller and found it at least as beautiful. Autumn came. We had to tend the cows in the meadows. The days were sunny and mild, the sky hung dreamlike over us. We lay on our backs and looked up to the hills. We felt contented. I composed ballads in those days, and Anna was always enraptured by them. I eagerly followed the varied careers of the poets and pictured my own future accordingly. As a rule, when I finished a poem, I introduced it with a romantic tale about a poet and never failed to draw comparisons. In doing so – I believe – the characters took on a clearer form than if someone else had described them to me. My stories sounded as if I had known Grabbe, Schiller and all the other great men in person. Someday, I thought, I will make my way up out of my obscurity and astonish the whole world.

Bit by bit, the household learned about my poems. Emma had come home again and listened to them a little. She always had a patient ear and was the most cheerful member of the family. It is true that she laughed at me but she took pleasure in the poems I recited. One Sunday, when I could contain myself no longer and read a verse to her with immense pathos, Leni said to me: "You will be another Goethe." But Max could not be allowed to know. My mother took no interest; she read nothing but the prayer book and the church notices in the Starnberg *Country and Lake Messenger*.

Our library grew and with it the danger of being discovered. But we were seized with a fanatical book-buying frenzy. We often threw caution to the winds; then we suffered tormented hours in fear of Max. "If I am discovered this time, I shall have to leave, or Max will kill me," I often said to Nanndl. She nodded and said, mechanically and perplexed: "Yes, you're right already." But we did not think about what was to come. Despite all of our precautionary rules we were never free from our eternal fear, and even the smallest sign of danger caused me to lose sleep. I racked my brains. And so did Nanndl. Our mother had once said to me that as a young girl she used to pray to the Virgin Mary to fulfil a wish within a certain time. But she went on thinking about her wish, and it was never fulfilled. She then told us that her sister Marie, by contrast, had a momentary fancy and never thought about it again, and you see, the matter ended happily. That was to give us a hint. We were constantly thinking about the danger and hoping, in this way, to banish it.

"Oskar," Nanndl announced to me very excitedly one day in the wooden shed, "the postman has been asking the shoemaker why he is always being sent things to be paid on delivery, and what is in the parcels..."

The postman! Our worst enemy! Known far and wide as a garrulous, vain bad-mouth! A man we never said hello to, because his face reminded us of Max so much.

The postman! Who all the village daughters that wanted to get married flocked around because of his impressive appearance and soldierly bearing, and who, knowing this, played the great man everywhere, had his finger in every pie and was, so to speak, the arbiter of public morality of the season. This midget of a discharged NCO, whom we had already taken prisoner, hanged, shot and quartered a hundred times in our earlier invented stories? He had said that? And he was still alive?

I ran to the shoemaker. "What had the postman said?"

The old man wanted to avoid this question. I pressed him. Finally he admitted: "The snoop asked why I was always sending for things. I was struck dumb and said I did not know what was in the parcels ..."

That spooked me. I ran back home. Told Nanndl. And I calculated: one way or another. This will come out! I must get away! Away! Escape then – but how? I turned it over and over in my mind. As I said earlier, we had an extensive special shop on the side, selling alcohol, braces, legumes, ribbons, chocolate, cigars and cigarettes and so on. So there were plenty of the things you would need if you were to flee. I found Eugen's reservists' trunk in the lumber room, placed it in the hayloft, and gradually filled it. I stole several pieces of soap from the shop, two bottles of methylated spirits, candles, a huge quantity of Maggi soup cubes, a packet of sugar, collar studs, writing paper, pens and ink. One half of the trunk was full. So then I fetched my shirts and got an old spirit-lamp from the kitchen dresser, matches, and a few towels; two tins of cocoa disappeared into my hands and then I packed the trunk full with my shoes and various bits of clothing, locked the trunk and covered it with hay.

Now I felt more at ease. At any rate, I was ready to escape. Yes but, you silly devil, I suddenly thought as I crept downstairs, to escape you need one thing above all else. Money! Once again, I was gripped by a terrible fear.

Where could I get money?

As my mind darted this way and that I suddenly remembered my savings book, which my mother had shown me last on my birthday. I already had three hundred marks.

With such a sum at my disposal, I am the king of the world, I thought. I immediately sneaked into my mother's room and poked around. I could not find a thing. The desired treasure-trove was neither in the wardrobe nor in the bedside cabinet.

But the cupboard on the wall, with the Madonna on it, was locked. That amounted to a silent assurance. The savings books must be hidden away inside.

But where was the key? I looked and looked. I could not find a thing. In despair I crept back to my bed and waited until my mother came upstairs. Luckily, the journeyman was at the pub. No sooner had my mother shut the bedroom door than I was at the keyhole. I was right. She said her evening prayers, went to the wall, raised the Madonna a little on one side, and pulled out a small key. Then she opened the wall cupboard. I knew everything and was content. I went back to bed with an easy mind. And just in time. The journeyman was already making his way upstairs, coughing.

The next day I got hold of the savings book. Nothing happened. Days passed, one after the other. My nerves were frayed. I slept badly. I plunged back into my books, but they could not hold my attention. The catastrophe could occur any day, at any hour. Nothing happened.

It must have been about three in the afternoon. When I had finished tidying up the bakery, I sat on the bench and slowly nodded off. All of a sudden, the door opened. Max stood there with a threatening look, and seized hold of me. "You!" was all I heard, and something about the postman, cash on delivery and cobbler. Then his iron blows rained down on me. Max dragged me up to the cupboard, turned out my pockets, then unlocked the secret door and hurled the books out. He beat me without pausing for breath. Blood was pouring from my skull. I clenched my teeth and shut my eyes. I sweated, then turned ice-cold, and still the blows rained down. Suddenly I fell flat on the ground. When I came to and looked around, it was quiet. The clock showed a quarter past four. I stood up, carefully brushed myself clean, slipped into the cowshed below, rinsed my throbbing head in cold water and refreshed myself. Back in the journeyman's room, I put on my Sunday best, got my savings book from the mattress of the journeyman's bed and made my way to Taufkirchen, because that's where the savings bank was.

I had made up my mind. I was off.

But first, the money. On the way there, I racked my brains as to how best to get the cashier to hand it over without causing problems. It was already striking five o'clock. I hurried on. At six, the cashier might be gone. Perhaps she had already shut up shop and gone for a walk. Once again, I was gripped by a terrible fear. I dashed ahead. I panted up the hill. From up there you could see far and wide over the fields. It was a clear, late autumn day. Manure wagons were standing in the stubble. Ploughs arched their way over brown farmland, drawn by slowly moving oxen. A soft stillness was all around.

But what if she did not give me the money? The thought shot through my brain. I was already wondering if I should not simply sleep in the woods and set out the next day. Nevertheless, I walked on, more resolute than ever.

As it turned out, the cashier really was still at the savings bank. She looked at me through her spectacles with aged, watery eyes, asked what I wanted, and sneezed. The cashier was a sixty-year-old spinster with the airs and graces of a kindly headmaster's wife. I played the part of a well-behaved, shy schoolboy and said to her, very politely: "Good day, Miss Waschmitzius, and greetings from my mother, I have come to get the money, because I am getting a new suit."

Miss Waschmitzius looked a little suspicious, but because I gazed at her with such desperate innocence, her wrinkled face lit up. "Ah ... Yes ... You're from Graf the Baker's ... Young Oskar? ... Very well, but you must sign for it," she said with questioning eyes.

"Oh yes," I said, with an even more goody-goody expression. "I know that already, my mother told me so ... Nobody else had time to come ... I am old enough to sign."

She scuttled off to the cash desk with the book that I passed her, counted out the money, and I signed.

"Count it again," she said. I did so. Three hundred marks. Ten twenty-mark notes and a hundred-mark note. "Yes, it's exactly right, Miss Waschmitzius," I said politely once more, and even tried to smile. Then I put the money in my pocket, said, "Thank you" and left. Out on the street I was seized by a feeling of triumph. I hurried out of the village and burst into laughter. A warm glow ran up and down my body. I was already looking forward to the train ride as everything was now settled and I was fully resolved.

When I got home, I crept to my room through the barn and eavesdropped for a while. Nobody made a sound. I had brought my trunk down from the hayloft and once I was ready, I went loudly down the stairs – I knew that Max was driving the muck-spreader to the field. Mother came out of the kitchen. She stood rooted to the spot and asked me, help-lessly: "What are you up to?"

"I am leaving," I cried back and once more I was on the verge of tears. I quickly slipped out of the back door. There was a lump in my throat. I could hardly speak.

Leni was loading manure onto the cart. As I passed by, she stared at me dumbly. I wanted to say something, but I felt ashamed of myself and looked away before running on.

I went down into the Etz valley to the jetty, to catch the steam-packet. On the way I met Nanndl. She asked: "Are you off?"

I nodded and looked at her. It was painful. She stood and waved to me for a long time. I had told her hastily that she should secretly send my books to me and, from time to time, something to eat. I would write to her via the shoemaker.

It was not until there were no more people about that I felt easier. It was as if I realized for the first time that I now had to rely on myself alone.

I gazed once more across the meadow at the bottom of the valley where the horses grazed, and everything came back to me, how we shot and played at Red Indians, destroying, chasing horses; I felt miserably weak. But these thoughts were vaguely mixed up with others: about the big city, the future. I swallowed hard and went on, resolute.

4.
IN THE CITY

In the train, among so many strange people, I tried to make as meaningful an expression as possible. I was very uncomfortable. I had come to town three times in my life until now. Once with my father as a seven-year-old kid, once with my godfather, and once with my brother Lenz for the Oktoberfest.

The question that was troubling me was lodgings. During my last days at home I had continuously searched through the newspapers for a furnished room. And now in the train my head was buried in the newspaper looking carefully under the heading, "Rooms to Let". I went back to the start again and again, partly out of nervousness, partly out of fear. But when I thought of my money and of the possessions I had brought with me, I felt better. I pictured a pleasant life as a poet. Something like this: a room with a divan. Nice and warm. I cook for myself and write poetry. In a short while, my works appear. Those at home will hear about me and come and visit their distinguished son. Three hundred marks! That seemed to me like an inexhaustible sum. I could live off it for years.

The trees flashed past. The fields spun by. Evening mist was already rising out of the valleys. The train roared. At the station I got off, went up to a man in a red cap and asked where I could find someone to carry my luggage.

"I can do that for you," he said, and felt the weight. I looked at the paper and said: "Take it to 59 Augustenstrasse, second floor."

"Have you already rented the room?" he asked me.

"No I haven't, but there it is," I said hesitantly, looking at the man who now took my trunk. "Look, the room is available at any time ..."

The man smiled. Obviously, he could see that I had come up from the country. That completely disarmed me. Helplessly, I said: "Yes, but what else can I do?"

The man took me good-naturedly by the arm, picked up my trunk and said cheerfully: "Come along – just put your trunk in the left luggage room and then go into town to have a look round the houses. Wherever you see a notice saying: 'Room to Let', go in and ask if you can rent it. When you have found a room come back here and let me know. Then I will bring you your things. So, now ... Here is the ticket. Don't lose it. Cheerio."

I gazed at this man in dumb admiration, gave him a tip of five marks, and went into town. I felt terribly uneasy. For the first time in my life I was experiencing what it's like to be homeless. A miserable, restless feeling sent me hurrying down the streets and alleyways. I greedily searched for "to let" signs. I found one in Zweigstrasse. I read it hastily, ran up the steps, and rang the doorbell. There was an enamel plate with the words, *Hotelpension Kronprinz*. A small waiter in a dress-coat opened the door, scrutinized me and asked what I wanted.

"Have you any rooms to let, please? I want one," I said, embarrassed.

"Yes, indeed." The waiter ushered me in with a gesture, that I should follow him. We passed through a long passageway to the back of the house, up several flights, then along a murky, narrow corridor, and finally the man opened a door, and stepped into the middle of a rather bare, cold room.

"This would suit you ... It's plain and not too expensive," he said.

"What does it cost?" I asked, already reaching for my wallet.

"Thirty marks a month," was his answer. "Then I'll take it," I said without stopping to think, and giving him a one hundred-mark note.

"How long will sir be requiring the room?" asked the waiter formally as he took the note. He took a notepad out of his breast pocket and wrote something down. "Well ... for three months ... But I don't know exactly ..." I stuttered. "Ah! ... Then you will be staying some time, won't you?"

"Yes, take the rent for three months at once," I said, and breathed a sigh of relief.

"Just as you wish," opined the waiter attentively. He stared at me so strangely that I lost my self-assurance.

"Can you turn the heating on? ... And my trunk is still at the railway station," I said, woozily. "Yes of course, we will send for it. Our hall porter will take care of it," the waiter said, soothingly, and continued: "I can also turn the heating on, if you wish. That always costs one mark and then – what was I going to say – of course, you always give the chambermaid a small tip for doing your room and bringing your meals ... Just as it suits you, sir..." He gave me a sideways glance, with a world-weary expression. He smiled submissively.

"What does that cost?" I asked and got my money out again. "I can give it to you now and then you can give sort it out with the others.

This once again struck the apparently worldly waiter so much that he replied very quickly.

"Good grief, one always gives three or four marks to each," he said unswervingly and smiled courteously, wanting to give a ten mark note back as change from the hundred.

"I see. Then here are another twenty marks, and now I have paid everything for the three months," I said, giving him back the ten mark note and another twenty. The man made an elegant bow and thanked me coolly, before saying, once again in a business-like tone: "I will tell the hall porter to fetch your trunk at once ... May I have the ticket? And then, of course ... One gives little tips now and then for one thing and another."

"Yes, thank you," I said and went on: "When he brings me my trunk, I will give him a little something."

The waiter said: "Very well, sir!" He bowed once more and left me alone. I sat down on a chair, without taking off my coat, and let my thoughts wander. After a while there was a knock at the door. The hall-porter brought in my trunk, took off his cap and stood there, as if he was waiting for something. I gave him five marks. He thanked me attentively and left. As I was unpacking, there was another knock. The chamber maid came in, smiling, gave me a printed registration form to fill in, set a pen and ink before me, and said in a wafer-thin voice: "Would sir kindly fill this in?" and tiptoed out of the room again. I hung my clothes up in the wardrobe, put the Maggi cubes in the table draw, placed the spirit stove inside the oven, the bottles against the wall, put a couple of shirts in the chest-of-drawers and arranged things to make the room a little more homely.

There was another knock. I said, "Come in" and the waiter appeared, asking: "Will sir be taking dinner with us this evening, or will he be going out?" He wanted to give me the menu.

I said: "No."

He said: "Very well," and shut the door behind him. I walked restlessly to and fro. It grew dark. I turned on the electric light, got undressed and lay down in bed. For a long time I lay there with a blank mind and I finally fell asleep.

Very early the next morning – I think – there was a knock at the door. When I woke with a start and asked what was up, the chambermaid said: "Will sir take breakfast in the room?"

"Er, yes," I answered drowsily, "but I am still in bed ... A little later!"

"Please ring for it then," said the girl, and I heard her steps die away down the corridor. I fell asleep again and woke up when the sun was high in the sky. The sounds of the city created a strange atmosphere in the room. I hastily jumped out of bed, washed and dressed myself. I wanted to get out into the streets as soon as possible. It felt repulsively unfamiliar here. I really did not know what I should do. I rang. Breakfast came. I swallowed my food in hurried excitement and went out.

The streets were littered with people. My first outing was to the department store. I poked around among the books. When the shop assistant came, I ordered a huge quantity and said they should be sent to the Hotel Kronprinz. Then I went on.

At the corner of Augustenstrasse I went into a café and sat down. The waitress came, put a cup down and asked: "Coffee sir?" I nodded. She poured the coffee, and asked again: "Cake?"

I said: "Yes," stirred the coffee, drank it and ate the cake with it. I thought: "What should I do now?" I could not leave yet. But country inn-keepers usually look askance if a guest sits on after drinking a single glass of beer.

I ordered another cup of coffee. With cake. Of course. All the time I was watching the guests sitting around me, to see how they behaved. They sat reading or playing cards at the table.

Bizarre, I thought, quite bizarre how much coffee people drink! Sitting around the whole afternoon and gulping down one cup after the other. And I drank up and ordered another. The waitress was starting to look amused. But what else was I supposed I do? I could not sit there for hours after ordering a single cup of coffee!! I ordered coffee and cake again and again, eating what was put before me with ice-cold earnestness. The waitress was laughing by now. It was embarrassing. I said out loud: "My bill!"

"Five coffees and five cakes – that makes one mark fifty plus one mark seventy-five, that's three marks twenty-five," the waitress calculated, suppressing her smile. I cleared off, fast as I could. Out on the street I suddenly had an idea. I walked to and fro in front of the café and looked sideways through the window. I suddenly noticed that a girl was setting water glasses on the table. I went back to the hotel, reassured. Aha, I thought, so you can also drink water.

The next day I came back and ordered water.

"We only serve water with coffee," came the answer. I blushed a deep red, ordered coffee and left as soon as I had drunk it. After this experience it was a long time before I visited another café, and it was much later that I first learned how these things are done.

But I had at least one great triumph at this time. I was hardly even settled in the city before I had business cards printed with the words: Oskar Graf, Author, Munich. To my mind, that amounted to a passport, and a step into a new life. I was what I wanted to be. Here it was, in black and white in letters that nobody could delete or alter. I went into the hotel and stuck my card in a prominent place on the door. I gave one to the waiter immediately and said in the jovial and confiding manner of a petty bourgeois: "There we go."

The money melted away shockingly fast. It got less and less. And that in spite of the fact that I never went to a restaurant for lunch – not to save money, but because of the embarrassing business with the café. And in spite of the fact that I made soup from the Maggi cubes on my spirit stove nearly every day and ate bread with tea or cocoa. It was incredible. After two weeks there were only about eighty marks left. But whenever I became really anxious about the future, I remembered that I had accommodation for three months. That meant, three months that I did not need a penny; just Maggi cubes, bread and methylated spirit.

I did not write home. I only wrote twice to Nanndl via the shoemaker. I enclosed a business card in the second letter. As my first appearance in print, that must impress her. And as her first letter showed, it did so. What's more, she also promised to send me money and food secretly. That was something to look forward to. I bought Schopenhauer's *Aphorisms on the Wisdom of Life,* sat every evening at my table, and read them aloud to myself. I did so with such eagerness and such stubborn conviction that before long I knew them all by heart. At the same time I was writing two plays. The first was called *The Fear of Others* and the second *The Ruins of Society. The Fear of Others* was about the meaning of honour in present-day society, and *The Ruins of Society* was about suspicion. Meanwhile I was beginning to get used to city life.

"Can you type out a play, if I read it aloud?" I asked one day, upon entering a typing agency in the square by the Sendlinger Gate.

"Dictation, yes. One mark fifty per hour," said the lady with the high collar. She led me into a cabinet-sized room. Within a fortnight – at the rate of several hours a day – I was happily in possession of the manuscripts for my first two plays. Now I really set to work. I wrote twenty letters a day. I bought all of the newspapers, magazines and Sunday reviews and looked in books etc. for publishers' addresses.

I wrote: "Dear Sir, I have completed a play and am ready to submit it to you for publication. It is a tragedy. I would accept one thousand marks. If you want to pay less, we can discuss the matter. It ought to be published promptly and is sure to be accepted for production at once, as it is very dramatic. With the greatest of respect, Oskar Graf, Author, Hotel Kronprinz, Zweigstrasse, Munich." I wrote more confidentially to the leading publishing houses such as Bong, Cotta and Fischer: "Worthy and noble publisher! A young man of talent turns to you in the deepest distress. I, the undersigned, have written a play that is likely to have a phenomenal success the moment it appears and sell lots. Please help me. I am living in extreme poverty and will give you my work at any price you care to offer. I hope to hear from you soon and receive payment. I will then supply the work to you immediately. Thank you in advance. I remain, Yours Sincerely, Oskar Graf, Author, Hotel Kronprinz, Zweigstrasse, Munich."

To another I wrote, asking: "Dear Sir or Messrs! Could your publishing house make use of a popular drama about contemporary life? I can, immediately upon your reply, send you two plays, each in four acts. I will accept any offer, but the plays must be published promptly. I enclose a stamped addressed envelope for your reply. Thank you in advance. I remain, Yours Sincerely, Oskar Graf etc."

I was showered with rejections: printed, typed and handwritten. It was outrageous. I sent the plays themselves. They were either returned quickly or not at all, until I wrote and inquired about them. These follow-up letters were usually rude: "Dear Sir, I assumed that you would be the only publishing house that would read everything and would help a young talent living in poverty. I hope to have your answer tomorrow. There are other publishers waiting. I must ask you to return the manuscript. It is a shame, but I must write to you in this way. Yours Sincerely, Oskar etc."

The manuscript then usually came back without a cover letter. I shook my head. It was no use. Oh well, I thought, they did not even bother to read the play. If they had, my name would perhaps already be on a theatre programme.

It was hopeless.

I looked around in the bookshop window displays. What was just out, what was being promoted? Comic tales by Georg Queri. I immediately wrote a volume of Upper Bavarian comic tales and offered them to all manner of publishers. None were interested. They did not even ask to see the manuscript. One wrote, after I went ahead and sent the manuscript: "Who would ever print and publish such stuff?" I returned to promoting my plays.

My money ran out. Damn it!

I wrote to Nanndl. Twenty marks came. She promised more. Thank God! I got down to work. More and more letters. And at night – Arthur Schopenhauer. *Aphorisms on the Wisdom of Life*.

No more money. Nanndl sent five marks and wrote: "I cannot send you any more. It's impossible. Also, don't send any more letters to the shoemaker. He won't take them."

What now? I had no peace. Night after night I read Schopenhauer. The lady in the next room, a baroness, sent me a letter: Dear Mr Graf, As your neighbour I would like to broach a subject, which I hope you will not resent. Much as I appreciate your diligent studies, I would beg you urgently and respectfully to read rather more quietly. Wishing you every success in your work, I remain Yours very Faithfully, Baroness So and So."

What was to be done? Damn it! Damn it! The bitch! Once again, I sent out *The Fear of Others*. I enclosed a long, imploring letter. Meanwhile I had also learned about mailing by registered post. That must attract attention. I waited. A letter suddenly arrived from this publisher. He replied that he had read the play with great interest, and that it showed very remarkable talent. He wanted to publish the work. This would cost four hundred and fifty marks. In return, the book would appear very soon and very well produced with a print run of 1,000 or 2,000 copies. As a special offer I would receive 25 percent of the sale price. I calculated. Victory was mine. Full of self-confidence, I said to the waiter, as he brought me a letter from another publisher on the following day: "Now they are queueing up because I have found a publisher! They always hesitate at first." He viewed me with a malicious smile. I turned away with an imposing gesture.

But where was I to get hold of 450 marks? I wrote an enormously long letter to Nanndl and at the same time one to the shoemaker, requesting that he do me this one final favour. As soon as the play was out, I would send him complimentary tickets and money so that he could see the performance.

And again, Nanndl wrote: "I have no more money. I can't." What was I to do now?

I had four marks left. I had only been away from home for six weeks. What was to be done? I was on the verge of despair, and at the height of ecstasy. Time and again I read the publisher's letter. Then came the contract and an urgent letter asking that I give a definite answer. I wrote confidingly: "Blessed publisher! I am delighted beyond measure that you discovered me. I will send the money as soon as I can. My sisters are going to send it to me, and they must first withdraw it from the savings bank. I kindly request that you allow me a little more time. I promise faithfully to send you the money soon. Yours in sincere confidence and gratitude, Oskar Graf, Author."

Now I had taken the decisive step. At the time Theres, my oldest sister, was in the city, learning the millinery trade. I had her address from Nanndl. However, because I was ashamed to go to her I had to arrange things so that we seemed to meet by chance, without any conscious effort on my part. So one evening I went secretly to the entrance of the business where Theres was learning. She was bound to come out at seven o'clock. I went and stood some distance from the entrance and watched every person who came through the gate. I paced up and down, tormented with anxiety.

At seven on the dot Theres came out of the gate with several work companions. After a short farewell she came towards me on the pavement, without seeing me. I walked towards her as though I was in a great hurry. When I was five paces away from her, she abruptly recognized me. She stood still for a moment, then said in alarm: "Oh Oskar!" I held out my hand with an air of defiance and tried to force myself to appear indifferent. And now the questions started: "What are you up to? Have you got a job? Where are you living? How's it going?" I evaded all here questions, acted all mysteriously, and just repeated: "I am writing."

"So ... what are you writing?"

"I have written two plays."

She shook her head: "All right, but are you earning anything?"

I said: "You will see in a month."

This made her curious: "What does that mean?"

"Yes well, in a month's time a book of mine is coming out..."

"Well, are you getting enough money to live on?" Theres asked me urgently. She continued, scrutinizing me closely: "And where are you living?"

"In Zweigstrasse, on the second floor," I said, curtly.

"How much rent are you paying?" she pressed further, looking at me more and more uneasily.

"Thirty marks a month," I answered drily.

"Where do you get the money from? And where are you staying? What are you eating?"

"Me? ... I mostly cook for myself," I said, stuttering a little. She was increasingly perturbed. One look of astonishment followed another.

"Can we go to your place now?" I would like to come today," she asked.

We went to the hotel. I was feeling sadder and sadder and bit by bit the truth crept out; I told her about the publisher, and that I had no more money. I grumbled about Max and everything else and said, pathetically: "My talent must not be wasted. You have no idea what a brother you have."

As we were standing before the doorway, Theres got a real fright and said: "What? ... You are living in a hotel? ... That's just not on! You can't pay for it! That must be really expensive."

"It's already paid," I said, again drily and defiantly.

"But how?"

"Well, three months' rent is already paid," I replied in the same tone. Then we went up to my room. Theres stood there absent-mindedly, just repeating: "Thirty marks! Thirty marks, my dear boy, my dear boy!" I then showed her the letter from the publisher and pressured her until the two of us were crying and she promised that she and Emma would give me the money for the publisher. I immediately cheered up and said, formally: "Someday, after I am dead, this will bring you silent fame."

I took her home. She gave me some money, and four days later Emma, who was at home, knew everything and sent me five hundred marks. I immediately sent off the publisher's fee, together with the undersigned contract.

Every second day I wrote an immensely long letter to my "publisher" and already felt like a great poet.

Three weeks later a few proofs came for correction, and a letter from the firm's official receiver, which disclosed to me that the firm had gone bankrupt and asked me if I had any claims. I felt as though I had been struck dead. I ran off to Theres with my sob story. I struck a tone that would have melted the heart of the stubbornest curmudgeon. But Theres was implacable.

"You have to get out of the hotel," she said resolutely, and promised to find a room for me.

"You have to find a real job," she said next, "writing will be the death of you." On the next day, during her midday break, she ran round to me and said firmly: "Come on. I have a room for you." We went down to Schillerstrasse together. A few days later I moved into the second floor at the rear of house number 16. Theres had already paid for the room. It cost 16 marks per month. We tried to get back the last half month's rent, but this was refused. I always hated haggling back and forth, because I assumed that the waiter might lose respect for me and no longer regard me as a wealthy gentleman and distinguished author, and because, once the money was gone, money no longer troubled me. Perhaps Theres failed to get a refund on the rent precisely because I did not support her persistent attempts to get the money back; I did not make the slightest effort.

The room in Schillerstrasse was rather gloomy and full of imitation German antique furniture. The landlady had a cunning lynx-like face and her eager attention made me suspicious of her from the first. It also seemed to me as though Theres had spoken to her about me, because I could not let go of the impression that I had been placed here like a naughty schoolboy who was under observation.

"So, that's all we can do for you. Now you must find a job or go back home," said my sister when we were alone in the room. She was on the verge of tears. Then she left.

My spirit of defiance rose up again. I wrote a rambling letter to Nanndl, begging for help. Several food parcels arrived, but no money. I started looking around for work.

There was a notice in the paper: "Lift-attendant wanted at once. Apply Röckenschuss, Block 2." I went and applied. It was a large textile business.

"What do you want?" asked an elderly man, looking me up and down.

"Please sir, I saw the notice in the paper, saying that you were looking for a lift-man."

The man smiled: "Yes ... But," and he looked at the business card I gave him. "But you are an author? And now you want to be a lift-attendant?"

I nodded awkwardly, then asked pleadingly: "Take me on. I will do the job well." After all sorts of questions – where are you from, what school did you go to – the man invited me to go off with the hall porter, who took me down a passageway leading through various buildings before showing me the place where I would be working. It was a four-storey shop on the Marienplatz. I made several journeys up and down and started work the next day. My wages were seven marks a week.

The same day I went to see Theres and told her about it. She softened again and promised to help me in any way she could. Actually I was deeply offended but I put a good face on it. Secretly I was thinking, one day I will distinguish myself, and then I will have revenge for all these humiliations and insults to my genius. I was constantly calculating ways to save money, but with seven marks a week I did not make ends meet.

Theres got Emma to spread the rumour that I had a good job in a bakery serving the Bavarian court, so that Max could do nothing to thwart my plans. They often secretly sent me food parcels.

When I started work on the lift it was February. I had to stand all day long from seven in the morning until six in the evening, with a two-hour lunch break, in an open, paved entrance. It was bitterly cold that winter. Hardly six weeks had passed before I was struck with a severe attack of rheumatism and was no longer able to get out of bed in the morning. I stayed in bed without letting Theres know, and told the landlady I was ill, and would she mind making me some tea? Three days later Theres happened to come by in the evening. I was lying comfortably in bed and reading.

"What's up with you then?" she asked.

"I have been in bed for three days already, I think it's rheumatism. My whole body is aching," I said.

"Did you tell them at the shop that you are ill?" Theres asked.

"No – I couldn't do that," was my answer.

"If you are ill, you should be in hospital ... If you stay here it will be the death of you," my sister groaned in disappointment. "Besides which, if you have not told them at the shop, you'll lose your job."

"I am just ill!" I hissed angrily and went on moaning: "What's it got to do with you! Leave me alone! What's the use of work that makes me ill! I'll find some other way to fend for myself."

Theres sat silently for a while, then started to weep softly: "But, Oskar! ... You cannot carry on like this! Either find a proper job or go back home! You'll go to rack and ruin! ... Only rich people can afford to write poetry! ... It's complete madness!"

"What does it matter if I go to rack and ruin!" I snarled angrily, turning over. I was suddenly seized with unspeakable hatred of all my brothers and sisters, and swore never to listen to them again

"Oh, Oskar!" sobbed Theres and shook me: "Just be sensible! You'll get there in time."

I turned around and held my hand out to her coldly. She finally went away, completely demoralized.

After about a week I was able to get up once more. I started reading again, wrote and frittered away my days one way or another. I was crushed with despair and gripped with self-disgust.

Then I had a new idea. I wrote jokes and sent them off. That might bring in some money, I thought. I had a few marks left, and Theres had given me something before she left. There was still food. So I could get by.

Wherever I went and whatever I read I wanted to exploit it for writing jokes. I recalled my school days. There was a boy who was asked to write a sentence with the word "hat". He wrote: "The hat is too small, because the head is too large." Another time he wrote an essay about poultry, in which he said: "The rooster jumps on the hen when he is feeling cocky."

The moment I thought of a joke like this, I hurried to typing agency by the Sendlinger Gate and dictated it to the lady with the high collar, had a letter typed at the same time and sent both of them to the *Meggendorfer Blätter* or *Fliegende*. Endlessly. I always wrote with passion: "Dear Editor! I have a joke for you. Please accept it. It is a good one, and I am sure it will make many readers laugh. I will let you have it for five marks. Yours faithfully, Oskar Graf, etc."

I went on sending them in without ever waiting for an answer. And I calculated the exact amount that I would ultimately receive.

One day I happened to meet Theres. "Do you have a job already?" she asked immediately. "Ha! I don't need a job! I am earning enough now," I said, self-assuredly.

"How?" she asked further. "I am now a contributor to *Fliegende* and the *Meggendorfer Blätter*. The first will soon send me two hundred marks for forty jokes and the second about one hundred and twenty marks," I told her, almost condescendingly.

"Yes, but are you sure? Have they already agreed?" pressed my sister with her pig-headed insistence.

"No, but I have sent them in, and now I just have to wait," I answered calmly.

"As if I care," she burst out finally, "I will never help you again! Do as you like! Some day you will realize that you won't get on in life without a proper job!"

Then she left.

It was beyond me how anyone could fail to grasp something as simple as contributing to the papers. I shook my head in disbelief.

6.

A VERY COCKEYED AFFAIR

At that time something happened that really tormented me for more than ten years, even though I managed to sweep it under the carpet along with all the self-made problems, idiocy and guilt in my further life.

That is to say, a letter arrived out of the blue from my brother Maurus in Kassel, which caused me great alarm. "Dear Oskar," it went, more or less, "I am coming to Munich, where I will look for a job, and I am looking forward to seeing you." He complained about things at home and went on to propose, "Now the two of us will help each other and save money. We will then go on our travels and buy books. It will be fine." But I was not at all looking forward to it. On the contrary, I was horrified. Now it will all come out, I thought, suspiciously. He will find out what is going on and will write home and tell them how I am living; then Max will come and beat me up and take me home to keep me under control.

I read the letter again and again. It was sincere and touching. But I did not believe a word. I expected only bad things from his coming. A dog that has been beaten mistrusts even the most well-intentioned person who tries to stroke him.

"Perhaps we can live together; and I will find work at your company," Maurus wrote in a further sentence. Oh my God! Oh my God, what was I to do?

I wanted to go straight to Theres, but then neglected to do so. No, I won't, I persuaded myself with an idiotic obstinacy, she will only go on about getting work again, and it will be just the same with Maurus. "You must get a job, without fail! Or else you must simply go home!" he will say, the same as Theres.

I racked my brains. At once I went off to the hated landlady and told her a complete sob story about unfortunate entanglements.

"You see, Frau Ulitsch, I am studying in secret! ... Only my sisters are helping me. If it comes out, I will have to go back home, talent and all! My oldest brother is a lout, as are all my brothers. One is now on his way from Kassel ... He has no job and no money and wants to live with me."

Frau Ulitsch understood at once. Her face immediately hardened; and she said to me in her keen, high-pitched voice: "No, no Herr Graf, that's not on! ... That's out of the question. No, you are such a nice, quiet man. But your brother cannot stay here overnight."

"Yes, of course, I don't want him to come either but, you see ..." I was literally struggling for breath and felt the sweat running down from my armpits. "But ... Please help me! ... I will tell you what, Frau Ulitsch, we will help each other. I will show you how grateful I am. I will pay more ..."

I was utterly confused. Frau Ulitsch glanced at me for a moment and declared that she would not demand more money from a lodger. No, she would not do that, but gentlemen had liked her rooms and had given something every year.

"A respectable gentleman knows what is proper in such a situation, Herr Graf ... And I like you. I am sure I do my duty as a landlady. Am I not right?" she squeaked.

"Yes, I realized that as soon as I came here," I lied with an air of innocence, and was already secretly calculating what she would ask. In the end, we reached an understanding. I told her everything and she took my side. "Just four extra marks, Herr Graf. That is not unreasonable," she decided, and I agreed to everything. Just to have an ally who would back up my lies. I was a little relieved after this discussion.

Two days later, Maurus arrived. I received him with simulated joy. It only occurred to him that I was so stressed about my landlady. I listened to his stories. He was so warm towards me. I hesitated again and again about telling him everything, but I always suppressed the impulse and cursed my landlady. She was so disgusting, so repugnant, that she did not allow visitors, I had to keep a sharp look-out on everything in the room. All in all, it was painful living here.

My brother had arrived in the early morning. We sat together in my room until noon. I felt like I was treading on hot coals, whereas he was blithe and unsuspecting. He set out his plans.

"You save money and I will find a job and save. We'll put our money together and be made men," was his constant refrain.

Frau Visutech was shuffling around outside in the passageway. Every now and then Maurus noticed my absent-minded nervousness. At last, we went out for dinner.

"I can sleep in your room tonight, can't I... You'll be off to work, in any case?" asked my brother.

"Well," I said, frowning, "I don't know, she might kick up a fuss... You'll see, she won't like it if you stay with me, but it's all the same to me... We are together now ... And tomorrow you'll find a room for the time being ... If possible, we can move in somewhere together."

I got up hurriedly and went out and drew the landlady into the kitchen. I told her the situation."

"And, please, please Frau Ulitsch, can you give me a few marks, five perhaps? I need to pay for dinner. My sister will come by tomorrow and pay for everything," I desperately insisted. She gave me the money, somewhat hesitantly.

"You can stay with me ... Thank God! ... She's such a cow!" I said, returning to Maurus. "You won't stay here long!" he said, as we went out. He asked me how much I earned a week, how long I worked at night and if I had had any success with my writing.

"So, 22 marks a week," he said, showing respect. "Hey, that's great! And Sunday off? ... Wow! You're in luck!" He smiled, then said cheerily: "Then you'll treat me to lunch today?"

"Yes of course ... I have not yet been able to save anything, but after half a year I'll have a nice little pile," I answered casually. He smiled mockingly and said: "Well if you pay for it... I'll get a nice lunch today."

After we had eaten, we went for a walk. He teased me about my poetry and started to laugh heartily again. He was in the best of spirits and talked incessantly. We finally arrived back in my room in the evening and I lay down in bed until eight. Meanwhile he sat down and read Heine. I got up at the appointed time and pretended I was in a rush to get off to work. He wanted to accompany me; I tried to dissuade him, but he was not to be put off. So we went to Seidl's, the bakery to the royal household in Marsstrasse.

All the way there I was boiling over with mistrust and fear and was beating my brains about how to keep up the deception. Before the shop, which had a small front garden, we parted company. I quickly went into the entrance and waited there a good half an hour. If somebody came by, I lit a cigarette and straightened out my clothes. At last I slipped carefully out of the doorway, looked in all directions, and walked towards Schwabing, where I sat down in a coffee-house until it closed, then tramped the streets again. I crouched down on a bench in the railway station, but a policeman moved me on. I spent some time in the waiting room, then continued through the city. I was freezing. I felt sick as a dog. I cursed myself out loud and loathed my deceit. It gradually got dark. I went to the English Garden and walked up and down along the deserted paths, hearing every hour strike. To pass the time, I recited a poem every now and then, and finally began to make rhymes myself. Near the Monopteros I wanted to take a leak and found a man asleep behind a bush. He woke up and stared at me dejectedly. I just stood there, not knowing what to do. The sleeping man sluggishly got himself together and looked at me more closely.

"Mornin'," he finally stammered, and rubbed his eyes.

"Mornin," I said likewise. "No roof over your 'ead neiver?" he asked in a Berlin accent. Then, apparently annoyed by my stupid scowl, he went on: "What you starin' at? ... Just lie down 'ere ... Snuggle up, that way it'll be warmer." That sounded so much like a command that I got a fright. I hesitated further. He was already curling up like a hedgehog, and nodded, as if to say: "Come on, greenhorn!" and lay down again. At first, I really did not know what I should do. I gawked at him as if possessed; adventurous thoughts bewildered me and I at once lay down beside him. He moved, coughed a little, then pressed his back hard against my chest and pressed his behind into the middle of my body. As he did so, he grunted contentedly. I wanted to recoil, but he wriggled after me directly and mumbled encouragingly: "'Ang on, boy ... Don't be so shy! ... Stay put!" And his arm suddenly groped back towards me. "Snuggle up! Snuggle up," he whispered and wanted to pull me even closer to him. It felt horribly creepy. I shivered and shuddered. I had never heard the word snuggle and God knows what lay behind this bizarre behaviour. I felt nauseous. I wanted to jump up but did not dare to do so. As he let go for a moment and began to grunt again, I carefully pushed both of my palms onto the dewy ground, hastily braced myself, and legged it like a persecuted fugitive over the gardens to the city. My heart was pounding, and blood raced through my veins.

Back on the streets, it was early morning; the houses were enveloped in a thick fog, the trams were already running, the streetcleaners were sweeping rhythmically, and here and there the blinds were being raised. The tower-clocks struck seven. I walked slowly to regain my composure, and only now did I think of Maurus and what the future held. I waited a little longer, until I found the first open baker's, bought fresh rolls and returned to my room just like a weary night-shift worker. "Hey, that was some night's graft again," I said sanctimoniously, and pretended to be very sleepy. My brother got up and I went to bed.

"I am off to the bakers' employment agency and will come back this afternoon," Maurus said, and went out. I breathed a sigh of relief, like a released prisoner. But I was tormented by anxiety. My mind was in a whirl. I jumped out of bed, got dressed, walked up and down, but could see no way out.

He had to go! He had to go, or I'd be lost. The words buzzed in my head constantly. I was in utter despair. Suddenly I had a quite extraordinary idea. I stood still, thought about it time and again – and then wrote a letter home to my arch-enemy Max: "Dear Max! I have found a good job here at the royal bakery Seidl and am earning good money. I have already joined the Catholic Journeyman's Guild and like it. I would like to ask you to write to Maurus and tell him to come home at once. He arrived yesterday from Kassel, has no money and no job and is rather down and out. He's also in poor health. I cannot take care of him so he must come home. And he won't easily find work here. Regards, Oskar etc."

When I returned from the post-box, I felt disgusted with myself. Deeply ashamed. I would have liked to spit in my face, beat myself up and knock my head in. I thought with alarm about what would happen again and saw no way out. I dropped onto bed in a state of confusion and did not wake until Maurus was standing at my side.

"Hey, I have already found a job and from now on I'll be living in Sendlingerstrasse ... It's only a place to sleep, but it will do for now," he said, very pleased with himself. It was as though I had been stabbed.

"I start work tomorrow!" He sounded refreshed. "But today we'll have some more fun, let's go!"

I got up, washed, and we went out for a walk. We discussed books and poets and got on warmly. We made plans for the future and laughed a great deal. We went to a coffee house and parted around seven o'clock in the evening.

"Until Sunday afternoon then," my brother said. I nodded and went. Unlike me, Maurus was very thrifty, almost stingy. He hardly ever treated himself, buying a Reclam paperback at most, and saved up all his money.[11] Despite his congenital lack of trust, every Sunday he brought his hard-earned wages to set aside and I wrote down the amount in a notebook. Each time he asked: "How much have we by now?" and I showed him the book.

But he did not stay in Munich for long. Max did, in fact, write to him and say he must come home immediately, as there was so much work. He said he was surprised, and I said the same. I advised for and against, as the mood took me. Finally Maurus quit his job and went home. He promised to send me all the money that he could get together from home and he was firm in his romantic resolve: when we had pooled the necessary sum, we would go off together.

"Yes" I said, and again "Yes". At first, I set the money carefully aside. But then Frau Ulitsch came for the rent, I had to pay for the dictation, and no more food parcels arrived. Slowly I started using up the money. At first, I did so with a heavy conscience; but gradually, I became indifferent, and once that happens there is no stopping.

I cursed the money again and again. All the money, and the ill-fated get-together with Maurus. More and more, I wanted to go back to Theres; I wanted to go and ask her for advice and help, but I let everything go as it did. I frittered away the days and wrote poetry.

Now and again I consoled myself with the thought, he knows nothing about it at present. It will turn out all right. You just have to take a job and pay back the money secretly. But I did nothing of the sort and did not make the slightest effort to find employment. I had no will of my own: the money just melted away.

Then I was often seized with a true sense of vengeance against myself. "You scoundrel! You crook! You thieving bastard!" I snarled inside, and to relieve the gnawing pangs of conscience I suddenly went out and gave five marks to a beggar, treated workers who were complete strangers to a beer in a pub, or threw a few marks into a church's poor box.

---

[11] The Reclam publishing house, established in Leipzig in 1828, is still well known for its cheap paperback editions of classic literature.

"He'll kill you anyway. Nothing matters, nothing at all," I told myself. "You are completely lost already! It makes no difference!"

Every now and then a mood of insolent defiance rose up in me. I met Theres and boasted about how well I was doing. I said nothing about Maurus.

"I am simply a genius! I am a poet and that's that!" I said, in an effort to justify myself to her when she started up again about finding work. "I don't need any of you!"

I worked myself into a rage over my unrecognized genius and lived in a state of indifference. Days passed by aimlessly for week after week. It was then that I realized for the first time that I was a useless, shabby character.

Maurus sent less and less. I often had not a farthing. I was glad about this situation. When I went hungry it seemed like a just punishment. Autumn came and Maurus stopped sending altogether. I spent the time in dull anguish. I read a lot, I wrote and composed poetry, but really, I was simply waiting for the coming catastrophe.

7.
SEARCHING

Unexpectedly, an illustrated newspaper bought eight of my aphorisms, and paid five marks. It had an intoxicating effect. My hopes rose. My plans ran wild. I immediately wrote a whole bunch of random thoughts, aphorisms, poems and sent them to every imaginable editorial department. They didn't take a thing. I had less and less to eat. Maurus' money ran out entirely. Theres openly declared her hostility. I wrote and wrote. I had to have something in hand, I thought, in case an editor asked for more material. I must have a selection!

I wrote right through the night. My days were restless, full of worry and hunger. And utterly alone. I wrote. I wrote. A tremendous sense of alienation took hold of me.

As soon as I met Theres, her yammering started: "You are a young, healthy man! We all have to work."

I went my own way. I did not know a soul. I didn't go to the pub. I roamed alone through the department stores, museums, exhibitions; I sat on park benches and waited for some human contact. But nobody spoke to me.

So, to work.

And I went back to my room and wrote. Ridiculous articles piled up, sketches, observations. I wanted to write a long book on education. Then I wrote more letters appealing to well-known authors. And moaned.

Maggi cubes, tea, bread!

But I just had to tough it out, I thought.

I read Tolstoy and all the books that Nanndl had secretly sent me.

My stomach rumbled. I paced up and down in my room, reciting aloud. Work! Work!

There was a book-binding company below me. Work! As what? What? A baker, maybe? Out of the question. If only because of Frau Ulitsch; besides, I had not even completed the journeyman's exam, so I would have to start as an apprentice. No, that was out of the question for a budding author.

Every day, the bookbinders and stitchers came out of the buzzing workshop, having a good old laugh. They were secure. They had learned something and were earning money. What was to be done? What was to be done?

If only I could find a single human being who was prepared to take me under his wing!

A bookbinder named Schmocker was living next door. Every evening he came home from work, made some cocoa, trilled a song, and now and again went out again. I managed to strike up a conversation with him. I knocked on his door and asked for a newspaper. He opened up, greeted me in a friendly manner and with an engaging smile: "Yes, certainly."

"I like to keep up with the latest news," I said in such an urbane manner that I surprised myself.

"Of course, yes, it's essential for an author like you," replied the little man with a walrus moustache. He collected together pages of the newspaper and went on to say that everything in it was a pack of lies. "But you need to learn how to read between the lines."

"Yes, there's plenty of lying in the world," I said mechanically, secretly referring to myself.

The bookbinder picked up a pamphlet that was lying on his table and offered it to me. It was Tolstoy's *Slavery of Our Times*. He carried on in a more assertive tone and in a distinctive Swiss dialect: "Ye see, thes man tells the truth, which is wha th' warld treats him as a luuu-natic. But folk tha hae naethin' ken tha' he is right."

I blushed. His words struck a familiar chord. I felt a kinship. I knew the little book and felt instinctively that the man wanted to draw me into a longer conversation. And at the same time, he stimulated my curiosity and interest. "Yes," I said, with a feeling of relief. "But who believes in Tolstoy these days? A few people, and they can do nothing against an entire world."

The bookbinder looked at me meaningfully and said, insistently: "But their numbers must grow, an' e'en if it starts wi' jist a few who stand up for th' principles in thes book, and attract others, th' few will become many, and the warld will be changed!"

I did not understand this. I stood there stupidly and asked, embarrassedly: "Are there people like that here?"

My neighbour also seemed to be expecting this question.

"Aye, of course," he said in a low, solemn voice. "There are quite a few of us here. Th' syndicalists are also wi' us. Dae you want tae come along? I am sure you'll be interested."

I was struck completely dumb. "So what is this society called?" I asked after a while. The bookbinder smiled: "It's nae society. We ur anarchists. We meit every Friday in th' *Glockenbach* restaurant. Fur a discussion evening. We'll also hae anither large public meetin' suin. We want tae hae it oot with th' Social Democrats. They ur jist bureaucrats who hauld back th' workers an' make fools ay them."

When he saw me standing there and looking dumbfounded, he went back to the table and took a second pamphlet out of the drawer and handed it to me.

"That tells ye everythin' we want. Read it through, and if ye like, come with me oan Friday e'ening," he said, before leaving me. I went back to my room and read Landauer's *For Socialism*. That was the second pamphlet that my neighbour had given me. The "Twelve Articles of the Socialist Federation" were on the last page, and below it a blue stamp: Gruppe "Tat" München.

But there was nothing about anarchists.

Anarchists, I thought, and vaguely remembered Luccheni, the murderer of Empress Elisabeth of Austria, bombings and terrible criminal associations.

I was already imagining a dark, hidden cellar; I saw masked figures, rolling the dice to decide the fate of this crowned prince or the other. I was overcome with an immense sense of excitement, a curiosity that stopped me from falling asleep, Landauer's arguments had been scattered to the four winds. I had to see for myself. I had to go there, they are criminals, you get a different name and disappear, so to speak, for the rest of the world. What could be better, when I thought of Maurus! Just go ahead!

The next day I got up very early, went out to the street, and looked for the *Glockenbach* Restaurant. On the way there, ghoulish images entered my fantasies: a cellar full of bombs, audacious figures, secret doorways ...

That was something epic, beyond my imagination. I had to find out for myself. Come on! Come on! I was on fire. I searched, in a fever. Damn it, where was this outlawed *Glockenbach?* I was walking alongside a stream. The sunshine glimmered on the rippling waves. There was a little hill beyond the far bank. A cemetery wall ran alongside it. I looked around. There was nothing to be seen of the *Glockenbach*. A policeman sidled up lazily. I went up to him, doffed my hat shyly, and innocently asked: "Excuse me, can you tell me where the anarchists meet round here?"

"What?" he said, "the artists?"

"No, the anarchists," I said. The policeman's face grew serious, and he became stonily official. He looked me up and down for a few seconds then said gruffly: "Come along with me!"

Now I was in for it. My heart was in my boots. I nearly burst out crying. I was taken to the station.

There was a strong smell of tobacco. Several policemen were sitting round a table. They turned phlegmatically when we entered, and one of them said to the arresting officer: "What's up with him?"

He whispered something into the questioner's ear and went out again. I stood there, feeling intimidated.

"Come here," said the officer on duty. "Sit down over there." He took a writing pad out of the drawer and began asking: "What's your name?" I stammered out a reply. When was I born, where was I from, what was my father, did I have an occupation? I answered one question after another and already saw myself in the deepest dungeon. The man took it all down. When he had finished his questions, he turned to me broadly, rested his arms on his hips and gave me a sharp look. Then he started lecturing me.

"How did you get mixed up with these people?" he now asked. I told him everything and started to whimper. When he saw how helpless I was, his expression softened. He even patted me on the shoulder.

"Young man," he said. "You are still young. Find a job and steer clear of those shady characters. They're people who don't want to work and make a living by all kinds of dishonest means."

I explained to him about my sister Theres, and that I had a terribly brutal brother at home and had run away from him. Now I did not know what I should do. He wrote down the address of the nearest employment agency and advised me to go along, as I was sure to get some small job as an office clerk or similar. "So," he concluded, "now you can be on your way. Remember what I told you and steer clear of that sort of thing."

I said, rather sheepishly: "Yes, oh yes" and "thank you" and went out the door, stupefied. The sense of depression fell like a stone from my heart. But I was delighted that my suspicions of cellars full of bombs and criminals had proved correct. I was so conceited with my perspicacity, but at the same time I was so dreadfully frightened that I could not still my curiosity. These anarchist blokes, I thought, they must have their secret dodges, and my neighbour must surely know how they come together in secret. I hurried off home and told him what had happened. The lively little man sprang out of his chair and ran up and down the room like a madman. "But Herr Graf! Herr Graf! What hae ye gain and dain? Think about it! ... I could gi arrested onie minute! Perhaps they're already comin' tae gie me! The polis! ... Damn it, damn it. That's sae stupid."

I waved my hands around and protested my innocence, but he caught me completely off guard with his words, snarled at me and stared me out reproachfully. I was disarmed and spluttered: "Yes, my God, if I had known that!" When he finally realized that I had not been asked about him in person, he calmed down a little. He took his overcoat down from the peg, put on his hat, and went out, saying: "I'll hae tae report thes at once!" And off he went. I likewise left, shaking my head and went into my own room, where I collapsed onto the sofa and thought about what had happened.

Out of all the Swiss man's rant, the following words stood out: "Thes could land ye in a lot ae trooble. Frae noo on ye are on polis records." What could that mean? I went to bed but could not sleep. Late in the night I heard the bookbinder return home. What was going on? It was all very sinister.

On Friday, the bookbinder said to me, casually: "We arenae meetin' until Friday next week. Ye can come if ye want."

This was getting more and more mysterious. I felt as taut as a rolled umbrella. But whatever. I had to see this, and they could not hang me just for going this once. If they tried to trick me into murdering princes, I could always say that I did not know how to throw a bomb, or that I had no weapon, or my sister would not stand for it, or whatever.

All week long I buried myself in *For Socialism*. That made some sense. But what had it got to do with anarchism? There was nothing in it about bombs or regicide. It simply repeated, quite harmlessly: "The Socialist Federation is a community of people who want to create a new society, inspired by an ideal." It went on about groups that were to build up this community, step by step; redistribution of the land and the revolutionizing of our whole way of life by the power of the spirit etc. Finally, much to my bewilderment, being unable to fathom it out, I came to the murky conclusion that these sly anarchists must use language in a peculiar way, so that no one would find them out. Perhaps this entire tract and the whole business meant something entirely different from the words on the page. A secret language, in fact. I felt satisfied with this thought and looked forward excitedly to Friday. That evening my neighbour came by, rather better dressed, and said in a friendly tone: "Ur ye ready?" I nodded. We left.

On the way my companion told me about the arrests and house searches that various comrades had already suffered and advised me to be careful. I said few words and looked serious. The further we got from our flats, the more anxious I became. But it was too late to back out. Secretly I thought, I'll go just this once, but then never again, I would rather move out so that this damned Swiss doesn't drag me out again. But my curiosity was out of control and finally got the better of me.

We entered a pub called the *Gambrinus* on the Sendlingerstrasse and groped our way through a dark corridor to a door. The bookbinder went ahead and opened it. I followed, trembling a little. We found ourselves in a dirty, smoke-filled hall, which looked bare and uncomfortable. Around 25 people were sitting around the table, drinking beer, talking about all kinds of things and smoking. We were hardly noticed. The Swiss approached one of the tables, spoke to a shaggy-haired man in glasses, and introduced me. When the man smiled at me and shook hands, I eventually smiled too. Several men who were already sitting there scrutinized me. Then we sat down. At one of the tables, the word "Expropriation" or "General Strike" cropped up a lot. Then a man with a pear-shaped face stood up, and it grew quieter. The man thanked us all for turning up in such large numbers, then sat down again. There was a pause.

I was more bewildered and excited than ever, because I was expecting the real anarchist part to start. Yes, I said to myself, they are really cunning. They are sitting here quite innocently in the pub's meeting room and any moment a cavity will open up and we will disappear into a dark conspirators' cellar. Meanwhile nothing of the kind happened. "Are you going to speak, Mühsam?" said a worker to the man who I had just met. Others were again talking indifferently to each other, about this and that. They were discussing social democracy and police spies, were telling stories about arrests, and then Mühsam spoke briefly about the objectives of the "Socialist Federation". When he had finished, leaflets were handed out. A skinny little woman went from table to table and sold the newspaper, *Sozialist*, offered various pamphlets by Kropotkin, Landauer, Most and Hervé. Then Morax – the man with the pear-shaped face – stood up and asked, "Who would like to volunteer to distribute *Sozialist* and do other propaganda work?

"We also need a volunteer to write our letters."

The Swiss nudged me. "Ye? ... Ye coods dae 'at, nae? Bein' as yoose an author...?" I stared at him rather bashfully and raised my hand like a schoolboy. I could not bring myself to speak,

Morax came over to me. Friendly. "Do you want to take care of it from now on?" I said, "Yes." And nodded. He at once gave me a pile of pamphlets, a bundle of copies of *Sozialist*, and told me exactly what to do with them. I was to hand them out to people in person and sell pamphlets at meetings, distribute leaflets, and take all deliveries of printed literature. He also gave me a rubber stamp with the words: "Gruppe *Tat* of the Socialist Federation, Meeting: ..."

I was to use this to stamp each leaflet and fill in the place, date and time of our next meeting. I kept on saying "Yes" and felt very proud of the fact that I was given such a responsibility so soon. Then the meeting came to an end. A few went through the door into the public bar. Others sat finishing their beer. A number paid and left, wishing one another goodnight. A half dozen of them joined us, including Morax, Franz Jung, Ida, Theo and George, who was simply called "Schorsch".

As we parted, Jung promised to come and see me. At the time, he had just brought out his first book, so I saw great personal advantage from making his acquaintance. I shook hands with each of them.

When I was left alone with the Swiss, I was very disappointed with this group of anarchists. Thinking about it all in all, my big illusions had vanished. Nevertheless, I was glad. Just because it had put me in touch with people.

"That's fantastic," I said to my neighbour as we climbed the stairs, clutching the package even more firmly. "Thank you for getting me such a good position." I pictured myself with an incredible amount of activity and regarded myself as indispensable to the movement. My talent had finally been discovered. Being involved in book-selling and newspapers, getting them directly from the publishers, all that was opening prospects for getting into print. I immediately sat down that night and wrote an article about oppression and justice, looked up the address in *Sozialist* and sent it off.

The next day — I had to tell someone about my happiness and success — I went to get Theres after work, for the first time in ages.

"I have a splendid job now," I beamed, smiling with the certain confidence of success, "I am now secretary to the Anarchists."

Theres stood there in a stare of alarm and stared at me in wide-eyed disbelief: "What – with the Anarchists?"

"Yes," I said and told her that from now on I would be involved in an immense enterprise selling books and newspapers. I gushed forth in my happiness.

"Selling books and newspapers?" said Theres, dumbfounded, murmuring and shaking her head. "Hm, hm..." But I wasn't listening. "And just imagine, how easily I got the job. I got to know my neighbour in the next room better, went with him and got the job straight away," I babbled on hurriedly.

"So ... Yes, that's very nice," Theres said, who now seemed to have grasped what I was talking about, and she asked: "What wages do you get?"

"Wages?" I said, staring at her. It now occurred to me for the first time that the people had not said anything about wages. "Wages? ... Oh, they haven't yet told me. I'll have to ask."

I was getting confused again. Damn! Fancy forgetting that.

"Is there an office?" Theres enquired further.

"No, nothing like that. Everything comes to me by post, and I sell it at meetings, and send out the papers, and have to deal with all the letters and other writing that the association needs," I explained to her.

Theres shook her head again and again, but said: "Well, well. Good for you." Then she asked: "So, you should enquire tomorrow what you will get and how it all works? That is the first thing to be settled when a business appoints a new employee."

"I can only sort that out at the next meeting," I answered. "The members are not there every day."

"Well, we will see," said Theres as she said goodbye, looking at me rather anxiously. I promised to let her know immediately or come around next Saturday in person to tell her everything myself.

I handed out lots of leaflets, sent one to Nanndl and wrote to her joyfully about my new career and happiness, but she should say nothing to Maurus. There were people sitting on the park benches. I went up to them and offered *Aufruf zum Sozialismus*. They glanced at the booklet lazily.

The following Friday, I shyly asked Mühsam: "Excuse me, Herr Mühsam, but my sister has asked what wages I will receive and all about my new position?"

Morax, who was sitting next to us, burst out laughing. Mühsam looked at me almost pityingly and smiled, explained everything to me and asked what other work I had. I stammered out one thing and another. I was literally sweating with embarrassment. I stood there like a terrified defendant before an angry judge. Finally — Morax had whispered the story to those sitting next to him — the entire room was laughing and looking at me scornfully. I had the feeling that the floor was going to open up under my feet. I must have stood there looking dreadfully stupid and red-faced. I was just waiting for someone to say: "Sit down." When I had finally collected myself somewhat, sitting next to my neighbour, I ground my teeth and angrily thought, I have screwed everything up again! To hell with it all! And did not utter another word.

I did not go to see Theres; in fact, I did not get in touch at all. I grew more and more conscious of my misfortune. Life was so difficult out in the world! You had to be so cultured, quick witted and hard boiled, so I thought over and again. My respect for anyone who found his feet was unlimited, even if I felt almost embittered about it. But I did not give up on the sales and kept writing new articles, which I sent off, never getting an answer. I collected all the verses that I had written and sent them to Mühsam, with a really stupid letter. He returned them to me with an introduction to his publisher, Steinbach. I was to cover the cost of printing. I was in utter despair and let the matter rest. I cursed everything and everyone.

I got to know my neighbour better and better. We visited the meetings and I gradually drifted into political circles. I got a halfway clear understanding of socialism, and I picked up a lot of useful information at this time. My horizons were broadening, and I become less tongue-tied thanks to the perpetual arguments with comrades and reading all the pamphlets. But I was in a bad way. And I was always haunted by the business of using up Maurus's savings; I desperately sought after some means of earning a living.

TWICE HANGED …

Jung came to see me often. He was entirely different to how I had imagined a poet. The first time he came I wanted to discuss poets and poetry with him immediately, as I used to do with Maurus. But he was not in the least interested; on the contrary, he hardly listened at first, and then he was really angry at such talk. "Rubbish, man!" he repeatedly exclaimed in his hoarse voice. He seemed to be repelled by any literary subject. His face was almost always gloomy, and when he really did laugh it sounded noisy and forced, involuntary and nervous. He argued with me in fits and starts and abused me as "bourgeois" when I shyly told him about my troubles.

"It doesn't matter a damn if you write a book or not! First you have to become a real man. Jesus! … It's all rubbish!" So he preached at me, all the while gnawing at a match. He came nearly every day. He was a riddle to me; everything that he said sounded strange. I never warmed to him. He looked at my books, ranted about Schiller, and told me to come with him. He smiled wryly and said in a mocking voice: "What's the use of Schiller these days – It's all baloney!" I followed him. He sold the books, took me to a public house, and we spent the money on drink. I let all this happen without raising any objection, because the last thing I wanted to be was "bourgeois". Whenever he had no money and I also had none, he grabbed hold of some books, and blurted out something like "Oh, Heine! Nobody reads the Jews nowadays!!" or "A revolutionary shouldn't have that boring Lenau at all." He took my volumes of Lessing and raged against reading the classics, took me to a second-hand bookshop and sold everything we had with us. I never dared to protest about this and joined him in all he did. He always pocketed the money and said gloomily, "Come on!" Then we went from one public house to another and spent the money on drink. If there was lots of money, we ordered huge quantities of cognac. If there was little, we drank beer. Towards evening we went to the artists' *Café Stephanie* and scrounged money from acquaintances.

I loved this wild life. It drove away deeper reflection. I was living in the shadows, so to speak. Mornings, I awoke with a terrible hangover. The whole world seemed nauseating and depressing. The only way to work off this feeling was booze, wandering about, and mixing with people.

In this way I got to meet all sorts of writers, artists and other café life. I sat there stupidly among them and attempted to put on a meaningful expression. They philosophized, argued and psychoanalyzed. I often listened attentively but did not understand anything in the slightest. They positively crushed literary greats and eternal values with a couple of words. I sat there like a young sweetie and said nothing. This was a new world. I saw a new way forward opening up.

When there were no books left, Jung taught me about pawning. We lugged everything that I could do without down to the pawnshop, which kept my head above water. A wild bohemian lifestyle began. We drank through the night at someone else's expense, played skittles or danced. If one of us had no money, another had.

The others were much cleverer and more agile than I was. When I gradually started to talk a little, they ridiculed me. They looked at me wryly, almost pityingly.

In the "Tat" group I got to know Schorsch better.

We often met, and soon grew close to one another. We read Stirner, Nietzsche and Kropotkin, and Schorsch explained everything quite simply. In no time at all, we were the best of friends. I grumbled to him about my problems and clung to him. He worked by the hour in cake-shops and when I told him that I knew bakery work, he advised me to go to the bakers' lodge.

"Somehow or other, you have to find the easiest way to keep your head above water," he said, "then you can do what you like with the rest of your time." In his free time he read or met his comrades. He was older than I and had a much harder life behind him. We often talked together for hours on end. He explained to me what it meant to be an individualist. It meant denying everything: the State, society, the law and the family and opposing ethical ideas and everything else invented by the bourgeoisie. Because those dogs had spent centuries refining their whole system with the utmost skill, adapting it to their own purposes to make sure that their comfortable lifestyle is never disturbed, that they can sit tight on their possessions, and that the foolish proletariat carries on working for them and making them even wealthier. He showed no passion as he told me all this, but did so rather drily, almost brainlessly. But his conclusions always convinced me. Everything was clear to me from the first moment. What the literary people, what Jung and all the café society said only confused me.

"Morality? ... What's that? ... A mental aberration!" he began, in the style of Stirner. He called everything that hems people in an *idée fixe*. I listened eagerly, and a lot of what he said literally sounded like a public announcement. I felt a little unburdened. My disgraceful conduct towards Maurus didn't weigh so heavily and strange conclusions began to form in my mind.

I went to all the anarchist meetings. The individual, so they told me, is a victim of society. I soon realized that this was a useful thought, as I interpreted it as meaning: you can do what you want, it is society that is to blame. You are merely its victim, with no responsibility.

Finally, finally I had something – but what was it? A new religion, an ethical system specially designed for me. I rejoiced inwardly. I felt abso-

lutely free. Yet with all this awareness, my life grew more and more desolate. It became unbearable to me. Things could not go on like that. Suddenly, I was overcome by an impulse to stand on my own two feet. I talked it
over with Schorsch. He gave me some tips for finding work. I went to the
bakers' lodge and left my name as a jobseeker. I felt a growing disgust at
the café society that I had been drawn into. In the end I only socialized
with Schmocker, my neighbour, and with Schorsch.

Since I could no longer pay such a high rent, I moved in with a
friend of Schmocker's, sharing a room in another street. He was stingy, vile
and pedantic. He spent the whole day imagining he could see bugs, was
constantly wiping down the walls and wanted to force me to do the same.
I left him to ruminate. What did I care about his imaginary bugs, if they
did not bite me!

From then on, the police visited me at eight in the morning every
Sunday and looked through my belongings for socialist literature. Always
two detectives. They poked their noses into everything, ripped out my
clothes and books, rifled through my suitcase, left everything in a mess
and then went away with a few leaflets and pamphlets. My roommate was
furious and kicked up a fuss. I kept quiet, went to Schmocker, and asked
him to calm down his friend. That didn't help much.

I hardly had a crust to eat and went hungry a lot. I went to the bakers' lodge every day. There were no open positions. Schorsch sometimes
brought bread, margarine and leftovers. My roommate had a good job. He
put all of his food on the table, and in the morning, before he went out, he
put it all on the open window, so that the bugs would not come inside. I
was hungry and took some of it. He kicked up a fuss. This made me angry.
I ate his cheese and said: "You skinflint!" The fuss turned into a scuffle. I
threw him to the ground. He seemed to submit and went off. But late in
the night he came home and went for me. I was already asleep. That drove
me mad. I leapt like a tiger from the bed and grabbed hold of him, howling
with rage. A bitter struggle began. The landlord came in and gave out to
us. The people below bashed on their ceiling. We did not stop until the
landlord separated us forcibly. Both of us went to bed covered in blood. I
gave my notice the next day.

Eight days before I moved out, a letter from Eugen, written from a
hotel, arrived like a bolt from the blue. He had come back from America
with his wife to fetch his illegitimate daughter. I hurried to the hotel. There
he was: a fat, bloated man with a skinny wife. He laughed in my face. I sat
down. He knew everything. Emma and Theres, who had always had a
weakness for him, had secretly commissioned him to set me back on the
right path. He treated me paternally, gave me some money, ordered food
for me, and promised to come in the next few days to discuss other things
with me. Then the couple went home.

Before leaving at the train station, he said, "If you do as I say, you will get what you are due." I waited in eager anticipation. Two days later – while I was sitting alone in my room – Maurus came, looking pale and depressed. As soon as he opened the door, I knew what was coming. I turned my back to the wall, expecting that he would half kill me. But he just stood there, white with anger and trembling a little. He hardly spoke, but his expression was terrible. I looked down.

"Have you really spent all the money?" he asked. I nodded.

"Wretch! Scoundrel!" He was so angry, on the verge of tears. "Wretch! Why did you lie in such a shocking way? Why didn't you tell me, you –." He stepped closer to me. It was all about to kick off. But no, I felt the cold sweat running down my armpits. I was ashamed, yet I was glad that he finally knew. I had stolen three hundred marks off him and spent the lot. He launched into the bitterest accusations. It overwhelmed me. I was struck dumb. His voice grew tearful. I also broke down and cried.

"Do you know what you are? You are the lowest crook, the meanest villain in the world!" he said at once. I looked up. He looked at me with all the scorn that a person could show. Then he was off. He hadn't thumped me once, true, but there had been an element of sorrow in all his angriest words. It was as though deep down he wanted to say: "Oskar! why were you such an idiot? Why did you block your own path forward?" I sat there. Alone. Utterly alone. Momentarily, it really seemed as though I were walled in by a hostile darkness.

I sobbed. I heard a noise outside. All of a sudden, I remembered the landlord and his family and my roommate, who might come in at any moment. I clenched my teeth, got up quickly, went to the wash basin, gave my face a wipe, combed my hair, and acted as though nothing had happened. I started to whistle and noticed that I was still trembling. I drove all thoughts of Maurus out of my head and went out.

I wandered the streets aimlessly for quite a while. It was far into the night when I came home. This time I crept softly into bed so as not to wake my roommate.

9.
AT THE MILL

I was packing my things ready to move out. Morax and Ida were there. There was a knock. My brother Eugen came in. He stood still, broad-shouldered and arrogant, did not acknowledge or greet my visitors. There was an uncomfortable pause.

"Have you time now?" Eugen asked bluntly. I nodded. Morax and Ida got up and left the room in silence.

"Come on," Eugen said curtly. I put on my overcoat and followed him. Out on the street he started to talk about his plans. "First and foremost, you have to find a decent job. You can go on writing your poetry at the same time," he said. I nodded again.

"I have just been with the manager at the Tivoli Mill and spoke to him. He would like to take you on. First you will have to do some hard graft in the mill, then you will get an office job. In the evening you can do a typing course and learn shorthand. Once you have a few years' experience in the office, you can leave and find a new job, if it no longer suits you. The people at the mill will not expect too much of you. We have been buying their flour for years and are among their best customers," he said quietly. That sounded good to me. I was pleased. I was very happy to hear it. Eugen asked me to go to the mill and see the manager as soon as I had moved into my new room. Then I could start at once. I asked him how things were going at home, and after our mother.

"Max is getting married in a week or two," he told me, "he has gradually admitted that he has a love child, a son, and there is another on the way. He is now very subdued and sanctimonious. Basically, however, he is calculating how quickly he can take over the property and turn us all out. But he won't find it so easy."

I said indifferently: "Well, that's none of my business any more. I have already been chucked out." Eugen thought about it. We went to a pub and had lunch.

In the afternoon we bumped into Schorsch on the street, together with another man from the "Tat" group. I took Schorsch aside and told him that I would visit him in a day or two. When we had left the two of them behind us, Eugen asked: "What kind of people are they?"

"Anarchists" I said. "What do they want, then?"

"We want the overthrow of the present state and the creation of a collectivist-communist social order. We want to put an end to wage labour. Everyone is to have the same rights and possessions. Exploitation must end. Human relations must be at the centre of our life. That's what we want," I said, though without conviction. At this stage I had given so many speeches in discussion groups that I had gradually learned to express myself in a way that I felt to be correct.

Eugen laughed. "What odd people you are ... In America there is nothing like that. That's sheer madness." I said: "We can talk about it later when something has happened." We went back to my flat. I sent for a porter to take my suitcase to my new room, and said goodbye to my old landlady, who had always been kind to me.

"You have to get all of that stuff about world revolution out of your head," said Eugen, "it will never amount anything. It's fine to think about it, but not to do it. That's madness. . . It will only get you into trouble."

"If nobody does it, then nothing will ever change in the world. If we admit that it cannot change, then we might as well put a bullet through our skulls," was my reply.

Eugen just went on shaking his head. "You are totally nuts."

I kept quiet.

"So, first thing tomorrow you can go and present yourself at the Tivoli Mill," he said, changing the subject. "Your move is sorted out?"

"Yes."

The next day I went to the mill. I was presented to the Managing Director in his office. He remembered me from home. He smiled good-naturedly behind his grey beard and said that Eugen had spoken with him, and I could start the next day. I nodded.

"Come with me," he said, and guided me down to the mill. We were greeted by the hum and whir of machine rigs. The whole building seemed to shake.

I was presented to a lean old hunchback, who shouted dreadfully loud.

"He's joining us tomorrow," said the Managing Director, just as loudly.

"Is that so? ... He's a weedy specimen," said the head miller, and smiled at me scornfully. The MD then left me. The head miller asked me all sorts of questions and then showed me the mill. It had four storeys. Everywhere you looked there were industrial sieves and grinders that gradually filled the sacks hanging at their sides. The workers stood there tying up the sacks and emptying the barrels of grain into the machines; they eyed me over suspiciously and apparently rather astonished. Their clothing was white from flour, as were their faces and beards. What struck me was how they all shouted in tremendously loud voices when they spoke. But you had to.

We then took the flour lift up to the loft. There were hundreds of flour sacks stacked up close to one another.

When the head miller had shown me everything, he led me to the mill gate and said: "Right then, tomorrow at six. Don't be late!"

I said thank you and went.

It was a lovely day. The trees in the English Garden were still bare, and wisps of thawing snow lay on the little strips of grass. The sky had the brilliant colour of spring. Drops fell from the roofs of the mill's outer buildings. I was in a peculiar mood. I was overcome with a desire to venture further afield; I felt suddenly attracted to meadows, hills and the open countryside, stretching to the horizon.

I wandered on thoughtfully, but aimlessly. Only now did I think of seeking out Schorsch. I knew that I was sure to find him in the café. I wanted to talk to him. I longed for human company.

I thought, quite spinelessly: if he tells me not to go to the mill, then I won't go. I was not thinking beyond this.

Then the thought shot through my head: tomorrow I have to go to work, but today I will carry on living in freedom. Boozing, making wild, playing the fool. Whatever. It was all a matter of complete indifference. Terrifyingly so. A desolate feeling of alienation had taken hold of me, of homelessness and solitude, of being cut off from everyone.

I walked faster. And I really did find Schorsch in the café. "What's up with your American brother now?" he asked me.

"Nothing," I answered, crestfallen. "Tomorrow I am to start working in the Tivoli Mill. I will get 22 marks a week."

"And what are the working hours," he further enquired.

"From six until six."

"Bollocks! I would never do that," he growled.

"Sure, but ... They won't give me any more money, and I don't know what else to do," I moaned.

"Oh well, just get on with it for a while," Schorsch said, then went on: "Once you get in the office, it won't be so bad."

I felt reassured and content with my decision and surrendered to my fate. "Christ, I would love to booze and raise hell once more," I then said. Schorsch looked at me and said, smiling: "Yeah, me too actually."

He at once asked me: "Did you get any money from your brother?"

"Yes, a little," I admitted.

"Right, let's go! Come on!" he retorted and left the café with me.

But a feeling of nausea had overcome both of us. Neither really knew how to deal with it. We went along aimlessly. To let off steam, we shouted at the passing cars, elbowed pedestrians and suddenly yelled out meaningless noises that startled passers-by.

We headed for a hostess bar in the centre of town and drank our money down to the last few marks. On the way home we started reciting Stirner loudly on the street, cursed bourgeois morality and parted in a gloomy mood. As soon as I got back to my room, I noticed that I had no alarm clock. It was already past midnight. I was seized by an uncontrollable rage. I started to swear loudly.

There came a knock on the wall. I swore even louder. A bed creaked. Then there was a knock at the door: "Herr Graf!"

It was the whiny voices of my landladies. They were three old maids, horribly sycophantic and bigoted.

"Yes," I growled and tore open the door. "What's the meaning of this? I told you that I have to get up at half past four tomorrow and every day now ... Why have you put no alarm clock in my room?"

"Yes, but Herr Graf... But Herr Graf!" whimpered the old maids and backed off: "Our alarm clock is not working ... Besides, we really will wake you up..."

"I would like to know which of us will oversleep," I snapped, and slammed the door shut. I heard the three maids shuffle back to their room, whimpering as they went, and threw myself morosely onto my bed. I soon fell asleep, without getting undressed. At about two o'clock I woke up. In an anxious fit. I listened out for a clock striking the hour. Nothing. It seemed as though the day was already breaking. I jumped out of bed and began running around, flinging the window open so I could hear better. Nothing. I started to swear again. Something moved across the way. I crashed about even louder. If I cannot sleep, those old sticks shan't sleep either, I thought in my rage.

And I was right. Soon there was another knock at my door, and a whimper: "Herr Graf, it is only two o'clock."

I wished the old maids good night with "To hell with it all!" I sat down at my table to wait until morning came. I heard a few more whimpers and sighs, then it fell silent.

The hours crept by slowly, unspeakably slowly. I was freezing. But it was also too late to sleep.

When the clock struck four, I set out. It was quite a long way, across the English Garden, and you could easily lose your way. But I wanted to be as punctual as possible on the first day. The air was cold. The trees had a ghostly appearance in the moonlight. My steps rang out. I arrived on time. It struck a quarter to six as I left the park behind me. It was still quite dark. The massive colossus of the humming mill towered up before me. Light from its many windows fell onto the oily river and threw shimmering reflections.

As I stepped through the gate I was met by workers. Once again, they gave me astonished looks. I followed them. We went into a shed, where we got changed. Then we went off to the mill. The head miller was already standing there, with his eyes on the clock. It had barely struck six when he started dashing about. Almost as though he too had been wound up.

The workers took the lift to the various floors. I had to stay with the old man. He growled at me as I stood there, not knowing what was going to happen, and thrust a broom into my hand. I swept mechanically, even though there was nothing to sweep. Then all of a sudden, the head miller shouted and waved at me.

"Stand over here, because the sacks will be coming down now, catch them and carry them off ... Over there ... And stack them up!" he ordered me.

I had to stand at the opening of a wooden chute in the ceiling and catch the sacks that were sliding down from the fourth floor. I hardly had time to grasp what was going on when a sack hurtled down and — wallop, I was knocked to the ground and flour spurted out of the ripped sack. I had neither the skill nor the strength for this work. The head miller stood there. I saw him effing and blinding, then go to the gutter, catch the sacks of flour and swing them aside. Anxious as I was to do my duty, I wanted to take the broom at once and sweep up the flour from the burst sack. But then the old boy turned and ran over to me: "Wait! You can do that afterwards."

Then he showed me how to catch the sacks. This went on all morning. By midday the palms of my hands were raw and stinging like mad. I showed them to the head miller. He smiled and said: "That will get better in time ... We have all had the same."

In the afternoon I had to carry sacks away from the lift with several other workers. They were for despatch. At first, I broke down. When they all laughed at me, I lost my temper. Then I got through it. I lugged the sacks, out of breath. By evening my back was raw and as I got undressed, my shirt clung to my broken skin. I cried inside and cursed my brother and the whole world. But I had to stick with it. And so it went on, day in, day out. The older workers got the best job, tying up the sacks, and I would not have dared to say anything. Over time, I even got used to the heavy labour. It is true that every single day my shirt got stuck to my bloodied back, but one day, I thought, my back would grow thick-skinned and resistant. To hell with it all!

Every evening I washed my back in cold water and rubbed in boracic ointment. One of the workers in the mill said to me, when I complained to him about my pain: "That's really bad. Your skin will not get any harder ... At first it always hurts."

In despair, I let it be, clenched my teeth, and lugged and lugged. I had to make the best of it. What else could I do? I had no more money, and on the third day I had to ask for an advance. The pen-pusher looked at me contemptuously and gave me ten marks.

I wanted to write Eugen a terrible letter but could not bring myself to do it. It might have ended up in Max's hands. He would have driven over and beaten me. I dropped the idea and slaved away. Every evening I dropped dead with exhaustion. My limbs felt like they had been crushed, I could barely lift my feet, my back ached, and my mind was a blank.

I gradually got to know the workers better. I did daft things, and they laughed. There were other jobs, also including the so-called skivers' jobs, such as sweeping out the cellar or spending a long time on the toilet. I soon got the hang of these tricks. Sometimes, when four or five us were stacking sacks in the cellar, we also got into a conversation. All kinds of grievances came up. The men grumbled.

"It will always be like that so long as the workers do not wake up," I said.

"Yes! ... Wake up?" the others started. "What can we do?"

"Make short work of it," I said, cheekily.

"Make short work of it, how?"

"Just knock down the head miller and the Managing Director and take control of the mill ourselves," I argued.

They laughed and said: "You're a really wild one."

I said: "So long as the workers do not rise up in revolt, nothing will change."

They all laughed again, but a couple viewed me with suspicion. I did not care. Better to go hungry and beg rather than slog our guts out like this, I thought.

But this only did me harm. From now on, the head miller treated me roughly. Someone must have ratted on me over my rants.

There was more and more work. I got on with it in total apathy, went home in the evening and calculated how I could get money together faster.

I never treated myself. I just wanted money so I could give up the whole damned business. That was my only thought. I could not care less what came next. Money! Always money! There was something wicked about it. It made you a thief and a dog. It dragged everyone down.

Schorsch often dropped by. When I lay cowering in my room like a hunted animal, he said: "It's bullshit, that job of yours ... You have to get out. Or it will break you." I was in a complete stupor and just nodded again and again. As I did not want to waste money, I did not buy an alarm clock and often slept just a few restless hours, made tea and then set out to the mill. Eugen did not show up any more. The occasional food parcel came from home, but with no accompanying letter.

The weeks went by. Overstrung and angry with everything, I lived in total isolation. Everything wound me up. My landladies had a little dog, which barked every time I came in. The three whimpering old maids paraded there and smiled fawningly. They said: "Herr Graf! do you want some milk? ... Shall we warm it up, or are you going straight to bed?"

Or they fussed about how bad I looked. So hunted and restless.

What business was it of these three old maids, of all people?

And whenever they stood there, the pooch would yap under some skirt or other. I could have spat at them all, I hated it all so much. The whole world disgusted me. I was so weary. Endlessly weary. What interest did I have in all their wailing? As for the dog, he was already driving me to distraction. I would have stuffed his mouth at the first opportunity.

One Sunday afternoon, when the three old maids had gone to church for vespers, I packed the little brute into my towel and flung it in the toilet. It squealed terribly, leapt out, and made a mess of the whole corridor. But from then on it always disappeared when I came home and hid itself away somewhere in terror.

The three said nothing. They just trembled.

Eugen came one day. I was irritated by how fat he was. His body language had become phlegmatic and Americanized, and he spoke lazily.

"You've really landed me in the shit!" I said bitterly. He looked a bit surprised but was otherwise unperturbed. He told me what he had already done in America and that he now had to see how he should feed wife and children. He seemed no better off than I.

"You don't seem too bothered about it," I repeated, grimly. He softened a little and even spoke to me in confidence.

"Hey, if you only knew how I am up to my neck in it ... I have started as a rep ... In fact, you could help me out with it," he said. He then took a longish, red case out of his waistcoat pocket and showed me a very small hand-held glass syringe, together with soluble tablets: a new patent that he had acquired from the manufacturer for sale. He explained everything to me and assured me that with hard work, we could get a good turnover.

"And where do I come in?" I asked.

He came close to me and got more animated. "Every woman needs one of these, don't you see? It will mainly be whores who buy them, and you know your way with them, don't you? ... You've been hanging around these people and you know the various cafés where they do business ... Do you get it now? ... You go in on Sundays or in the evening and sell the syringes over the tables... There is good money to be made ..."

He gazed at me. I saw this man of the world, suddenly brought down, small and helpless, and thought with a bitchy satisfaction: so you're also in the shit. Good. Good!

For a moment I was overcome with the desire to burst into raucous and cruel laughter. But I refrained and said morosely: "I don't know any whores and I don't understand what you're on about! ... You'll have to manage for yourself ... It would suit me fine not to see or hear from any of you again."

He was quite cool, stood up and recovered his superior attitude: "Good! I have done what I could for you... If you want to leave it at that, it's all the same to me."

Then he was off.

I carried on slaving away in the mill and heard nothing more from home. Jeez, if only the whole damned world would sink into hell! This thought whirred through my head. I was sick to death.

Such was my mood when I met Schorsch on Sunday.

"Come on," he said curtly. "We're going to Italy. Get ready." I looked up at him.

"Have you the money?" I asked.

"I have enough for the journey to Locarno," came the reply. I imagined that you'd need hundreds of marks for such a journey.

He asked: "How much money have you got?"

"Just my last week's wages, and I have to pay those three unmarried housewives today," I told him.

"Rubbish!" he exclaimed resolutely, and with a determined swing of the arm. "We'll just scarper."

We went to my room and waited until the old maids had gone to vespers. We chucked everything quickly into my suitcase. Schorsch jumped on the lid and forced it shut. I locked it. Then we packed what we most needed in a cardboard box and went out.

"I just want to see if we can get something to eat from home," I said to Schorsch in the tram. He stared at me in disbelief. "What? Now? You're mad!" He was outraged.

"Come on, I'm just going to call home on the off chance that Nanndl comes to the telephone and I'll ask her to bring us a food parcel on the quiet. It'll be all right. There's no one else there. It'll work, just wait and see," I said quietly, and added reassuringly: "I'll definitely be back by evening. Then we shall at least have something for the journey."

He gave himself a face-slap and exclaimed: "My God, you are a nit-wit! Such stupidity!"

But I would not let him stop me. I carried out my plan and it really worked out for the best. That evening I came to the café with two gigantic food parcels. We said goodbye to a few acquaintances and went to the station. At ten-thirty the train carried us off into the night.

Schorsch gave me a fabulous description of Switzerland.

"There are no policemen, it is all faithful and democratic," he declared. After a while we fell asleep. In Bregenz we were woken up by the Swiss customs officials. In the morning light we reached Zurich, where we had a wait-over of several hours, so we went to see something of the town. Around four we set off again for Locarno. I had never travelled so far in my life. Suddenly I started arguing like a madman with my companion about the direction of travel.

"We're going the wrong way! We're definitely going the wrong way!" I shouted and blustered at him.

It was only when we steamed into Locarno that I calmed down. "What a job it is travelling with you," sighed Schorsch with relief. We got out of the train and used the last of our money to find a lodging for the night at the *Hotel Alpino*. The next day we wanted to seek out some comrades at the communist colony in Brione, to get accommodation there.

10.
FREEDOM AT LAST

The sky was deep blue and seemed tremendously near when we woke up. The hotel courtyard was strangely quiet and reminded me more of a monastery than a guesthouse. In its centre, a dilapidated fountain reared up, gently purring and splashing. The tendrils of wild grapevines climbed up the walls. Open corridors connected the stone stairwells running around the hotel floors. This meant you had to enter the courtyard to access the hotel.

We ate what was left of the food we had brought for the journey, went below to the porter, collected our baggage, paid and went out to the street.

"We now have precisely four francs," said Schorsch. We weren't bothered. We felt indescribably at peace with ourselves.

Life itself was clad in a richly coloured dress, which made us feel at home. Pretty, tanned Italian girls scurried past, the clumsy trams hummed peacefully along the narrow streets, coarse-looking men leaned broad-shouldered at the street corners. The shopfronts had a blissfully bright and open appearance and the sun, high in the sky, shone in splendour over everything.

We wandered deeper into the town and sat down on a park bench in the Piazza Grande, where we dozed off. A shabby-looking man came up to us and said something like: "Papiero, cartonaggia?" We thought he was a wandering journeyman who wanted to join us, and I immediately started talking to him in a mish-mash of Munich dialect and scraps of Italian: "Ah! Lazzaroni too! Niente, not us! We are resting here and then we're off to Brione to meet some friends."

The man now pulled out his police badge and said: "Polizia!" We understood at once. He also gesticulated wildly with his arms and made it clear that we had to follow him. So, we followed him.

"Ah," I said to Schorsch with a malicious smile "So this is what goes on in free Switzerland. Aha!"

We plodded on mechanically. The sun shone and there was a clear blue sky above us. Everything was multi-coloured and warm, beautiful and new, apart from this sleazy dog who was arresting us. You meet his type all over the world, I thought. It is all the same, whether you are in Munich or in Switzerland.

At the police station they were most interested in how much money we had. Curiously, nobody asked for identity papers, and that was a relief, because we had not bothered with these in our hurry to leave. I possessed a bill of lading that had been stamped very many times, a Bavarian certificate of residence, and a notification of discharge from Karlsruhe General Hospital in the name of my brother Maurus. I suspected we'd be put in solitary confinement and – because Schorsch had already mentioned this possibility – that they would dump us over the border. But they could only speak a few words of German and did not seem to be taking the matter seriously. A short, fat man on a revolving chair flipped through a dictionary, searched and searched, before finally reading out loud, "Un-gefähr?"

His speech was rapid and muddled, and we simply answered again and again: "Not Lazzaroni!" We finally told him where our comrades were living and were dismissed.

"I suppose it is a bit freer than it is with us! ... That's fine with me!" I exclaimed with satisfaction, as we left the gloomy building.

Going up the hill above Minusio towards Brione, a man, who looked like a gypsy, strode towards us.

"That's Theo!" said Schorsch and shouted the name out loud. He laughed and came up to us beaming and open-eyed. In fact, it was our comrade Theo from the Munich "Tat" group. He had fled from Munich when he got called up for military service, and was leading a natural life here, more or less according to anarchistic principles.

Apart from him, another three comrades were there. We were delighted and hurriedly told him about what had happened to us. Slowly we climbed higher and higher. The flat house roofs of Locarno and Minusio sank further and further beneath the treetops. The lake stretched out, broad and shimmering. A steamboat cruised lazily across the water. The flat, square houses of the villages on the far shore stood out in the crystalline air and the softly rounded loins of the Italian foothills undulated peacefully in the sky ...

Theo took us to his abode and fetched the other comrades. His girlfriend Grete gave us something to eat. We decided to go and stay at the Christian colony, "Love", whose members Theo knew. It was a modern house, built like a villa, with a vineyard and many vegetable beds. A pious community lived here according to Christian principles. The Elder greeted us gently and provided us with a room for ten francs per month. We brought in our luggage and settled in. Meantime it was evening.

Feeling dead tired but liberated, we lay down on the mattresses. When we had been lying there a short time, we suddenly heard a fussy whisper behind the partition. We listened more attentively and looked around the room, which was really a boarded cubicle. Behind the partition that separated us from the adjoining cubicle, there was suddenly a scratching sound, as though a cat was sharpening its claws. It gave us the creeps. The room was lit up by a full moon. Above us, we noticed a metal-plated hole in the wall, which had probably once housed the flue-pipe. I nudged Schorsch, and whispered to him softly: "Can you hear it?" He nodded. We listened again and for some reason we fixed our attention on the hole in the ceiling, as that seemed to be where the whispering and scratching came from. Then, all of a sudden, a face appeared in the opening. We saw it clearly. Then another face appeared and disappeared. There was more whispering, and again a face appeared. We stayed still, but we were ready for a fight. Involuntarily, I thought of the scary story about the Spessart Inn[12] and similar goings-on. And because gruesome stories had always fascinated me, it was natural for me to imagine all kinds of nonsense.

I crept closer to Schorsch and breathed into his ear: "Nice people, these Christians! Let's go and have it out with them! No messing about!"

What business did these blighters have in watching us at night, why were they whispering, and what were they talking about? They must have been crooks hiding behind their Christian masks, or – more probably, as our comrades had told us about spiritualism – they thought we were ghosts. We were very tired and gradually got terribly angry about these scoundrels who would not let us sleep. I nudged Schorsch again, and whispered softly: "Come on, let's get up and make all kinds of mysterious signs." We sprung out of bed at the same time and started making an unholy row. We recited mystical verses, rhapsodized over the moon, knelt like Muslims and went about like ghosts. Finally we stripped naked, danced and made incantations, without taking any notice of what was going on in the hole. And just as intended – the noises diminished, the whispering ceased, and no face reappeared. It became quiet. Laughing, we got back on our mattresses. Aha! We thought, though we were not really sure why.

Finally we fell asleep. The next day we told our comrades what had happened. They just said the people in the Christian colony were cranks, rather confused in their ideas, but our comrades did not know anything more specific. They did tell us that sometimes they held spiritualist seances and belonged to a sect.

We climbed up a mountain and cut down stout cudgels, which we took to bed, and we listened again. Sure enough, the whispering and spying did start up once more. But then it suddenly stopped for a while. Quickly, and in unison, we threw our cudgels at the wall with all our might, then lay still and listened intently while pretending to snore, as though deep in sleep.

It worked. First it was deathly quiet, then the faces reappeared in the hole; the eyes stupefied with terror. We stifled our laughter. There was an excited chirruping above, then we heard a door open and there was a

---

[12] *The Spessart Inn* is a ghost story about two travelling journeymen, dating from the eighteenth century, adapted for cinema in 1923 and 1958.

knock.

We were ready for anything. Nevertheless we called out fractiously, as if we had been woken from a deep sleep. "Yes! ... What's up?!"

"Something has happened," someone whimpered. We crawled out of our beds, grabbed our cudgels and hid them under our bedclothes. Three men stood there in their long nightshirts, trembling with fear. One of them was flashing a light in the corridor. They wanted to start a search. Grumpily, we said that they should spare us such idiocies and leave us in peace. We went back to bed. We were secretly in fits of laughter. We heard them shuffling around like ghosts for a while, then we finally went back to sleep. But from this point on, there was no more whispering and gawking through the flue-hole that night. It happened occasionally, but we got used to it and let those people do as they liked.

Now we saw another ghost every evening and often roused the entire household. Actually, a white cat was prowling about; a nightly phantom that wandered through the vines. But we did not just want to create a bit of excitement for its own sake. We were stirring things up with calculated intent. We had no money and did not know how we were going to pay for our accommodation. Each time the colony's Elder approached us we got the jitters. We could see what was coming in his eyes, but we covered it up by telling him the most fantastic stories. The good man could hardly get a word in edgewise; we were the most daring and inventive fibbers. Shaking his head, the master of the house withdrew.

No money! So, to work! I shuddered at the thought of the mill.

Apart from us, our circle of comrades included another six people: Gobmaier, a genuine son of Munich with some rather peculiar and confused ideas about housing settlements, his wife and young lad. Then there was Jenke, a painter and decorator from Saxony, Giuseppe, a locksmith from Munich, good-natured, with a military bearing, and a permanently awkward smile on his lips. And lastly, Theo with his Grete. Each of them had built their own dwelling and only worked now and again, so they could devote their leisure time to their own free development. Actually, they were all people with an inner calling, one could even say they had an artistic bent. What mattered was the inner spirit, and the true task of a genuine anarchist meant: to shape his outward life according to the law of his innermost desires, in the utmost freedom, without limitation, and as far as possible untouched by "culture".

Theo was the leading intellectual. There was much discussion. We made plans for a future anarchist settlement in Brazil.

Gobmaier was the most practical of all. He was a paperhanger by trade, but there was nothing he could not do, and he regarded the ability of a person to produce all of life's necessities for himself as the mark of progress: a person should build his own house, make his own clothes, cultivate the land. He worked incessantly, and in his leisure hours he wrote naive verses about Lago Maggiore, poems on freedom and ideas. Jenke was a radical vegetarian who abandoned himself to nature, painted miniatures and justified vegetarianism in his diary. He was very gentle and spent a lot of time observing his theories on digestion and trying to make them plausible to others. He was almost fanatical about this, even if fanaticism seemed ludicrous in such a gentle soul. When we visited him, he read passages from Nietzsche or Forel. But everything came back to vegetarianism. Once, when I read Zarathustra's "Night Song" aloud and with great feeling, he said, quite ecstatically: "No question about it, the man was a vegetarian!"

"Very nice," I once said, when he showed me his little pictures. That made him angry; he showed me to the door and started to expound on nature to me. He placed his hands in front of his eyes like blinkers and said in his Munich accent, as he looked out at the landscape: "There, I see blue, don't I, and that's how I paint it. I'm dead good at it. It's a gift of nature."

I nodded repeatedly. When we went back into the house, he declared: "You just have to be a bit skilful to do that kind of thing." Giuseppe, who lived with him, took no notice of this. In fact it seemed to me that he was secretly having a laugh. He was generally austere and always working on something practical.

The ties of comradeship were loose. Everyone lived for himself. We were held together only by our convictions. There was no place for anarchists in countries with governments, in cities and in this civilization. That meant starting from scratch somewhere or other, where absolute freedom made such a life possible, where such communities could be created. For this reason, the scheme to emigrate to Brazil became more urgent with every passing day. We got together every evening and read and discussed Kropotkin, Landauer and Proudhon. It often got heated, but we understood one another. Everyone worked during the day.

We had no money. The landlord pressed us. I cursed all of Switzerland. In Ascona there was work with a man called Gräser. But he paid no wages. He just provided food and accommodation and rejected all contact with "culture". There were quite enough settlements of that kind. This was profitable for people who already had some property, sometimes highly profitable, because deserters for example, or Russian revolutionaries, were forced to work for these drones without wages.

There was every type of human being there: revolutionaries, vegetarians and painters from every point on the compass, disciples of open-air health regimens, and lastly writers and devotees of nature with long hair, who wore no clothes except a shirt and sackcloth. Some full-blooded vegans had a large settlement at Verità, known as "The Blueberry", where they proclaimed the cult of naturism, free love and a "new humanity".

They stuck propaganda sheets written in verse form on all the trees, inviting people to join them, but woe betide anyone who smelt of soap, or brought any, or worst of all, smoked ...

Our need for money became more and more acute. We worked a few days for Gräser. Then a master decorator in Locarno gave us some painting jobs. Nanndl sent money. So we got by.

"To hell with this life," I moaned one day during a discussion. "It's just the same as anywhere else." Schorsch moved out and built himself a couple of rooms in a mill, planted vegetables and finally found a job as a pastry cook in Locarno. Suddenly, I hated the whole set-up; I called Jenke a "grass-muncher and digestive-tract revolutionist" and shut myself off. I did not like this placid life and all the discussion. I spent my last francs buying a supply of groceries and showed my face no more. I lay on my mattress all day, reading and writing. Sometimes I tramped through the surroundings alone.

One day, as I was getting on the bus in Ascona to go to Locarno, a man sat next to me who seemed very familiar. The Leipzig *Anarchist* had published his picture a short while ago.

A French-speaking companion was talking with him. So I could observe him at my leisure. The man was small and had a long, well-kempt grey beard, which covered half of his chest. His eyes moved restlessly behind his glasses, and his entire face was thickset, with sharply protruding cheekbones. Only his forehead rose smoothly in the shadow of his hat.

The pair of them got out in Locarno. I followed them. I got closer and closer to them. The little, grey-bearded man grew nervous. I came right up to him and tapped him from behind on the shoulder, causing him to turn around in amazement. He looked rather confused.

"Excuse me, but have I the honour of addressing Prince Peter Kropotkin?" I asked, rather awkwardly, and with a slight laugh. The man nodded amicably and scrutinized me briefly. At the time, I wore only trousers and shirt, always going barefoot, and had long, flowing hair.

"Excuse me," I repeated rather hastily, "my name is Graf. I am a socialist and saw your photograph in the Leipzig *Anarchist*."

"A young comrade," Kropotkin now said to his companion, introducing me. We gradually got into conversation. I praised Kropotkin's books and told him about the movement in Germany. The two of them listened with interest.

"Do you write for socialist newspapers?" asked the Prince, when I made a passing mention of my literary efforts, and he gazed at me.

"No, just for comic papers," I replied. The two of them cast their eyes over me again and smiled a little. Nobody knew what to talk about next. I felt uncomfortable. I said something about my German comrades in Brione and said goodbye where the road turned off.

"Hopefully we will see each other often," I said as we shook hands, then ran off in a hurry. I reached Brione breathless and, in a state of feverish excitement, I told my comrades what had happened. They were all in raptures. They wanted to organize a ceremony of homage and visit the Prince immediately.

"That sounds like the German Veterans' Association celebrating the anniversary of Bismarck's death," I protested. That hit home. We quarrelled. They felt offended for some reason and, rather doggedly, they tried to justify themselves. "Honouring intellectual achievements, which can be of great service to all of humanity in the future, is a very different matter from the deferential cult of royalty and rank that is instilled in people, which does nobody any good and just stupefies the masses," Theo argued again and again. He went on: "If we feel compelled to honour Kropotkin openly, I would say we are doing this almost spontaneously. It's just common sense."

"The German Veterans' Association does things spontaneously, too," I said maliciously.

"Sophist," shouted Theo, casting angry glances at me.

"In the past the people had the Kaiser or some such creature. Now you have set up another God for yourselves," I said, standing up, and added wryly: "It's always the same story, men must have some authority, or else they perish." We parted; half divided by an invisible barrier.

German revolutionaries are an odd bunch, I thought, as I strode through the dark; they are like eternally craggy twenty-year-olds with their stodgy idols, Don Quixote come to life, with the everlasting urge to become a Nazarene.

A heavy fragrance hung in the night air. The moon heaved through fleeting clouds. Deep below, Locarno was speckled with light, reflected in the pale lake, which stretched out peacefully like a silvery-blue rug, and the sky above was infinitely distant.

Shortly before I fell asleep, I sat up suddenly and said out loud to myself: "It's all madness! I have to get out! It's all filth."

11.
THE BREACH. AND BACK TO THE SWAMP

There's always a fly in the ointment. To hell with Italian Switzerland! There were too many lizards. I had a phobia for these loathsome creatures since my childhood. I could run a mile if such a reptile suddenly appeared anywhere near me! And here the rocks were alive with them, heaving down on you like a single swarm.

And when it rained there were vast numbers of salamanders. They were even more disgusting. They stood there motionless, with the head raised a little, giving you an icy-cold glare. I hardly dared go out alone any more, stayed on the high road, and finally, in spite of the glorious weather, lay in bed until late in the afternoon; in the evening I ran down to Locarno and collected Schorsch from work. My debts mounted daily. Whenever I went to the garden gate the master of the house stood there and whined: "Herr Graf, when are you going to pay?" I calmed him down and asked for a bill, saying I had to send it home. That was of course all a lie and no money ever came. But what else could I do? The most plausible excuse was that the post had been delayed. When even that was of no further use, I gave him my family's address and said he should write himself. As I had expected, still nothing came. The situation became even more awkward and distressing. I wrote to Nanndl. A letter came, saying that she had sent twenty marks, *poste restante,* to Locarno. I showed the master of the house the letter every day. And every day I went to the post office in Locarno. Still nothing came. Nothing at all. Every day the post office clerk took out a bundle of money orders, leafed through them phlegmatically, and said indifferently: "Niente." I lost my temper, raised hell, called the whole postal service a pack of thieves and idiots, and was arrested. After three hours' detention in a bare room, a German post office clerk came and quizzed me.

I told her about my trouble and showed her Nanndl's letter. She was very friendly and was herself lost for an explanation. Suddenly, something seemed to dawn on her.

"The money might have been sent to Lugano by mistake," she said, giving me an endearing look. "What has that to do with me?" I raged. "Calm down, Herr Graf. I will enquire there at once," she said politely. My gloomy expression only made her smile. I blushed and felt embarrassed, but to hide my lack of self-confidence, I lost my temper again and grumbled: "Yes, but why did nobody do that ages ago, I've been inconvenienced long enough!" The young lady smiled again:

"You've certainly been inconvenienced."

"I'd like the complaints book," I interrupted. Quite suddenly I had recalled what my father once told me, that you can make a complaint in a special book in any German post office. This book has to be presented to the government after the end-of-year financial close. Just you wait, I thought as this occurred to me, I'll cook your goose for you. I rejoiced at this newly acquired weapon and was already mentally formulating my complaints. But nothing could fluster this young woman, who continued to smile. She got up and gave me a form, on which I had to write my exact address. "So," she said, "I will enquire immediately, and you are sure to receive your money in a few days."

She remained standing, eyed me up once more, and said with the genial but firm tone of a schoolmistress: "Herr Graf, Germans always behave abroad as if the world revolved around them! ... That is a big mistake."

I was taken aback, and stared at her, lost for words. Then she left me. A policeman came and let me out. I went down the dark corridors and out into the street as night was falling. When I reached Brione, I at once sought out Schorsch and made a terrible scene over his boasts about free Switzerland. "A fine people, these Swiss gentlemen! A pack of postal thieves and spies, vegetarians and cranks! Old maids and moralizing professors!" I argued, to which my comrade replied, time and again: "You're a complete idiot!"

Thankfully, by the time I arrived back home it was late at night, and my housemates were already asleep.

Very early the next morning there was a knock at my door. I leapt out of bed and was already looking forward to finding out that my entry in the complaints book had worked! But the postman who stood there gave me a summons from the police. I was to report at eleven o'clock, it seemed.

"Police spies! Spies wherever you look!" I snarled and cursed Schorsch and the whole of Switzerland. I got dressed, made tea and went down to Locarno. The landlord was standing at the garden gate again, with his usual whinge. "I have to report to the police," I yelled at him. He recoiled in shock.

At the police station they showed me a long letter that my brother Max had written to some high office claiming that I had come under the influence of anarchists and that our mother was crying her eyes out. He demanded my immediate deportation. One again, the police officer could only speak broken German. He sat there completely unperturbed on his swivel chair, pushed the letter over to me and, wholly indifferent, busied himself by thumbing through a thick volume without troubling himself any further about me. They will probably demand my identity papers now, was my first thought, already getting used to the idea of being deported. On the other hand, I calculated, at least you'll get out of this shithole of a country on the cheap. But the gentleman on the swivel chair did not seem to want anything to do with me. He did not even listen when I said: "He's just denouncing me!" He carried on looking through his book, unhurried. Then another gentleman arrived, looked at me calmly, and asked if I was working. I made out that I was writing for newspapers and working as a freelance author, adding that the letter was written out of pure hatred and vindictiveness, and when I saw that the man was listening to me calmly, I started telling him my entire life story. When I was about halfway through, the man laid a piece of paper in front of me, with something about a tax on foreign visitors, and asked me to sign it. I did so and was released.

Out on the street I exulted over Max's failed attempt. I felt entirely reconciled with the police and the Swiss nation, looked out for Schorsch, and told him all about it. Then we went to the temperance restaurant at the train station.

We had been there several times and had met a radical *Grütlianer* who always liked to expound his theories on *Schwyzerdütsch*.[13] It was always the same story. We no longer listened to what he said but were simply amused by the way he said it.

The more heated he got, the more we egged him on. His theories boiled down to the idea that the workers would, over time, take possession of the soil and the factories, and that the standard of living would rise steadily, and property would cease to exist.

"In the communist state it is aw' the sam' if I'm here or there, everything belongs tae everyone," he sermonized, illustrating his point with drawings on the floor. For him, Zurich and Bern were the most advanced cities in the world. But he hated Locarno, because there were no public conveniences. He got so wound up about this deficiency that he threatened a bombardment of the city by the working class. He emphasized the distinction between freethinkers and socialists.

"Och aye," he said. "Th' freethinkers! ... Th' freethinkers are a totally different kettle ay fesh tae th' socialists! ... Th' free-thinkers struggle against God, but th' socialists, th' socialists, they fight against th' whole system." Etc. We bit our lips in an effort to hide our laughter. "And as for Switzerland! Switzerland is something else altogether," I said, in deathly earnest, but he always responded with the stereotypical turn of phrase: "When it comes tae nations, that'll aw be sorted oot when th' socialists tak' th' helm!"

Finally we, or at least I, left the "dry" restaurant deep in debt. I can

---

[13] The Grütlians were a Swiss socialist sect focused on workers' education; it later merged with the Socialist Party. *Schwyzerdütsch*, the Swiss German dialect, is an endless source of amusement for German speakers north of the Alps.

still see the upright, corpulent landlady looking me over and saying: "Ah, but I can see I am dealing with an honest man!" as I spoke movingly about how my debts were piling up. I left my overcoat behind and never came back. The ground was starting to burn under my feet. Every day I went to the post office and steered well clear of the temperance restaurant. The money didn't show up. There was no escape. I was already half resigned to my fate. Completely dejected and outraged by the tedious business at the post office, one day I bumped into Kropotkin again. I told him about it all and showed him the letter from Nanndl. He became embarrassed. "I don't have a penny. I've no idea what to do," I said. The good man became more and more embarrassed and flustered. I wanted to calm him down and say: "I don't want anything from you. I didn't mean it that way." But he had suddenly turned away and was gone. I never met him again. I just spotted him from a distance sometimes.

Finally, the twenty marks arrived. Finally. I paid five francs to my landlord and with the rest I bought *Palmin*,[14] macaroni and sugar, bread and some butter. Then I shut myself off from the world and lived off my supplies as best as I could.

Our community in Brione decided at last to emigrate to Brazil. I was against it and called it an escapist fantasy. There were impassioned discussions. Even here, I did not show up very often. Sometimes I did not leave my room for three days on end. My landlord was waiting around for me to pay the rest of my debt. I avoided him. My supplies ran out. I ate sorrel and even tried roasting it but threw up at the first attempt. Whenever my housemates sat down to eat, I secretly sneaked out if I could no longer bear to stay within my four walls. Bored and aimless, I wandered around the area and went to Locarno of an evening to fetch Schorsch. We argued in his hut until deep in the night and I urged him not to go with the others to Brazil. At the time he was starting to copy Michelangelo and showed me his efforts. I liked them, which encouraged him. But apart from that, he would soon get what the emigrants were counting on, a small fortune.

I ranted: "What are you going to do in that dump over there? Were you born to be a lumberjack? Are you a farmer?"

He nodded and admitted, I had a point.

"It's the same all over the world. Us proles can clear all the rain forests and cultivate the land, we can graft, and we can sweat, but in the end the State will come and tax us, make us its vassals and take away all the fruits of our labour.

"It's the same racket, wherever! I'd sooner be a tramp in a more comfortable country..."

---

[14] A cheap brand of margarine that is still sold in Germany.

He was on my side, entirely. We went to see our comrades. We faced a hostile attitude. Schorsch vacillated again. I got annoyed.

"Just go back to your urban swamp!" Theo told me. I called him a coward for wanting to escape to the rain forest. "You might as well go and open a monastery, if you won't take up the struggle against our own countries," I ranted. We argued the point angrily, back and forth. And then parted on hostile terms. Three days passed without me leaving my room once. I immersed myself in all the socialist literature I could, to the best of my ability. I learned a great deal in this way. It slowly dawned on me that we must go to the masses. Often, as I was reading, I thought out expansive plans, which made my emotions run hot and cold. Schorsch did not come. I crept down to his *molino*. Everything was locked up. I went up to Theo. Only Grete was there. She greeted me with suspicion. "Where are the others?" I asked.

"They went over to Italy," she replied curtly. "Damn it!" I snarled, and thought they were already off.

"Why don't you tell us what you have in mind?" Grete asked tetchily.

"What am I supposed to have in mind?"

"All kinds of things! ... You want to turn Schorsch against us, so he goes off with you," she said in the same tone.

"What does a revolutionary want with Brazil and the rain forest?" I asked, surly.

"The same old song," she snapped at me.

"When are they coming back?" I returned.

"In about eight days," Grete answered.

"Christ! The whole lot of them can go to hell" I swore, and left.

After eight days, Schorsch and Theo came back. They had hiked all the way to Milan. My friend was fully in favour of Brazil again. It was time for me to take a decision. We took long walks and I talked to Schorsch about his talent as an artist. We argued it out, this way and that. Our comrades were too torpid, too moralizing and muddle-headed for our taste. Besides which, my debts were piling up intolerably day by day. And monotony was once again setting in. I got no post; we were in the middle of nowhere and had no idea what was going on in the cities. It was too quiet, too comfortable, too dreary. Blue skies alone could not alter that. Not one bit!

"We'll go back to our urban swamp then; I won't miss any of this cretinous back-to-nature stuff ... I would rather leave it to vegetarians and other philistines! ... That's no way to live!" I said in total disgust.

Schorsch nodded. He also hated this self-satisfied cosiness. If we drank a little schnapps and lots of wine, some of the anarchists would suddenly kick up a storm of indignation. And if we smoked, they called us decadent.

We wanted to live, and it seemed to us, they just wanted to scheme. Brazil was rubbish. We went to Theo.

"So," Schorsch said straight out, belching his last schnapps. "Now I'll tell you what for: "We're going back to the swamp." He blurted it out with feeling, but like a petty-bourgeois philistine who has suffered a sudden attack of self-awareness. I could almost have smiled.

Theo grew pale with anger. Then he smiled scornfully and looked at me.

"We are no Napoleons! Not even in our imagination," he mocked.

"Me neither," I retorted, unmoved. From this point on, we were rather alienated from each other. An invisible barrier.

Schorsch wrote asking for money from his brother, who was looking after his property for him. Nobody knew our intentions. I packed my boxes and smuggled them down to the *molino*. Schorsch had already given up his job at the patisserie in Locarno a fortnight earlier. After a wild drinking session in a restaurant we passed by Jenke's – the philosopher of the digestive tract – and bawled out pub songs. Then we looked for Theo and told him what we were going to do. He and Grete did not come and see us off at the station. We boarded the train and it set off.

"We've got a long and fun-filled life stretching out before us. Man!" I said to Schorsch with a sense of relief and breathed out.

We arrived in Munich on Whit Sunday. The next day, I spent my last mark on my fare home. When I arrived in the town, people gawped at me. I was like a wild man, all bedraggled with my long hair. I felt like a stranger in these civilized surroundings. It was a glorious day. The vast clear sky spanned far and wide over Lake Starnberg. It all seemed so familiar, so close, it was as if I had never been away. I got out of the steamship in Leoni and climbed up the hill. In the distance I saw two girls in their Sunday best, coming towards me with a well-dressed man. They laughed and chattered in boisterous high spirits. As I came closer, the three of them screamed in unison:

"For heaven's sake! Oskar! Oskar!" The laughter died down at once, as each of them took on an embarrassed expression and looked me over in astonishment. They went with me to the village, surrounding me so that no one could see me. They were ashamed of me.

We entered a small cottage. Theres and Emma had rented it and taken in mother. Max had married and was living in our old house. Eugen had travelled back to America with his wife and children.

I was received like a lost son. Max let it be known that I should not show my face, or else he would beat me up. The next day I went up to Munich with Maurus and took a job as a baker.

12.
THE GREAT LEAP

Work, save and to hell with it all – again. That was my basic principle. Just to get away. As far away as possible. Where to didn't matter. Munich is a dump! Away! Away!

I was vaguely aware that Jung was in Berlin, and that literary activity was possible there. So that's the place to go! A really big change had to happen. Something to get me completely out of my current rut. So I started my job in Munich. For me it was not a big thing, just a means to an end.

Schorsch attended a painting school, had set up a studio, and engaged models. They robbed him, took advantage of him and picked fights in his studio. I rarely dropped by. I was working relatively long hours. From eleven at night to two o'clock in the afternoon and often even longer. When I got back to my room I sat down and wrote short stories until I fell asleep. I lost touch with the anarchists. I had no time.

Meanwhile, Maurus was also working in a Munich pastry shop and made friends with Schorsch. It was a lopsided relationship. Maurus was bitter and twisted. He read a lot and had the manner of an urbane man of the world, old before his time. It's easy to imagine that he harboured suspicions towards me over the smallest details. Nevertheless he visited me on Sundays and sneered: "I had a new suit made for me, I bought new ties, and I've almost saved a thousand marks." For him, I was a person with no willpower and no character, and it was a bad idea to get involved with me. He took every opportunity to throw the business about the three hundred marks in my face. "I bear you no grudge," he usually added, with a malicious undertone, "you mean nothing to me. I couldn't care less what happens to you ... But old Schopenhauer was right: a person's character does not change ... That's a very good insight." Then he smiled maliciously and twisted the knife ... "And he says another fine thing, so completely correct ... How does it go ... Yes ...

"Something like ... Once one has been deceived by a person, and trusts him ever again, that means one is throwing one's money out of the window ... Hahaha! Yes, that is very fine indeed. Very good!" He then broke into raucous laughter and seemed to gloat over the fact that I could say nothing in response.

I was dead tired. He started to read aloud to me. I closed my eyes. He bragged about how hard he worked and what he had achieved, and said again and again: "Yes, work ... Earning money through your own labour ... Yes! Ha-ha ... That's not so easy, ha-ha ..." Then he was off. I borrowed books off him. He gave them to me. But he was very keen on his books. I forgot to give them back on time. I had borrowed a little money from him to get started and wanted to pay it back when I had some more. He was not reluctant to lend it to me, but he kept pressuring me and said: "Oh well, the money is gone anyway, I know what you are like ... You're a very profligate man, when you know you can swindle someone else." Finally I argued back that he was cajoling me. I got angry and stayed out of touch for a while. One day as I was asleep, he thumped me with his umbrella before vanishing in an instant. The bust-up was now complete. We did not meet again.

Schorsch blew all his money and was working as a pastry cook once more. We only met each other on Sundays. Models came and borrowed money. We went for walks and got together with some of our friends in the café.

The journeyman was cunning. He had a bloated face, small, slitty eyes and a sugary, falsetto voice. He was very chummy with the master baker, because the latter had a small branch store, and the journeyman aspired to become a master baker himself in the near future. He belonged to the species of men of whom it is said, they trample on the people below them, and creep up to those above. When the master came home at midnight and looked in at the bakery, his diligent assistant always said: "Oh Herr Doll, we'll manage comfortably. You can go to bed with an easy mind. The stuff is nearly all baked. At Ettaler's we always had three times as much to do, and there were only two of us, myself and the apprentice."

How a master baker loves to hear such words. Herr Doll said straight away: "All right, yeah, just get on with it!" He belched a few times, stuck his finger up his nose and prodded the fermenting dough, saying, "That's done already, has to be worked out quickly ... Don't let it sink." He bared his teeth for a while and then went off to bed. When he was gone, the journeyman grabbed the dough and, in a sulk, muttered a few unintelligible words like, "He always has to find fault" and threw the dough on the kneading board. Then the mad rush started. I weighed the pieces, the apprentice put them in the dough machine and spread them out for the head journeyman. Then we had to cut rolls and twist pretzels and so on. Early in the morning the master came and helped make buns. I had to prepare the various types of dough. When the master was there, his assistant drove us hard – the apprentice and me – and played the industrious worker. At night I often casually said it was real drudgery in this sweatshop, and that we had to work hard for our money, while the master was guzzling beer and pigging out on roast pork.

"Do you know what Oskar was saying tonight?" the journeyman would usually say to the master, as he was making buns.

"No, what?" the master asked inquisitively, without looking up from his work, smiling maliciously to himself.

"He said it's real slave labour working for you, while you have it easy," his assistant informed him, in an innocent tone of voice, and then the creep carried on with a supercilious smile: "He's just not used to hard work and seems to think you can get to be a master baker overnight ..."

"Oh yes. That's young people for you these days ... They always think you can just make it in the blink of an eye," the master interrupted, with his loud, beery laugh. "In my time they worked eighteen hours a day for just one guilder a week. Whereas nowadays workers are pure thieves!" And then he usually told his life story. He was thick-set, stout and sure of himself. The journeyman nodded now and again, as if he felt called upon to back up the master's assertions. I usually kept stumm on such occasions and suppressed my resentment. Once the baking had been done, I had to deliver the bread. Until two in the afternoon I rode around to the various customers on my bike, fully loaded. Once I was done with this, I went into the bakery, scraped my troughs clean, filled them with flour and made the sourdough. Meanwhile the apprentice swept out the bakery, keeping close by my side. He was a distant relative of the master, and it was his job to make sure I did not take any bread with me. At first, I innocently put my ration of bread to one side in his presence. It was customary that you were allowed to take half a pound of bread with you. But I needed a ration of three pounds. The apprentice complained. The master dropped spiteful hints. But I thought, why shouldn't I eat, if I am hungry? If I have to work hard, I have to eat a lot. I was soon sick and tired of the way the master needled me. Since it was not officially sanctioned, I made off with the bread in secret.

"Go and get me some cigarettes," I usually said to the apprentice, shortly before leaving, and while he was out, I stuffed my pockets full of bread and got dressed. I kept cool as he eyed me suspiciously and disappeared. "Bunch of hypocrites!" I swore out on the street and calculated how much money I had saved. Up in my room I made cocoa, ate a few rolls, started reading, or wrote until I fell asleep. The landlady came in, shook me awake and said kindly: "Do go to bed Herr Graf!" So I got undressed, lay down, and slept like a log. At nine in the evening, before they went to bed, the owners of the house woke me. I got myself ready and went back to work.

In the meantime, I had bought a dove-blue suit, a pair of yellow moccasins, and shirts. I was pleased with my new possessions. I had earned them with the sweat of my brow, which made them all the more precious.

One Sunday I went to see Schorsch again. He lived in a small studio flat in the extension at the back of a house in Schwabing. When I passed through the corridor at the front of the house and looked up from the courtyard, the windows were open. Two girls waved down to me and were shouting very loudly. One was wearing a blouse, the other was stark naked. An aeroplane hummed in the air and was attracting their attention. A terrifying noise came from above. I ran up the stairs and went in. Inside, it looked like the aftermath of the Battle of Sedan. Herring tins, crates, dirty buckets were everywhere, and the table was covered with paint pots. Combs were lying about, dirty cups everywhere, and the two models were bouncing around like crazy. Schorsch was sitting calmly on the sofa and painting a landscape; he laughed now and again, or moaned about the noise. I revelled in this bohemian life. I made friends with the girls. We went for a walk. In the evening we went to the pictures and then back to Schorsch's studio. Lollo made tea in a herring tin and asked me if I had ever worn such ragged shirts as my friend. I didn't even think of getting some sleep – I wanted to go straight to work from there.

"That's enough, you'll have to get out," Schorsch said resolutely to the girls.

"Of course, two girls can't stay with one gentleman," said Lollo. Schorsch looked on, helpless.

"You'll have to go," she then said to her rival. "I was here first." Schorsch and I sat there stumm for a while. The girls bickered. Suddenly they started to fight, pulled each other's hair and made a tremendous spectacle, until Schorsch got up and intervened.

"Get your things and sling your hook," he threatened. The girls pleaded with him. Lollo came over to me. "Don't you agree, Herr Graf, that the one who has been here longest has the right to stay." At last everyone agreed that the two would move out the next day. I had to go to work.

"How long are you going to put up with that crud?" my comrade asked me on the way out.

"Not much longer," I replied mechanically.

"Get yourself an office job," he returned.

"I really have to get away from Munich. I want to go to Berlin, there's more I can do there," I answered. On the way home, I figured out how long I could hold out without a job, racking my brains for ways to earn a living. Everything was so disgusting, so parochial.

It was already half past ten. I hurried to work. Weeks slipped by. Lazy and indecisive, I let the time pass. I bought a lottery ticket. The draw was to be made a week later. The top prize was 10,000 marks. Salvation, I thought. Nothing. I sent sketches to various magazines. They were all returned. I often met Lollo and frittered away the afternoon.

I slept at night.

Away!

Away, I thought, away, as far as a train will take me. One day I met Morax. He told me that Jung had gone to Berlin and was living there. He had already published two books, it seemed. Yes, Berlin, no less, I told myself.

The apprentice had snitched on me again. Now the master turned up to work in the bakery just before I left, so he could watch me. I grew furious. I accidentally scolded my hands with lye.[15] I had to sit it out for two weeks and got sick pay. But every three days the master sent to ask when I could start again. When my hand had healed, the journeyman sneered: "Taking a fortnight off work for such a trivial thing!" The master held back, though he did say sometimes: "Oh yes, young men these days! They are so thin-skinned."

Or he asked directly: "How did you live for those two weeks?" So that's the way the wind is blowing, I thought, and said innocently: "Well, you've got to put a few pennies aside so long as you are working."

"A little splash of caustic soda isn't so bad if you can get a long holiday," the journeyman joked while twisting the pretzels, and the master laughed. I carried on working calmly. Just another three or four weeks' wages, then I'll chuck it in, I was thinking.

"You're a right pair of creeps," I said one night to the journeyman and the apprentice. "You tell the master everything, who laughs behind our backs at our disunity. He profits from it."

"What? ... Who told you that? ... What do you mean?" the master's loyal assistant blustered, and then turned red, because I had struck home.

With a dismissive gesture I said: "I've nothing to add. That's what I think."

"We've been working together so long, and now you start carping," the journeyman whined hypocritically, adding: "I'll certainly not make life difficult for you."

"All right, all right," I said in a bitter tone, and shut up. The journeyman's face got even redder: "If you want, we can have it out."

"Good," I said, ready for a fight. We carried on with our work in silence.

It was Saturday night and Sunday morning. And more than usually busy. In the time between baking the rolls and waiting for the pretzels to rise, I used the slack period to get my trough in order. I rushed down to the cellar and fetched up one tub of flour after the other, emptying it into the trough. Meanwhile the apprentice sat there idly eating his night rations. The rolls were done.

"Oskar! Come and do the pretzels," the journeyman shouted. I rushed down to the cellar, wanting to bring up the last tub of flour. "Right away, just one more tub," I shouted behind me. I was dripping sweat. "Get up here!" screamed the journeyman.

---

[15] Lye: the caustic soda used to give pretzels their crisp outer crust.

"Tell Andreas to get up there," was my hasty reply from downstairs.

"Now!" came the threatening cry. I hurriedly climbed the stairs with my full tub of flour, ran to the trough and emptied the flour into it.

The blows rained down on me. I hurled the tub at the journeyman with all my strength, so that it smashed. The apprentice screamed in terror. Now I was in the grip of a wild fury. My body trembled. There was no holding me back now. I raged. Dripping in blood, they fell upon me again. I howled out loud, grabbed the coal shovel, and now it was like a fight to the death. The journeyman retreated into the oven room. I threw the lamp to the floor, rushed into the darkness and hit out at everything indiscriminately. The pretzel boards were smashed, lye gushed out from the pails, and the trestles crashed to the floor. The pair of them now screamed for all they were worth from the bathroom. I battered the door and smashed in the window. Then the two stopped snivelling. I chucked dough and filth in all directions. I wanted to break everything! But the door was bolted and too strong. I shouted through the smashed-in window: "Scabs! Dogs! I'll do for you". The pair of them whined: "You're crazy!" Again, I battered the door with the coal shovel, so that a board crashed in. They both shouted me down, rousing the household. In a flash I saw the entire baker's family standing there in their nightshirts, whimpering. Other tenants were also standing outside in the corridor, horrified. The master baker raised his candle, lighting up the demolished oven room and started, as he saw his entire batch of pretzels lying in filth, to wail like a child. "That's just great. Oh yes! For the love of God, Oskar, you've gone berserk. Just look, everything is ruined! ... Calm down! Quiet! ... Lord almighty!"

"Who wants to have a go? I'll squash him like a mouse!" I yelled like a madman and growled: "Those scabs! Those filthy scabs! I'm off! I'm off, right now!" I flung myself at the bathroom door again: "Open up or I'll smash everything to pieces! Open up. I'm going. I'll be off! Just give me my clothes! Now!"

The whole courtyard was seething. They threw my clothes through the hole in the smashed window. I caught them and got dressed. Nobody dared come close. The two captives screamed incessantly: "He's off his trolley! He should be hauled off to an asylum!" No one heard them, everyone outside was wailing and squealing.

"Well, that's all got to be paid for," whined the baker's wife. "For all I care!" I bawled at her, flung down my apron and got ready to go. Terrified, the people outside made way, and I ran off in haste.

Morning was already breaking out in the street. The houses stretched out, drowsy and glum. Drenched in sweat and splattered with soot, filthy from head to foot, I rushed blindly on and went to find Schorsch. He was still in bed.

When he opened up, he almost recoiled in shock.

"I've finally packed it in!" I said, dropping into a chair. Then, after a short pause, I told him what had happened. He shook his head, simply saying: "That will really drop you in it, if the master decides to get nasty." I wasn't listening. "The best thing for you to do is to disappear out of Munich for a while," my comrade continued. I nodded, half asleep.

"Get off to Berlin," Schorsch repeated, "it's ten times better for you literary types. Besides, Jung is there." That settled it. I washed myself and Schorsch got ready. As we went out to the sunny streets, I was overcome by a feeling of utter freedom. It was as if I was walking on air after struggling through a sea of sludge. After a short stroll we ate in a pub and got everything I needed for my departure.

Once again, as previously in Locarno, I set out into the dark night at ten. Standing at the carriage window, whose surfaces rattled with the clatter and roar of the train, I let out a yell of sheer joy.

Away! Away! Far away! The words shot through my veins and my blood surged.

The railway tracks beat out the rhythm, "Berlin Berlin!" and as if by some strange miracle, the city rose in my imagination as a mighty cathedral.

13.
A GUEST

I arrived in Berlin with three marks and twenty pfennigs. I only had a vague idea of what I was to do. I had Jung's address, but it took a while to find him. When I finally did, I moved in with him and we went drinking. I met all kinds of new people. There was much discussion in the circles we frequented. Psychoanalysis was a major topic, mixed up with all sorts of social ideas. I came into contact with the new literature. Horribly awkward, as I was, people had little idea where to start with me. I had a rather hard time of it. I looked up this person and that and got money or food. After gradually settling into this environment, I began to work as a writer again, published a number of verses in magazines, and was perpetually out drinking with Jung, Oehring, and various other newcomers. When our money ran out, we went foraging far and wide. This time I became skilful. I went to people and told them that Jung and the others had been locked up for doing a runner from some restaurant or other and needed to borrow the money to pay off the outstanding bill. In the end I was known everywhere. People avoided me if they could. For example, when I showed up at the *Café des Westens*, they looked at me and went into a huddle; once, I even heard them call me "the master cadger".[16]

Outwardly I was reduced to a pitiful condition, shambled around and felt embarrassed wherever I went. I soon got into a quarrel with Jung and his wife, and went to sleep at Oehring's place, whose father was a high-up official with the telegraph service. When I rang the bell, the old gentleman usually came to the door himself, looked me over hurriedly, left me standing there and called up: "Richard! The delinquent's here!"

This man hated me from the first. On one occasion when I was sleeping at Richard's again, the old geezer suddenly kicked up a row in the next room. In a trembling, emotional voice he blustered: "I am like Samson! I am supporting the pillars of this house! But just wait! One day I will be unable to hold them up and then the whole edifice will crash to its ruin!"

He always played on the emotions. He thought Jung and I had corrupted his two sons. When we were in Richard's room, we heard his voice wailing through the house: "Helpless in the face of corruption! Helpless! My sons, my pride and joy!" He was a gaunt, grey-haired man, whose

---

[16] The *Café des Westens* at 8/19 Kurfürstendamm, a coffeehouse from 1898 to 1915, was a meeting place for turn-of-the-century artists and intellectuals. It was known colloquially as *Café Größenwahn* meaning the café with "delusions of grandeur".

nerves had been worn ragged by his long years of service. His wife was paralysed and sat the whole day long in a tall armchair at the window. Richard and Fritz were studying, but they spent most of the time loitering in literary circles and writing verses.

Jung helped me in any way he could, but we never really understood one another. When we got into discussion, I usually stared at him stupidly because I did not understand a thing. Then he got angry and called me a "cretin" and a "moron". He speculated on the stock exchange, managed partners' offices and was the editor of a trade newspaper. When I was at home with his wife, I had to sing Bavarian folk songs to her, or else we went to the café and lay in wait for people who had money. There were often ugly scenes at Jung's place. The two of them came to blows. I got the blame for it. Usually after such a bust-up Jung and I went off and drank for two or three days on end. I had broken all ties with home. I clung to Jung. Finally, the two of us quarrelled. For a while, I secretly went to sleep at Richard Oehring's and went out with the two brothers. I frittered away the time. I was disgusted with myself. I was unhappy. We often attended anarchist meetings or spent our days at fairgrounds. Nothing happened. I borrowed money off Richard and went looking for a room. I wanted to be alone and my own master, and to start something or other.

The news of the Sarajevo murder shook the world. Telegrams announced Russia's mobilization. Then Germany's. A tremendous outburst of rejoicing swept through the streets. Everything was in a whirl. Mobs gathered and the barracks were crammed full of volunteers. Cars full of officers roared through the streets and were hailed with enthusiastic cries. Trucks heavily laden with military clothes, boots and helmets rattled by. A bunch of people gathered and attacked a café with a foreign name, smashing everything to bits. In one square a yelling rabble hunted down a man, beat him to death, and sang *Deutschland, Deutschland über alles!* Grey regiments heaved their way down the long streets, acclaimed by the people, by the bourgeois, by elegant gentlemen, and ladies. It was a terrifying hustle and bustle. Day and night, the air was humming with the music of patriotic songs and gruesome stories about spies and the first clashes with the enemy.

"Now we're in for it!" I said.

"Everything will be wiped out," said Jung.

The intellectuals in the *Café des Westens* looked dumbfounded. Everything that had been so important yesterday had come to an end, at a stroke. Everything was in suspense. Countless men volunteered. Nobody quite knew why.

"A fine state of affairs. We should join the *Betoneurs*," said Jung. He was frantic. I did not understand the word or understand him and gazed at him vacantly. I went to Oehring. The Director of Telegraphy received me ceremoniously, with open arms: "Come in Herr Graf! Now, in this hour, we must put aside all personal discord. We are Germans! Germans! Come in!" And he led me into the parlour, where Richard and Fritz were sitting with their mother. That had never happened before. The table was laden with dishes of food, fat boxes of cigars and cigarettes. The two brothers looked at me, flummoxed.

"I stand behind you to my last drop of blood, my sons, you are my everything!" the Director of Telegraphy called out, and, pointing to me: "Herr Graf here is also going to volunteer for service in this hour of need. We cherish the Fatherland deep in our hearts." He raised his wineglass and exclaimed, almost as though singing: "For God, our Kaiser, our Fatherland and our honour! Courage!"

At first, I stared blankly, then I could barely hold back from laughing. Nonetheless, I could not suppress a dull feeling of unease. I did not know what was the matter. But something was paralysing every decision that I wanted to take.

The Director of Telegraphy gave his two sons some money, and we left. Now I was completely stultified. The two of them went off to the Wrangel Barracks, wanting to volunteer. The business made me uncomfortable. What was I doing there? I saw countless volunteers in the barrack yard. Every single face was beaming. I said to Richard: "You know what? This is just too boring for me! If they want me, they will come and get me soon enough! I'm not going to run after them!"

We had lost Fritz in the crowd. For a while, we whistled for him, but in vain, then we went off and looked for Jung. "What's this crap got to do with me! I shall go back to working as a baker," I said as we walked along. Richard did not know what to say. "And in any case! If I must join up with the military, I'd rather go to the Bavarians," I continued.

"That's no longer even possible," said Richard."

"Why not?" I asked, baffled. "All of the trains have been commandeered for troop transports. You can't get to Munich now," he replied.

I went to Jung and asked him what I should do. "Volunteer ... It will all be all right! Liège has already been taken. It'll all go like clockwork," was his answer. And then he added: "Paris will fall in no time at all." I no longer knew him. He was no different from the dense masses that wandered through the city belting out patriotic songs in a wild warlike enthusiasm! Weird. Where had all his anarchism gone?

The *Café des Westens* was empty. Jung no longer showed up in the bars where we used to go boozing. He and his ilk had totally disappeared. I was left entirely on my Tod Sloan. What had happened to all those people who had taught me that an anarchist should, under no circumstances. serve the State, and above all had to refuse all military service, absolutely? They had all run off in their droves to the barracks, as volunteers!

I was overcome by a tremendous disappointment, anger, hatred and disgust at all those windbags.

But how was I to manage from now on? I was still living with the Jungs. There was Margot, his wife, and her old mother, who was always moaning. We went to the *Café des Westens* to find someone we could tap for money. There were just a few apathetic guests and senile rakes there. Margot finally managed to squeeze some money out of the waiter and said: "Let's go!" And we went. Out on the street she called for a cab, and we drove to the quarter near the Silesian Station. As we drove, she talked about one of her friends, who was working in a small cellar next to a *Pischinger* cake factory.[17] We went there and found seven packers sitting at a long table, putting the chocolate-covered ready-made cakes into packaging cartons. We said a friendly hello to the girls, and said the boss had been called up, and we'd be running the business from now on. Then we took a whole load of full cartons down from the shelves and carried them off to our cab, telling the girls that we'd received a big order. We then drove back to the flat in the Berliner Strasse. At least we now had enough to eat for a while. That was all on a Wednesday. The next day we picked up another load of cartons, and I said to Margot: "That's our lot now." The week was coming to an end, and the staff had to be paid. It all looked very bleak.

The streets were bristling with people. One victory after another was being proclaimed in bold print on the newsstands. It was getting hot under my feet. I heard that you could volunteer in another state. I went to the Wilmersdorf police station and volunteered for the Third Infantry Regiment in Augsburg. They gave me a voucher for the train journey. I rushed off to Jung's, packed my possessions, went to the Anhalt Station, boarded the train and arrived, after a four-day journey, in Munich. I never even thought of reporting in Augsburg. There was still plenty of time. I wanted to go home and see Schorsch and wait to see what turned up.

It was a beautiful journey through half of Germany. Almost idyllic, the kind of image presented by the country's patriotic student fraternities. Red Cross personnel waited at all the railway stations and stuffed us full of food. Entire carriages were littered with leftover bread, bits of sausage and crumbs of cheese.

At any rate, there's plenty to eat in wartime, I thought, recalling the stories that my father had told me about the campaign of 1870-71.

Munich was as quiet as the grave. It was almost a relief. There were no mobs to be seen, the streets were empty – though admittedly, it was the middle of August – the trams ran as ever, people were out and about, Tietz's department store was still there and so was the Palace of Justice.

---

[17] *Pischinger* cake is of Galician origin, made with layers of chocolate and wafer.

I went to Schorsch's mother and asked after him. He had gone to Augsburg as a cook, but was now in hospital, she told me. Dog tired, I went to find a model and slept at her place. I knew that Max, my oldest brother, had joined up long ago. I did not want to meet Maurus, not at all. So I could go home. On the third day I stood at our open kitchen door and laughed aloud: "Well now, we have a nice rumpus on our hands.

"It'll all be fine and dandy!"

I couldn't care less. They could have their war; it was none of my business.

Max's wife was there, the children were loafing about, and Theres, Emma and our mother had moved back into the old house to help out. They all hung their heads and expected something terrible to happen. Our mother had a calm expression, then a few furrows appeared on her brow and she said, neither happy nor sad:

"Yes ... I remember how the men went out in '70. No good ever comes of it."

"How about you then?" asked my sisters.

"Me? They can come and get me. I'm not going to run after them," I said. I had to report to the Mayor, and shortly afterwards I was sent off to Munich to enrol.

"Train."

Many of the villagers laughed at me

On 1 December 1914 I had to report at the Supply Train Corps' Barracks in Munich. We were led to the clothing stores and were given our uniforms, boots and various other bits and pieces. And so it began.

14.
SOLDIERING

It was hilarious in our barrack room. Forty-five of us were there with one NCO. The first few days were full of variety. At last, when we were completely fitted out, we went out into the barrack yard. Drill.

Our corporal was a dumpy little man and an ornithologist; or, translated into plain man's German, he sold birds. He had a dashing manner, and we learned well with him. But I couldn't help breaking into laughter at the slightest provocation, and that altered his mood terribly.

"What have you got to laugh about?" he yelled at me. That made me laugh even more, without knowing why.

"Have they let you out of the loony bin?" he stammered. I laughed even more. He told me to stand aside. So long as the drill went on, I stood there and looked on. Sometimes the corporal cast a threatening glance in my direction, but I could not help it, the little man was so comical when he got angry. If you just looked at his head, and how it got redder and redder, he looked like a sausage that had swollen up like a child's balloon. His crumpled little cap glistened and sat on top of his head, as if glued there.

The next day we started to learn the various salutes. We had to goose-step past the NCO and salute him with our hands raised to our temples and with our eyes fixed on him. Once again, I laughed at this nonsense. The corporal swore. I laughed louder. He snarled at me. I laughed even more, so much that I could barely stand up straight.

"Stand back again!" roared my superior. It was no use. I went on laughing. At school, we once had to form a sentence containing the word "bounce". I said to a simpleton: "We put short fat people on the plank and bounce them in the air." I was thinking of something like making frogs jump, which we used to do sometimes. Now, as I marched past, I simply could not get this childish memory out of my head. I literally saw the NCO's bullet head bounce up in the air and suddenly explode with a bang.

Again and again, again and again, I had to march past with my hand to my temple and my face turned towards the corporal. My laughter got so loud it was like a fusillade. The NCO jumped up, spluttered and squealed. Suddenly I fell to the ground with laughter, still holding my hand to my temple, and my gaze fixed on the completely perplexed, angry NCO. Everyone laughed. The NCO took out his notebook and took down my name. "Step aside" he yelled.

At roll call I was reported to the cavalry captain. "Why can you never stop laughing?" he asked, in a peremptory tone.

"Forgive me, Captain sir, I have always been like that since I was a child," I answered respectfully.

The captain wagged his finger at me and growled: "You wait! You with your juvenile laughter! We'll cure you of that in the dark cell!"

"Oh," I said stupidly. Then the captain roared at me and swore like he was going berserk. Grumbling to the sergeant major, he said: "Let's send this chap over there for three days! Make a note of it."

After the roll call, as we were cleaning our boots and tidying our clothes, the corporal came off duty and yelled through the door: "Graf! Get out here. Now!" and I ran out to him. He told me to take off my apron and follow him. I did so.

Then we went into the kitchen. I was given two standard issue bread rolls, then I was taken off to the guardhouse. The NCO blustered all the way there, saying I had no idea how to behave, and that I was a downright disgrace to the entire company of recruits.

When I was presented to the sergeant major in charge of the guardhouse, he looked me over contemptuously, and said to the corporal: "Wet behind the ears." Then the corporal left. The sergeant major prattled on at me about the rules of behaviour for the arrest cells, then took me up to the first floor, and locked me in a cold, dark cell. Three days on bread and water in that hole gave me time to reflect. Why have they locked me up, I kept thinking, when they need men? Why was my "Oh!" such a crime? It was cold, boring and pointless, languishing in this cell. When I get out of here, I decided, I will say they should just send me straight into the field. They certainly need people for things other than imprisonment.

The day after I was released from arrest, I had to sweep out the NCOs' quarters and polish their boots. When comrades came by, they laughed at me sheepishly. I laughed with them, but I got the clear impression that none of them liked me any more. The next day I was sent to the stables at five in the morning. The corporal showed me everything that I had missed during the three days and I already felt somehow cut off from the others. You idiot, I thought, you idiot, now they've got their eye on you and will certainly give you the worst jobs. But after a few days the corporal's interest in me faded and I was treated just the same as the others again.

When we returned to the stables one day and got ready to do our duties in the middle stable, one of the old servicemen, who seemed to have long experience in the job, suddenly winked at me and said: "Come on!" He took me by the arm and whispered again: "Don't be such an idiot, working yourself to death like that!" We were standing on the steps leading up to the hayloft. The middle stable was almost dark and only used for getting dressed and undressed. The old boy silently beckoned, and I followed him up to the hayloft.

"You're the one they threw in the hole on the very first day, aren't you?" the old boy asked, when we were alone up there. I nodded, dumbly.

"Now listen," he then advised me. "The corporal has a liking for those who get a move on, and if you are smart, you can get on his good side again and you'll have a cushy little number with him. See the hatch in the loft up there. When the corporal calls up, 'Throw down the hay!' push open the trapdoor and throw the tied hay-bales down one after the other, fast as you can, until he shouts: 'Stop!' Then close the shutter again and come back into the stable. Do that every day starting tomorrow and after that you can sleep up here until it is time to go out riding."

I soon saw what he meant, and right enough, when I heard the call of "Throw down the hay", and my comrades came running out of the horse-stalls, I was already throwing down the hay-bales. The astonished corporal was standing below and laughed with satisfaction, calling out to the others: "That's what I like to see, he's fleet of foot and nimble in the knee." From then on, I did indeed have a nice little number. But one day, when it was time for drill, I did not show up and he noticed. The NCO told the others: "A right cheeky little monkey, that one!" and then kept a sharp eye on me.

Because I could still not help myself laughing, I was always sent to clean out and groom the horses that bit and kicked. I used to go to the corporal, stood to attention, and said innocently: "Permission to leave the ranks, Corporal."

"Get on with it then!" he said. I ran off and went to the canteen. That wheeze was discovered, too, and from then on, every day after duty I had to sweep out the NCOs' staff room and clean the boots of all 20 corporals. I had to do extra drill, because I still laughed, or peel potatoes in the kitchen after I had finished sweeping out the staff room, which took until noon. There was plenty to eat in the kitchen, and I quickly made friends with all the cooks, which meant I got the largest helpings at mealtime and had a nice little number there too.

I was given a very sensitive horse, who liked to throw its rider. I enjoyed that. I was a fairly good horseman and never got told off during riding lessons. I even laughed out loud when I got thrown from the saddle and remounted the nag with double the pleasure. The corporal liked that, and he said to the faint-hearted: "Look at him! He shows no fear, and that's why he is good at it! You need to be bold to be good at riding, boys!"

Just wait, I thought, I'll pay you back for bullying me, and I kept on tickling my nag in his tender parts, just when everything was going well. And sure enough – the horse planted his rear hooves firmly, bucked up angrily in front, and threw me with panache onto the thick carpet of wood shavings, which flew everywhere.

Or he threw me forwards, just as I liked. "Lad! Lad!" blustered the corporal, who couldn't help laughing. "Lad! You'll spoil the whole review! Get up! March! Quick about it! March!"

Easy does it, I thought to myself, I'll pay you back for the cleaning and potato-peeling details. Then came the ride past the captain. Right in the middle of the finest German slow-trot, I tickled my nag again and up I flew. It spoiled the entire review. The corporal got a good dressing-down and from then on, I was sent to the coal cellar. Down there I worked with an old boy who sucked up to the cellar sergeant and was constantly taking snacks: the first at nine, the second at eleven, then lunch, a third at two o'clock and somewhere between half past three and five the last. Then we were off duty. That was a pleasant enough life.

"The best thing you can do is report for service in the field. I'm telling you," the old boy said to me. "There are heaps of cushy jobs out there if you know how to get them." So I went straight to the corporal and said, with an air of soldierly self-sacrifice: "With your permission, Corporal, if there is a transport to the front, I would like to go with it as soon as possible."

The corporal looked at me with a strict expression, and rebuffed me: "Just you wait, lad, I'll find you a job that will kill off your impudence! You'll never have it as cushy as you've had it in the coal cellar. Mark my words! Your turn will come soon enough, just you wait!"

The old boy in the cellar laughed when I told him this and said condescendingly: "It's not so bad! No one can play tricks on you there!" Then we went off to the canteen again. And so the days passed by.

"Who said he wanted to go into the field the other day?" yelled the corporal a few weeks later, and already had his eye on me. I stepped forward immediately. A few others moved up. "I only need two," the corporal commanded, pulled me out of the ranks, and asked: "Who else?" Another baker, called Dreier, joined me. A first lieutenant from the Engineers received us in the corridor.

"Report at three o'clock in the orderly room of the Railway Battalion," he said.

We were given new uniforms, went to the orderly room, had to collect two horses from the collection point and were from now on assigned to the Railway Battalion. The few days before being transported to the field, we let our hair down, lounged about a lot, went drinking on the town and acted all superior towards our barrack-room comrades. Finally, on the fifth day, we were called back to the Railway Engineers' orderly room and presented to a major, ordered to pack our things, and at one o'clock that night we travelled with the staff of the Railway Corps (that was the unit to which we were now attached) to Insterburg, on the border of East Prussia.[18]

---

[18] Now Chernyakhovsk, in the Oblast of Kaliningrad.

There were eight soldiers and two officers, the major and the first lieutenant, as already mentioned. We got out at Insterburg. We had to take the staff baggage into the town and were allotted quarters in the barracks. It was the deep mid-winter, and snow lay thick on the ground. We had very little to do. Just a little horse-grooming and collecting rations each day. The rest of the time we roamed through the town, which had been somewhat ravaged by the recently expelled Russians. Notices posted by the enemy commander, General Rennenkampf, were still stuck to the walls of the houses. Generally speaking, the people were neither well nor ill-disposed towards the military; instead, it seemed as though they were sick and tired of all the hullabaloo. You could buy genuine white bread and cheap sausage. The barracks, which we shared with the East Prussian Home Guard, was overrun with lice.

15.
DONE FOR

At the time, I had the curious habit of asking everybody, almost mechanically in the middle of a conversation: "So tell me, how old are you?" I suffered from such bad manners since childhood. For instance, as a boy, on every occasion – whether or not appropriate – I used to burst out with the phrase: "Wow, forty thousand marks, that's a pile of money!" and my father gave me a good box me on the ears for my trouble, even though he hardly ever beat me. But I'd come out with this exclamation again and again, until one day I replaced it with another. Enough already.

In Insterburg we had to line up every third day for roll call in the corridor at our staff headquarters. The lieutenant gave us the necessary orders, then the major came and inspected everyone from top to bottom with stern eyes, yelled at us for badly polished boots or bad posture, threatened us with arrest, and that was the end of it. We went to the kitchen, ate and lounged around with nothing to do in the town, came back and played cards until late into the night. Our staff occupied the first floor of a deserted private house, and we had to stay in the kitchen during the day, take telegrams to the post office every now and then, and run various messages. Almost every day the two officers drove in a car to the front and did not return until late at night, sometimes not until the next day around noon. They went no matter how deep the snow, so that their two drivers grumbled and swore. Those of us left behind were therefore free to do as we liked, got up to all kinds of mischief, and were often at a loss how to kill time. There was Peperl, the clerk who later became our corporal, the two officers' batmen Ginhart and Hartig, and us two privates of the train. Peperl, whose real name was Schwedes, was a young surveyor's assistant from Lower Bavaria, had passed his exam as a one-year volunteer, and was very officious. He was supposed to be in control of us when the officers were absent, but nobody took any notice of him. His appearance itself commanded little respect. He had pouting lips and chubby red cheeks, was barely 22 years old and his tongue was too long, which hindered clear pronunciation. We used to call him "Chickenshit" because he was so nervous. A rough word from anyone would intimidate him. We chuckled at him, and when something went wrong, when we were scolded by the officers, we cursed him. He was always our scapegoat, and that often unhinged him completely. Then he'd grin, get flustered and start whining: "I can't do anything about it! ... I already told you, but you never listen!" But then we all raged against him and ranted murderously: "Whatever ... You're the NCO! ... You dropped us in it, nitwit! ... What happened to comradeship? ... We won't forget it! ... Just wait, next time there's trouble, you can forget about any comradeship on our part!" That drove him to despair. He whimpered and literally cried. He was soft as a baby's bottom and did whatever we told him.

Around about the seventeenth day of our stay in Insterburg we unexpectedly received a cask of rum from the commissariat. It held fifteen litres. We sat down at once and began to drink. Filling our field canteens. Our card game grew livelier. The major's batman threw in his hand and staggered off to the kitchen tap and doused his head under cold water.

"Oh yeah," sneered the lieutenant's batman, and threw in his own hand. I took a great draught of rum, snorted like a horse, and stared vacantly at someone or other. "So tell me, how old are you?" My tongue felt heavy and my head was in a whirl.

"What a useless lot you are, roaring drunk after a drop of rum," blustered the lieutenant's batman. He filled his canteen and drank the lot in a single gulp. My comrade Dreier laughed uproariously.

"So ... So tell me, ho-ow old are you-ou?"

"Idiot! Why do you keep asking that stupid question? Just try asking the major how old he is, you moron!" yelled the lieutenant's batman and continued: "We've had quite enough of your shenanigans."

Dreier burst out laughing again. The major's batman was hanging on limply to the splashing tap.

"He's sagging already," said Dreier indifferently. The other man at the table lifted the canteen to his lips again and gulped noisily. All of a sudden, he was lying on the floor stiff as a board, making a noise like a death rattle. Dreier got up, staggered over to the tap, filled his canteen and emptied it over the drunk's face. He winced and gulped but stayed lying on the floor.

"The speaker," I gasped, staring into space, wrinkling my brow and suddenly opening my eyes wide, as if testing myself. I was still all right. I could still see everything, Dreier was back at the tap, the major's batman Ginhart clinging to the spout and Hartig was gurgling on the floor.

"Come on, turn off the tap and leave those two where they are, drink, drink!" I roared at Dreier.

"Drink," he said, back at the table again, and took a huge gulp from his canteen. We stared at each other through glazed eyes.

"So tell me, how old are you?" The words slipped out of my rum-sozzled mouth again.

"Jesus, you're one crazy son of a bitch," yelled Dreier, shaking his head and laughing. Hartig threw up, Dreier bent down and gave him a kick: "Oy, you! Get up, man!" Peperl, who had drunk the least, stood there quaking in his boots and repeated: "What if the major comes? What if the major comes?"

"For Christ's sake! How drunk can a man get?" growled Dreier. I sat, glued to my chair, and groaned in a deep voice: "Drink, man! Drink!"

"I'm off! I'm off!" cried Peperl, and left the kitchen.

All of a sudden, the door was flung open and both of the officers appeared. Ginhart groaned, Hartig vomited again, Dreier stood shaking by the cooker and stared. I had pulled myself to my feet and staggered over to the major, fell helplessly against his chest, and bawled drunkenly: "So tell me, major, sir, how old are you?"

I felt the lash of a terrible yell. The major pushed me away in utter disgust. Then the two drivers took hold of me.

The following morning I found myself next to Dreier in my bed in the barracks. We stared at each other in amazement. The two drivers were quarrelling loudly with Peperl, who was on the verge of tears. "You should have known that would happen! ... It's all your fault! You're the NCO in charge!" They swore terribly, then told us what had happened. Peperl collapsed on the bench and groaned: "I always have to carry the can, even when I can't do anything about it!"

"Come on, pull yourself together," Dreier said, and suddenly started laughing. The drivers jumped up indignantly and laid into us. I just lay gormlessly on my straw mattress and didn't say a word. Although it did dawn on me that this time, we would get a big fat punishment.

"We will all pay a heavy price for this," fulminated the smaller of the drivers, "all of us, not just you!" Peperl suddenly stood up and said, almost resolutely: "I shall get myself transferred. I can never serve as a corporal here." He then left us.

"We'm all done fer noo, I'm telling you," snapped the elder driver in his nasal Viennese dialect, "After all, yaouw can't carry on loike that when yaouw knoo that the other comrades wull suffer fer it as well!"

In the afternoon, there was a great to-do, and on this occasion the major began to have doubts about my sanity for the first time, in that he came up to me in a threatening manner and said: "It seems as though an inmate of the lunatic asylum has been smuggled into the German army. We certainly picked a right one!"

Everybody involved was punished with 27 days' field arrest. How they arrived at that figure, nobody knew. The major's batman got an extra three days' for a mere trifle. Shortly afterwards we went to Gumbinnen, then Lötzen in Hindenburg's headquarters, and we finally landed in Marggrabowa, right on the frontier.[19] Already in Gumbinnen our staff had been considerably enlarged. Prussian soldiers joined us, an office was furnished, and at Lötzen there were 17 of us. The adjutant was changed, and a new lieutenant arrived from Munich with his batman. The Viennese driver

---

[19] Today Olecko, in eastern Poland.

was replaced by a stuffy Mannheimer. It was summer. We could go bathing, and Dreier and I had hardly anything to do. The lieutenant seldom went riding, so every morning I saddled up his chestnut horse and rode around the countryside until midday. I did my best to avoid the officers. But if I did happen to run into them, there was generally trouble. I was entirely "done for". So I did not show my face at all. My comrades were alarmed and took charge of my duties. In Marggrabowa I got dysentery and was sent to the collection point for invalids, and from there to the reserve hospital at Goldap. Because I refused to take any medicine, the doctor threatened to send me straight back to the front, which would have suited me just fine. Only half recovered, I was sent to report at the commandant's communications HQ.

"Where do you belong?" asked the duty lieutenant. I told him my unit. The man covered his ears. "Your battalion left for the Carpathians long ago. Where are your reserves based?"

"In Munich!"

I was given a pass and took the next train home passing through Berlin. I got out, wanting to see my friends. Jung was at the front, as were the two Oehrings. I only saw Cläre, Richard's girlfriend. She was delighted and found me accommodation. I stayed for three days. During this time I went to see Oehring's father. He had gotten old, really old. He threw the door open and received me with a hearty handshake, led me into the parlour and brought food and cigars. I got all kinds of news about my friends from him. Alfred Lichtenstein had fallen.[20] Fritz Oehring had been taken prisoner. The old man hung his head dolefully. His crippled wife cowered in her armchair by the window. She said nothing, simply staring blankly into space. "Yes, this war," I said.

"This war," the old man interrupted, stirring to life, "it has brought the essential to the fore. It will be the making of German youth." And in an instant, he towered up and gesticulated with his arms, as he had done in younger days: "Destiny makes us great! Many enemies, much honour! Here on the home front, our hearts and souls beat as one to the end with our lion-hearted boys, who stand in the thick of battle and in victory!" He began to tremble, the tears flowed down his cheeks. He shook me firmly by the hand and gave me a packet of the best Havana cigars.

"Brave warrior," he said, "take this little gift as a modest token of love and gratitude for your heroism," and his voice vibrated with emotion once again. "Oh – God willing – my heroes will once again sit in this

---

[20] Alfred Lichtenstein was a German expressionist writer of Jewish heritage who contributed to the reviews *Der Sturm* and *Die Aktion*. He fell during the battle of Vermandovillers in the Somme on 25 September 1914, at the age of 25.

room." His eyes glanced over his sick wife, who sat there motionless. "And thankful parents will listen to their tales, drinking from a fountain of youth and strength!" He was now sobbing openly, without restraint; he shook me once more by the hand in farewell and groaned: "Thus, we hope, the German nation will be the world's salvation!"

I gazed at him, I gazed at his wife. Strange, I thought, really strange. His words seem to come from another world, completely alien to me. I was deep in thought as I walked out to the street.

In Munich the sergeant major in the orderly room was dumbfounded. He said to me: "You're back already?"

"Yes, sir, sergeant major, sir," I said. I could see that the man felt some respect for me, as he had seen nothing of the world beyond Munich.

"Report to the senior physician and get yourself examined," he ordered, because he was worried that I might spread dysentery. I was declared in need of a thorough rest and given an immediate furlough. I went home. Many things had changed there. My brother Max had fallen, my sister Emma had a terminal lung disease, and our old house now belonged to the strange wife and children of my dead brother. My mother and sisters were already thinking of moving back to the smaller property where they had previously been living.

Maurus had not yet been called up and was still working as a cakemaker in Munich; Nanndl was training as a hairdresser in the city. I didn't visit either of them.

There was an atmosphere of hostility on all sides in the house. It was obvious that things could not go on that way. I really had no idea what to do with myself in the place, and every day the feeling of unease increased. My mother slaved away all day long, as usual. She even baked the bread, since there were no journeymen left. Her hair was already turning grey. Every now and then she dropped into a chair, dog-tired, and groaned: "I've had enough of this shitty war! ... Maxi is dead, and everything has changed hands ... I've slaved away for 35 years and now I'm not wanted ..."

Her face was a picture of bitter disappointment.

The young widow was lazy and went around with an air of bereavement all the time. Each day she grew fatter.

When my furlough came to an end, I reported back to my unit's orderly room, but was re-examined at the urgent request of my anxious sergeant major and sent to the military hospital at Oberwiesenfeld. They said I had chronic gastritis. Schorsch, who at the time was in charge of garrison duty at the district HQ, visited me a few times. He followed the news in the papers, and always said when we argued: "It will drag on for years, you'll see."

"Then we'll all be mercenaries, robbers and murderers ... That's all right by me," I said. What should I care about tomorrow or the next day?

Back at the orderly room, I was received solemnly by the sergeant major. He enquired after the state of my health and then asked, "Do you want to return to your unit? Your major has just written to us." I was delighted at the prospect of returning to my old mates, was given a fresh uniform and left the very same night. Fortunately, I was assigned to a troop-transport heading to the east, which was instructed to drop me off in Marggrabowa. Given my lack of experience with trains, I might easily have ended up somewhere quite different. It had been the same story on the journey back from the front. But then I just trusted to luck and always followed the crowd that talked about Berlin or Munich.

Nevertheless, an incident occurred. Namely, we stopped in Schwandorf and I went to the toilet. Meanwhile the train left with its passengers. Highly agitated, I ran off to the stationmaster and reported myself. A telegraph was sent and the whole troop-transport had to wait for me in Marktredwitz. The platoon commander, who was a junior veterinarian, raised hell and threatened me with every imaginable punishment. But I was not in the least bit intimidated, because from my point of view, I was not under his command. I was simply a passenger. I said impudently: "I'm not under your command, not at all!"

The junior vet was absolutely furious and yelled like a murderous firebrand: "What! Just you wait! You won't forget me! I'll report you to your staff officer! We'll see."

I stared at him brazenly and got into the carriage. He wanted to wind me up for the rest of the journey, but in fact he seemed to accept the fact that I was responsible to no one but myself. He was my bitter enemy but did nothing to harm me. Admittedly, I figured that the major would have me locked up immediately upon hearing about the business, but I didn't really care. Curiously enough, it seemed as though the veterinary gentleman had forgotten everything by the time we arrived.

I found our staff very comfortably accommodated and considerably enlarged. Only Dreier, Peperl and the small driver were left from the old crew. Even the first lieutenant had fallen out with the major, I heard. He went with his batman to the Western Front and a very nattily dressed lieutenant took his place.

16.
"FOR SPECIAL DUTY"

The first few days passed without anyone really noticing I was there. Then I was used as an orderly and had to sit in the office and take telegrams to the post office. I usually stayed out for a long time, even though the post office was only ten minutes away. I was far more interested in the tea-rooms, the local people and the devastated houses. I searched through their rooms, which had been turned inside out, nosed through books, and read them. Not a single soul asked after me. They had no use for me. The major's batman was taken ill. A replacement was needed. Everyone made himself scarce. Nobody wanted to take the post, which meant being locked up for the most trivial mistake.

Peperl came to me and said, gravely: "Graf, you must become the major's batman. Get yourself ready and go up to him. But don't act the fool, or we will all be in disgrace and I will end up carrying the can for everyone again." I did as I was told, dressed, and went to the major.

"At your command, major, sir! Excuse me sir, I am to be your bat-man," I said and stood to attention, my hands planted on the seams of my breeches.

The major looked me over and drawled: "Ye-es." I stood there for a moment, unsure of what to do, then I stuttered: "I should like to inform the major that I have no talent for the post. I have never done anything of this sort."

"Then you'll just have to learn," said the major curtly, and dismissed me. I went downstairs, lay on my mattress, and continued to read. Peperl came and asked: "Are you his batman?"

I nodded. Peperl laughed, but immediately put on his serious face again, and said, sympathetically: "It's not so bad, if you know how to han-dle the major. A great job! ... You'll have nothing to do and all day to do it." I, on the other hand, was of the opposite opinion. I started to argue about it: "You reckon? ... Then why would no one else have it, if it's so great? ... I shan't stick it out for long, I guarantee. I suppose you thought you could just pimp me out?"

Peperl's face turned scarlet with rage. "I suppose you think I'm go-ing to be the batman? I can't help it if the lieutenant gives me the order."

"Get out! Get out!" I jeered and turned away. "You're a bunch of de-ceitful scoundrels!" Peperl jumped up and snorted: "Enough of this. It's not up to me! I've nothing against you!"

"Right then, right-ho!" I scoffed and buried myself in my book. "You'll see right enough how long I last as a major's batman!" That was too much for Corporal Peperl. He ran out of the room, slamming the door on his way. The officers' cook came a while later and said, I had to help him. I followed him up to the kitchen. He showed me how to wait at table. Then the gentlemen came to dinner and it all started. I was very shaky, spilt the soup, put my sleeve in the vegetables when leaning across the table and was generally useless at this difficult job.

"I am a private of the baggage train and stableman! ... I know how to give the nags their fodder, but not this bunch of clowns! What business is it of mine!" I raged at the cook. He was an upright master plumber from Berlin, who never got agitated. He cut off a piece of meat and held it in front of me. "Eat, man! Just keep cool! Keep cool!" I ate and shut up.

"We're packing up tomorrow," said Peperl, "the officers are already setting off today. You must travel by car with the major."

"Nice! Very nice!" I grumbled and went back to the cook. The major looked in at the kitchen door and called me. I followed him into his room.

"Pack up my things and get yourself ready," he ordered crabbily, and stood watching me. That made me nervous and irritable, but what could I do about it? When I had packed his trunk, he sat down at his desk and wrote. "And now go and fetch my grey coffee pot from the kitchen," he said, with his back turned to me.

"Yes, sir," I said respectfully, and disappeared into the kitchen. I had not understood the order, because I was not really listening to what he was saying. I just repeated "Yes sir" and "Yes major". And now the search started. At last, I found what I thought he wanted. It was a grey acetylene lamp. I went back to my superior's room, held out the lamp, and said: "At your command, major!"

He clapped his face and exclaimed: "I told you to fetch the grey coffee pot!" He glowered at me. I stood there in stunned silence.

"Go downstairs. You're no use to me," he snarled. I performed a clumsy about-turn and went out the door. And that was the end of my career as a batman. Once again, I was the fifth wheel on our staff wagon.

We went to Lyda. When we moved in there, Peperl and I had a furious argument. From then on, we were bitter enemies. I had been ordered to go and find a padlock but couldn't find it. Peperl kept coming back and finally threatened: "Watch it! ... Graf, if you don't bring me the padlock, I will have to report you!" He gave me a shove and I suddenly lost my patience. Before long I threw everything I could lay my hands on at this jumped-up little corporal, threatened him in the most abusive way and went for him with a drawn bayonet.

"I'll run you through, you son of a bitch, you miserable bastard," I hollered, and he bolted off like a rabbit. He just made it to the train and shouted from the carriage window: "That'll cost you a spell in the guardhouse. Just wait!"

"You can stand me up against the wall, for all I care!" I roared and went back to my cattle-truck.

We drove through a desolate landscape, furrowed with trenches, and stopped in Waca, which consisted of a mansion and a few houses. There was a pond nearby. The whole scene was lonesome and idyllic. Spring was already in the air. I sought out distant quarters for my horses. The others prevented Peperl from reporting me.

Pleasant days of idleness turned into oppressive boredom. I often lay all day long in my hammock, which I had purloined somewhere or other, and read. At that time I had convinced myself that in Germany no one had to serve for more than two years, or three in the cavalry. Every day I told myself that I should assert this right, war or no war. You served out your two years and that was an end of it. This became a fixed idea with me, and I was wondering if I should just report to the major and, if that's the case, announce: "With your permission, sir, my two years' service are up. I am going to join the reserve!"

I also promoted this idea to my comrades. They called me a lunatic and laughed out loud. But I stuck to the letter of our National Service Act and could argue the case so convincingly that the others even began to reconsider and said: "Well, yes, actually, if you take it literally, no one could stop you ... The law is the law!" But a moment later they laughed scornfully and said: "But you're totally insane! ... You're talking rubbish! It's entirely different in war-time!"

"What do I care about the war? ... Did I start it? ... I'm just stating the legal position!" I defended myself. "On the first of December I am joining the reserves!"

"The war will be over by then in any case," said Römer, the little driver, to console me. "Let's wait and see!" I said sarcastically and was pleased with myself. One day we were sent closer to the front. Around 50 kilometres from Kaunas. We were permanently quartered in the baggage train. Artillery thundered in the distance, and on clear days we could even hear the faint rattle of machine guns. Companies of the Railway Engineers, Prussians, which were under our staff's command, lay ahead of us. Then we heard about losses. One company, which was very near the front, suffered especially badly. We retreated again. Then all of a sudden, Kaunas fell. It was said that the major was the first to enter the city in his car, and that he was later decorated with the Iron Cross, First Class for this action.

Kaunas took a terrible battering. We advanced to the shore of the Memel, unloaded, and walked past trenches filled with corpses and through smashed-up forts over the Memel bridge into the city. There was a colossal heap of rubble on the edge of the far bank. We saw a tremendous number of drunks cowering beside the debris. Poles, Jews, soldiers, girls, children, women – they all hurled abuse at us, and all of them were drunk. Infantrymen drank from field canteens and crockery; the locals drank from buckets, incessantly. They were all laughing and reeling. We saw people creep out of the ground with frothing vessels; they gathered in groups, shouting, drinking, making a racket. It was a demolished brewery. Only the cellars remained intact. We jumped into the crowd and slipped into the cellars. We found indescribable scenes down there. There were huge parades of people before the beer casks. They were holding buckets, field kettles and empty tins beneath the casks and making a drunken din. One infantryman took a pickaxe to a cask. It splintered open and the liquid fizzed out and splashed all over the reeling mass of people. Everyone was taken by surprise and waded towards the squirting holes as the tide of beer rose and rose. We climbed out to the open air again, soaked to the skin and reeking of beer.

By the time we got back to our quarters we were hammered. We left everything in complete disorder and lay down in the ransacked rooms. Peperl stood at the door, in despair and almost in tears, begging us to obey his orders: "This is no time to relax! Sort everything out! We'll all be locked up!" Nobody was listening. The whole room was spinning in such lovely circles.

The next day, the major and the lieutenant came back from the front by car. Peperl had taken care of everything. He had even stabled my horses for me, his enemy. Which was fine. We lay low. There was little to do. For the most part we lounged about in the lovely city. I poked around the ruined houses and brought back anything of use for our staff office: paper, files, carpets and clocks. Among other things, I found a magnificent stamp album.

Peperl took a fancy to it and wanted it for himself. "To whom does the album belong?" he timidly asked Dreier.

"Graf," Dreier replied.

"So ... Would he be prepared to give it up?" Peperl asked again.

"You'd better ask him," Dreier retorted.

The zone commandant had seized the beer and forbidden access to the brewery. The beer could be bought at the station for 40 pfennigs a litre. But none of us had any money. Dreier came to me: "Oy you, Peperl wants your album."

"It's worth a fortune," I bragged, although I knew nothing about stamps. Peperl had been listening at the door. I noticed him. Suddenly he burst in and stood there, abashed. I played the enemy. Turned my back. Peperl nudged my comrade.

"Ask him yourself! What has that to do with me?" growled Dreier. Turning deeper and deeper red, Peperl embarrassedly asked me:

"Graf, won't you let me have your album?"

"You can have it for 300 marks," I tossed at him. Peperl sighed audibly, keenly examined the object, then went out again and into the orderly room.

"Just wait, we'll make the nitwit fork out big time ... That will be enough booze for the entire staff," I said to Dreier, who was immediately won over to my side. We told the others. They went to work on Peperl. That evening he told us he would soon receive a pay-out from his savings. We pricked up our ears.

The next day Peperl came up to me again and said: "All right Graf, I'll give you 200 marks."

"What!" I thundered. "I'd sooner throw the bloody thing in the fire."

"All right, let's say 200 and a round of drinks for the entire staff," suggested the little driver, Römer. Peperl turned around, scratched himself, and thought it over. "Anyway! ... What about this pay-out?" we all shouted in unison.

Peperl got all in a tizzy again, then protested: "I haven't got it yet!"

"Then at least stand us all a decent drink!" a few shouted. The ice was broken.

"All right Graf, 200 and a round of drinks? ... And we're back on good terms?" Peperl conceded; and he held out his hand to me. "Oh for God's sake," I said, pretending to be dissatisfied, and accepted. Then we went off to the station. A wild boozing party began. Peperl was unsettled.

"Enough already! That's quite enough now! Enough, enough," he whimpered. But we weren't listening. We ordered round upon round. Peperl sat by, utterly defenceless and his face pale, and paid mechanically. Dreier, Römer and I were the last men standing. Peperl had slipped out secretly, and the others had also left. We sang boozing songs and set the whole beerhall in uproar. Finally we left, badmouthing Peperl horribly. We had to be back in our quarters by nine. And it was already way past. We pissed in a corner. All of a sudden, Dreier made a bolt for it, dragging Römer with him.

"Graf, watch out! It's the major and the lieutenant!"

I was startled. The two officers were already standing there. Alarmed and confused, I wheeled around and stood to attention, without first putting things back where they belonged. The two officers stared at me, speechless, and shook their heads in disbelief. "This chap is not normal," said the major, and the lieutenant yapped: "Run along home, you nincompoop!" I did up my flies in silence, and went on my way, feeling a right Charlie. I suddenly started to run. The two of them had vanished down a side street.

The next day, I was summoned to appear before the lieutenant. I got a right beasting. "You're a disgrace to the entire Bavarian Army!" he bellowed again and again. I had to do a dozen about-turns in the office and was given four days' "severe arrest".

From that point on I was not considered normal. It was already rumoured that the major was thinking of having my sanity tested. But we made a big advance and the time slipped past. Vilnius floated by like a memory from an enchanted fairy-tale. Russian religious devotion was a new experience; I shall never forget the golden domes of the churches.

The others chased after skirt. I read. I was already known as: "Brother Loony".

17.
THE STRUGGLE BEGINS

A letter came, telling me that Jung had deserted and was now in a lunatic asylum. A rumour was circulating in the staff that a regiment had mutinied near Kaunas; near Vilnius the troops had flung their rifles and medals at the feet of their commanding officers and said: "We won't be shot down for the sake of an army loaf!" The drivers told how Russian prisoners, who were being employed in the front line, were going on strike. They refused to get out of the railway carriages; they were freezing to death by the dozen, refused to eat, and were only brought back into line by being beaten. The air was thick with rumours. What's more, every railwayman had a grudge against our major. "We'll get him at the first opportunity," they muttered.

It was bitterly cold. The water that we fetched from the nearby spring had an icy crust on its surface by the time we got back. My feet had frostbite. I stood rigid and motionless in the cattle-truck, unable to resist the cold that took hold of me. On and on we travelled through endless snowfields. At one station the major looked into our cattle-truck. I was fetching tea from the kitchen, so I wasn't there. The stable boy was asleep. He was given a "severe arrest", which he had to sit out at the end of the journey. He sat there pudding-headed, saying over and again: "I'm done for ... I'm done for ... They'll enter it in my army book. It's all up with me. I have a family." He had already been a groom in civilian life, working for barons and counts.

I said: "I've had about all I can take of this racket."

The other said: "I'm done for."

I said: "Shit!"

We finally reached our destination. A dump called Rakischki. It was a tiny village. Our baggage train stopped far out in the snow fields. We had to unload. I was frozen stiff. The others brought me schnapps and hot tea. I got moving again. I took my horses down from the wagon. The stable boy reported himself sick. That meant I had to take care of his stuff, too. The others helped me. We lowered the baggage wagon. I harnessed the horses, tied the two belonging to the major and the lieutenant's chestnut to the back of the wagon and set off. The officers had gone ahead with their two drivers. Peperl and the others drove into the village in a lorry to set up quarters. I got moving with all my baggage on my own. Baggage trains passed by, lorries rattled, frozen reinforcements shovelled away the snow.

At first, I kept a sharp watch on the officers' horses. Then I was overcome with the cold once more and complete indifference set in. It was a long way. I sat there stiff as a board on the box, cowering in my fur coat, and let the harnessed horses in front jog on. When I arrived, the officers' horses, which had been tied to the back of the wagon, were gone.

The lieutenant came: "Where are the nags?"

"Disappeared," was my answer. The officer started to yap like a terrier: "If those horses are not back within two hours, I'll have you demoted to a second-class soldier, placed under severe arrest, and immediately sent back to your reserve battalion. Stand to attention, soldier! ... You blithering idiot! What were you thinking of!"

I stood rigidly to attention. The lieutenant did a bobbing about-turn in his own operatic manner and went back indoors. I stayed where I was. Peperl ran up to me: "Oy, Graf! Graf!"

"They can do what they like. I'm frozen!" I grumbled, clenching my teeth and rubbing my hands to warm them up; I unharnessed the two draught horses, led them to a room at the back of the house and tied them up for the time being.

The rest of my comrades came running: "For God's sake, man! You're crazy!"

"I'm freezing!" I yelled back.

"You snivelling wretch! Come on! We'll help you look! Do you really think we're going to get ourselves locked up in severe arrest for such nonsense!?" they all moaned. By the evening we'd got the horses back. A passing supply train had caught them. A junior officer was riding the major's horse. After I had brought back the recovered horses and they were safe and sound, I went and reported the fact to the lieutenant.

"You'll pay dearly for this, you blighter!" he hissed again. Then he made me do several more about-turns before dismissing me.

The struggle begins, I thought on my way out. The next day Peperl summoned me. He gave me a strange look. "What's up with you? You're trembling and pale as a corpse?" I asked. "You're in for a stiff punishment," he whispered.

"Really," I said, "so it's starting already ... Very well."

"The major's away for three days. You must go down to the lieutenant. He's standing in for the major. But it will still be reported to him," Peperl further informed me. I stared at him. He didn't dare make eye contact.

I went down to the lieutenant's office.

"So there you are," he snarled at me, and read out a type-written sheet, which stated that I was sentenced to an immediate three days' severe arrest. "Is that all?" I thought involuntarily, remained standing to attention, and listened. "Right!" snapped the svelte lieutenant. Then Peperl came and took me to a nearby Russian town hall. There he got the duty sergeant major – a good-humoured old boy from the Erzgebirge – to register my arrival, and left me, feeling downcast. I smiled back to him, but he was still silent and nervous, almost like a shy child.

"Reet then comrade, come on. There's a little room at' back. It's still warm, just wang um wood ont' fire," said the sergeant major with an un-soldierly cheerfulness, and he shut me in a dark room containing nothing except a wooden bunk. There was some firewood left. I stoked up the fire, lay down on the bunk and gradually dozed off. All of my limbs were fee-bly languid. We received the same food here in detention as we did when on duty. We had to chop and split firewood for our cells, which took about two hours a day. There were some fifteen of us in detention, plus a Polack woman, who had been locked up for whoring. Little Jewish boys brought us cigarettes and Russian white bread. The sergeant major was a decent man. He was easy-going about everything. Two old home guards, also from the Erzgebirge, guarded us and looked in. One of them fetched books for me from our quarters, which I read by the skylight.

"This is brilliant," I said, "I'm never leaving. Why should I care about the bastard staff?"

"Everyone's sick 'n tired of this long bloody war," the old boy said, with his kindly, troubled face. There he stood, stooping and melancholy, like a man who would let you do as you pleased.

"If we onny knew what it wor orl about," he said, "it won't be over until they've destroyed everything. I said it all along. Owd or young, ah said to our Gustav, we'll get nowt if victory comes ... The bigwigs will get together and sup their champagne as ever when it's orl o'er, and us nobod-ies'll be ruined ... It's one big swindle, comrade, just one big swindle ... Us ordinary blokes don't mean each other no 'arm, it's the bigwigs whoa are behin' it orl! ... A swindle, nowt but a swindle ..." He put his hand in his pocket and pulled out a plug of chewing tobacco, cut off a chunk, and put it in his mouth.

He spat it out with a sulk and shook his old head ... On the third day I was released and reported myself to the lieutenant. All my comrades looked at me askance, almost fearfully.

"Well I hope that's knocked some sense into you," the lieutenant de-clared, "but there's more to come. Dismissed!" And once again, the famil-iar about-turns.

A mysterious letter arrived from Berlin. It said: "Don't write any more! Jung broke out of Dahlem. On the run. Police searching high and low." I did not recognize the writing. I only knew that Schorsch had been discharged from the District Command in Munich and had settled in Ber-lin. So I did not write again and waited. Nothing came. I learned through the grapevine that Jung had indeed escaped from the asylum and had been discharged soon after his recapture. He had been declared insane, because he had deserted. He had gone to Schorsch in Munich, but the police soon caught up with him and Schorsch did five weeks in gaol for aiding and abetting him.

This unsettled me. I wanted to know what had happened. I wrote a note: "Private of the Train Graf requests that the Major grant two weeks' furlough, as he needs a week to attend to private business in Berlin and another for family business at home." I hesitated, carrying the note around with me for three days.

"Crumbs, why aren't you doing anything?" my comrades on the staff asked me.

"I am off duty after my arrest," I replied. They shook their heads doubtfully and kept quiet. Anxious, they took care of my horses. In the afternoon I let the officers' horses run free for a while, and the lieutenant's chestnut ran off again. This time, the lieutenant's words were softer: "You should be ashamed of yourself!"

"Excuse me, lieutenant sir, it just happened," I said awkwardly. He lost his temper again and dismissed me with the order to bring the nag back at once. We all looked, and once again, we found the beast. The lieutenant wanted to hush it up, but the major found out about the business anyway. The lieutenant received a mild reprimand, and that was it. One evening I put my request for leave on the major's desk. The next day, Peperl appeared breathlessly and panted: "You have to report to the major." I did so.

"You asked for a furlough," he said, with my request in his hand. "A furlough is a reward. I cannot grant it to you after the way you have behaved ... And in any case," he raised his voice threateningly, "I have been meaning to have you locked up again, because of the lieutenant's runaway chestnut, you slacker! ... I'll have your sanity tested! Get away with you!"

I had to do an about-turn and left, stepping out of the office with a smile on my face, and up in our attic-room I wrote another note: "Private of the Train Graf requests that the Major grant a punishment on account of the runaway chestnut," waited until the evening and put the scrap of paper on the major's desk again. Nobody knew about it.

All of my comrades were giving me a wide berth. They were scared witless. Just one of them, an Alsatian, spoke to me now and again. I said to him: "The war will never end unless each and every one of us starts to rebel."

"What will ye gain by struggling against a solid mass? They'll just stand y'up against th' wall and shoot ye, or send ye tae a fortress gaol, where ye'll die a slooow death," was his reply.

"One way or another. It's all the same to me," I said, and added: "We're still treated far too well. It will have to come to the point where they need to whip us like dogs, then we'll rise up against them. When the oppression becomes unbearable, then the change will come."

"Ye're right abit 'at," he agreed in a whisper, "but watch out ... thaur ur traitors a' place. Actin' oan yer ain is a bad idea, nae leest coz it is pure useless. Th' swindle just carries on."

"Then the others can carry on with it. I've had enough," I said. "Can't you two just shut up!" the others snarled from their straw beds. We said no more. In the morning Peperl hurried back, pale as a corpse and gasping for breath. He exclaimed: "You have to go down to the major. He looks like a rabid dog." I laughed. The lieutenant met me in the courtyard, and said, scornfully: "You blithering idiot!" I straightened up and entered the major's office.

"Three days' severe arrest!" came at the end of a torrent of abuse. Peperl led me back to the town hall. He always did this with an officious formality, not daring to look me in the eye, and did not answer any of my questions. The old boys from the Erzgebirge welcomed me with the same matter-of-fact friendliness. I liked that. Carry on, I thought, carry on. Why should I care what they put in my army record? I shall tear it up in any case. I don't give a damn about my reputation with the military brass.

Out of sheer boredom, I scribbled all over the walls of my cell and wrote in every corner: "Down with the war!" or "The masses won't do it! The individual must act!"

I thought, if only the inspecting officer comes by and sees that, then there will certainly be a big row and more punishment, which was all right with me, because it was much nicer in here. But there was no raid. After my release, a draught horse died of colic. We dragged him out of the stable and left him lying on the ground. When I reported this to the lieutenant, he said, quite cynically: "The nag must be flayed! Flay the horse and bring me its hide!"

"I beg your pardon, sir, but I am no butcher," I said.

"Shut up! I'm ordering you to flay the horse! Dismissed!" he said brusquely.

I went upstairs and lay down on my straw mattress. Evening fell. "You have to report to the lieutenant," said Dreier as he came upstairs. I was sick and tired of all this back and forth. "Have you flayed the horse yet?" the lieutenant asked grimly.

"I can't. It makes me sick," I replied. We glared at one another for a few seconds. The lieutenant looked like he would explode at any moment. I stayed calm. "If the nag is not flayed by tomorrow afternoon, you'll be sent to military gaol," the officer sneered all of a sudden.

I repeated, in the same tone as previously: "I beg your pardon, sir, but I am no butcher."

"Get out," he yelled. I went up and lay down to sleep again. Early the next morning I went back to the lieutenant and repeated once more: "I beg your pardon, sir, but I cannot flay the horse."

"Get out! Get out of my sight!" he bellowed and shouted after me:

"Fetch two Russians from the equine hospital and get them to help! But get on with it!"

I went to the equine hospital, grabbed two Russians, gave them each a pick-axe and shovel, and said: "Russki! Russki! Hole! Hole! Here!" And I made signs to them. The two of them understood, dug the frozen earth, and made a deep pit. In the meantime I picked up an axe and hacked off the head and hooves of the dead nag, which was frozen solid, and flung them into the pit, followed by the rigid body. Then we covered it up. At midday the lieutenant came up to me: "What's up with the nag?" and he looked at the place where the black earth was piled up.

"He's lying here, lieutenant, sir," I answered and looked him calmly in the eye.

"And the hide?" asked the slim man, red with rage.

"Begging your pardon, sir, but the nag was frozen through, and his guts were hanging out behind him," I said. "The hide!" he yelled.

"Even the Russians couldn't manage it!" I told him, unmoved.

"Very well!" began the lieutenant, now in a rage, and stepped towards me menacingly:

"So you want a fortress arrest? You are welcome! What do you want here anyway? You! You!"

He was now trembling with anger.

"I've been wanting to say this to you for a long time, lieutenant, sir, I would like to be sent to another unit, as I just get one punishment after the other here. I do not believe I am suited to staff duty," I said coolly. "I see! ... Hm ... You'll have time to think about that in the fortress, my lad!" the superior officer ranted at me and carried on in the same tone: "What do you think this is!? What makes you think you're entitled to special treatment!? What have you got into that head of yours, you blithering idiot!"

"Well ... I suppose you could send me back to my reservists' depot and then they could put me in another active unit," I said, unmoved. That dumbfounded him for a moment. He gave me a silent and deadly look. Then he said curtly: "You wait! You'll see soon enough," and he went.

Two days passed.

"Go to the stable, for Pete's sake! Or they'll lock you up for ten years!" wailed my comrades. I did not budge. "I'm sick! It doesn't matter one way or the other," I answered, obstinately.

On the second day, at five o'clock in the afternoon, I was summoned to the lieutenant.

"Report back to me for active duty within one hour," was the short order.

"What's up, lieutenant, sir?" I asked innocently. "Dismissed! Get out!" he thundered in reply.

"Very well!" I growled resolutely on my way out, almost under my breath. Once again all of my comrades looked at me with a peculiar, silent alienation, as if they were afraid of me. After approximately ten minutes I came, ready for active duty, to the lieutenant's office, stood to attention, and said: "At your command!"

The lieutenant turned around instantly, looked me in the eye with utter contempt, and said in a spiteful tone: "I see! ... Now get off to the Prussian Reserve Army Railway Company Number Two, so you can learn how to use a shovel!" I started to tremble a little, but immediately straightened myself up again and said: "I should like to inform the lieutenant that I will never follow the order!"

The lieutenant moved a step forward. A Prussian officer, sitting at the other desk, bounced up like a snapped mattress spring, and the two roared in unison: "Whaaat?"

The door to the major's office opened, and the major burst in, snorting: "What's this I'm hearing? ... Whaaat? ... Insubordination?" And his eyes drilled into me. I turned around, shaking, and said again in the same tone of voice as before: "I should like to inform the major that I will never follow the lieutenant's order!"

A babble of voices fizzed around me. The major pointed at the door, threateningly: "Get out! Get out!" My whole body at once flushed hot and cold and I lay down on the straw, without even unfastening my kitbag, smoked one cigarette after the other and waited for whatever would happen next.

Night had fallen outside. Nobody dared go to bed. I calmed down and, bored, I read the Jewish calendar that I had found in a house in Kaunas. Several people's footsteps tramped up the stairs. A light shone through the crack in the door. The lieutenant came and shone his pocket torch on me.

"I see! So you're lying up here!" In a snarling tone he hurriedly read out loud an immensely long arrest warrant. I took no notice. A Prussian NCO wearing a helmet and two soldiers with fixed bayonets stood behind him in the gloom. I vaguely caught something about immediate incarceration and temporary custody in severe arrest owing to insubordination. I lay there calmly and listened, without taking the cigarette out of my mouth. That was not boldness, but rather nervousness, a feeling of resignation and submission. The colour drained completely from the lieutenant's face, and his eyes drilled into me. When he had finished reading, he asked: "Understood?" I nodded.

"Will you follow the order?" he asked again, quickly.

"Yes," I said with indifference, and nodded.

"Then at least take that damned fag out of your gob!" he yelled.

"I must finish smoking it first," I said, calmly. The lieutenant winced, then stopped to think for a moment. I could clearly hear him gnashing his teeth. Then, without giving me another glance, he turned to the three Prussian soldiers and ordered: "If he does not obey and follow you within five minutes, report to me below!" He strode noisily through the open door and slammed it shut. The Prussians looked at me, helplessly. After a short pause, the NCO said to me in a muffled tone: "Comrade, don't do anything stupid! Come along with us!" I got up slowly, sought out two pieces of army bread and took them in my woollen blanket.

"Will you follow us?" he suddenly asked, speaking formally again.

"You can see I will," I said, wrapping my blanket around me.

"Crumbs, what have you got yourself into?" the NCO said, now in a more sympathetic voice. The soldiers, who had been standing there stiff as posts, shook their heads. They let me go out in front and brought me back to the town hall.

I still remember everything very clearly. Snow lay deep on the ground and we ploughed through it in silence. The wind blew bitterly cold around the corners of the houses. It was pitch dark. Only the razor-sharp line of the NCO's pocket torch showed the way. All the way, the song *Es geht bei gedämpfter Trommel Klang* went through my head, and I was overcome with a sombre spirit.[21] Odd, that it never occurred to me that they might stand me up against the wall or cart me off to a fortress gaol; it only crossed my mind that this must be how the Russians are transported to Siberia. And then – yes – then, I don't know why, I suddenly imagined that spring had come, and that I was walking over the wind-swept meadows of my homeland as they burst into life: I felt blissfully happy and suddenly started to sing:

"Ein Vöglein sang im Lindenbaum
in lauer Sommernacht!"[22]

At first, I just hummed the tune, but then, it seems, took a great liking to my voice and, although I now remembered that the NCO and two privates were behind me, I sang out cheerfully. The three men acted deaf and dumb and simply tramped onwards. They let me sing; I imagined that they were actually enjoying this bizarre gaiety. The exertion of ploughing on through the snow brought me into a sweat, however, and I panted for air; I abruptly stopped singing ...

It was eleven at night by the time we reached the cells.

---

[21] A song set to music by Robert Schumann: "The soldier. He walks to the sound of a muffled drum."

[22] A German folksong: "A little bird sang in the linden tree / In the warmth of the summer night!"

"Back again already, Graf?" said the sergeant major, and dismissed the three men.

"I like it so much at your gaff," I said, laughing.

I was put in my old cell, lit a cigarette, walked rather nervously up and down, and shone the light of my match on the walls. Under my graffiti, someone had written: "Quite right."

I settled down contentedly on my bunk and only fell asleep after all manner of thoughts had whirled through my head.

18.
YOU'LL BE AMAZED

On the first day the home guardsman came in early with a canteen full of tea and said: "Sup up, comrade! There's actually sugar i' it today ... It does tha good to get something warm inside theur int' morning ..." He put down the mess tin and went through the open door, locking it on his way out.

I had a couple of slurps and left the rest as it was. Lunch came. I did not touch it. For supper, there were a couple of slices of sausage. I put them aside and ate nothing. The same happened on the next day. I ate nothing.

"Taste no good?" asked the home guard.

"I have no appetite," I said, and left all the food. The third day came. It was agonizingly long and distressing. I didn't eat a thing. You're bound to croak, I thought, and worked myself into a rage to avoid temptation.

"Ea' up, comrade," said the home guard, worried and almost imploringly. "Tha'll peg out on our watch." The sergeant major came by and asked: "Can't you eat?" I said: "I'm not in the least bit hungry."

"Are tha poorly?" enquired the sergeant major. I shook my head, smiling cheerfully.

"No, it's just that I can't eat, otherwise I'm fine ... It'll be all right, sergeant major," I said, innocently. My stomach rumbled. Hold out, I ordered myself caustically, and suppressed the tummy trouble. Polack boys came and secretly sold me cigarettes through the skylight. If it was too risky to hang about, they slipped away without a sound, but they always came back. I stood all day at the window and blew the smoke through the grating, so that nobody could smell it. It was very easy-going. The guards never checked what I was up to.

On the morning of the fourth day I heard unfamiliar voices at my door. The district commandant's lieutenant entered my cell, accompanied by the sergeant major. I was told to stand to attention and report, but I just lay on my bunk. The officer blamed the kindly sergeant major and bawled me out.

"Why are you not eating? Are you ill?" he asked, giving me a sharp look,

"No, I'm just not hungry, lieutenant, sir," I said in a flat tone.

"I see! ... Are you aware that we can force you to eat?" the lieutenant threatened.

"Sir, yes sir, but you can't make me hungry," was my answer. Then the man lost his temper.

"You're obviously a right little malingerer," he raged and then said, scornfully: "Well, we've got the better of others. You'll eat soon enough!" All along the corridor he ranted about applying violence. In spite of myself, I thought of the 500 Russians who had been beaten into working and eating at the front.

But I ate nothing. The third day was the worst, and that was over. My stomach had grown used to hunger. I went on smoking and lay on the bunk. I shall soon collapse, I thought. And so the fourth and fifth days passed. I heard our lieutenant outside: "Has he made up his mind to eat now?"

"No lieutenant, sir," the sergeant major returned.

"Oh well, let him go hungry, if it amuses him," said the lieutenant, and he went away. The sergeant major came back to me, depressed.

"Please ea', comrade," he beseeched, almost paternally.

But I could not be moved. Freedom or death, I thought, and carried on starving myself, smoked or lay on the bunk and dozed. An East Prussian private of the train was delivered into the neighbouring cell. He sang all day long, then knocked on the wall, and chatted with me through the afternoon out in the yard as we were chopping firewood.

I felt a slight weakness being out in the fresh air. At last, I thought.

I carried on smoking. The sixth day came and went, the seventh and eighth, without me sensing any imminent collapse. Only I grew weaker. The home guards and sergeant major were frantic. "Comrade, what's wrong with you? Just tell us! Do you want to report sick?" they asked, dolefully.

"I'm fine," I replied amiably, and smiled contentedly.

"Hm, hm, hm, awful," murmured the sergeant major, and all three left the cell, shaking their heads. As I dozed on the bunk, the walls slowly started to grow blurry, and all the objects in the cell seemed to float. But I still had my senses about me, and I could still clearly hear the East Prussian in the next cell, singing:

We sit between four walls, all right
and moan about this torture.
Here we must feel contrite, contrite,
on stale bread and water.

The monotonous melody penetrated through the walls, and here and there, others joined in. It droned in my ear, and in the end the entire building seemed to hum with these gloomy verses, which I have never forgotten:

Our curtains are braided with iron,
barbed wire surrounds the yard.

They've robbed us of our freedom, freedom,
this dungeon treats us so hard.

And should our friends call on us
the gaolers won't open the cage.
Then we start to cuss'em, to cuss'em,
And murd'rous loud is our rage.

Our days of sorrow are over,
Our days of sorrow gone by.
Now raise your glasses of beer, of beer
Our days of sorrow gone by.

The major rode over and inquired if I was now eating. No, they said. He rode off again.

I started to wonder. I became unsettled. Nothing happened. I did not collapse. On the ninth day, around midday, I knocked at the door. The men, anxious, came and opened it.

"I would like to be deloused," I said. All of their faces were once again a picture of cheerlessness. Several shook their heads silently. I was told to collect my things. Two home guardsmen took me by the arm and led me carefully through the Russian village, as though I were seriously ill. I saw Dreier and the little driver, Römer, on the street. They looked away. I summoned up all my power to look desperately serious. In the delousing station the two home guards helped me to undress and carried all my clothes into the delousing machine. I got into hot water. In the bathtub next to mine there were soldiers on leave, who chatted and laughed. And now I felt a sudden weakness. It spread from my feet up to my head. I broke into a cold sweat.

"Comrade," I said hastily to my neighbour, "I feel dreadful, haven't you got a drop of rum?"

The home guardsmen were speaking with the delousing orderlies. My neighbour handed me his army flask. It was genuine field-issue rum. I took a large gulp and quickly handed back the flask. I shivered all over. I turned dizzy. I had a blurred vision of the home guards running back, tried to stand up and fell back into the tub with a splash. I heard a loud buzzing around me. Later, I woke up in a warm room. A doctor was leaning over me, manipulating my eyes with an instrument. But everything was in a whirl. Someone asked me again and again what was my birthday and what day it was. They rubbed something into my forehead. It smarted on my skin, and a sharp smell penetrated my nose. I opened my eyes wide. There was the doctor in his white coat and behind him a medical orderly and one of the home guards.

"Are you ill?" asked the doctor. I shook my head, wearily. "What day is it today?" he repeated. "I don't know, I don't know," I stammered, with fixed eyes.

"When were you born?" he asked again.

"I don't know, I don't know."

"Have you a mother still? Are your parents still alive?"

"I don't know, I don't know," I said, utterly exhausted. Everything was so woozy, so fluid, nothing mattered. Night had fallen when I woke up again in my cell. How I got there, I knew not. They had wrapped me in woollen blankets. I was fed up, utterly fed up. Back in this hole! There's nothing for it, I will have to croak, or they will not let me go, I thought, spinelessly. My eyes closed again.

Next morning the two home guardsmen carried me out. I opened my eyes. The sergeant major stroked my forehead and said, emotionally: "Tha're goin' hoam to thy mother, comrade." They loaded me onto a transport service lorry, drove me to the railway station, and handed me over to a hospital train. I was still half asleep. Dreams came and went. I felt fresh air again, then warmth and a bed. Noises penetrated the wall of sleep. The smell of medicines rose up through my nostrils. How long this went on, I have no idea. I woke with a start, saw the smiling face of a nurse quite close, and fell asleep again.

Something was stuck in my throat. I opened my eyes wide. The nurse was spoon-feeding me with semolina. I spat it out violently, right into the nurse's face. She spluttered and screamed. But I fell straight back to sleep again.

This dreamlike state continued for nearly a fortnight, they told me. Now and again I opened my eyes, saw strange faces in white coats and fell asleep again. Gradually I recovered and, even when I was awake, I let the nurse spoon-feed me. The doctor in charge came and flashed an electric torch in my face. I stared into the piercing beam of light. A cold hand stroked my forehead.

Slowly, my strength returned. I became conscious of my surroundings. A man was constantly leaning at the window, tugging at his hospital gown. Others were running round and round in fast circles.

One of them suddenly fell down and struck out convulsively, screaming and roaring. A whimpering voice in a corner howled ceaselessly: "I am mad! I am mad!"

Then he broke down, sobbing: "Holy Mary! Holy Mary!"

Every now and again the patient in the next bed broke into a nervous twitch from top to bottom, sprang up in bed, and ground his teeth until they cracked. A young man in the middle bed on the other side, who was propped upright, jabbed the air with an outstretched finger and screamed:

"Neu-Ulm! Neu-Ulm! Neu Uuuulm! Ha! Neu-Ulm! Neu-Ulm!" And finally there was a man who jumped out of his bed every now and again, as though doing the St Vitus dance, ripped his clothes from his body, took his penis in his hand, and stared at it.

Meanwhile two guards walked among them placidly, and at mealtimes I saw nurses handing out dishes. Or else two doctors in white coats strolled from one bed to the next, examined the patients, and gave my neighbour an injection.

New patients arrived. There was a terrible racket all the time. Plates were thrown at the walls with a crash. One patient spat at anyone who passed by. One man or another turned on him in a rage. The attendants intervened. He was put into a straitjacket and taken to another ward.

I was given meat for the first time, jumped up with a start and raised my hands in self-defence: "That's the horse! The horse!" The nurse wanted to force me to eat. I threw the plate, food and all, at the wall.

The attendants came and threatened me.

"That's the horse," I said doggedly.

"You're nuts!" they yelled. But I refused all meat. They brought me sponge cake and red wine. I ate the cake but refused the red wine.

"That's blood! Horse blood," I said, pushing it away. The nurse shook her head. The attendants laughed and drank the wine. Then I was allowed to get up. My knee still trembled when I took just a few steps. All day I sat on the edge of the bed, stared out of the window, and did not say a word. When I went out, two attendants accompanied me, one left, one right, and waited at the lavatory door. I was taken for examination. The doctor questioned me. "Why won't you eat meat?" was the first question. "That's the horse! They sent it after me," I said. "Which horse?" asked the doctor.

I told him about the horse that I'd had to flay, and the guts that trailed behind him, and I told him that ever since, any thought of meat made me sick.

Had the major been right to punish me?

The physician raised the question quite frankly. He was flattering, like a comrade in a soothing mood.

"From a military standpoint, the major had done the right thing. From a human standpoint, that's another matter, but this is not the place to judge," I said, tactfully.

"Oh well, yes. Well, you're being sent home to your mother," said the doctor, and two attendants took me back to the mental ward. I went back to my bed and stared out to the whiteness of the courtyard. In the evening there was a large L on my temperature chart. That meant I was to be transported in the hospital train.

But the NCO in charge of the train hated me, because I would not lift a finger whenever there was anything to be done. One ambulance after another collected patients and sent them homewards. New patients arrived. But I stayed on and on. Weeks flew by and I was still there.

One day, at 12 noon, the general physician's spurs clattered down the corridor to the hospital's secretariat. I was in the corridor as he went past.

"What? You're still here?" said His Excellency. He did an about turn and went to the NCO in the bureau. There was a big row. The same evening I was driven to the station in an ambulance and travelled by hospital train to my homeland. A medical orderly watched over me for the entire journey. Three doctors came by and tried to question me.

"I don't know" was my answer to every question.

Blithely I lay there on my gently swinging mattress and stared out at the jarring countryside.

Our train passed through Berlin and stopped at Görden near Brandenburg on the Havel. In Berlin I wrote a military postcard to Cläre Oehring and gave it to some man at the station. I did not expect it to reach her. I already knew where we were going and gave her the address, asking her, if she possibly could, to visit me. No sooner had the train started again, than I forgot all about it.

I arrived at an auxiliary hospital with wounded soldiers. We were bathed, given fresh clothes and lay down in the beds allotted to us. Then the nurses bustled in bringing us frankfurters with potato salad.

What am I doing with the wounded? I thought. The nurse passed me a plate of frankfurters. Splat! It hit the pristine, white wall.

General uproar. The nurses came running in, looked at me in astonishment and assailed me with questions:

"What's the matter with you? Can't you eat it?"

"That's the horse," I said calmly. General shaking of heads. The doctor came, went from bed to bed, questioned each of us and was very friendly. "Well, what have you brought us from Russia?" he asked and smiled. "I had a dose of gastritis once, doctor, sir," I said.

"Oh, and now? Are you in good health?" he asked. I nodded and laughed. The doctor's expression changed slightly.

"All right, but in that case, why did they send you here?"

"I don't know ... They just sent me here," I answered.

"Hm. Oh well, we'll just have to wait for your records to arrive," said the doctor, looking at me. Then he moved on.

On the second day they brought beef and vegetables for lunch. Once again, I threw the dish at the wall. And once again the nurses came in, assailed me with questions and looked at me sympathetically.

"That's the horse," I said once more.

They gave me pancakes, scrambled eggs or sponge cake and I was allowed to get up. Whenever the doctor came, he smiled at me amiably, and I laughed back.

Finally, my records arrived. I had to go to the doctor's office.

"Now then Graf," he said, in a very friendly tone, after I had sat down next to him, "let's try some simple arithmetic." He had a large folio sheet in front of him, and asked: "What is two times two?"

"Four, doctor, sir," I answered. "Good, good," he murmured, approvingly.

"What is the difference between a dog and a roof?" he asked rather more anxiously and observed me keenly through his shining spectacles.

"The roof is above, whereas the dog runs on the ground," was my answer. The doctor wrote everything down. He turned to me again and showed me an apple: "If I cut this apple into four parts, what is each part called?"

"A quarter, doctor, sir," I answered promptly. Once again, he praised me, and the result was recorded on paper.

"And if I now cut each of the parts in half, how many parts do I have?"

I hesitated and looked at the questioner. He encouraged me again, and actually cut a quarter of the apple into two: "Well? Well?"

"It's odd, sir," I said truthfully and wiped my forehead with my hand, "but it's as though my mind has been wiped blank. With the best will in the world, I can't say."

The doctor looked at me critically, smiled a little and finally drew a line with his pen across the paper. Then I was put on the operating chair and examined. Once again came the curious manipulation of my eyes. And that was it. I was allowed to go.

"We shall send you home to your mother, what do you think?" the doctor asked, smiling at the door.

"I'd rather stay in the military, sir," I said in reply, "at home they have nothing to eat, and I am just surplus to requirements."

In the dayroom, they all clamoured around me with questions about my illness.

"I don't know, only the doctor knows," I answered. And – why were all the patients standing at the end of the bed, staring at the same thing? I went round and looked at my temperature chart. Next to the printed word, "Diagnosis", was written in fresh ink: "Idiot". And then behind it, a question mark. Several of them gave me odd looks. I burst into wild laughter, literally danced about and infected the entire room with my gaiety. The nurses let me do as I pleased, and they thought I did not notice, they just sighed: "Good grief, the poor boy!"

When the doctor came by on his rounds, I stood broad-chested and said cheerily: "Good morning, doctor! Filthy weather we're having today!" or "We had a fine old time last night, it was fabulous, I'm telling you."

Because I was always in a good mood and made everyone laugh at every opportunity, I was treated accordingly. That delighted me. "He's a fool, that Graf," said the Hessians, and the Prussians and Brandenburgers nudged each other knowingly, and laughed: "A young dope!" So the days passed. I was now also writing letters. Mainly to my friends in Berlin. And one day Richard Oehring arrived from Berlin. He was promptly seized by the doctor, who cross-examined him in detail. Afterwards, when I was allowed to walk with him in the garden, he told me, looking deadly serious, the strangest things.

"They regard you as mentally deficient. But it's all up with you now. At any rate, be prepared for a long internment ... I didn't know what kind of sickness you were claiming to have and just told the doctor what I knew about you," he said, giving me a fixed look. He left me feeling rather depressed. That evening, I was summoned to the doctor.

"Now look here, Graf, it appears you're a rather intelligent man," he said, as I went through the door, "you are a poet and have been published in magazines, according to your friend."

"That's not correct sir, that's not me," I said stiffly, with a frosty expression. A few seconds passed.

The doctor softened: "Just sit down ... Let's have a little talk." He moved his chair very close to me and looked into my eyes with paternal kindness. Then he grasped my shoulder as though he wanted to shake me out of a deep dream. "Now, imagine I am your friend, Graf ... Talk to me as you would talk to Oehring."

I sat there stiffly, almost breathless, staring at him stupidly. "But you are a poet," repeated the doctor more and more urgently. "Graf! ... You, Graf! ... You have been published in magazines, haven't you, Graf?"

I drew a little breath.

"That's not me, doctor," I repeated.

"Just look at me! ... You see, I am a man like you ... It is my duty to cure you as soon as possible, that's all," said the doctor mildly, almost pleadingly.

All of a sudden, I bent down into his face, which startled him a little, and shouted loud, and even louder:

"You're the worst of criminals! You only heal us so they can keep using us as cannon fodder! You are worse than any General or Kaiser, because you only use your knowledge to ensure that there are more people to get killed! ... The Generals, the Kaiser, the entire General Staff do what they are trained to do, but you, you, you have been trained for something quite different, and allow yourself to be used for the grossest outrage. You bring men who have been hacked to death back to life, so that they can maim and murder all over again! ... You are a pimp and a whore!"

The doctor had sprung to his feet, appalled, and took hold of me: "Pull yourself together, Graf! You are seriously ill!" He stammered helplessly. But I never shut up. I had also stood up and roared at him. I was overcome with boundless rage. The doors swung open.

"You're totally unhinged, Graf!" the doctor said, and led me to the doors. Two orderlies were already standing there with my things. The nurses peered in nervously and I vaguely saw patients pushing forward behind them. I stood still, trembling; there was white foam on my lips.

"We're sending you to a sanatorium," the doctor said in a monotone, and the orderlies took me between them. I had calmed down a little.

Everyone left, feeling embarrassed. Many looked at me as though I was a ghost or the devil. We left the hospital and walked through the park. An arched gate suddenly appeared. Above it was written, in large letters: "Royal Prussian Mental Asylum Görden."

We passed by some red houses, fronted by a wire mesh fence. Inside, extraordinarily demoralized people were wandering around. We finally stopped before such a house. "Ward 4" appeared on an enamel plate. One of the orderlies unlocked the door. We followed. The door was bolted shut behind us. A few steps. Another door, also unbolted and bolted. We were greeted by a terrible hullabaloo and clouds of smoke.

An old man was standing on the table with eighteen pipes of various sizes, which he was tossing about like a juggler. People ran around, laughed, whistled, smoked or sang. "That's Austria! – Long live Wilhelm! – Here is Hungary! – Death to her! – That's Thuringia – Saint Peter is pouring puke on the world – Hallelujah, Dominus!" yelled the smirking old man with the pipes, and slammed the table, making an almighty racket. A few men stood there and spat at him, tugged at his jacket and swore at him. He swore back and repeated his crazy ranting.

I leaned against the wall and burst into ringing fits of laughter. Now they noticed me.

"Come on, Sepp!" said a tall man, taking me by the arm. They all broke into a braying laugh. We went around in circles. The noise grew louder. The old man flung his pipes around in the air and caught them again, jumped down to the floor and started to cry raucously. One man fell down in convulsions, ripped his clothes, and bit himself. The orderly grabbed hold of him and carted him off. A young man ran crying from one corner to the other, shouting: "Don't shoot! Don't shoot! Dooon't …!" He flung up his arms and covered his face.

Another started preaching loudly. Everyone laughed, cried, screamed or sat dozily in the corner and stared listlessly. I was taken to the dormitory and told to lie on a bed and wait for the doctor. I kept bursting into lurid laughter. The doctor allowed me to get up. I could go to the dayroom and was given something to eat.

We sat at long tables. Everything was firmly riveted to the table. The crockery was made of tin. There were no knives and forks.

Some shovelled salt by the spoonful into the fruit compote, others first spat into the nicely cooked grub and then gobbled it down. One patient kept battering his plate on the edge of the table and slopping his food over the others. I had to keep a sharp lookout. If you looked away, your food was gone. I sat stupefied by all this chaos and roared with laughter again and again. The walls almost echoed with my laughter and it infected the others. Often, the entire room laughed in unison.

The old man with the pipes was the centre of attention. He always swore in the most shameful manner at the doctor as he made his rounds, threw his pipes at him and spat at him. Then he was prescribed a course of prolonged immersion. He struggled hysterically, screamed, cried, begged, scratched and howled like a bird wounded with shotgun pellets.

After a few weeks I was moved to the first floor. This was a so-called non-acute ward. The dormitories were smaller. There was a calmer atmosphere. We were given paper and allowed to play cards. At two in the afternoon we were all allowed to walk in the fenced-in garden.

20.
THE SEQUEL

There were five of us in our room. Leow, a Berlin locksmith, was in the bed next to me. There was a tall Jew called Mayer, a watchmaker from Cologne, who suffered from hysterical fits, and finally a student from Berlin, who barely spoke a word to the other patients.

Leow helped out in the kitchen. There was very little to eat. Leow stole bread and sausage and shared it with us. And so we all became friends. All, except the student. He always stood apart and one day Leow stormed into our room and said that someone had betrayed us. The student constantly kept company with the orderlies. We grew suspicious. We told the patients in the other rooms about this gentleman. Everyone avoided him.

"He has to go," said Leow, who was now banned from helping in the kitchen.

"For God's sake, don't cause a fuss," pleaded the emaciated watchmaker, trembling like an aspen leaf.

"The scoundrel!" I said.

Mayer stood guard when we were alone together. We engaged a man from the neighbouring room as our spy. His job was to eavesdrop on the student's conversations with the orderlies. And right enough: Hanisch – as the student was called – had told tales on us.

Leow clenched his fist and whispered in my ear: "We'll get him today." I nodded.

We went into the dayroom. I was suddenly overcome with an indescribable fury. All of our comrades were ready for a bust-up. I rushed around the tables, faster and faster. The orderlies already had their eyes on me and took up their positions in the corners. Then Hanisch emerged from the lavatory. With a bound I sprang at his face, clawed his cheeks and tore him to the ground. A terrible uproar arose. The orderlies swooped down on me, but all of the patients were in a rebellious mood and came to my aid. The door opened. A dozen orderlies came in from the "acute ward". They wrenched our arms behind our backs. We were given injections in the shoulder, then taken off for prolonged immersion. Leow lay next to me in the pool. He made signs to me, shook his fist: "Revenge!" An orderly came and dealt him a blow.

We were defenceless, lying there stark naked in a pool of water heated to 40° Centigrade. The room was full of steam and slippery. Three orderlies walked up and down by the window. If one of us tried to get out of the pool, they simply pushed him back in. In other words, we just had to lie there, lie still, and wait.

We had to eat lunch in the water, but none of us was hungry. Languor set in, then weakness, unutterable weakness. Terrible wailing sounds came from cell doors on one side. Shouts, screams, curses and prayers. It was only after the third day, when I was totally exhausted, that I was pulled out of the pool and put to bed. From then on, I did not utter a single word. I had been separated from Leow and other people I knew. The doctor came and felt my pulse. The gigantic orderly told him that I had destroyed the entire dayroom and torn off Hanisch's cheek.

"Is that true?" asked the doctor. I held my tongue and gave him an angry look. I held my tongue for five months. I did not even speak to myself. I met my comrades again in the garden. Leow came, wanting to tell me what was going on. I held my tongue. Mayer came. I held my tongue. They were all horrified and said that I was dumb.

Either I get my freedom, or I'll kick the bucket, I thought repeatedly, grinding my teeth. I suspected everyone. Every one of them was my enemy. If the doctor came by and wanted to speak with me, I made a sign that I wanted to write something. When I got a pencil and notepaper, I wrote down what it was that I wanted. Just before I was due to be transported elsewhere, I attacked another man I hated, a sapper, and screamed with excitement. I was given another two days' prolonged immersion, and the same business repeated itself. As I lay in bed and the doctor stood before me, the orderly reported: "He rebelled and smashed the place up ... The sapper is in a bad way."

"Why did you do that?" the doctor asked with an angry expression. I wanted to speak but could only stammer.

"Come, come now, you see, it is quite good that you wreaked havoc like that ... At least you can speak again," said the doctor, smiling. I stammered out a few more incomprehensible syllables and started to laugh. "We're transferring you to your homeland now," said the doctor, and left.

I was allowed to get up again. Fascinated, my comrades crowded round me. I wanted to speak but was unable. I burst out laughing again. Then the orderly came, took me to the changing room and gave me my things. I was told to get ready for a journey. A member of the Brandenburg home guard took me to the railway station. The train journey went through Berlin. As we were leaving the Anhalt station, I waved to an officer, stammered a request for a light, and held out my cigarette. The man started swearing at me. My escort explained the situation by pointing to his forehead. The officer laughed and gave me a light.

We visited Jung, Schorsch and Oehring. I laughed on and on. The orderly was jovial and treated me like a child.

That evening we continued our journey. We all met up again in the waiting room and drank lots of beer and cognac.

"Idiot!" Jung yelled after me

The others shook their heads like lunatics.
I laughed.

21.
SET FREE

My relatives visited me at the sanatorium in Haar.[23] When I stammered and laughed convulsively all the time, they started to cry. They did not know what to make of me and left depressed.

I found myself in a rather more peaceful environment here. One of the patients was at war all day long, explaining to everyone the position of the trenches and the state of the troops, moaning about the "swine" at district command HQ and sometimes slapping the priest or an orderly in the face. Then he was given prolonged immersion in the acute ward. Another spent the entire day producing bills of exchange from scraps of paper. Another constantly compressed his ear like a rubber ball while opening his mouth so wide that his jaws cracked. He claimed that the gas in his head was doing this. He was an average-sized Lower Bavarian with a cartilaginous face, who had escaped from the asylum no fewer than five times, once making it all the way to his native village. Once there he took a rope and ran to the nearest pear tree, fastened the rope, made a noose and poked his head through it before his family, local firemen and the village policeman came to arrest him. "I'll hang myself on the spot if anyone touches me!" he threatened, until at last his pursuers withdrew empty-handed.

Late that night he resurfaced in Haar. He answered all the questions and rebukes of the doctors and orderlies with fits of laughter: "Something is stirring! Things can't go on like this!"

They had to cut open the body of a Munich master bricklayer because he was convinced that he was pregnant. He was quite "normal" when he arrived at the asylum, but all at once he got into bed and whenever anyone passed, he lifted his bedspread, exposing his stomach, and cried: "There, it's long gone! ... Can you feel it, it's kicking already."

At mealtime, when the plates were set out on the table, another patient came up, put down small scraps of paper and said to each of us: "There are your bread, meat and fat ration cards. Now you can eat! So eat away!"

"August" or Lorenz Heppenheimer as he was really called, the sergeant major, was the star attraction, so to speak. One day he had crept out of his trench on the Western Front and started marching, as he was, all the way home. On the way he got hold of two sacks and hung them over his

---

[23] The sanatorium, on the outskirts of Munich, still exists. Since 2006 it has been called the *Isar-Amper-Klinikum München-Ost*.

shoulder. Then, whenever he found a dead or wounded soldier, he would go up to him and cut all of the buttons off his uniform and collect them, until the sacks were full. He was arrested not far from Strasbourg and taken to the lunatic asylum. His strength was legendary. He had been an acrobat and the proprietor of a travelling circus. It was even said that he had knocked over the mounted policeman, horse and all, as they tried to arrest him. The orderlies were afraid of him. Once, in a moment of agitation, he had bowled two of them over and halfway killed them. The only way to handle him was with kindness.

For a while he smashed every window with his bare fist, and when the orderlies threatened him with prolonged immersion, he went along with them quietly, saying: "Oh well, I'm dirty anyway." He always called the doctor "Max" and addressed him with the familiar *du* rather than the polite *Sie*. He was a brilliant chess player and always won. And he knew a whole load of card tricks.

If anyone asked August about where he was born and his family background, he came out with some fantastic stories. He was born as seaweed in the deep ocean and joined the gypsies; he owned horse-stables and treasure beyond your imagination behind the asylum. When he was weighed, he said, with deadly seriousness: "Oh no, I've lost another seven hundred hundredweight," and he sobbed like a child.

One day his mother came to visit. She was old and grey. He embraced her and introduced her to "Max", saying: "This is my lover, my sweetheart!"

"Really," laughed the doctor, "how old is she then?"

"Nineteen," said August suggestively, making a lewd gesture. On another occasion he carefully tied his right hand with a handkerchief. The doctor came and asked: "Well, August, what seems to be the trouble?" The doctor wanted to take hold of his hand, but August pulled it away shyly and plaintively, winced and wailed: "Ow! Ouch! Ouch!"

"So, why have you bandaged that hand?" the doctor inquired.

"Because I like it better than the other one," August said, whimpering. This man was my friend for the entire year that I had to spend in this peaceful lodging. We lay together in the garden, performed magic tricks, or else August told his stories. True enough, from time to time other inmates joined us; there was a medical student in a strange state of mental confusion and a trainee teacher from the Rhineland named Hobrecker, who treated everyone with cigarettes and came out with grand maxims. For some reason, however, I avoided nearly everyone else and associated with nobody but August.

Gradually, what with all of these conversations, my tongue loosened somewhat. The doctor brought me paper and books. I read a great deal and took notes. One day, Schorsch came from Berlin to visit. I was suffering from headache and a runny nose. The diagnosis was suppuration in the frontal sinus. This meant that I had to go twice a week to the garrison hospital in Munich, escorted by an orderly. My nose was cut open and I had to apply nasal spray.

One day the doctor came to me and said: "They will probably take you in at the garrison."

"I am not a soldier, doctor," I said. He gazed at me.

"Do you really think, sir, that after a year and a half in a lunatic asylum, I can simply pick up a rifle and start playing soldiers again?" I continued. Without answering this directly, the doctor asked: "Do you want to go on leave?"

"That sounds to me like you are just putting the dog on a longer leash," I answered.

"Do you want to be set free?"

"I am free," I said, and added with more emphasis:

"Even if you keep me here for years. It makes no difference. I am free. Nothing bothers me any more."

"If nothing bothers you any more, then you can go back to soldiering," interjected the doctor in a superior tone.

"As soon as I see an open meadow, I'll just break loose, and if you send me to the reserves, I'll say: I am no longer a soldier and I shall clear off. So, either I will come back here, or I'll land in prison." The doctor paused to reflect for a moment, fixing his eyes on me.

Days passed without anyone taking any notice of me.

One day, in the middle of the afternoon, the sergeant major attached to the army hospital came and gave me permission to go on furlough. I hesitated, but finally took my leave. There were no acquaintances of mine left in Munich. At home and in the village, people regarded me with something approaching terror. A few days later I received a card from the sergeant major with the following message: "Since your discharge from military service has already been agreed, you are requested to present yourself here. You are required to reimburse the ration-money that you have received. It will be paid back to you at your reservists' depot."

I went to Haar in mufti and without the money. The sergeant major thundered at me. But there was nothing he could do about it. I was given my army book, which contained no comments, and was free to go. August was discharged at the same time. His mother had come to collect him. The three of us walked through the gate into the open, into freedom. The road was mucky with slush. The snow was melting, and the sun shone large and high in the open sky.

August had refused to part with them: the two sacks filled with military buttons dangled from his shoulder and he tramped through the puddles in the worn-out sandals that he had worn all the time in the asylum, splashing up the sloppy filth. When his mother swore at him, he said resolutely: "I'm heading into the mountains!"

And he is probably still wandering there today, this blessed man, free of every inhibition, without a care in the world ...

In Munich we drank what was left of our money and parted. "Come with me," said August from the bottom of his heart and looking into my eyes. For a moment, I thought about it, hesitating.

"You'll turn out fine!" August repeated.

His old mother stood there, smiling at me. My thoughts swayed this way and that. Suddenly, as if in a dream, I shook my friend's hand and left. Sometimes, as I sink deep into thought, I see August standing before me, just as I left him.

You stupid devil! You fool, I tell myself. Why did I not go with him?

Part Two

STEP BY STEP

1.
ONE MADNESS ENDS,
ANOTHER BEGINS

And so I was back home again, free from the military, and could make a fresh start.

It was quiet in the house and quiet in the village. Since the death of my brother Max, the property belonged, according to my father's will, to his widow and the three young children. My two older sisters still lived together, and our mother with them. Theres managed the business, mother baked and did the housework, Emma was so sick that she had to stay in bed most of the time, and the widow mourned and had grown very stout.

Nanndl, meanwhile, had finished her apprenticeship and had stayed in the employ of the hairdresser in Munich. Maurus had been in the Vosges for some time and we had heard nothing from our brothers Lenz and Eugen in America since the outbreak of war.

I had more or less lost touch with my old friends and hadn't made any new ones. Schorsch sometimes wrote from Berlin. I occasionally got news from him about Jung and Oehring.

The war went on.

Quite frankly, now that I was back in my own life, so to speak, I hated being suddenly wrenched from a routine I had grown used to for years. A human being who is forced into a multitude easily loses whatever fragment of willpower is left to him, allowing himself to be pushed this way and that and, over time, thinks about nothing other than the immediate future. In the barracks, in the field and in the asylum, it was the same: nothing mattered. Nothing needed to matter to a person. And the *massenmensch* soon learns how to exploit this. He fills the hours and the days as comfortably as possible, and all he aspires to is: how can I get the cushiest number and the most to eat?

For the past few months, work had been relatively plentiful. Now there was a downturn. The rainy season was starting. Gloomy days followed. Unemployed, uncomfortable, and unconcerned, I loitered around. The villagers looked at me askance and grumbled:

"That bugger's back home! Others have to risk their necks."

I had been to Munich several times to look for work as an assistant. Each time I came home without success. Theres grew impatient.

"It's not possible that you can't find anything, you're just not looking properly," she said one day. "This can't go on, loafing around at home the whole time! ... The whole village is talking about it! ... When all the menfolk are at the front, you must be able to find something! ... You're just not looking seriously! You don't want to, that's all it is!"

I had no answer. The only thing that stuck in my mind was that, once we reached the age of majority, we were to inherit a sum of 2,000 marks. The thought had been buzzing around my head for some time. I wanted to get my hands on the money as soon as possible. I did not for a moment consider how I would use it. Just get the money, I thought, then you'll be a made man. I hankered after money from my earliest youth, aspiring to be as rich as possible, not to buy possessions, but simply to waste it. Money was only there to be spent, not for any other purpose!

So I said: "Yes, I will look for something, but I want my inheritance now."

Theres looked me directly in the eye, with an obvious air of superiority. She knew me.

"Your inheritance?!" was her thrusting reply. "You won't get that! That's taken care of. It's tied up in the mortgage on the house. So there's nothing you or I can do about it."

"So? ... Yeah, well!" I was still muttering as I went up to my room. I came back down a while later in my best suit. Theres gave me some money. My mother simply said, wearily:

"If only I'd drowned my children in their first bath, or in a sack full of stones like new-born kittens! Then I'd have saved myself all this worry." That was her stock expression whenever we siblings fell out. Nothing annoyed her more than arguments.

"All right! For God's sake, I'll find something soon enough! Don't get so upset!" I said in a surly voice, trying to calm her, and left.

I took the steamer to Starnberg. The lake looked old and ugly. The train was already waiting at the station and was soon chugging through the rain-swept countryside.

In Munich, I did not go directly to the labour exchange in the baker's lodge. And this because Hobrecker, the Rhenish trainee teacher whom I had met at the Haar sanatorium, had written to me twice, telling me that he was now in Munich. He had been discharged from the military shortly after me. He came from a well-to-do bourgeois family in Remscheid in the Rhineland and was about to do his teacher's exam. But not long after his return home he ran away and used the money he had taken to rent an elegant room, and he bought a social directory. When his money ran out, he supported himself by writing begging letters to all the barons, aristocrats and directors of the Chambers of Commerce, in which he claimed to be a military invalid in the direst straits. And he was so good at it that almost every day he received registered letters containing banknotes. Only very rarely was he asked to go and collect the alms in person. He was a sociable man and was lucky here too.

"My dear fellow," he exclaimed when I told him about my intentions. "You want to get a job? ... No thank you very much. That's not for me!" He laughed condescendingly, paid for my coffee with a show of ostentation, and invited me to spend the night at his place. That's not a bad idea, I thought, as we arrived at his room later. It was an extremely comfortable room, well heated and homely. Hobrecker ordered tea from the landlady and served bread, butter and sausage. While we were eating, he explained his "system" to me. He had noted down a huge list of addresses on a sheet of paper. A few of these were underlined in red, many in blue and others with ordinary pencil. The red ones were difficult to extract money from; the blue ones sometimes invited him to dinner and gave money as well; and those underlined in pencil were still to be tried out. My friend approached all of these people and, for this purpose, he had drafted various standard letters, which he copied and mailed in batches.

"My dear fellow," he said again after giving this explanation, "it's all very simple! ... Why shouldn't these old fatherland-fogeys cough up? ... I advise you to do the same! Do it! You can have my addresses, if you like!"

I thought: as a side-line, perhaps, but not permanently. "What do you mean permanently?! When you can do no more here, just go somewhere else!" Hobrecker lectured me. Well, that was undeniable. I was in full agreement. You could sponge off of the whole of Germany in this way. That made sense. Even if the idea revolted me. Then we slept in the same bed and next morning I got up in a hurry and made ready to go. "Have you any money?" asked my host, yawning sleepily. I nodded. "Give me some then! You can have it back twice over this evening," he said.

My illusions were already disintegrating. I grew suspicious but said nothing and gave him ten marks after we had arranged to meet again.

It was cold and damp out on the streets. I felt very ambivalent. I could have spat at myself. I envied every road-sweeper, every cyclist, every single person going about their day-to-day business. The thought raced through my head that they are provided for, they know what they are about, whereas you are just a nobody. A lame helplessness had taken up residence in all my limbs. I wandered on aimlessly. I wanted to look up my sister Nanndl. She had also been in a similar situation. Max had once taken her to the city without more ado and they went from shop to shop, asking if they needed a young assistant. In the end he dropped her off at a confectioner's. After six weeks she had to go into hospital. When she was discharged, she did not go back home but instead found herself an apprenticeship with a hairdresser and was still there. Yes, I would look up Nanndl. As the two youngest, we always trusted each other the most.

Suddenly, though, I abandoned this idea and made another decision. I set off for the labour exchange but on my way, I changed my mind again, and instead I went drowsily into a coffee-shop that I had previously frequented now and again and idled away a few hours there. The owner recognized me and asked if I had a job. For some inexplicable reason I lied, told him about literary successes, that I was working in an office and I even spoke about being wounded. When I finally left, I felt even more wretched. I groped onwards without purpose. It was already late afternoon. I was supposed to meet Hobrecker at this time. All at once, I entered a house and rented a room.

"Have you a position, sir?" inquired the shrivelled landlady, surveying me critically. I nodded.

"Yes, I am starting on Monday," I said without giving it a thought, and paid the rent in advance. The woman handed me the keys, piously forbade all visits by women, and left me alone. I heaved a sigh and sat down on the plush red sofa. "Idiot!" I said to myself under my breath. "Why do you do such stupid things?" I was annoyed about my lies. Why had the woman looked at me so suspiciously? I really did not know where to start. It was cold and ugly here. It was getting dark. I suddenly jumped up, went shopping, bought rabbit meatloaf at a butcher's shop, went to a pub, thoughtlessly scoured the newspapers, drank my beer, paid, went back to my room, and went to bed.

After long reflection I finally came to a decision. You simply have to find a job tomorrow. Otherwise you'll have to do a runner, I told myself. Theres had given me 60 marks and I had 25 left. I could still do a lot with that ... I woke up feeling dejected. Everything was strange and inhospitable. It started all over again: I would look up Nanndl, I would meet Hobrecker, I would go to the state library. It also occurred to me that I could go to the baths. Then I decided to write a short story as soon as I got up. I would dictate it in a typing agency and send it directly to a magazine. All of a sudden, the bizarre idea occurred to me that I should ask the landlady if she knew of any job opportunities. I would tell her everything. Once again, I changed my mind. "This war! This damned war!" I snarled, pointlessly. There was a knock at the door.

"Herr Graf?" Would you like a coffee?" murmured the landlady outside.

"Yes, I am just getting up!" I answered and heard her shuffle away. I quickly jumped out of bed, got dressed, and went out after drinking the coffee. It's curious how much more determined you feel once you have something hot in your stomach. I went straight to the bakers' lodge. Sheepishly, I presented my papers. "Discharged from the military? Completely?" asked the man at the counter. I nodded, looking at his enormous goitre. "Would you like to work at a biscuit factory? ... You can start immediately," he said, looking at me with a glum expression.

He gave me a card with the employer's address. Amazing coincidence! The biscuit factory was approximately five minutes' walk from my lodging. I presented myself at once and was to begin the day after next.

"Very well, Herr Graf, then it's settled? ... Get your things from home and come to us! ... I can definitely count on you, can I?" said the master baker, amiably. This was a new world. My superior was calling me "Herr Graf". So I really was a free man. That felt good.

I went back to my room in good spirits.

"I will be back tomorrow," I said to the landlady. She smiled again, a rather odd smile. She did not seem to believe a word. As I was about to leave the house, she said, almost sneeringly: "Look, Herr Graf! ... You forgot your writing paper and soap!"

"But I'm coming back tomorrow ... I don't need them!" I answered innocently, and left, without worrying any more about her. I took the midday train home. Theres was delighted. My mother packed food in my case.

"You see! I said it all along: there are plenty of jobs, you just have to look properly," Theres said with a hint of ridicule, and added: "So now you'll manage without your inheritance."

Embarrassed, I grimaced at the corners of my mouth and replied, in a disinterested tone of voice. "All right, all right, I didn't mean it like that." I travelled back to the city that same evening. I entered through the front door but upstairs, when I tried to unlock the door to my room, it was double-locked. Alarmed, I tried again. Nothing. I knocked. Inside, something moved.

"Who is that?" growled a deep man's voice. "I am Herr Graf! ... Your tenant!" I answered. "I came back this evening ..."

"Herr Graf?" ... I don't know any Herr Graf! ... What do you want?" he called from inside, sounding annoyed.

"Well! ... I rented the room only yesterday! Let me in!" I cried, dumbfounded.

"Just a moment!"

Now I heard some muttering and the voice of my landlady. The pair opened the door. The woman was holding a light and the man – it turned out to be her brother – put up his fists, as though he were spoiling for a fight. But when they saw that I had a heavy suitcase in my hand and heard me say "Thank the Lord" they became friendlier and apologized.

"You see, Herr Graf, all sorts of stuff goes on these days," the man said. "You must forgive us ... Three of our lodgers have made off already and were later captured." At the time, it sometimes happened that deserters rented a place for just one night and disappeared the very next day.

"Yes! ... Yes, but that's another story!" I said, and went off to my room, laughing.

I couldn't find Hobrecker the next day. I left a note, on which I wrote my address and: "Be sure to visit me at eight o'clock one evening in the next few days. Definitely!"

For the rest of the day I sorted out my room and wrote to Schorsch in Berlin, giving him my address. Pleased with myself, I went off to bed and turned up for work the next day at the biscuit factory. It consisted of dirty, narrow, very hot underground cellars in which some ten assistants worked. There were also women working there. The whole place was slippery with syrup and dough. The stink of ammonia hung in the air and stung our eyes.

People took little notice of me. One man showed me how to fill the electrical kneading machine's enormous vat with dough, explained how to start it up, and away it went. Clank! The belts clattered, the motor hummed, voices screamed, whirred into one another, the oven shelves rolled unceasingly in and out, the assistants' rolling pins made a dull thud, the tin trays rattled, steam and dust and sweat reigned supreme.

I clenched my teeth and worked, as dull as an ox.

2.
"LABOUR, NOBLE GIFT OF HEAVEN"

The biscuit factory had, in fact, been an ordinary bakery. The owner had adapted it, so to speak, in the war. He was a member of the Bavarian parliament and a town councillor with the Centre Party. The numerous field hospitals all needed biscuits for the wounded. There was no money to be made at the time with bread, so the man threw himself into the manufacture of biscuits and soon secured the most extensive opportunities for contracts to meet the army's needs. That made him rich.

I now worked in these cellars every day from six in the morning to about half past seven in the evening with a two-hour lunch break. We were expected to give our all, and from the first day I made the mistake of working too hard. My predecessor made about 32 hundredweight of dough, I made well over 40. And just when I wanted to slacken off a bit after the first rush, it was no longer possible. The owner now decided to start making *lebkuchen* and appointed two new biscuit makers. I could hardly pause for breath. I started work each morning feeling almost lame all over. It was already bitterly cold in the streets, so when I descended into the cellar and stood before my dough-making machine, the heat did me good. But later it became unbearable. It always took a while to get used to it.

The electric light burned all day long, and yet it was half-dark. Condensing steam hit the walls and ceiling without end. That meant you had to watch out that you did not slip on the wet floor. All in all: half-light, stench, filth, dough, dust and steam, the whole room seemed to be coming to the boil. Heat! All-consuming heat!

The day started. I ran with my tub into the flour storeroom. Which was ice-cold. The door and windows had been removed. I filled the tub, ran back into the hot oven-room, out again, back again, filled the vat, poured in the fluid made from powdered milk and melted fat, added sugar and crushed ammonium, pulled down the cast-iron kneading arm, and switched on the machine's engine. Then up to the chilly courtyard to fetch syrup. Four or five buckets of syrup, that was enough. My arms ached.

I always slipped up when extracting portions of dough from the vat. My knees ached from the effort required to remain upright. My body trembled. And so it went on, a second and third time. But after a while I was seized with rage, a senseless, dogged rage – and all of my physical weakness was forgotten. Sweat oozed from every pore.

My shirt and trousers got wetter and wetter. Eventually, my clothes clung to me like a second skin. Big fat drops of sweat ran from under my hair over my forehead and into my eyes, from my cheeks and nose into my mouth, from my shoulders to my chest and into the dough, from my chafed armpits to my hips, down my legs and into my hot shoes. I was turning into dough myself. But now I was into the swing of things, with a uniformity of movement. I slaved away mechanically.

My tiredness was gone. But when midday struck, or it was knocking-off time in the evening, when I switched off the machine to get changed and go to eat or return home, I could barely put one foot in front of the other. It even hurt slipping on my jacket. I would have gladly dropped to the floor and fallen asleep in the sticky filth.

I groped along the street as though in a dream. I gobbled down my lunch at the Catholic Journeyman's Association and then gobbled down a second helping, just to pass the time. I finally got up again and staggered back to the hell of the factory cellars. And so it went on. The cold air stung me. It was as though the skin of my face was being torn in two. I never ate in the evening. I dropped onto the sofa like a sack of potatoes, crouched and cowered there, tried with all the care you could imagine to pull my boots off my swollen feet, unbuttoned a single button on my waistcoat and finally tore off my clothes, threw myself on my bed and slept, slept, slept!

I was uncouth at work. People avoided me and left me in peace. They all hated me, and I hated all of them. I worked like a machine. Nobody molests a machine, they just let it run. I once screamed abuse at the master baker's wife when she came in the cellar.

I did not know her. She was wearing a dazzlingly white embroidered apron and perfume. "Get out you stupid cow!" I snarled and she vanished in horror. Everyone stopped work and made long faces. The master came and demanded an explanation. "Yes! Oh yes!" I said with a clipped voice and a snarling expression. The master said nothing and moved on.

"Oy you," bellowed the senior journeyman. "You can't just do that!" I looked at him in the eyes, full of hate and ready for anything, and cried provocatively:"

"Can't do what? What! Whoever gets in my way has to clear off!" The man smiled maliciously and turned way, shaking his head.

They were all creeps here, all organized into the Catholic union, every one of them a hypocrite who sped up as soon as the master appeared. It almost seemed as though each of them was watching his neighbour, waiting for the chance to stab him in the back. Only the packers, all women, who sometimes came downstairs, were brazen. They stole like magpies. There was little supervision. Only the master's old father, a wizened, grumpy grey-headed man, sneaked around from time to time, eyeing us suspiciously. We had to be on our guard against him. He even rifled through our clothes in the dressing room to find out who was stealing the most. But there were a thousand dodges and we soon learned them. As time went on, I certainly learned how to get by in the company. I munched lebkuchen and biscuits all day and drank the instant milk. I cut holes in my jacket lining above the breast pocket, and always filled it, before going home, with biscuits, sugar and flour. There was a broad double-doored cupboard in my room, which had a spacious, locked drawer beneath it. Bit by bit I filled it completely. I carefully arranged the stolen biscuits and lebkuchen in layers.

I thought to myself: one day you'll pack in this shitty job, then at least you'll have something to eat for a while. Make hay while the sun shines.

I wanted to get hold of as much as possible, wall myself up in a mountain of edibles, save some money and then take it easy. Saving money, though, took time. My weekly wage was spent before I knew it. Coal and firewood, this and that, every day a double helping in the Catholic Journeymen's Association and the debts started mounting again. And it was the third winter of the war. There was hardly anything to be had. I had no time to stand in queues at the shops. So, I said to myself, a wise man provides for the future.

I was living completely alone. Hobrecker visited a couple of times in the evening, talked big like Rhinelanders always do, told me where you could get a meal, and always wanted to borrow money before he left. One day I punched him for no good reason, just frustration; I caught him in the face with a juicy left hook and started shouting at him, and he disappeared immediately. I had to calm down the landlady and her brother who came rushing in; he was a pushy good-for nothing, I said, and they should not let him in again.

Nanndl visited me once and then a second time. One of her fellow workers came with her. I had first met her at the Haar psychiatric hospital when my family visited me. Her name was Luise; she was slim and had a pert, freckled face. During the visit, while the others cried, she laughed. I liked that. Later, when I was sent on leave, she turned up. I literally fell in love with her and often slept with her. When I had to go back to Haar to settle my military discharge, Luise was – as if she had fallen from the clouds – also there. She told me that she was pregnant. "Good," I said, then we must get married. "I will find work as a baker and it will be all right." Luise laughed and left me. When I met her again in Munich, she took back what she'd said about being pregnant and, strangely, I didn't hear from her again.

And so our love ebbed away.

Now we were sitting together again, as though there had never been anything between us. Only as we were about to part did Luise whisper to me, unobserved: "Come to the Isar Bridge tomorrow evening. At half past seven. I'll be waiting." I looked at her questioningly and nodded.

The next day, dog tired, I hauled myself to the rendezvous. Luise was smiling again. We linked arms and went into a side-alley. She suddenly burst into tears and laid her head on my shoulder.

"I really am pregnant – but not by you," she said, and told me about a little romance she'd had with her boss. She had started as an apprentice with him at sixteen; when she was seventeen, he had seduced her; and now, aged eighteen, she was carrying his child.

"So that's why ..." I shouted, and a light came on in my head. "Yes, so that's why I didn't want to get you mixed up in my unhappiness," she answered, and ran off abruptly.

I did not follow her. I just stood there, thought this way and that, then went home. I was sad and didn't know why. I remembered the nights that Luise and I had spent together. A vague unease rippled through my limbs. I no longer felt tired. An annoyingly noisy tram rumbled past and flooded me in its light.

"You could so easily have taken her home again," I muttered to myself in a half whisper. I suddenly turned into another side-alley and walked into the city. I strode along faster and faster, and when I had reached the Müllerstrasse I spoke to the first prostitute I met and went with her. Disgusted, and without a brass farthing in my pocket, I left her. The following morning I plunged into work again, fed up after a sleepless night. I thought about Luise every now and again, staring into space. She had given me her address. But I never wrote to her again.

You have to get out of this filth, I told myself day after day. Something's got to give. My energy was on the wane. Sometimes I arrived at the factory late. Christmas was approaching. That meant overtime. Often, I didn't get home until nine. Brain and body had been through the mangle. I was hostile and abhorrent, even unto myself.

And now my nerves. It always started in my lower spine. The sharp, stabbing pain radiated outwards and upwards, penetrating my head and my brain. It settled above my eyes like an iron clamp and pressed like a leaden weight. Every now and then this cursed trembling started up and flew into all my limbs. And, from time to time, my stomach was as though hollowed out. Then it seemed to swing around in my body like a dead weight hanging heavily from my throat. All of a sudden, I became ravenously hungry, but as soon as I started to eat the food stank and I became nauseous. The room went into a spin. My intestines rumbled noisily and incessantly.

I was up to my neck in filth and slime. I myself was pure filth. Terror, disgust, horror and frustration, hate and dread raged inside. What was causing it?

"You've got a dose of the clap! You've been infected! You've had it!" The thought rushed constantly through my brain.

I ran to the doctor. He was a square-set, grumpy old codger. You could see from his expression that he suffered from piles. He examined me superficially and muttered something incomprehensible under his breath.

"Doctor, I slept with a prostitute ... I think I've been infected!" I wailed tearfully. The doctor took no notice and lazily examined my genitals. "Are you with the services?" he asked at last. He looked at me contemptuously from head to foot. "No, I was discharged several months ago ... I work in a biscuit factory and do not have to do further military service," I stammered, and asked further:

"Do I have a venereal disease, doctor?" Again, the doctor ignored my question.

"Why did they release you from duty?" he wanted to know.

"I was insane."

The doctor gave a slight shrug.

"So where were you last?"

"In the asylum ... And afterwards ... I had ulcers in my sinuses ... My head still aches, doctor," I moaned confusedly.

The doctor suddenly became animated. "Aha ... That's it! ... Hm-hm! ... Then I'll prescribe some menthol ... Snuff, you understand ... That will clear your head, you understand," he said, now surprisingly energetic, and went on, pointing to my genitals: "There's nothing wrong with you downstairs ... It's only your nerves. Indeed, indeed! Get this made up at the chemist's. Take one of the tablets daily before going to bed, and take plenty of the snuff, you understand! ... That will clear your head!" All of a sudden, he seemed very diligent and even escorted me to the door with a look of downright anxiety.

I collected the prescriptions. Menthol. And bromide. I returned to the cellars somewhat calmer.

I took the bromide. I took the menthol snuff, which gave me a perpetually runny nose. But my feeling of unease did not let up. My landlady and her brother were often disturbed at night and woke me up angrily. I laughed and screamed in my sleep. The bromide gave me palpitations. I threw it away.

I went to a second doctor.

"Nothing serious ... A touch of the nerves ... You shouldn't smoke so much and you should live sensibly and eat well," he said. He was on the staff of a local military hospital and only worked in his practice on the side.

"I can't go on like this, doctor! I've had enough," I said.

"Oh come on! ... What would our soldiers at the front say? ... Pull yourself together!" he reprimanded me. I went back to the drudgery of the underground caverns. My feet swelled up and I had to take a leak all the time. I worked like fury. We were captives here, like in the war. Stopping was out of the question, let alone going home.

And so I got through the days. You'll croak eventually, and that will be that, I thought lethargically. "I'm too much of a coward to hang myself, so I won't kick the bucket that way ..."

3.
ALL OVER THE SHOP

There were always only two ways for me to deal with an ugly situation. Either I went off my head sooner or later and, for no apparent reason, smashed everything to pieces, or else I tried to do it by means of hypocrisy and peasant cunning. I now wanted to get away from the biscuit factory, but at the same time I feared for my immediate and short-term future. For the time being I wrote a letter to the master baker, mentioning my sinus troubles, sent my landlady with it, and stayed home.

But when you exert all your strength and then suddenly let go, your energy gives out entirely. I had to work again, damn it. It could not go on like this. I turned it over and over in my mind.

Once again, I thought about the business with the inheritance, and Hobrecker's "system". I did actually write a few begging letters to barons and company directors. But I only got a reply in one instance, with a five mark note enclosed. Obviously, I had not written insistently enough. Everything has to be learned, I thought.

In the newspaper I read: "Money lent and loans arranged at shortest notice against adequate security. Box Number 53 248."

I sat down. "Esteemed Company!" I addressed myself to the Box Number. "With reference to your advertisement in the *Münchner Neueste Nachrichten*, I beg to request a considerably large loan. As security I will be receiving an inheritance of 2,000 marks. Looking forward to your earliest reply, I remain, Yours sincerely, Oskar Graf, Author."

I likewise looked through the matrimonial advertisements. "Young lady of good family with apartment and private means, ideal temperament, handsome appearance, well-educated, seeks exclusively man of good standing and solid position with a view to matrimony."

I read several similar classified ads and wrote to a young war widow with one child, to the lady of ideal temperament, and to a penniless nurse of aristocratic background who was seeking to marry. I did not waste much time in thinking. "My dear and esteemed young lady!" I began. "I am an invalided soldier and author with good prospects of being published in the near future. My current income is moderate, but publishers of standing are already interested in my work.

"Later," I arrogantly emphasized, "my career is likely to be highly remunerative, but for the time being I must find a sympathetic wife of financial means, with whom I would be able to cohabit. I have seen twenty-four summers and have no physical defects. I shall be glad to provide further personal details and await your kind reply with affectionate interest. In deepest love, your very devoted Oskar Graf, author."

I was downright proud of my letters. I thought back to the ones that I had once written as a boy to manufacturers and those that I had written in the past to publishers and said to myself, smugly: "What progress! You have learned a lot!"

And I was already picturing everything: sitting in a comfortable home and writing. The wife cooks, I am composing poetry and moving in all kinds of social circles. I also receive my inheritance upon marriage, and everything is going swimmingly. When I had posted the letters, I felt more optimistic. The following day, I returned to work.

I was in a strange state of suspense the whole time. All I could thing about was coming home in the evening to find the various replies. My heart beat in a perpetually optimistic excitement.

And in any case – an author must have a prestigious wife at his side! It's the making of the man. He can entertain. He is seen in the theatre with his wife – and God knows, with men in such short supply at the moment, you can get a really good catch, I calculated. Besides which – all of the great poets got their material from women! That's where they got their inspiration! Schiller says that, and Goethe above all! They all say the same, one way or another. I was almost cheerful at work and in the evening, I often sat down and, despite all my fatigue, I wrote a poem or sketch.

One day when I returned home there was a business card on the table. On it was written "Director Hartmann, Tengstrasse 34 III, would like to meet you." As I was reading, my landlady came in and told me that a man had come by and would return at half past seven.

"Director Hartmann? Would like?" I muttered to myself and reflected. I washed, put on my best suit, made up the fire and waited in suspense. At the appointed time the doorbell rang. I opened the door.

A short, rather fat man with a puffy red face and red hair introduced himself as Director Hartmann.

"Oh yes ... My name is Graf," I said in some confusion, and led him into my room.

"You wrote to me regarding a loan, Herr Graf," the gentleman said in a muffled, almost hurried tone, and took out my letter. He had a curiously high, feminine voice. He helped himself to a seat and went on: "As stated, Herr Graf ... Now I have met you ... I can arrange the thing ... If I may first ask, how do things stand with the security? ... I could procure any sum of money for you at a moderate rate of interest."

My heart beat. I gazed at the man. Money! Money! The word flashed through my mind: any sum of money! "You are currently in employment here and probably want to become self-employed?" the man asked, and looked me over cunningly.

"Yes, and oh yes, I am soon to come into an inheritance! ... Two thousand marks! ... It's like this: I am the son of a master baker in Berg on

169

Lake Starnberg ... But the inheritance is tied up in the house," I stammered.

"Aha ... ... You come from out there by Lake Starnberg? ... I see, from Berg? ... Yes, I know the place. You have come of age, haven't you? ... And I expect the property has already passed to the heirs?" the gentleman further inquired, casually.

"Yes, I haven't been at home ... My elder brother, Max, fell in the war. The house actually belonged to him, and now it belongs to his wife and children. We siblings get our share of it," I informed him. The company director seemed completely satisfied.

"Well, Herr Graf, as I said, the matter can be easily arranged. Now I have met you ... I prefer to see clients in person first ... Bring me an extract from the land register – you will get it without any trouble from the Starnberg district court, if you write to it – and then come back to me. Once I have the extract, the whole business can be settled in three or four days," he explained, got up, and shook my sweaty hand.

"The interest I charge is hardly worth mentioning," he repeated at the door.

I flew back to my room. I felt like a new man. Now then! Another life, a new beginning. I revelled in the knowledge that I was transformed into a rich man and wrote immediately to the Starnberg district court. Above all, I took a fiendish pleasure in the fact that my folks at home would learn nothing about my machinations, as Director Hartmann had told me.

I fell asleep that evening in a blissful state and cheerfully ran off to the biscuit factory in the morning. Work went like a breeze. I sang through the humming and roaring of the machines. I had completely forgotten about the marriage candidates. Nevertheless I ran home every day to check if any letters had arrived. One day I found a note. "I'll be at the *Café Arkadia* this evening, important. Come, I shall wait until you turn up, Georg."

I was thunderstruck. I often went completely off the rails because of these sudden visits. They wrenched me out of my daily train of thoughts.

When he last visited me in Haar, my comrade told me strange things about the so-called "Scheidemann peace", about Franz Jung and the Oehrings, about Liebknecht and the secret Spartacist League. Now and again I learned something about him and my friends from his letters. He had exhibited some of this oil paintings with *Der Sturm* in Berlin, Jung had become the editor of a business paper, was writing novels, was well known with the Spartacists,[24] and worked on advertising for the Cigarette

---

[24] *Der Sturm* (The Storm) was an influential *avant garde* art and literary magazine founded in Berlin in 1910 and published until 1932. Starting as a group within the Independent Social Democratic Party of Germany, the Spartacus League (Spartacists) formed the nucleus of what became the Communist Party of Germany (KPD).

Cartel on behalf of his paper. Every now and then I received a copy of the magazine Jung published, *Die freie Strasse*.[25] It carried all sorts of verbose, complicated essays and extracts from novels, which, as far as I could understand, proselytized something like absolute individual freedom, the complete transformation of the relationship between men and women, and an ethical system based on psychoanalysis. I didn't understand them but thought them immensely significant. I immediately wrote similar essays, sent them to Jung, and received rough, incomprehensible answers to my stupid letters, which went something like this: "You can send the product of your unparalleled idiocy and sexual repression elsewhere. We have nothing in common."

Now Schorsch was there. Something unusual must have happened, and he would be able to tell me about everything. I asked my landlady again. Yes, the gentleman had called, yes, he was from Berlin.

I ate nothing at lunchtime that day, and the hours dragged by far too slowly. In the evening I found a letter from the lady with the ideal temperament, enclosing a photograph. Her handwriting was steep, which conveyed a rather comical awkwardness. On ivory paper she wrote that I should appear at eight o'clock the following evening on the corner of Goethestrasse. To identify herself, she would carry an illustrated newspaper in her right hand. The photograph showed a lady in a low-cut dress and slim neck; she had a rather mature appearance, from which you could clearly see that she had gone to a lot of trouble to make herself look younger. Her hair was voluminous and appeared to be jet black. "Minna Sauer, 1917," was written obliquely in a corner of the photo.

Extraordinary! Hot and cold sweat ran over my body. I did not look at her face. I glanced at her naked shoulders and breasts. I felt agitated.

But there was no time for that now. I changed hurriedly into my best suit and travelled to the *Café Arkadia*.

Schorsch was seated there with Lollo and Betty, two models that we knew in the old days. He greeted me with a hearty laugh. He had rather glassy eyes and he looked horrible with his square head and close-cropped hair. I sat down quickly. The two girls giggled and overwhelmed me with questions. I just answered, "Yes, yes" all the time and laughed along with them.

"Hey, what's up with you? What are you doing?" Schorsch asked, and gave me a hefty smack on the shoulder. He stank of schnapps and belched.

"Nothing, what would I be doing? ... I'm working in the biscuit fac-

---

[25] *Die Freie Straße* (The Open Road) appeared from 1915 until 1918. Politically anarchistic, the magazine was also at the forefront of the Dadaist art movement.

tory. And what are you and Jung and the others up to?" I started to ask. "Why have you come here?"

"I had to deal with the Vice Squad all day ... The scum!" he growled and ground his teeth.

"The Vice Squad?" I asked, astonished, and wanted to hear more. But at this point the girls nudged each other and whispered something about "stupid tarts", looking at another table. Two well-dressed bourgeois girls were sitting there, whom Schorsch – as I later found out – had also arranged to meet there. They kept looking our way and seemed very annoyed about the two models. But Schorsch and I did not worry about them and he told me his story.

Sometime earlier he had received a letter from a friend of Finny's, in which she said that the latter was now in the workhouse, and Schorsch should help. Finny had also been a model and had lived for a few weeks with Schorsch during his time in Munich. Then she became a waitress in a wine bar, and finally ended up on the street. One day she was arrested by the Vice Squad.

At that time Franz Jung was arguing for the complete liberation of women as a first step in the transformation of society and considered that women should be protected by the State, so to speak; moreover, Schorsch was no less convinced that this was central to the revolutionary cause. So when he received the letter in question, he did not hesitate to swing into action. He was always ready to take action against current legality and statutory institutions. He went to a lawyer in Berlin, who counselled him to enter a marriage of convenience with Finny and then to divorce her again after her release. Everything had been arranged to the point that there was a chance of success. Schorsch travelled to Munich, went to the Palace of Justice to speak to the presiding magistrate and was kept waiting for quite some time. To pass the time he walked up and down the corridor and read the case notes in the courtrooms. And there, among other names, he found that of an old acquaintance who was likewise being charged for prostitution. He went straight into the public gallery, stood up in the middle of the judge's deliberations and started to defend the girl in a thunderous voice. He was reprimanded, flew into a rage, and was threatened with arrest. He shouted all the louder. The girl was sentenced, and as Schorsch tried to speak to her in the corridor, the detective from the Vice Squad pushed him away. He then got into a scuffle, swore and shouted, and that ruined the business with Finny. Because of all things, this same detective was in the anteroom of the magistrate Schorsch was dealing with. He had barely entered the room when the man said: "You again! We know you already. Under the circumstances, there is no way your request can be granted."

In order to loosen his tongue, Schorsch had been at the schnapps

172

earlier, and attempted to protest vehemently. But the haggard old judge simply raised his hand and said brusquely: "Be off with you! You stink of schnapps. I will not tolerate it!"

Finny's case was thus lost and the whole thing came to nothing.

"Scum! Scum! That's the State for you!" Schorsch cursed.

"Yikes, you should have seen that coming!" I said, finding it difficult to calm him down. Betty looked around, bored. Lollo said of the judge: "What a mean bloke!" I grew impatient and wanted to hear something – finally – about Berlin, the prospects for peace, and our chums. Just then, one of the bourgeois girls at the neighbouring table stood up and came over to us, with a weak smile.

"That's Selma Igl," Schorsch snarled. "You remember her, don't you?"

"Really?"

I racked my brains. Selma Igl gave me her hand. She cast a venomous glance at the two models. I made room for her.

Yes – now I remembered.

Schorsch had got to know Selma before the war, through a lonely-hearts advertisement, dated her throughout his time in Munich, and I once wrote her a love letter, without telling my comrade about it. We met.

That was it! At the time, she said to me: "Let's be quite frank, Herr Graf. You are too young for me."

We then parted, without any ill will. But remembering such incidents is no pleasant matter. I now regretted this entire meeting with Schorsch. We could not talk about anything.

"So, how are you, Herr Graf? ... Come up and see me some time ... One knows so few people," Selma Igl said to me, and, turning to Schorsch: "You must go now. It is time."

Schorsch paid, noisily. We got up and went to the railway station. I walked with Schorsch, between Lollo and Betty, and Selma and her friend walked behind us.

"Don't give her my address," I whispered to my friend. He nodded, half asleep. We said our farewells. The train departed. Lollo and Betty left; Selma's friend said cheerio. The two of us stood there, alone. She asked after my address. I dodged the question. Once more she asked me to visit her. I agreed.

"Hm, yes, old Schorsch ... My God, hm," she kept on saying mechanically, and nodded reflectively. I said the same. It seemed as though both of us wanted to get away from the other. We parted at Stachus.[26]

---

[26] A large square in Munich, officially named Karlsplatz since 1797, but still known to natives as Stachus, after a pub that was once at one corner.

"You really will come and see me, won't you?" Selma Igl called again from the tram.

"Yes, yes," I said indifferently. I hurried on, numb and depressed. It was bitterly cold. Everyone stared at me because I had no coat. Despondent, I buttoned up my thin jacket and ducked down.

I had the feeling that this insignificant episode had made a complete shambles of my entire life up to now. I was furious with Schorsch. I gnashed my teeth and could not think straight.

Thick snow was falling. The streetlamps cast a strangely yellow light. People were passing noiselessly. All of the voices and sounds were muffled. The trams purred by sluggishly.

"Oh hell! I must get hold of the money, then everything will change!" I cursed and trudged on.

I don't know why but I was suddenly seized with a need to take my revenge. When you have money you can put one over on anybody who has injured you in the past. It's always the same: one against the other! That was my last thought as I clambered into my cold bed.

4.
MONEY! MONEY!!

Schorsch coming had really messed me up a lot. I wanted to begin a life as a freelance author at long last, whatever it took. If *they* can do it – by which I meant my friends in Berlin – you can do it too, I thought.

First of all I wrote to Minna Sauer, saying that unfortunately I was prevented from putting in an appearance at the appointed time on the corner of Goethestrasse on this occasion, but I would be in touch in the next few days. In fact, I no longer felt any desire to meet her, because other things were on my mind. Every morning, every afternoon, every evening I hoped to receive the land registry extract from the Starnberg district court. It never came.

"They cannot refuse it. You are of age," Director Hartmann had said. I was ever hopeful, never sure. I was making new plans time and again for using the money, if only the whole business went well. During my lunch break I went into town in my dirty, shabby coat and looked in the clothing shop windows. Then I started calculating. You must have this, that and the other. What'll it cost? Hm, I was already feeling confused again. It seemed there would not be enough money. I calculated afresh, divided the sum differently, and thought about whether I should give up or keep the job. My mind was fully occupied with such deliberations.

Nothing from Starnberg. I had already half given up hope and was considering other options. One morning I was suddenly struck with the thought: you are an author, and what's more "young, ambitious and a war invalid". Certainly, Hobrecker's system for pushing through life was not to be dismissed out of hand, but above all, you had to stick with your own sort.

I now started writing begging letters to all kinds of literary types and, lo and behold, I was referred to the Society for the Protection of German Authors. I was advised to apply to the Society for a long-term loan. I immediately sat down and wrote a toadying, lickspittle letter to the Society. It sent 60 marks. I took courage, because Dr. Kurt Martens, who was then head of the Society's Munich branch, had added a personal letter in which he advised me to apply once more to the treasurer of the Society's benevolent fund. The 60 marks were just for temporary, immediate assistance. He was sure I would get a larger loan. He would support my application.

That was good advice! I took heart: Germany takes care of its poets! So I sent off my application. The reply said that I should present myself at the secretariat within the next few says. This time the letter was signed by a Dr. Krell.

My heart was in my boots. I was seized with panic. I felt a pang of guilty conscience, because I knew very well that my begging was a seriously dodgy and fraudulent act. Still: what's done can't be undone; if I stop now, they will probably make enquiries and involve the police. I therefore went to Dr. Krell's home. It was a very elegant flat. Parquet floors and beautiful old engravings on the walls. Bookshelves reached from the floor to the ceiling, filled with the most luxurious volumes. A housemaid announced my arrival and the doctor appeared in a morning suit. He dragged one foot slightly. I introduced myself obsequiously and awkwardly and was ready to tell him my sob story.

The gentleman with the chiselled face looked at me rather contemptuously and asked me to wait. He disappeared through the high white door. I stayed standing on the parquet floor, behaving myself. I did not dare to sit down on the silk-upholstered antique chairs.

That was the bane of my life. In such an environment I always lost the capacity to think straight, and everything was left, more or less, to chance. I gawped stupidly around the room and waited. The doctor opened the door and said: "Please." I trod clumsily into the next room and remained standing, as if I was waiting to be given instructions by the gentleman, who now dropped into a large leather armchair with the air of a man of the world and leafed, or so it seemed, through files about me.

"Please, won't you sit down?" he asked distantly and surveyed me with a curious gaze once again. I went to the table and extended my hand; somewhat surprised, he gave me his, and I finally sat down.

What gracefully slender hands he had! He was wearing a ring with a long jewel on his left hand. And this wonderful apartment! My God, so this is what it's like if you actually get published!

"You have already published material in *Der Sturm* and *Die Aktion*?" the doctor asked and looked at me again.

"Y-yes."

"But you earned nothing. As is well known, *Der Sturm* and *Die Aktion* do not pay for contributions ... How have you made a living? By writing?"

My face reddened. I stammered:

"I have been working in bakeries, sir, and now I am working in a biscuit factory, but I am ill now. I once had a piece in *Jugend* and in the *Münchner Illustrierte Zeitung*."

The doctor raised his head and looked me square in the face. "Where did you study?"

"Er, er, in Munich – and – and then private study."

"Were you in a grammar school?"

"Y-yes," I lied.

"In which, then?" the man asked, suspiciously, it seemed to me. I

176

turned pale. I broke into a cold sweat. I did not know what to say next.

"In – in the Löwengrube ... I'm not sure now exactly ..." I rattled off broken phrases, grew hopelessly confused and stopped short.

"Is that so? We shall of course confirm everything by making inquiries," the doctor simply stated, getting up in a rather dismissive manner and escorting me to the door. "You will then hear from us."

I ran down the stairs out into the fresh air. I literally fled. Now you're at the end of your rope, I said to myself, and imagined the police arriving one morning:

"Herr Graf, you've been going around begging. You'd better come with us." And then – yes, what always happens to good-for-nothings like you.

I walked along, feeling crushed. I remember such moments in vivid detail. Always more in fear than in regret. It was an indescribable self-loathing that became my lord and master, as disgust followed fear. Sometimes these moods of contrition lasted for days. I could see no way out of the situation and did what I often did at home when I was a young scallywag and Max found out something that was bound to mean a good thrashing. I crept into my cold bed and simple-mindedly repeated the Lord's Prayer. If you confess and recant and become a decent person, then everything will turn out right in the end, I reflected.

And then – never again! Never again!

Every night I dreamed about the police, my sudden arrest, and in the morning, I awoke fearful and in bits.

I already wanted to write a penitent letter to Doctor Krell asking him, begging him earnestly, not to take any further action against me. I racked my brains. Flight, and nothing less, would solve the problem, I sometimes thought. But where to? I remembered that there was a war on. All the frontiers were closed. We were enclosed by a wall.

And so the days passed by.

One morning, shortly after eight, the senior assistant came running down from the shop, screaming: "Graf, you're wanted upstairs!" I was overcome with panic. I was petrified. "The police!" flashed through my mind like the crack of a whip. I staggered down the corridor and up the slippery steps. The postman was standing in the entrance hall and handed me a registered letter from the Starnberg district court. The landlady had sent him over. Quivering, I signed to acknowledge receipt. I opened it hesitantly. It was the excerpt from the land register.

My blood ran hot and cold. I glanced through the letter thoughtlessly. Yes! This is it!

I ran back down to the steamy bakery and worked like a fanatic. Everything was banished from my mind: Dr. Krell, the police, fear, disgust, confession and communion.

Money! Money! Heaps of money! The thought raged incessantly through my mind. On the very same afternoon I hurried to my room and sent word to Director Hartmann. He made an appointment for the day after next between 12 and one o'clock in a vending-machine restaurant at the railway station.[27]

"As I said, Herr Graf," the little man resumed, "the matter is sorted." He gave me back the report from the land register: "I have a gentleman who will pay you the money immediately ... My commission is 200 marks ... Further charges are not worth mentioning."

"And when will I get the money?" I asked eagerly, while staring vacantly at the director.

"In two or three days ... As soon as I have received the confirmation from Starnberg," he replied, and added lightly: "And as mentioned, in the meantime, my commission is 200 marks." I felt helpless and looked embarrassed. The director understood the situation immediately, and said, with reassuring frankness: "I see, you don't have it at the moment? ... It doesn't matter ... Just sign here ... We can sort it out when you receive the money ... I trust you."

I was thrilled at the thought that this stranger should have such confidence in me, of all people. I wanted to show my gratitude.

"I can give you the report from the land registry as security, sir," I said. But the man looked at me the way a wolf looks at a sheep and smiled with a kindly superiority.

"But Herr Graf! ... I wouldn't hear of it! We will settle the matter when you get the money!" he said cheerfully, and continued in the same manner: "So, as I said, Herr Graf, I will let you know immediately, when the time comes, you can depend upon it. And I also wanted to say ... I had a coffee and two cakes. That is added to my expenses, of course. One mustn't worry about such trifles ..."

"But of course! That goes without saying," I cockily replied, paying for him as well as me. I signed the paper he put before me without even thinking about it.

Hartmann was really a man you could trust. On the third day I received a card from him. I asked the master baker for some time off and went into town. Once again, I met the director in the vending-machine restaurant at the station. He received me with a very cheerful air. Another gentleman, wearing a dark horn-rimmed pince-nez on his fat nose, sat by

---

[27] *Automatenrestaurants*, pioneered by the capitalist Ludwig Stollwerck, became common in Germany at the turn of the nineteenth and twentieth century. The concept was subsequently exported to America. They were self-service restaurants with seating, in which the dishes and drinks were held in coin-operated vending machines, so that customers need have no contact with service personnel.

him and looked at me with prying eyes.

"May I introduce Herr Stahl," said Hartmann, and the man with the fat nose shook my hand. "Delighted."

"Well now, Herr Graf, the main event is about to start," exclaimed Hartmann, and this time he paid himself. "Let's go! Everything will be done within an hour." We left directly and went to the house of a Herr Teilhaber in Bayerstrasse. We sat down at a round table in leather reclining armchairs in the solidly bourgeois apartment. As far as I could gather, Teilhaber and Stahl were partners in a firm. First one, and then the other, read the excerpt from the land register. They talked to one another in a low murmur. Finally, Teilhaber turned to me.

"So, you want money against this, Herr Graf? As a special favour I can offer you seventeen hundred marks ... You can have it at once in cash," Teilhaber added.

"Seventeen hundred?" I asked, astonished. "But it says here two thousand?"

Herr Stahl intervened: "Yes, of course Herr Graf ... But you have to remember, we are bearing the risk ... Suppose, for example, that the wife of your dead brother goes bankrupt, we lose everything, but you still have the money, you see? ... But you are a young man and you will get cash in hand right away? ... So, what do you say?"

I couldn't think of anything to say for the moment. Hartmann nudged me. The other two men spoke to one another again.

Director Hartmann whispered in my ear. "I would say yes, Herr Graf! ... I'll tell you what ... We'll try for eighteen hundred, how about that?"

I nodded again.

Hartmann acted as my friend and ally.

"Herr Graf suggests eighteen hundred marks ..."

"No, no, absolutely not! ... We'd rather drop the matter," answered the two money lenders dismissively, and Herr Stahl was already getting up. My hopes were shattered. I felt quite sheepish.

"All right. I am satisfied," I said, before Hartmann could speak. "Seventeen hundred then ..."

"I thought so ... But as I said, you don't have to! ... You can think it over," Teilhaber resumed. "On no account do we want to put you under pressure." That also made me feel more confident.

"Good. Seventeen hundred it is!" I repeated, with a sigh of relief.

"Good," said the two money lenders, and Teilhaber counted out seventeen blue hundred-mark notes on the table. I stared at them, vacantly. The banknotes were all I saw. My heart thumped.

"Now then!" said Stahl with satisfaction, rubbed his hands together, and got me to sign something. I got up hastily and pocketed the money.

The two money lenders shook me by the hand and Hartmann left with me.

"That didn't take long ... And now you owe me three hundred marks altogether. Two hundred for the introduction and one hundred for my expenses," he said, quietly. I was overcome with horror and rage. For a moment, time froze. The man chattered away, showed me the paper that I had signed and went on and on about his 300 marks.

"Yes, all right," I finally gasped, paid him and said goodbye immediately.

I was at most half satisfied. I had to recalculate. I had reckoned on 2,000 marks and received just 1,400. Stupid, very stupid!

But my sulk did not last long. I was ready for action. In all my life, I had never had such a pile of money in my hands. All of a sudden, I had become a really rich man. Now for a new life – something quite different, something almost unthinkable.

Fantastic schemes whirled through my mind, burning me like fire. That very afternoon I bought a patent leather cigarette case, leather gloves, a purse made of crocodile skin and a wallet. I went into the best shoe shop and left with a pair of patent leather shoes that had special grey inserts for buttons. Then silk socks, half a dozen at once. I had to have four shirts at the very height of fashion, and finally, for good measure, I bought a large and a small suitcase before returning heavily laden to my room.

The cash had unsettled me greatly. I had all kinds of ideas. Very strange! Now this wicked feeling about money started all over again. Actually, I just wanted it to be able to write calmly and to be carefree. But now that I had reached this goal to the extent that I could come and go as I pleased – all at once I started to be greedy for a thousand frivolous things. The craziest desires sprang up by the day, by the hour. Now I felt an immediate need for things I had never even thought of before!

I wanted to see something for my money! I wanted to have things in abundance!

I held out for one more day in the biscuit factory, then sent the landlady, once again, with a sick note.

"Yes, everything is all right, they said, and they wished you a speedy recovery," she reported to me on her return. I felt relieved, jumped out of bed, got dressed, pocketed all of my money and went to Nanndl. I loved her more than anyone. She never asked me to justify myself and did not worry about me at all. She laughed and was jolly when she saw me and was pleased to know things were going well for me. That was all.

"I've got money now, Nanndl," I whispered to her in the hairdresser's salon. "I want to buy a suit and an overcoat, come with me."

"Great!" she yelled, full of joy. "All right, wait for me by the Isar Gate at 12 o'clock!" Luise had hurried over. She smiled, and I also smiled casually, then left the salon. All morning I wandered through the department stores and shopped. Ties, a skiing sweater, books, leather writing pads, a nickel-plated tea infuser, knives and forks, arts-and-crafts cups, an umbrella.

I bought indiscriminately. Whatever caught my attention, I took. The hours went by far too slowly and the money melted like butter in the sun. I sat down in a coffee house, ordered pen and paper, and wrote a letter to Emma. "Dear Emma! At last I am in a position to repay you the money you lent me for the publication of my book. I am sending it to you today. Please let me have a receipt. You already know things were going badly at the time. I had to pay and then the publisher went bankrupt. But that won't happen again. I have always thought: one day the time will come when you can repay those 500 marks. That time is now. Perhaps I will send it all now, it depends on whether I can. Kind regards to Mother and Theres, Yours, Oskar."

I went to the post office with a sense of triumph. But I was changing my mind. I had already spent enough money. So I sent just 100 marks. Then I met Nanndl. We blithely made our way to the store and bought a dark green, modish suit and a light, greenish-brown *paletot* overcoat.

"You look really chic now," said Nanndl, looking at me. "Now you just need the right hat to go with it." She had to go back to work. I immediately entered the nearest hat shop and bought a black velour hat with a ridiculously broad brim, so as to appear a little artistic as well. To pass the time, I went into a cinema, and only got home after the front gate had been locked.

I hastily locked the door behind me, turned on the gas lamp and lit the fire. Then I spread out all my new possessions across the floor and looked at them. I gazed at each item again and again. I felt a hot flush.

I strutted up and down.

Now you have everything, it will be plain sailing. Now you're a somebody, I thought: the world is your oyster, you can start to live! Nanndl had given me good soap, *Eau de Cologne* and hand cream. I washed myself from top to tail and put on my new clothes. Proud and sure of victory, I stood in front of the mirror by the glow of the lamp, put on my big hat, held the umbrella stick coquettishly in my hand in the manner of a celebrity about to be photographed.

Yes, I was an entirely different man. What's more, I still had 600 marks and wanted to send Emma some more money. But I could do that later. The 600 marks was still a vast sum.

I looked at myself again in the mirror. An immense feeling of satisfaction oozed through my body. I decided to visit the doctor the next day and register for sick pay, because I lacked the courage to give my notice to the master.

That was the path of least resistance. After all, if things went badly, the doors were still open, I could go back to work.

You can break free without too much trouble, so there is no point in burning all your bridges, I reflected.

5.
THE COCK'S COMB STIFFENS

I went to the doctor. "Suppuration of the frontal sinuses," he said. I knew it. I had kept this illness as a souvenir of wartime service. And a very congenial affliction it is too: you are more or less permanently ill, so you can go to the doctor whenever you like and he will, without fail, certify you "unfit for work". You get a more or less bad headache now and again and some pus in the nose. And that's it.

I now had to visit the doctor twice a week. He dabbed my nostrils with cocaine. One day he cut away some small pieces of tissue and pulled them out with a wire sling. It bled profusely. My head whirred for quite a while, then my brain felt clear. I was to rinse it out twice or thrice a day with a boracic acid lotion, and I was not to smoke cigarettes. But I did not stick to this.

Since I had been cut, I took my illness very seriously and considered myself almost a martyr to my head. I told everybody about it: my landlady's family, strangers sitting opposite me in the coffee house; and I wrote home about it.

I could now use my time as I liked and received sick pay. I felt very enterprising. One morning the postman brought a registered letter from the Society for the Protection of German Authors, signed by Dr. Krell. My papers were enclosed, and the letter said, more or less: "In consideration of your petition the SDS has resolved that it is unable to provide you with further assistance."

I reflected for a moment. Then I breathed a sigh of relief. So that was that. I'm well out of it, I thought, and tore up the letter.[28]

I started thinking about women again. Now that you are so well turned out, you'll make a conquest in no time. That was my idea. I made a date with Minna Sauer to meet the very next day outside the *Café Arkadia*. And we did indeed meet up as planned, that is, we saw each other immediately, but we walked past each other for a long time and checked each other out with friendly looks. Now and then she smiled and then her eyes twinkled. I trembled and did not know what to do with myself. I fumbled my way past her again and again. I was hopelessly in awe of her thick fox

---

[28] Max Krell (1887-1962) also wrote under the pseudonym Georg Even. He became an editor in the novel department at Ullstein Verlag in charge of authors such as Bertolt Brecht, Ernst Toller and Lion Feuchtwanger. Krell achieved his greatest success in 1929 with the release of Erich Maria Remarque's novel, *All Quiet on the Western Front*. In 1936 he emigrated via Switzerland to Italy and lived as a freelance writer and translator in Florence. His memoirs appeared in 1961 as *Das gab es einmal*.

fur. Underneath, a snow-white lace frill peeped out modestly. She wore a tight-fitting costume that made the most of her figure and high, brightly shining patent leather buttoned boots. I now felt warm inside and at ease. I was entranced by such a discovery and kept picturing how I would carry myself in her company. What a fine-looking couple!

A discreet fragrance wafted towards me as I approached her again. I breathed haltingly, finally plucking up courage and, tipping my hat, went up to her.

"Excuse me but are you by any chance Fräulein Sauer?" I asked with a beating heart.

"Yes ...? ... Herr Graf?" she replied with a high, somewhat chirping voice and an engaging smile. "I could hardly recognize you," I stuttered awkwardly. "I have been walking up and down for such a long time." I looked at her shyly.

"Oh, yes – I saw you already," she replied with a polite self-assurance. We had broken the ice. It was as though the floodgates had opened. Hot blood rushed through my veins.

"So ... That's wonderful! ... Won't you join me in the café? We can talk there," I said more confidently, and in order to throw off my embarrassment I seized the handle of the heavy coffee-house door and pushed it open. But then something very stupid happened that unsettled me completely. Namely, I wanted to let her go first by stepping back quickly, but I was too slow. She was right behind me and I trod on her toes, then let go of the door handle in my horror, allowing the door to slam into us.

"Oh, oh," she twittered, grabbing hold of her dislodged hat.

"Oh my God! ... That was really stupid!" I snorted and quickly picked up my hat, which had dropped to the floor: "So sorry! ... Forgive me!" I stood there stupidly for a moment. She made an effort to stay friendly, smiled again, stepped ahead, and I trotted behind her. Thank goodness she had taken the lead and was walking up the stairs to the brightly lit gallery where, instinct told me, the better people were sitting. I hung up my hat and was about to take off my paletot coat. She unbuttoned her fur and looked at me rather curiously, as if she was waiting for something. But then the waiter came up and took her fur coat and jacket and my overcoat. Finally we sat down in one of the booths. There were table lamps with red shades and wine was being served. Once again, I felt thoroughly embarrassed. Because, since my youth, I could never rid myself of the feeling when going into a hotel or a reputable wine bar – or any place with wine and waiters – that it must be horrendously expensive and only there for seriously rich people; so I glanced with ill-disguised terror at the price list standing in the middle of the table, thinking with ever increasing alarm at the small amount of money I had brought with me. I secretly started adding things up. The thought buzzed through my brain, if this is what it costs to look for a wife, it will use up your last few hundred marks, and you might not even find a wife. Meanwhile I was smiling again and asked, almost gaily: "So, what will you have?"

I was already feeling a lot easier, as the prices were not quite so exorbitant. Anybody could come in here! I remembered that I was wearing a brand-new suit and looked at the other customers rather brashly.

"A Turkish coffee! ... It's cold outside!" she said, and I noticed that she had a long tongue and pronounced "s" with a lisp, like the English "th". Then she smiled again.

I looked at her more closely, unobserved. She was a really handsome woman. She was one of those well-dressed and rather pushy bourgeois ladies, a fashion I like, and which commands respect in me. Delicate lace and an elegantly tied blue ribbon peaked out from under her low-cut, V-necked blouse. Her skin was very white, and a good deal powdered. She had rings on her fingers!

The conversation was going nowhere. The waiter brought cups for the Turkish coffee and cakes.

"It's so cold today," she repeated.

"Well ... A terrible winter we're having! ... But it's warm in here," I answered. She looked at me closely.

"How old are you, Herr Graf?" she asked. I reddened and almost lost my temper, because I had already told her in my letter!

"I am now twenty-four, and you?" I asked.

The corner of her lips curled a little. She did not answer, saying only: "Then there is quite an age difference between us ... I am looking for someone rather more settled ... You won't think ill of me because of this, will you Herr Graf?"

"Yes – so there is nothing in it for us?" I asked nervously and made an effort to look innocent.

"So you see, I really want to find a gentleman in a secure position ... I have a beautiful home ... I have never moved in artistic circles," she said, coyly.

"Hm! ... Oh well, it can't be helped! ... Perhaps it could work though! ... But of course, I don't want to press you," I said, manipulatively. But she shook her head and smiled again, ironically.

The Turkish coffee arrived in unfamiliar contrivances. Now I felt a new source of anxiety. Up to now, I had been hiding my red hands under the table, then these confounded contraptions appeared! There was no point in paying them any attention for the time being. My female companion was already serving herself. For better or worse, I must do the same. I desperately observed how she worked the thing. Cold sweat was running from my armpits. You will never manage to do that, I told myself, as I was about to bring my hands out from under the table. But thank goodness, at this precise moment my companion said: "Shall I pour you one?"

"Y-yes, will you please," I said, in a real hurry. A lead weight fell from my stomach. I looked at her in wonderment. Christ, I mean really, what a woman. She really seemed magnificent! Pity! Christ, surely she must feel something for me! I started again.

"You know, you ought to realize that an author must start as soon as possible, when he is young ... It is true that it is a hard until you succeed, but that is why I need a wife ... I do not mean to deceive you," I said in good faith, and went on to describe what might come to pass as attractively as I could. But nothing could persuade her to change her mind. In the end I grew visibly irritated at her persistent shaking of the head and her sceptical smile. She always returned to her "gentleman with a good position" and the age difference!

Several awkward pauses in our conversation had already occurred. In the end she resumed: "Well, it's getting late. I must go home, Herr Graf."

Although I was glad, I tried to persuade her to stay a little longer. It was no use. I waved to the waiter. "Everything together," I said, grandiloquently.

"No! ... No! ... I will pay my own way, if you please!" she interrupted. She was plainly offended. The waiter hesitated and I looked at her, equally uncertain.

"But I insist!"

"No, and twice no! What are you thinking? I cannot allow it!" She was almost ferocious in her refusal as she took her money from her silver purse, saying to the waiter: "I had a Turkish coffee and two cakes."

I allowed her to pay, paid for myself, and we left.

"I never allow a gentleman to pay for me," she blathered indignantly, as we left the café. I walked beside her in stupefied silence as far as Goethestrasse. At the corner she told me I must go now. I doffed my large hat, shook her hand, promised to send back her photograph, and left.

The streets were still bustling with life. Snow was falling. People hurried by. I was in low spirits. Everything seemed so pointless. I shambled on aimlessly. Then I found myself at Stachus. I was suddenly seized, once again, by that strange restlessness. I turned into Sonnenstrasse and continued on to Müllerstrasse. I was forever shyly passing by the prostitutes who prowled around here. I did not dare speak to any of them. Once or twice I looked up as a girl got closer. I was gripped by a tingling sensation. My throat felt as though caught in a noose. My face was flushed. I went with the first one to speak to me. Scruples had no effect. I was powerless to resist.

Deep into the night, after I arrived home, I wrote Minna Sauer a long, soppy letter: "You have made me unhappy, dear lady! You have rejected me, and I do not know what I have to live for," I wrote, with many variations on the theme. I put her photograph in an envelope and sent her the letter the next day.

I started writing poetry again. I sent manuscripts to every conceivable journal. I wrote through the night and slept through the day. That aroused in my landlady the impression that I was ill. I finally got up from bed late in the afternoon, got myself together, drank tea, ate biscuits and lebkuchen and disappeared. "To my sister," I said, when the landlady saw me going out. In fact I was almost afraid of meeting Nanndl. I lounged around in the coffee-houses with live music, sought out shady dive bars and ended up in the Müllerstrasse. It was strange – as soon as I had left a bar and seen a girl, I gave it no further thought. I brooded on my vanishing money with a sense of horror. But it was useless. It didn't even help to go out with just a limited sum of money in an effort to resist temptation. I could not hold out, always slipping back to my room – however late it was – to get more. And I'd start roaming all over again. I wanted to walk myself tired, I wanted to freeze my ardour – yes, what didn't I want?! As soon as a girl appeared, sweat broke out of every pore. Something pushed up from my stomach into my throat and got stuck there. I no longer knew, should I walk on, stand here or cry out.

My money evaporated in this way. In order to get by on the cheap, I usually walked around until dawn before going to the red-light district. Scattered, huddled and frozen, whores still trudged here and there, having done too little business through the night. They made straight for me. They demanded a lot less to spend the night with them, and if you pretended to walk on, they lowered their price even more.

"Yes, yes! Let's go!" was all I could say when one of them stopped me. She took me by the arm, I felt her swelling hips and no longer noticed the cold. All the tiredness was gone. My blood boiled and raced through my veins. I wanted to walk faster. She growled something or other. I slowed down and then, when we finally reached the dark stairwell, I fell upon her, clutching her body and groping her. I started snorting and spluttering. She only managed to get me into the bedroom with the utmost effort. She hardly had the chance to light the gas-lamp. I literally ripped her clothes from her body. Her white, flabby body peeped out of her lace underwear. I clung to her tightly. Everything was a haze. I was burning hot. However much she talked, laughed, moaned at me or pushed me away it was no use. She could go through my trouser pockets at will and take all my money. I did not see it.

I just fell upon her again like a burst sack. Only when I was back out on the cold, gloomy street did I recover my senses. I was ashamed to be seen by the people sweeping away the snow and crept past them timidly. I pulled my coat-collar up around my face and as soon as there was not a soul in sight, I started running and landed in my room dripping with sweat. I did not light the lamp. I did not want to see myself. I stood there as though shell-shocked.

Once I had written a poem with the following lines:

A man at twenty has lost his soul,
A mongrel mix of beast and child.
And all that saves him: the desire to rise above,
new heights to climb,
when he is touched by the light
that suddenly breaks forth
and leads him on to grace, to life ...

Drivel! The very next evening it was the same story! I wanted to send my sick sister Emma another 400 marks – and my money was nearly all gone.

Money! Damned money, that was to blame for everything. It was sheer hell!

I clenched my teeth and sobbed. I thought of my mother. Since her twentieth year she had got up every day at four in the morning, worked and worked until she was ready to drop, and then went to bed at ten. She was already in her sixties, had chronic foot ulcers and suffered, yet rarely grumbled. She had brought eleven children into the world and was devout, entirely devout!

I thought of my brother Maurus at the front, and my sisters. They all had to live, had the same blood, and yet they made their own way?!

"You are the very worst, the very meanest of criminals!" went incessantly through my empty skull. I was still standing in the middle of my room. I was overcome with an indescribable misery, a terrible hopelessness. I put on the light, went to the wash basin, stripped naked despite the cold and washed myself from head to toe again and again. Fanatically. After drying myself off I felt better for a moment, but just one fleeting moment. Then everything fell apart again.

I stood there shivering, my limbs frozen blue. It was as though I could see my body slowly putrefying. I threw myself on the sofa and sobbed.

Why had Minna Sauer rejected me? I would have done *anything* for her! I would have accepted anyone, anyone! I was finished!

Outside the day dawned grey before my window. An ugly sky. The tram hummed past down below. Yes! – Yes!! Yes, my mother was right: you should drown your children in their first bath or like new-born kittens in a sack. Throw in some stones and – ssst! In the water they go.

I wanted to be dead, just dead. I did not know how to carry on.

6.
MARRY AND DESPAIR NOT ...

I loafed about endlessly. The days melted away, devoid of meaning, dull and stupid. I often slept until evening. It cost me the utmost effort just to visit the doctor. I lounged in coffee houses, wandered the streets, spent money without purpose.

I didn't want to see anyone. Even my landlady's family irritated me. I woke up grudgingly and went to sleep grudgingly.

Then one day, Selma Igl came to me. Schorsch had sent her my address from Berlin after all.

Her face was ugly and haggard, her eyes protruded. She had asthma and rattling breath. She asked how I was and why I never came to see her. I made the excuse that I was sick. We drank tea and talked about Schorsch, about the bad old times. I talked incessantly without thinking. Just to kill time. I avoided eye contact. Later, I escorted her to the tram stop. She admired my suit, showing respect for everything that covered my body.

"Don't you agree, Herr Graf, there are so few people with whom one can talk! ... But you must come and visit me again soon! Really!" she said, as the tram departed. "Yes," I answered mechanically. No, I thought. I went straight back to my room and lay down on my bed. My one solitary wish was to see nothing and hear nothing. I lay there and gazed at the ceiling until my eyes closed themselves.

In the end there was nothing else for it: work.

I went to the doctor and claimed to be in rude health. He picked up the nickel-plated funnel and looked up my nose.

"Yes, yes, it is healing up quite nicely," he muttered, "but you must carry on rinsing it well." Then he wrote on the doctor's certificate, "fit for work" and let me go.

Now it was a matter of getting back into the swing of things at the biscuit factory, because once I had stopped doing a job, that had always been like an end to it. Starting there again seemed to me like begging for pity and mercy. In any case, I had been betrayed and sold; I preferred to start elsewhere, even if it was just as bad.

I tried to return to the biscuit factory three times, and three times I turned around again. In the end though, I summoned up all my resolve, and went to the master. In the shop they looked at me askance.

"I see! ... You've been sick? ... What was the matter with you?" enquired the ossified shop assistant, who had been working there for 20 years. She regarded me with undisguised contempt. I meekly gave an answer and – to my surprise – I immediately won her to my side.

"Aha ... ... Suppuration of the sinuses? ... Dear God, you've had it bad ... I know that from our master. He had it too and had to go for an operation," she said, and her expression became far more sympathetic. She then reported my presence to the master. I already felt more confident again. I wanted to describe my illness to my fellow sufferer, the master baker, in such a way as to arouse the maximum sympathy. I entered his office shortly afterwards with the most long-suffering face and wanted to start whining immediately, but I could not get a word in edgeways. The master turned to me with his sober, busy face and said dryly: "So, you are back to good health, Herr Graf? ... Can you start work again?" And when I nodded, he added casually: "Have an operation, that's for the best! ... Go to the consultant Dr. Mahr, he treated me. Then you'll soon be rid of it." He spoke with the clear intention of closing the discussion quickly. I nodded, disappointed, held my silence, nodded again and left.

I was to start on Monday. It was Saturday. That meant I still had one and a half days of freedom. I hurriedly bought sausage and a bottle of red wine for my mother, went to the station without thinking what I was doing, and travelled home. Only when I got out of the train at Starnberg and boarded the steamer did my head clear a little. Now at last I was capable of thinking straight and already regretted what I had done.

The thought ran through my head: there was little doubt that, in the meantime, my sisters had learned about the machinations with my inheritance. There will be a row, accusations and in the end, a total breach. Why the hell had I come? I felt like a criminal who is no longer in control of his bad conscience. I wanted to unload something and did not even know what.

But nothing out of the ordinary happened. I had already learned about the changes that had taken place at home from Emma's letter. The same thing had happened as when Max had married. After trouble and strife with my brother's widow, Emma, Theres and mother went back to the little house that they had already rented previously. They had now taken it completely on lease and once again had opened, just as then, a small dressmaker's with an associated millinery and cleaning business. My mother ran the household, Theres made hats and dresses according to Emma's instructions. Emma herself, meanwhile, was completely bedridden.

My mother was standing at the stove stirring a simmering pot of chickenfeed as I stepped into the small, low-ceilinged kitchen. She had just scrubbed all the floors and her skirt was still wet up to her knees.

"Hm, that you? ...? Come on the one o'clock steamer?" she asked, as always.

"Jesus, it's him?!" Theres said at the same moment; she stood there in the doorway of her sewing room, and looked me up and down. Emma also called weakly from her bed upstairs: "Oskar? Is that you? ... Come up right away!"

I put down my overcoat and suitcase and went up to her. Pale and shockingly thin, she was lying on white pillows. Her breathing was clearly audible. She smiled weakly but became animated as soon as she saw me.

"Oh, boy! You look really swish!" she called, admiring my new suit. "Where do you get the money from? ... You surely can't save that quickly?" Again and again she said gaily: "You look so handsome! Really handsome!"

I now knew that they had no inkling of my financial dealings and my spirits rose; I told all sorts of fibs about my new-found wealth. She listened and her face glowed with happiness. Then she became more thoughtful.

"Yes," she finally said, "you are a child of love ... Perhaps you'll be a famous man one day, after all."

So much talk had exhausted her. She sank deeper into the cushions and started to cough, more and more, worse and worse. Great red spots appeared on her sunken cheeks.

"It'll soon all be over for me ... The local doctor said I had acute tuberculosis last time he visited," she gasped indifferently, adding: "You needn't give me the rest of the money any more ..." She spat out thick phlegm with some effort, and each time she said: "You see! ... It's red. That's all coming from my lungs." Panting, she lay back and stared at the ceiling again. I held my tongue. Her chin quivered a tiny bit. Her dark, deeply sunken eyes slowly grew moist with tears. She pressed her thin, bloodless lips together.

"Yes, yes," she repeated after a while with the same sad melancholic airiness, as though talking to herself: "Yes, you'll soon see, it'll soon all be over for me." I was relieved when our mother now called me down for coffee. I stood up quickly.

"Ah, what nonsense. You're not going to die. You'll get better again!" I said like a chump and went out of the bedroom.

Downstairs, we spoke little as we drank our coffee.

"Emma looks very bad," I simply said. Theres did not reply and our mother made a pained expression. We could not find anything to say. Our mother wanted to know if I went to church now and again, and casually told me that Moni – that was the widow of my brother Max – wanted to remarry. "So everything goes into someone else's hands?" I asked casually. "Aye!" sighed mother heavily and wiped her wet eyes with her apron. Theres went back to her sewing and mother got the chickenfeed ready. I looked around the room. Everything here was low, oppressive and poverty-stricken. It was quite different in the house where we were born, which was spacious and comfortable. Here, we all got in one another's way. I finally got up uneasily and went back upstairs to Emma. I said goodbye with forced cheerfulness and left the little cottage shortly afterwards. I arrived back in the city utterly wretched and distraught. Nanndl had asked me to come and visit her on my return and tell her about Emma. I did not go. I did not start work on Monday, either.

I let everything slide. It was almost as if one thing had suddenly ground to a halt without anything new starting. A few days passed, then I wrote another letter to the master baker and sent my landlady to deliver it. I wrote that I had decided to have an operation right away, and "unfortunately I would have to give up my job because of family circumstances"; he should just send me my certificate discharging me from the army as unfit for duty and a reference. The lady had barely left before I regretted what I had done again. I thought of chasing after her but let her go.

Just to have something to do, I kept going to the public library, borrowing books, carrying them home, and then returning them unread. One evening I went to see Selma Igl. She was delighted. She had a nice room and all kinds of books. She raved about Cäsar Flaischlen and Nietzsche's Zarathustra. The room was comfortably heated, and she had mincemeat and sausages – an extraordinarily rare thing at that point in the war. She was a bookkeeper for a gravestone company, which was doing a roaring trade at the time. In her free time she took piano lessons and was buying a piano on an instalment plan. She played classical music for me all evening. I did not know the pieces, but she told me. I expressed great admiration, although up to this point I had not the slightest understanding of music. From then on, we met each other often.

Quite unexpectedly a letter arrived from Schorsch, asking me to go to Selma and let her know he was getting married.

"Be a good bloke and help me out on this," he wrote. I went to Selma. She had also received a letter and was crying horribly. I tried to comfort her. It was no use. She just sobbed. I was completely helpless. Listening to her heart-breaking yammer, I was overcome with a sense of pity utterly alien to my nature. I crouched there awkwardly, thinking about the sentence in Schorsch' s letter.

I could not make head nor tail of it.

"Now I am alone. Utterly alone!" shrieked Selma again all of a sudden.

"My God yes, my God! In the end, we're all alone. Everyone is alone! That's just the way it is. But you have a piano and books? ... And – I come and visit now and again," I said, wanting to get out of there. Then she started sobbing again. So in the end, I stayed.

By the time I left early the next day, I had promised to marry her. That's what he must have meant by that sentence in his letter, I thought sullenly all the way home.

Back in my room, I drowsily sat down at the table and wrote to Berg asking for the documents I needed to get married. I wrote home in vague terms, and since my landlady's family was always complaining about "ladies' visits" I gave my notice and moved to Schwabing.

Soon after, we married.

The marriage was unhappy from start to finish.

7.
BAD LUCK AND BAD COMPANY

It all started rather strangely. I rented the room in Schwabing with what was left of my money roughly four weeks before our wedding. We wanted to live there as a couple and arranged this immediately with the owners when I moved in; they agreed.

It was still the hardest of winters. After catching a cold, I got cystitis but did not do anything about it. When I woke on the second day, I suddenly noticed that I had wet my bed. Alarm and shame drove me from the bed in a panic. I hastily put on a new shirt, threw on some clothes and wrung out the wet sheet. On no account should my landlady notice. I kept as quiet as a mouse until finally at midday Selma came from the office to visit me.

"You! ... Guess what – I have – I'm ill! I don't know what it is ... Fetch the doctor, now," I whispered to her. Shocked, she quizzed me. I explained hurriedly. She went straight off to the doctor. As best I could, I set my bed straight and got back into it. My odd behaviour seemed to have already attracted the attention of my landlady's family, because they had been shuffling about suspiciously in the corridor for quite a while, muttering. But for the moment that did not bother me, although it would have been terribly embarrassing if, for example, someone or other had stepped inside and asked what was the problem. Yes indeed, what could I have said in my confusion? Entirely flustered, I would certainly have turned bright red and stammered in answer: "I am so sorry, I have, I have – wet the bed ... It, it – I don't know, it just happened all of a sudden ..."

But, as already mentioned, for the moment, the thought never even entered my head. Something else entirely was troubling me. I thought back to my dissolute life up to now, the whores and girlie bars and all the nights of lust. Now you've done it, you stupid bastard, I grimly thought to myself. You've gone and gotten infected and you're ruined for life! You've got your just deserts, you filthy cockroach!

But I was overcome with a dreadful horror when I thought of Selma. Now you've infected her! Both of us are finished! There! That's all your doing!

At last, Selma came back with the doctor. She waited out in the corridor while I was being examined. I sat up in bed and gazed at the doctor helplessly.

"Doctor?" I asked in a low voice: "For God's sake doctor, I have gotten myself infected! And I'm getting married ... Have I got VD? ... That's my bride-to-be outside!" The doctor carried on examining me closely, asked question after question, finally smiling. I looked at him in despair and completely at a loss.

"No, no Herr Graf," he answered quietly, and seemed to be making fun of me. "No, that's nothing serious ... You do not have VD. You've just caught a terrible chill and should not drink so much before going to bed, do you understand? ... A slight case of cystitis. It can cause bed-wetting ... Above all, you should keep warm and perhaps stay in bed for a few days. Take this three times a day ... All right?"

"So you are quite sure I don't have VD? Really?" I asked, still rather doubtful, because I had accustomed myself to my imagined affliction. Such a rapid change in fortunes was too much for me. The doctor could not help smiling again and asked if I had often wet the bed, and when I said no, he answered ironically: "Don't worry about it. You can get married, Herr Graf ... It will clear up soon enough." Then he said goodbye. I felt like a redeemed sinner. "It's nothing," I said to Selma, and told her everything. But the owners of the house had already grown so suspicious that they returned the rent and told Selma they wanted me to move out that very day. I could see from their faces that they were disgusted with me. So I got up, looked around and this time rented two rooms a few doors down the street for the same price. The new landlady was a haggard old spinster with a hawk-like face and a son of about eight.

"Aye," she said with a rasping, unadulterated Swabian accent. "Ah'll myek an exception fo' yee. As ah said, ah only deal with respectable people ... Yee can move in together with your wife after the weddin' ..." And once again she looked me over with extraordinary interest and repeated: "Ah hope ah am gettin' honest an' decent people. eh, Herr Graf? ..."

"Yes, for sure," I replied with confidence and she was satisfied. She was also really nice to me when I was on my own, but every time Selma came, she was strangely transformed. She did not leave us alone for a minute. She always came in on some pretext, fumbled around, went out again looking offended, and came back shortly afterwards. This repeated coming and going became a real nuisance. Selma was annoyed about it. I calmed her down. Everybody has their own crazy ideas. That will all change once we are married, I said. However, the nearer the time came, the more nervous the landlady seemed to be. Above all else, one thing about her was really ghastly: she was – let's put it like this – obsessively clean. Every day, every hour she found something new to complain about. She was really eagle-eyed. And it's just a fact that when you are constantly under the watchful eye of a governess, you get quite shaky. Once, when I was writing a letter on the table, I forgot to remove the tablecloth, and there was an ink stain that could no longer be hidden. The doughty woman noticed it immediately. She interrogated me with the frenzied zeal of a fanatic. Incredible. Normally she always had an almost whiny tone of voice, now suddenly she was the exact opposite.

"Herr Graf!" she cried, now a little gentler. "Ah'll say it once an' just once only, yee'll hev tuh replace the tablecloth ... Ah am aaal alone in the warld ... Ah canna afford it, as lang as ah live ..." But when I said, I thought that the stain could perhaps still be washed out, her friendliness was over.

"What?! ... What d'ya mean? ... Wash it yeut? ... Nar na, Herr Graf, nar na! Ah've nar na use fo' lodgers leek that!" Then she started all over again, this time even more violently. She cackled so much that I could not get a word in edgeways. In any case, I always hated quarrelling. In the end I promised to pay for the cloth and told Selma about it the same evening. She was furious. It took a lot of effort to calm her down again. We did not have a brass farthing left. Finally I decided to take a few things to the pawnshop and settle the business.

The landlady looked at me in an almost menacingly suspicious manner when I left with the package the next day. Out on the street I bumped into Hobrecker, who was delighted at this unhoped-for encounter. He had long since forgotten how I had knocked him about. He was my chum once again, heart and soul. I hastily told him everything. His jaw dropped in astonishment at the news of my impending marriage, went with me to the pawnshop and then back home. Frau Ulbrich – as my landlady was called – was already waiting. I paid what I owed, the price of a few days' peace.

Hobrecker now visited me again every day. He often came very early and told me about his "financial campaigns". He was also due to come into some money and wanted to cash it out in the same way I had done. But that seemed to be no easy matter, and despite his explanations, I couldn't make out why. At any rate, he told me, he had started the legal process.

He was currently working as an insurance agent. Some shady general insurance agency had engaged him. Without further ado, he then sought out all his former benefactors and, with his customary finesse, played the part of the honest war invalid, who now had finally pulled himself up by his bootstraps. He then talked to those people until they bought an insurance policy. He pocketed their premiums at once and spent them on himself without another thought. In this way he enjoyed the high life, ate in the best restaurants and spent every evening in the artists' watering hole, *Simplicissimus*.[29] Everywhere he went he spoke about his im-

---

[29] *Simplicissimus* is the name of the protagonist in Hans Jakob Christoffel von Grimmelshausen's 1668 novel Simplicius Simplicissimus, considered the first satirical novel written in German, and was the name of a Munich-based satirical review published from 1896 until 1967, with a hiatus from 1944 to 1954. Its writers were regulars at a bar that was renamed after the magazine in 1903 and was widely known as the "Simpl".

minent fortune; people believed him and extended him credit, yes, even the waitresses lent him money. I envied him. Selma hated him.

Every evening he took me to *Simplicissimus*, where I got to know all sorts of people. Painters, cabaret dancers, failed businessmen, talented pimps, drunkards, cocaine addicts and casual whores, pushers and students, arts and crafts girls and pacifist poets. Each had his own way of getting through his life. They talked about ethics, humanity and art, and about soap and other black-market goods that were on sale there by the wagonload. They all scrounged off each other. You could find gossip, business, eroticism, obsessions, morphine and cocaine here. Everyone judged everyone else, spoke his mind freely and expected to be given a hearing. They were all swimming downstream, so to speak, clinging to their own nonentity.

Every now and then someone bought a round for everyone, because he fancied a girl from the cabaret, and then after closing time the whole party went to an artist's studio, laden down with wine and schnapps, and there would be a frenzy of dancing, drinking and arguing. I thoroughly enjoyed it all, and besides – I wanted to be known in artistic society, and to know my own way about it. I regarded it as the start of my literary career.

This way of life was expensive, so every day I carted stuff down to the pawnshop. I never came home at night. My landlady observed my behaviour with suspicion. She grew increasingly hostile.

Before long I had nothing left to pawn. Luckily, I met Marietta, a little girl with an adventurous past, who in those days recited poetry in *Simplicissimus* and was famous among all the artists. She went with me every evening after closing time, told me all sorts of stories and often gave me the last of her money. Such an acquaintance made me feel exalted as an artist and I completely forgot about my marriage plans. I was totally cut off, completely lost in this "sphere".

But at last, the wedding day arrived. Selma took a significant advance on her salary from her boss, we redeemed the most essential items out of pawn, and moved in together. Selma was at work during the day; I wrote, and since some magazines had already printed a few things, I started to view the world through rose-tinted spectacles. Yet when the first of the month arrived, we could not pay the rent. Once again, I packed a few things together and set off to the pawnbroker's. This time, however, Frau Ulbrich planted herself at the door and did not let me out.

"Wheor are yee ganin? Yee cannit gan yeut until yee hev paid," she screamed, her face white as a sheet.

"For heaven's sake, where do you think I'm going? To the pawnbroker's! So that I can pay you," I shouted, and turned on her: "Get out of my way and let me go!"

"Nar ah winnet. Ah winnet allaa it!" she snarled, blocking the door.

I was overcome with rage. "What!" I bawled even louder and pushed her out of my way. The doorbell rang. I flung the door open. Hobrecker was standing there. I rushed out and pulled him with me. The landlady screamed after us.

When we got back half an hour late, both rooms were cleared right out. The Ulbrich woman had taken all our belongings. I went to her to ask what was going on but could not get a word in.

"Thor! Neeo ah am safe! Yee'll neet git your things until ah hev been paid... Tek that, yee!" Her voice cracked and she shut up.

"There's the money! I will move out today! Give me my things back or I will call the police!" I called to her emphatically, putting down the money. She counted it and then suddenly started laughing sneeringly.

"And?! ... Wey aye! ... Wot abyeut the netty yee broke? Wot abyeut the curtains yee damaged? ... Pay fo' everythin' an' then yee can leave an' ah will give yee back your things... Neet befawa!" she scolded me and took me to the bedroom, showing me the slop bucket, which had a slight crack, and the curtain, which was a little frayed. She unbendingly insisted that I would have to compensate her for the damage.

"No, I'm not paying! Give me my things back!" I repeated, resolute. "I'm going straight to the police! Then we'll see!"

I left her standing there and went with Hobrecker to find the nearest policeman. He kept saying it was none of his business, but finally, after much persuasion, he followed us. But he left the screaming woman again without changing a thing. I stopped him: "And if I just go for her and take my things by force, what happens?" He just shrugged his shoulder and said: "You can try, but then she can sue you for trespass ... The best thing is just to pay up and move out." Then he went.

So, this was the State! Pay up and then you can live in peace. Resist, and you will be punished. One way or another, you've got to pay.

I shut the bedroom door and asked Hobrecker what he thought. "Man, I haven't another farthing. All I can do is go for that bitch, take my stuff and get out – or else I must pay. Hmm!" I said and went on, anxiously: "And what am I supposed to do about Selma? ... She's upset as it is with all this endless back and forth."

My mate had a wry smile.

"Hm. Bad luck! Bad luck! ... The joys of marriage," he joked, pertly. I lost my temper.

"For Christ's sake, idiot! Give it a rest, man!" I snapped at him. "We at least have to get things sorted somehow or other before Selma comes back ... So, what do you think? Have you any money?"

"No – my entire wealth amounts to one mark and twenty pfennigs," he answered with a shrug of the shoulders, though he now also seemed to be giving it some thought. We stood there for a while totally clueless. "I've got an idea," Hobrecker said all of a sudden and made a face as though it was the most brilliant idea ever, "Let's have a look at you." He scanned me from head to toe, looking at my suit and shoes.

"You could probably get 20 marks for them ... I know the pawnbroker. He's a fair and decent chap ... Look, just get undressed and go to bed for the time being ... I will pawn the whole lot and come straight back; then we'll pay, get back the things she's confiscated, and it will all be all right. Clear? ... I will tell the man he should put the suit and shoes aside and I will be back for them shortly. What do you think?"

I thought about it. I still owed the landlady 27 marks. He could also take my hat, Hobrecker said, and my wallet was worth something.

"Good," I said and did as agreed. Hobrecker took my keys and went off with my things. I hastily got into bed and waited. I was freezing cold and pulled the blankets over my head. The yappy singing of the Ulbrich woman penetrated the walls. She sang overpoweringly loudly, and there seemed to be a cry of hysterical triumph in her voice. I harboured romantic thoughts of revenge. Time went by. I got more and more nervous. I thought of Selma. She was sick; her health was in bits. Oh my God! Oh my God, what had I done? Whatever had I started? I hadn't loved her, nor had I hated her. I had just married her because I felt pity for 15 minutes and now the whole business had brought misery on both of us. Why had I not just left that night, simply run away?

Everything had turned sour.

I wanted to talk to Selma, today. Everything was clear. But it was impossible! You must, I told myself stoically, it must be so, the whole affair! Maybe it's precisely because your life has been so pointless up to now.

I now heard the keys creak in the outer door. I did not know how late it was and was worried that it might be Selma. But it was Hobrecker. I could already hear the Ulbrich woman arguing with him in the corridor. But, against Wilhelm Hobrecker from Remscheid, resistance was useless. He was a marvel, a phenomenon.

"But my dear lady! ... Do calm yourself! Don't get so excited, you dear little lady." I heard his incomparably calm voice overpowering the landlady's nagging, and with that wonderfully rich tone of voice that had earned him so much trust, he added: "There, you have your money. Everything in its place! ... You were quite right, of course ... My friend is ill. He has taken to his bed. Surely you don't expect me to leave him in that condition? ... Do be reasonable, you dear little thing! ... Herr Graf will get his belongings of course, won't he? There now!"

And sure enough, where I had failed with fury and anger, he had succeeded. The Ulbrich woman had calmed down, and my friend entered the room smiling. "Have you fixed everything? ... Wow!" I called out, deeply moved, and he nodded.

"Everything ... I've brought some cigarettes. She's cooled down," he answered, and because I heaped praise on him, he became self-assured and wanted to settle the whole business with the Ulbrich woman. I was simply to stay in bed, and it would soon be sorted, and then we'd be off, he said. I gave him a free hand. But after just a few minutes he came back in.

"Can you believe it? Just now the creature was being quite reasonable ... You have to beg her pardon and give your notice, she says ... She won't deal with me, the toad!" he reported. Now I'd had enough. I was out of bed with a single bound.

"Get undressed! Get into bed for the moment! We'll see about this!" I shouted, beside myself with rage. He did so in a flash. I threw on his clothes. They were much too tight and too short for me. I bounded into the kitchen. "What do you want now, Frau Ulbrich?" I shouted. "Are you going to be obliging, and give back my things, or do I have to smash everything to pieces ... Right now!" I raged. She shouted and threw her arms around wildly. Her child ran off for a policeman.

"Yee hev neet given your notice!" she insisted.

"Like hell I haven't! Get my things! Where are they! Get them!" I yelled, and since I couldn't see them in the kitchen, I rushed to her bedroom door, charged against it with all my strength, and pushed the screaming, scratching nag out of my way: "Open it or there'll be trouble. I won't tell you again! Come on! Open up!"

The Ulbrich woman had reared up again.

"Good," she said, and opened the door, "Gan an' git your rubbish! ... The police will git yee aaal reet. Yee should be ashamed of yersel', yee scoundrel!"

I took no notice of her, picked up my things and carried them off to our room.

"Swindler!" she blubbered and looked though the open door. She hesitated for a moment and then she rushed into the room like a flag fluttering in a high wind, went right up to Hobrecker in the bed and really let loose.

"There! So that's ha yee carry on wi' your friend! Ah forbid it! ... A-ah forbid it! Ah know it! Ah'll tell your missus! ... The policeman – ah'll tell the policeman ... It's a filthy business! ... Yee carry on wi' men! Yee, yee, yee depraved man!" The words gushed out of her mouth, a scandalous torrent of abuse; she was tearing her hair out with rage and threatened to attack Hobrecker, who simply burst into laughter. Finally, when it became obvious all this was to no effect, she flew from the room like a Fury.

"Hey! Wow!" I exclaimed, shaking my head, and had to laugh myself.

"There you have it, petty bourgeois rage! The petty bourgeois is the most immoral in the world!" said Hobrecker, in his urbane way, and got out of bed with a shudder. The suit changed hands again. We quickly packed up belongings destined for the pawnbroker's and listened for a few minutes. Hobrecker quietly opened the door as we heard plates clattering in the kitchen; I ran ahead, yanked the door to the corridor open and he was off with a single bound.

After a while, the landlady's boy came back. It seemed that the policeman had also told him that domestic disputes were none of his business. Once again, the Ulbrich woman was howling to the high heavens. Her bad luck delighted me. All of a sudden, I was all in favour of the State again. I was triumphant at the thought that it was not at the beck and call of every nagging old bitch.

When my friend came back, I made for the door at the speed of lightning. But so did my landlady. We bounced into each other like two over-inflated footballs. She flew against the wall with a groan and held her head, whimpering. Before she knew it, we were both back in my room and had bolted the door. She battered it with her fists like a mad woman, but we did not pay any attention. I had heaped up my things together. Then we marched one after the other like beasts of burden past the furiously gesticulating Ulrich woman and out of the house. All of the other house-tenants had opened their doors and followed us with black looks. Down below, in the middle of the street, we put down our baggage to stop and consider the situation. "So, you wait here with my things and stop Selma from going upstairs ... I will look round for a flat," I said to Hobrecker, and disappeared around the corner. I took a room with two beds on the third floor of a house in Schellingstrasse. It was thick with dust. It stank of decay. Nothing was properly set up. The old, completely white-haired land-lady was friendly to the point of sycophancy when I said: "Good, I'll take the room. I will move in straight away." Taken aback, she agreed and immediately set to work with nervous energy.

Selma was already with Hobrecker.

"Everything is sorted! ... Don't worry ... I have found a nice room," I exclaimed, and we marched off. When we arrived, the new landlady was even more agitated. She had hurriedly dusted the furniture and put things in order, to some extent. "I'll do the room tomorrow," she whimpered, before disappearing. Hobrecker also left us. I promised to visit him at his room the next day. Steaming with sweat, I immediately started unpacking and arranging our things. Selma crouched on a bed and cried; a broken-down heap of misery.

"Lie down! Just take it easy! Everything will turn out fine! ... My God, we are where we are! Come on, get into bed, come on!" I said to her soothingly. She undressed mechanically and lay down. I hastily hung a few pictures on the walls and went to bed myself.

The sound of Selma's groans and sighs pierced the darkness, then she broke into fits of coughing, sat up, gasped for breath and finally, as the attack was over, she fell heavily back into her pillow and burst into uncontrolled, loud and despairing sobs.

"Selma? Selma?! For God's sake, calm down! ... It's painful for me too," I told her soothingly, and caressed her with a trembling hand. My chest felt tight. Gradually, she calmed down again.

I lay as straight as a rod and my eyes bored ceaselessly into the pitch darkness. A nearby church struck. Sleep would not come. All of a sudden, I felt stinging bites in my feet and scratched them. They got worse. Selma was also scratching now. Breathing hard, she threw herself onto her other side, lay still for a few moments and started to rub, scrape and scratch again. And now my entire body was itching. "Damn! Bedbugs!" we murmured to one another. I stood up and turned on the light. When we lifted the blankets, the loathsome black bugs were crawling all over the place. "For God's sake! And now this!" Selma simply exclaimed before dropping to the cold floor. She was at the end of her tether. For a moment I was at a loss. Then I packed everything up again and started swearing like crazy. An audible whimper came from next door, a shuffle in the corridor, then yellow light fell through the frosted glass of the bedroom door, and the landlady announced herself. Selma threw on her clothes. I opened the door and swore at her. The old lady stood there in her dressing gown and apologized profusely. She brought back the rent money and implored me to keep quiet.

We walked up and down the whole night through, occasionally leaning against the furniture for a few minutes, looking out the window, waiting, waiting. Finally, a grey daybreak came. We heard the tram, the clatter of shutters being raised, the trundling of carts, footsteps, and voices. Selma got washed and went to work. I started looking. A friend from *Simplicissimus* had mentioned a bedsit flat to me a few days earlier. I went round and rented it. It was a large, airy and friendly room with a small box room to the side. The flat also had the most essential furniture, and there was no landlady on the premises; we rented it directly from the owner.

I went to Hobrecker, breathless and overjoyed. We borrowed a two-wheeled wheelbarrow and by noon we had finished moving. I telephoned Selma and shared the glad tidings. In the evening she came home and fell, exhausted, into a chair. She cried and cried. I let her get on with it. I thought that was for the best.

I went round tidying things up. The owner of the house was a friendly woman who let us have use of the furniture without payment. Finally, finally our own home, free and with no strings attached. I was overcome with satisfaction and delight. I was happy, really happy about it. Now you can work, you can do or not do as you please. Now you can start to lead your own life, I thought.

Then I remembered Selma. That's right, now I was married. That's right, I am no longer alone. For the first time it occurred to me that someone was living with me, day in, day out. I turned and looked at her. There she was, broken down, cowering in the chair, crying her eyes out.

"Rotten luck! Rotten luck!" I said "But we'll stay here now! Come on, everything will turn out fine! ... The devil can take literary society. All of it! In the end, a man is always alone. ... Come on, let's go to bed! ..."

8.
LITERATURE BEGINS

Now I withdrew more and more, did not go to *Simplicissimus* and did not answer when Hobrecker was at the door. All of a sudden, I hated everybody.

It was almost as though I wanted to determine, once and for all, the course of my future life. Misery was closing in on me from every direction and there were few ways out. Writing was more than uncertain and the experiences I had had with fixed employment were not attractive. But I had to get money at all costs. First, to put an end to the eternal trips to the pawnbroker's and second, to put our marriage on a tolerable footing.

Money, that was always the Alpha and the Omega, wherever you turned. Money was fortune and misfortune. As time went on, for me, money had really become like a demon that controlled my life. It was all nonsense, what the poets and philosophers talked about morality, ethics, strength of character, idealism and God knows what other fine qualities. In the final analysis, these qualities were subordinate to money: money created them or annihilated them at will. Mankind had invented something to which he must, sooner or later, submit, without further resistance, body and soul. If he had no money, he was a nobody; if he possessed it or earned a good income, it was easy for him to be virtuous and humane.

Realizing this, I slowly started to look around for openings. Before the war I had attended a typewriting course in Munich and became quite friendly with the teacher there. I looked him up again and he allowed me to type my own manuscripts at the lessons, on paper I brought with me. Now and then this teacher heard about vacancies in offices; perhaps he could get me a job. But nothing of the sort happened. Editors continued to return my contributions, while Selma's income was not enough to make ends meet, and I started pawning again. I grew anxious, frightened.

At the time, a mail order bookseller advertised books in the newspaper, for purchase on the never-never. On payment of the first instalment you get an author's entire works delivered immediately. I had an idea that promised salvation. I got in touch. Everything was as stated in the advertisement. I pawned my umbrella and ordered the complete works of Heinrich Mann with the proceeds. Two days later I received the six half-linen bound volumes. I took them straight to the nearest antiquarian bookshop and sold them. It all went smoothly. I now worked out an extensive purchasing plan. I ignored Selma's objections.

So, what else could you get from the mail order company? The complete works of Heinrich Mann, Nietzsche and Dostoevsky, *Weltall und Menschheit*, all saleable goods, for which antiquarian booksellers paid good money.[30] I was already counting on unheard-of profits. "Perhaps you won't need to go to work any more," I said to Selma, sure of success, but she always shrugged her shoulders dubiously and replied: "Yes, but how are you going to keep up the never-ending monthly instalments?"

"That? ... Oh, that will sort itself out!" I said to calm her, and never gave it a second thought. I ordered quantities of books through acquaint-ances, to whom I handed over the money for the first instalment, and was fully occupied selling them. Selma's face grew increasingly anxious, but I bought all kinds of things in an attempt to get her used to the benefits of my business transactions.

I met two artists and talked them into taking books on my behalf. They both generously said, "Yes, of course." I gave them the money for the down payment. One of them received a visit from an investigator, who wanted to know if the buyer was really in a position to pay. That scared the man, so he gave up the book business. The other spent the money on himself.

The investigator had made me uncomfortable. I did not like all of the customers for the books living so near to each other. It looked suspi-cious. But who did I know outside Schwabing?

Perhaps I should look up Nanndl? She knew that I had married, but never came. At home they knew nothing at all. But no, it was no use going to Nanndl, after all, she was also called Graf. Suddenly I decided – now, because I had some money – to go home. I wanted to find out what my family thought of Selma. As it happened, it was Saturday. Selma came home from the office at one o'clock. We agreed not to say anything about our marital status and set off.

I felt very uncomfortable when I stepped back into the little cottage, but I put on the happiest of faces and acted the man of the world. I deliber-ately avoided being alone with Theres. I could see in her eyes that she had a good deal to say to me – and not the best.

It was the same as ever at home. Our mother was working, made coffee and said what she usually said. They had made up a bed for Emma in an easy chair in the sewing room. She raised her head, looked at me, looked at Selma, and looked at me again.

"Yes," she then said to Selma, "You know, miss, that Oskar always will always need a mother or a woman who acts as his nursemaid until he learns more sense. Perhaps he'll grow out of it and be quite different ... Nobody comes to any good with him ... All of us Grafs are weird, but he is the weirdest of all."

---

[30] *Weltall und Menschheit:* A popular history of exploration of the natural world, elegantly bound in *art nouveau* style.

"Yes, I had already noticed," joked Selma. We carried Emma out the back door in her easy chair and chatted with her. It was a lovely warm day. A clear blue sky. Starlings sang in the leafless trees. The sun shone brightly. The air was aromatic, laden with the scent of earth freshly broken by the plough ...

"This is the most difficult season for me," Emma said, breathing heavily. She looked at me again, as though she wanted to say: so, what is your latest idiocy?

Her features were more sunken than ever. It looked as though nothing but the thinnest layer of transparent skin covered her bones. That almost cheerfully sad serenity unique to dying people shone in her eyes. She was still talkative and lively. She was interested in everything: in the movements of the armies, in the latest fashion, in cooking and speeches in the Reichstag. She read lots, for what else could she now do?

"Oh yes, Scheidemann," she said thoughtfully. "I like him. He is perhaps the right politician. He recently said in the Reichstag: 'Guard your hearts more carefully than your gates' ... That's wonderful ... But I still like Bethmann-Hollweg even more. He is a true public servant. He is not vain. Thoroughly sound ..." We talked about all sorts of things. It seemed as if she wanted to stray far away from the present, and it was good to sit next to this peaceful soul. I forgot about everything unpleasant.

Selma now started coughing again and gasped for air. Taken aback, Emma asked what was the matter with her. Then , just for a moment, thin wrinkles appeared on her smooth brow.

"You should not get married, Miss Igl ... And especially not to *him*," she said with her weak voice, and looked at me anxiously. She laid back her head in the puffed-up pillows and looked silently into the sky. Her face was sad. "Well ... Everyone must know what's best for himself," she murmured. "Yes ..." And after a while she said: "Life is so short, and just when you think it is now finally starting, it's all over ..."

She was very contemplative now. We left her alone and went into the kitchen. We stayed overnight. I slept in Maurus' room and Selma with Theres. She suffered another bad asthma attack. Everybody was troubled, and on the following day our mother took me aside and said to me: "You cannot marry her ... She is seriously ill." I nodded in embarrassment and was anxious to go. Without having mentioned that we were husband and wife, we left them. Theres escorted us to the steamship. As we boarded and set off, we called: "Herr and Frau Graf thank you for your hospitality!" Theres stared and smiled in shocked astonishment. The next day I wrote a letter of explanation, and a late wedding present of 25 marks arrived.

The letter from home said: "You must get by on your own now; we have never been able to tell you what to do. We wish you and your wife every happiness and hope that you will lead honest lives." My mother had written underneath, in her crooked, laboured hand: "Dear Oska, I have had truble with my children and work from early morning till late at nite till I come to my grav. Say your prayers and go to confession and become an onest man, lov, Mother."

Selma was not there when I read this. I walked up and down in the large studio. I was on the verge of tears. Every which way I looked, I saw ruin. It was as if I had entangled myself in an invisible, clinging net, from which there was no escape. There was a knock. I ran to the door and opened it. Hobrecker stood there laughing and came in.

"What do you want?" I yelled at him. "What do any of you want with me?" He asked, this way and that, what was up with me. I did not answer.

"Gosh, I can see you're in a bind," he said after a while, "we can find you a way out ... You can get something from the Red Cross ... Register with them ... And ... And they also have a War Fund to help out workers by brain ... Yup! I picked up something there ... It's child's play."

"I don't want anything more to do with this begging, I am looking for work," I hollered at him, but Hobrecker was unruffled. He told me that at the Red Cross there was a man with a long nose, some sort of Germanic artist with literary interests. I would be sure to get something from him. And as for the War Fund, there was a bunch of motherly women who might even find a job for me.

Now I paid more attention. He gave me a cigarette. I grew peaceful, made tea, and he fetched bread and artificial honey. I read some poems to him and showed him what had been published.

"You must take all that to the Red Cross and the War Fund," he advised me, "They're sure to be impressed by anything in print." He gave me the addresses. I felt more cheerful when he left. On the other hand, I did not want to go the Red Cross and the War Fund, so I tried with humble, grovelling letters. A few days later I received a letter from both by the same post, asking me to appear in person. I set out anxiously. At the Red Cross I presented myself with the long-suffering face of the honest, sturdy peasant.

"So you were a worker? A baker? ... And now you are writing?" asked the man that my mate had described and peered at me through his pince-nez with interest. I showed him everything that had been printed. The man seemed to light up. He started up a friendly conversation about literature. I looked at him closely.

Him? At the Red Cross? Clearly a well-educated man? Perhaps he's a doctor? Who knows what could come of it, I reckoned, groping forwards.

What did I think of the new poets, he wanted to know. "Well, they write such intellectual poems. That's not what I want to do," I said, walking the line between caution and self-confidence, and when I noticed that he was pleased with my answer, I went on more boldly: "You know, they are not real people ... They are just coffee-house poets."

A beggar develops remarkable intuitive powers; he immediately aligns himself with the person standing before him. He sniffs out the person's attitude of mind, his inner disposition. I had hit the target. The man grew more animated.

"Yes," he said, "they have severed all connection with the people." There was something down-to-earth, something Lutheran-Germanic in the way he said it. He referred to the war as the most powerful adventure of the nations, the well-spring reinvigorating all peoples. A new ethic would arise from it. I was perfectly in the picture.

"So where were you at the front?" he asked again. "Did you see a lot of action?"

"Yes," I said, "but I'd rather not talk about it." He seemed to take this as the natural modesty of the true, proven hero, which is precisely what I wanted. I had won him over, completely. He gave me 30 marks. I had to sign a receipt. As I was about to go, he invited me to visit him again. He knew a professor, who could perhaps help me.

I ran down the steps, literally jubilant. It's always the same, the slightest success bolsters you up. I went straight to the War Fund. I was received there by a tall woman with grey hair and a couple of warts on her face, who appeared to be an aristocrat. She had a masculine voice and sharp eyes. I had to explain things over and over again and finally fill in a form. "Things are not going well for me, Madam," I said with seductive honesty, "but others have it much worse ... You only have to think of those poor men at the front ... If you could just help me out this once."

I wanted to stick with the tactics that I had used to good effect at the Red Cross.

The lady took the questionnaire that I had filled in and glanced through it. "So you are already married?" she asked and smiled a little for the first time. She gave me a motherly look. I nodded. I also smiled, sanctimoniously.

"So what do you need most urgently?" she asked. I pretended to be shy, as if I the cat had got my tongue.

"I have a few items of clothing ... You must need some, surely?" she said, and without further ado she stood up, went to a wardrobe with sliding doors and took out a long frock coat without trousers and several ties. Although I was rather disappointed, I heartily thanked her with the utmost obsequiousness. That got her.

"Let's see if we can accommodate you. Come by every Thursday, and sign here please ... You can get your money outside at the cash desk," she said. This unexpected change of circumstances transformed me visibly.

I left the office with many clumsy bows and thank-yous and received another 30 marks. On the stairs I immediately put on the black frock coat and a tie, as I did not want to go out on the street with such a huge bundle of clothes. That would make me look too much like a beggar.

I returned home in triumph and told Selma. "Sixty marks! Imagine, sixty marks in one day," I exclaimed. Selma said nothing and showed me the reminder letter demanding payment from the mail order company, which had been lying in the post-box. I added it up quickly.

"Eight times seven are fifty-six," I groaned in disappointment. "My God, how stupid."

"And that will go on month after month," said Selma. I went gloomily to the post office and sent off the money.

Once again, I was writing through the night. Selma slept in the next room. I had applied to the *Münchner Neueste Nachrichten* to write book reviews and was in luck. My contact there was Doctor Kurt Martens.[31] He sent me a very friendly reply and invited me to visit at the editorial offices. He gave me books immediately. I read them, wrote the reviews and sold the books. I also brought in a few anecdotes and articles for sale. That spurred me on. I then tried to get some work as a reviewer with the *München-Augsburger Abendzeitung*, also with success. But in this case, I always had to return the books with the critique. I got five to seven marks for each piece. I wanted to earn as much as possible as quickly as possible, so I didn't bother reading the books. I just praised them and that was it. I went into bookshops, got hold of their brochures and cobbled together something plausible. This went very well. Everything was printed, although occasionally abridged due to lack of space, and because the fee was based on the number of lines, for the most part I got less than hoped for. That often annoyed me. But I told myself, "it's easy money" and "you've got a foot in the literary door".

My literary efforts seemed to be going better in general. For example, an article appeared in the *Münchner Neueste Nachrichten* in which I described a wartime experience. Two days later a statement from a Professor Oskar Graf was published in the same place, saying that he was not the same person as the author, and I received a letter signed by both the editor and the professor asking me to change my name, as he was the official war artist with the General Staff and was under an obligation not to publish anything about the war. What a lot of attention I was getting! I was delighted with this and immediately changed my name. From now on I was

---

[31] Kurt Martens (1870-1945) was an author of many novels and short stories, and a frequent correspondent with Thomas Mann. He committed suicide in Dresden the day after the city's destruction by the RAF.

called Oskar Graf-Berg. I didn't like it, but I had to be accommodating.[32]

A little later I met an acquaintance from the artistic circle at *Simplicissimus*, the painter Carlo Holzer.[33] He told me that nobody in Schwabing liked my new name. Holzer was a man who had absorbed everything of Stefan George body and soul, so to speak. Not only did he recite the poet's verses at every opportunity; even his voice and his movements were somehow "Georgian".[34] The man was all for sound effects. He stood on the street deep in thought, puckered his brow, gave it further thought and then said, all of a sudden: "Oskar Graf-Berg? That is a profanity! Simply call yourself Oskar Maria Graf." He pronounced the word "Maria" with great deliberation and significance, as though he had hit upon the world's deepest secret.

"Oskar – Maria – Graf," he repeated with emphasis.

"Yes! There's posh! Oskar Maria Graf," I yelled out, all at once enthusiastic. "Highly practical. Now, when I write crap, I am called Oskar Graf-Berg, and if I turn out something decent, I am called Oskar Maria! Nice one! Fantastic!" The artist, a little stunned at such a philistine attitude, smiled and went on his way.

But despite all this literary effort, I was still pressed for cash. I had got myself into a fine witch's cauldron with the book orders. I had to pay monthly instalment after monthly instalment.

They were the cause of quarrels with Selma.

I had often stopped by the War Fund to ask about jobs. One day I went again and was asked to go directly to the Chairwoman. She said to me, very amiably: "Go at once to Number 2, Karolinenplatz and ask for Privy Counsellor Bruckmann. He might take you on as his private secretary, if you acquit yourself well. I gave you a strong reference."

I thanked her and went. All along the way, I revelled in the romantic notion that I would now be received by very fine people, much like the classical poets of old. I pictured myself as a modest, young, talented man moving in the society of elegant, brilliant ladies and gentlemen, who found me fascinating. In a word, a vast and beneficent world stretched out in my imagination.

---

[32] Oskar Graf (1873-1958), an artist of the naturalism school, was a war painter under the Prince Rupprecht of Bavaria; in the Second World War he was the sole German war painter in Italy.

[33] The portrait of Oskar Maria Graf reproduced with Graf's 1965 Foreword is by Jakob Carlo Holzer. Graf published an appreciation of his work in 1925.

[34] Stefan Anton George (1868-1933) was a symbolist poet. He also translated the works of Dante Alighieri into German.

With my hopes at fever pitch, I arrived at the house in Karolinen-platz. A gentleman with a dignified and worldly-wise air and an elegantly trimmed half-length beard received me and explained his requirements. He seemed to take a liking to me.

"You will spend most of your time at the typewriter, don't you know ... But you aren't averse to carrying crates, are you? ... You have a strong build," he said and held me spellbound with a semi-ironic grin, which made me feel awkward.

"Yes, even as a fourteen-year-old kid I carried sacks at home, I used to be a baker ... I also worked in a mill and carried sacks weighting two hundredweight all day long before the war," I replied without hesitation. I wanted to make the best possible impression.

"Well ... Well then," said my future boss, clearly satisfied, "sit down right now at the typewriter. Let's see how you type."

I did as asked. The typewriter was a completely unfamiliar machine and what I typed was not visible. I got the jitters when the gentleman started to dictate. I typed unsteadily and as fast as possible to show how quick I was. I was convinced that I was making one mistake after another. After a while, the gentleman lifted the rubber cylinder and looked at what I had typed.

"Hmm? ... I thought you said you could type quite well?" he asked. I turned red and stuttered in my confusion. "Y-yes, but I have never used this machine. I don't know how it works ... I would have to practice," I stammered and looked helplessly at the gentleman. "No – no! There's no time for that," he said curtly, and dismissed me.

I did not go back to the War Fund to tell them the news. I sullenly strolled round to the employment office at the bakers' lodge. There were no vacancies. I went there every day. In vain. The outlook grew ever greyer around me.

9.
A FLASH OF LIGHT IN THE DARKNESS

Summer moved on. The streets basked in the late August sun. The air hung heavy and already a little autumnal and dreamlike. I often squatted in a state of indecision on a park bench until five in the afternoon and gawped at the hustle and bustle all around. I always had a book in my pocket, but never read it. I just stared into space. My mind was a blank. I did not want to think any more. Children romped noisily in the grounds, women scolded, girls bobbed past, old men sat around and talked. The birds sang in the trees and the dull rumble of the streets wafted over; everything went on as usual. When I closed my eyes, it was like sitting in a warm glass case with countless beetles crawling up and down and scratching the walls. Constantly, with irritating industriousness, in such a way that it made me totally thick-headed. A nearby clock struck the hour.

"Christ, five o'clock again!" an old man murmured beside me.

"Yes, time flies by like crazy ... I wonder how it will all end ... You don't even dare think about it, or else you'd string yourself up," said another bored man, and when I looked at him, I saw that he was a war cripple with a hideous looking face. I stood up and went.

Thoroughly jaded, I waited in the flat until Selma arrived. "Have you found anything?" she asked.

"No, there's nothing," I replied, shaking my head. We hardly spoke to one another. We were both depressed. On one such evening I found a telegram in the letter box. "Emma has died, come down, Theres."

It was as though a gust of wind had suddenly blown my brain out of my head. And then as if my skull were filled with lead.

"Emma has died, Emma has died, hm, Emma has died," I babbled over and over again to Selma. She took the scrap of paper and read eagerly.

"Hm, and we don't have a penny ... But you must go home," she said. "We cannot buy a wreath, but you must go home anyway ..."

I fumbled my way into the bedroom and mechanically searched for something I could pawn. I needed five marks. Early the next day I travelled to Berg.

"Hmm. She died so suddenly," I spluttered out, standing in front of my mother in the kitchen. Theres came. We simply looked at each other in silence.

"She's over in the mortuary," our mother said sadly, and started crying. Tears welled up in Theres' eyes, too. "Hmm, so sudden," I muttered numbly. "So sudden."

"She still had to suffer so much," sighed our mother, turning to her work again. "Now it's over. Better that way than if she had gone on suffering." She wiped her eyes dry and gave me a cup of coffee: "Go on, drink it ..."

Then I found out how Emma had died. Our mother was busy making plum jam when the death-throes began. Theres was dressmaking, as usual. Emma was lying upstairs, above the workroom, and spoke until the end. The hole for the sheet metal-lined flue in the ceiling had been opened up so that they could always hear if the patient needed anything.

"Steadfast she was," our mother told me about the dying girl. "When I brought soup up to her, her face has already swollen up, and her whole body contorted, but she never complained ... Steadfast to the end.

"Then when I started making the jam, she said all at once: 'Crumbs, Mother, you make such fine plum jam, really! ... Fiddlesticks, I am dying now! ... Cook it long and slow, you know ... And don't spare the sugar ... It'll all be over soon ... Do it right, Mother ... I am dying and you'll have something good for winter, but do it right ... Mind that you boil it for a long time ... I won't be here much longer ... Where is Nanndl, call Oskar on the telephone ... How much sugar did you use, Mother? ... Resl! Resl! Come quick, the end is coming ...'"

Theres went straight upstairs and, when our mother followed, Emma was already dead. Theres showed me a piece of paper. Written on it in pencil, in shaky handwriting: "Everything belongs to Resl, keep well, Emma." She had just managed to write those words.

I read the message more in gloom than in sadness, and said, dejectedly: "Yes, of course, everything belongs to you." I finished my coffee without saying much. A depressing silence had fallen over the house. From time to time my mother sighed heavily.

As I sat there, I remembered everything. I remembered the letter Emma had once written to me when she was already bedridden.

"Dear Oskar," she wrote, "I keep building castles in the air in my warm bed. Our cottage is very nice now, and they are spoiling me rotten. I always think, one day we'll all come together here, and it will be nice and cosy. Maurus will open a patisserie next to Resl's hat shop, Nanndl will do the ladies' hair and you will help out a bit and have a nice little room under the roof where you can write poetry. We are all a bit weird, but if we weren't, life would not be worth living. You see, I'm daydreaming again. But it's nice to daydream. After I die, look in every corner, dear Oskar, perhaps I'll have stashed away a pile of money for you. That would be great, wouldn't it?

"I now have a new doctor in Perlach. He's a quack. He has prescribed me a litre bottle of medicine. It's already doing me some good. He thinks I should be better in three months. But I don't believe it. I would just like to see us all back together peacefully in our house ..."

And then her face came to mind, her cheerfulness. Her entire life ran through my mind: how beautiful she was and how coquettish, how she was a ballroom queen, how she once, when I came back from Ticino and everyone was telling me off, said to me with her warm tenderness: "My God, Oskar, you just take your place and don't let them get under your skin ... You belong in this house as much as any of us. Nobody can kick you out ..."

And I remembered every word that she said to Selma and me that time. She had been bedridden for nearly two full years, and she had always known that each day was taking her closer to the grave.

It was all so vivid to me that I momentarily refused to believe she was dead, and then it hit me like a leaden weight when I realised that yes, of course she was.

I could no longer stand it in the house, so I went alone to the cemetery in Aufkirchen. I stood there, hesitant, before the glass doors of the mortuary. I only looked at the wreaths laid over the coffin. I felt a slight flutter pass over me.

There come moments – we want to erase such events from our thoughts, we do not want to acknowledge them – but suddenly we confront them full on. I pressed my face against the glazing in the doors and lost all self-control. Her shrunken upper body in its stiff white lace dress peeped out from beneath the mass of wreaths. Then – I was now freezing cold and starting to cry as I opened the door and stepped into the chilly, pitiless room and up to the bier – yes, then I saw the withered, yellow neck, the slender head with its smooth, sparse black hair. There lay the rigid face with its pale-blueish transparent skin, a skeleton already, the eyes half open, and around the thin, colourless mouth two little wrinkles, as though a faint smile had suddenly been interrupted.

I stared at the dead girl through a drizzle of tears. "Em-m-ma! E-e-Emma-Emma!" I stammered, sprinkling the corpse with holy water all the while, again and again, just to keep my mind off my trembling limbs.

"Em-m-ma! Emma! Emma-Emma won't you ever come back to life, Emma?!" I howled oafishly, howled and howled. Now the church clock struck with a resounding bong. I literally jumped with fright, then wiped my eyes in shame and ran out of the mortuary. I stole out of the graveyard like a chicken-livered schoolboy who has just done something dreadful. I think that if I had met someone – anyone – I would have run off.

It was only when I was on the path through the field leading to Kempfenhausen that I finally slowed down, and calmed down. I headed through the sparse woodland that runs along the ridge. As boys we often waged bloody wars there with schoolchildren from the neighbouring villages during their lunch break. You can see right across the lake from here.

I lay down in the soft grass and stared for a long while into the blue.

214

The sky was bright and distant. A vast stillness hung heavy over the land. Summer heat penetrated my body from all sides. Birds were singing in the trees; indistinct voices reached me from afar, crickets chirped, broke off and began again. The ship's bell rang clear across the lake.

Emma lies up there now like any other human, as we all will one day. Tomorrow we shall bury her. Over time she will crumble in the earth, her face, her eyes, her teeth will turn into excrement, into nothingness, and my mother will turn the earth on every All Souls' Day and plant geraniums or nightshades and water them. The water will trickle down to the corpse, to her decayed bones, which the worms will still be gnawing ... And people will say: "What lovely flowers she has planted ... beautiful."

It stuck in my craw. My eyes were open, yet I saw nothing; the same thought kept coming back.

"Life is so short, and just when you think, it's finally starting, it's all over ..." I recalled Emma's words and saw her lying in her bed with her sad smile.

"If it is all really like that, why should we live, when the very beginning determines the end?" came the voice from the dark recesses of my mind. A strange sadness, one that seemed detached from reality, gradually took hold of me. I absent-mindedly pulled a piece of notepaper from my breast pocket and wrote:

To us damned by blood
the prayer of comfort in putrid darkness and earthly torment:
Though we all die lonely and mocked, O God, thus have we risen up to you!
It cannot be that seed is sown, earth blossoms and fruit ripens, all for naught!
Deep truths circle around the infinite axes of pain and murmur their dying deeds
into my ear ...
And yet, a day shall dawn long sought in vain
A pyramid shining through the desert haze
Mercy shall bear away all earthly pain
And years of accursed greed – grace shall erase.

I was sweating now. My sadness was extinguished. I felt a kind of sullen rebelliousness rising up in me. I jumped up, looked over the fields, over the lake, and was quite calm. Inexplicably, I now felt sure of myself. Just before I reached the village I stood still for a moment and quite suddenly, as though I were defending myself against somebody, I said in a way that was both childish and proud: "It's all untrue! ... It's totally different!"

At home I met Nanndl for the first time since my marriage, who had come back from Munich in the meantime. She was shattered and cried almost the whole time, so that I could not even talk to her.

"Won't Maurus get time off?" I asked my mother.

"Yes, he'll come just in time," she said.

"He won't be in time for the funeral, though," said Resl.

The evening passed in almost complete silence. Nobody wanted to make eye contact. Nobody wanted to talk. The funeral took place the following day. Many friends and relatives were there. My mother stood at the grave, worn out. Moni, standing by me, howled as though she had lost her nearest and dearest. Then Resl and Nanndl also burst into her tears. My mind was elsewhere, and I did not shed another tear. I was just annoyed that I could not buy a wreath. Everyone looked at me, and their looks were not the kindest.

I left home in a lighter mood. Only when I got back to the city did the depression return. About a week later, at last, I found work at Rauber's bread factory. As usual, it was night shifts again, including Sundays. The vast factory halls were like ghost towns. Only two ovens burned and, apart from me there was just an oven-hand (the head journeyman) and an apprentice. Consumption of bread had fallen due to coupon rationing. Previously there had been ten assistant bakers, now three of us did everything. There was plenty to do. I was in charge of the kneading machines. The worktables were placed such that we had our backs to the ovens. We slowly roasted. It was too hot to wear a shirt. So we worked only in trousers, with naked torsos. Sweat ran down our skin and boiled. I got sores on my back, just as had happened in the mill. Tiny blisters appeared. After a while they burst and burned ferociously. When I got home my shirt was stuck to my skin.

I wrenched it off in a single movement and poured cold water over my skin. That cooled it. But as soon as I stopped, my body started to burn and itch worse than ever. I slept on my stomach. Thank God! It was not yet autumn. That meant I needed no blanket in the hot bedsit and did not need to tear it from my back on waking.

In the evening, when Selma came home, she woke me up. We sat together, saying little, and from time to time I glanced anxiously at her swelling body.

I left at about seven-thirty.

Now we always had bread.

10.
THINGS GET MOVING

One day the gentleman from the Red Cross met me on the street. I wanted to avoid him, but he came up to me with a friendly air.

He wanted to know why I never got in touch.

"I'm working again. As a baker. Again." I said. "Oh really?" He sounded interested. "And are you still writing poetry on the side?"

I nodded.

"Can't you come and see us some time? Maybe in the evening?"

I shook my head: "No, that's when my work starts."

"Well ... Perhaps during the day?"

"That's when I sleep."

The gentleman looked at me.

"Or perhaps you can come to us on a Sunday?"

"It's the same problem. I can't manage that either," was my reply.

This disconcerted the man a little. He wanted to know what it was like being a baker.

"Hm," he finally said, "that's just too hard on you ... You should have something a bit easier."

I looked at him with the concealed contempt that a worker always feels when someone quizzes him about things of which he knows nothing. He didn't notice this at all and started up again about the professor who had expressed interest and might help me.

"Did you know, everything you write is so original, Graf," he said, almost as though he was a friend. "You write because you are driven to write." He praised me and drew comparisons between me and Gottfried Keller. He said that Keller had been a State Secretary for all his life, and that it is quite good for a writer to have work, because then, everything he had was rooted in solid earth. I nodded all the time, and now and again I said: "Yes, of course, quite right, yes," though secretly I was thinking: it's easy for you talk. You live off the fat of the land and lecture others, who have to do hard work on empty stomachs, about how fine it is to slave for others. Why should I care?[35]

Nevertheless, in the end, I promised to visit him one afternoon.

I was fully occupied. On no account did I want to give up the book reviews. I ran around editorial offices during the day to fetch the books, then took the ones they gave me to the typewriting school, where I typed

---

[35] The Swiss author Gottfried Keller (1819-1890) is best known for his romantic novel *Der grüne Heinrich*, translated into English by A.M. Holt as Green Henry, published in 1960.

out the reviews and finally went to bed at five or six in the evening, before doing a full night shift at the bakery starting at eight o'clock; it was a terrible rush. Sometimes I nodded off while working the dough; my eyes closed, and my arms refused to do any more. From time to time the oven-hand complained. I repeatedly had to draw on reserves of nervous energy to tear myself out of this feeble state.

"It's too hard for you," the gentleman from the Red Cross had said. I thought about it and grew more and more irritated by and grumpy about this life of toil. By chance I learned that the General Post Office was looking for temporary pre-sorting clerks. I simply stayed away from Rauber's, begging for a reference and an invalid card in a tortuous letter, and after about a week I went to the post office. It really was much better there. Some 40 or 50 of us sat in a large hall. Each of us had a shelf divided into several pigeonholes, into which we threw the sorted letters. All kinds of people worked there. War invalids, non-professionals, impoverished pensioners, casual workers and intellectuals. The working hours were from eight in the morning until midday, then we were free until eight in the evening. And from eight until midnight, or the alternate shifts. Sometimes you got a whole day and a half free at a stretch. That was sweet.

It was sociable, too. You could skive off. We often stood, five or six of us together, outside the lavatory and smoked cigarettes while trading in goods. Everything imaginable was on offer: soap, butter, hoarded meat, watches, old suits, ration coupons, bread-cards, shoes and even, on one occasion, a complete suite of furniture. One of us stood watch and warned the rest of us if a manager was coming, while we traded. A handshake, and done! A signal from the look-out and we were in the lavatory in a shot. Inside, we coughed and snorted as though dealing with the call of nature. Once the danger had passed, it was back to business as usual.

I wanted to stay there. If you prove yourself, I thought, perhaps they'll keep you on and without too much trouble, you can become a postman.

After all, what would you get from all these people who had showed an interest in you? Lugging crates for Bruckmann, and who knows what the professor might have wanted! Nobody cares about anyone else these days.

But a postman! That was certainly a nice little number! I had always liked receiving things in the post, and as for delivering mail from all over the world? Ideal, actually. The postman strolls about all day long, without wearing himself out, sees everything, hears everything, he gets inspiration and even commands some respect. That seemed to be a uniquely suitable profession for me.

But my bad luck returned.

In one of my recent reviews, which I had delivered to the *München-*

Augsburger Abendzeitung, I had written about a book by Albrecht Schäffer. I got him mixed up with the Rhinelander Wilhelm Schäfer, who I knew to be coming up to his sixtieth or seventieth birthday. My piece started with the words: "In this new book the venerable old poet has once more bestowed upon us a glorious blossoming of his mature and serene art ..."

The publisher sent a letter to the editor, which he forwarded to me. They wrote that "in the review by Herr Oskar Graf-Berg, he described Herr Albrecht Schäffer, who is currently enjoying his thirty-ninth year in the rudest of health, as a venerable old poet." The editor did not have anything to add, but from then on, he gave me no more books.

Misfortunes never come alone. A little earlier I had sent an article to the *Münchner Neueste Nachrichten*. It did not appear. I had often written to Dr. Martens. And it still did not appear. Then I wrote ceaselessly. First cautiously, then urgently. No answer came, and no more books. Unhappy about this, I decided to turn directly to the editor-in-chief. Payment then came in the post, but without any further explanation. Everything was ruined. My literary position, which I had laboriously struggled to achieve, was teetering. Something had to be done. I decided to become independent as a writer and went to see Hobrecker.

"So," I said, after I had boasted about my literary successes, "guess what? I'm starting a magazine! ... Will you join?"

"Hm ... Quite an ambitious project then?" inquired Hobrecker.

"Absolutely! Something really big!" I nodded, and asked: "What about your inheritance? ... Have you got it already?"

"No, but soon."

I presented everything in the most attractive light.

"You can have as much money as you like but of course I must be your chief contributor," Hobrecker replied, already assuming the role of the all-powerful media baron. He took out a manuscript and began reading: "Leo just left the bar. He shivered. He had left Ruth and torn himself away from her cherry-red lips. Hell, thy name is woman, he thought. He grasped the polished revolver in his right pocket and released the safety catch ..."

I hardly listened. My thoughts were all over the place.

"Good," I said, feeling cornered, "we can still discuss our collaboration. But will you definitely let me have the money? Can I depend on it?"

"What do you think of the opening?" he asked.

"It's obviously not right for a magazine, but I know you can write good articles. That's what I need. Look, tell me straight, say: 'Yes' ... I need to know ... Just think, man! You've just been idling away your time and I will set you up, I'll be of incalculable value to you if I put you in print!" I pleaded with him. He beamed.

"You can always depend on Willy," he said boyishly.

On the next pay-day I took my hard-earned week's wages and had 500 bright yellow, ostentatious letterheads printed with the following inscription: Neuland / A Journal for the Literature of Self-Revelation / Published by Oskar Maria Graf / Neuland Press, Munich.

So now I was at one and the same time: writer and my own publisher! Now the door to fame was opening. I did not have a clue what the "Literature of Self-Revelation" might be, but it sounded good and meaningful.

When I showed Hobrecker the letterhead; he was entranced. He immediately promised to invest his entire fortune "in the enterprise". This gave me a great lift and I said confidingly: "Do you know what? ... You will be the Managing Director."

He was as happy as if he'd been awarded a medal.

Actually, I was unsure what to do with the magazine. But that did not bother me in the slightest. For me, the main thing was to publish my poems. Everything else would work itself out, I consoled myself.

I put an advertisement in the newspaper. "Journal for new humanity and ethical literature seeks young, talented contributors."

Whole bundles of replies arrived. I felt a tingle of pleasure every time I read through a new pile. I felt like a much sought-after man, a power in the land, yes, almost epoch-making. I returned the manuscripts with an accompanying letter in the style of a well-established editor: "We have read your submission with interest but regret that we are unable to make use of it as our next issues are already full up."

I wrote to my friends in Berlin. Jung answered rudely, Oehring not at all, and my letter to Schorsch came back stamped "Not at this address".

I appealed to Thomas Mann. He sent me a postcard with a very friendly greeting and wished the new venture lots of success.

I was over the moon. Selma grumbled; our money had run out.

"It's going forward with giant strides," I exclaimed. I did not listen to her objections. When a man's brain has been seized by an obsession and by stupidity and ambition in equal measure, he becomes reckless. I abruptly stopped going to work at the post office. Once again, I spent every evening in the artist's watering hole, *Simplicissimus*. Everyone had heard about my plans. "What is *Neuland* exactly?" they asked. I made the most idiotic statements, in all earnestness.

"Well, literature," I said for example. "You'll see." My instinct told me that you must avoid looking small. Men of letters are born sloganeers and charlatans. They live by their self-conceit, always looking to outdo their peers.

But I was not quick-witted enough. They looked at me askance. They smiled pityingly. I fell silent. A group of people had already gathered around Hobrecker, who kept him fully occupied. He gave me the slip. Whatever I did, he no longer listened to me and smiled in the same way as all the others when I set out my plans to him. I cursed the arty vermin.

"Bourgeois!" I said contemptuously.

I got into an indescribable rage, but I kept under control and did not want to let him go. But he distanced himself. The group had won. One day my landlady told me that Hobrecker and the whole gang had gone away. In *Simplicissimus* I learned that all the drinking pals had gone to Remscheid to collect Hobrecker's fortune. I retreated into a sulk. That was the end of the magazine and publishing house *Neuland*. The letterheads gathered dust. A friend met me in the street and told me that Hobrecker was back.

"Everyone in Schwabing is living off him at the moment! ... He's gone bonkers, writing cheques all the time ... Even for two or three marks. They're doing the conga round the bank! What a chump! ... Sekt parties every night! A primary school teacher who's gone totally crazy!" he declared.

"So much for your friends," said Selma. I did not rise to the bait. To find some outlet for my rage, I sent the manuscripts, which were still arriving, back to the senders with coarse and nasty accompanying letters.

I thought of the gentleman at the Red Cross again. In the end, I looked him up. His wife received me. She was tall and scraggy and wore a washed-out reform dress. Everything about her, from her plaited hair to her shabby sandals, had something embarrassingly neat and frugal about it. From the moment I first saw her I took an instant dislike to her elderly, skinny face, which seemed Protestant, somehow.

"Indeed, indeed! Yes, how wonderful to make your acquaintance. My husband has told me so much about you. He will be home shortly. In the meantime, come and sit down in the parlour," she gushed, and led me into a small, homely, freshly cleaned room. She smiled, apologized, and carried on dusting the furniture. We chatted. She was very patriotic and spoke constantly about Germany's greatness and invincibility. Among other things, I learned that she was descended from an old Prussian family and had a brother who was an officer on the Western Front.

Then her husband came in. She rushed out to the hall passage and the two whispered to each other busily. This made me feel uneasy.

Now the two of them spoke loudly to each other and finally came in. "So, good for you! You've come at last! ... And what are you doing now?" the man asked in a slightly paternal tone.

"I'm out of work at the moment, so I found the time to look you up," I said with a feigned innocence. He inquired about all my current circumstances and then started to talk about literature again. He went on and on, and I agreed with everything he said.

"Now, the professor that I told you about is at the local university ... He is the trustee for a scholarship. You must make his acquaintance," he said at one point.

That stirred my interest. A glimmer of hope passed through my brain.

The wife brought supper. I had to stay. They offered porridge with stewed apples and green salad. I got stuck in. "Does it taste good?" the wife asked, gratified. I nodded cheerfully and gulped it down with much effort. Nevertheless, I praised the food beyond all measure. The woman gave me another helping and was overjoyed to find such a naturally healthy, unspoilt young man.

Finally the two of them said goodbye to me, deeply moved, and I was relieved to get out on the street.

When I got home, I found a letter from Schorsch, sent from the Dutch border. His wife at the time, the artist Maria Uhla, since dead, had also signed the letter.

The letter contained some mysterious hints and finally said they were coming to Munich. I was delighted and, at the same time, depressed. Yet another upset, I thought.

I wrote a contrite letter to the biscuit factory, asking if I could have my old job back. Yes, they replied. I went straight away. The old people were still there. They quizzed me. I told them a pack of lies.

It was back to the old routine. From early morning to the evening, every day. Just Sunday off. I generally slept the whole day.

When I thought about it, it seemed to me that having once entered this inferno, I must return to it again and again. Walking home late in the evening I was often seized by the desire to grab a knife blindly and run amok. One day a man suddenly spoke to me, out of the blue. I looked up in surprise and stared at him. He was a syndicalist from the "Tat" group. He walked down the street with me. We exchanged some reminiscences, then he turned to the war and the labour movement. "All the leaders have betrayed us and sold us out!" he exclaimed bitterly. "Nothing will change so long as we all stay holed up like cowards ... The bloodhounds won't give up on their war ... The workers must start all over again. We must struggle for every ounce of freedom, there's nothing else for it."

I nodded and kept quiet.

"What difference does it make if we are slaughtered at the front or here at home! ... At least if it's here we'll know why we have been smashed," he added. He sounded angry and fed up. He was the first to tell me about the secret meetings of the radical socialists and urged me to come.

I nodded again. My blood ran warm through my veins. I felt a vague determination. He was expressing my own feelings. The next day – I had only worked three – when Selma tried to get me up, I just lay in bed.

"I've had enough!" I snarled in a strangely harsh tone and turned over in bed. She asked what was up. I gave no answer. She started crying. I did not move. "I can't go on like this," I snapped. "Then at least go to the doctor's and report sick," she moaned.

Yes, if you like, call the biscuit factory ... Then I'll go to the doctor," I replied. She left, feeling glum.

In the afternoon I went to the doctor and was signed off as sick. Shortly after I got back to our flat, there was a knock. When I opened the door, Schorsch and Maria Uhla were standing there. I was beside myself with joy and excitement.

"Hey! Thank God! At last, real people!" I cried, overpowered by emotion, and let them in.

They needed men for the war, whatever shape they were in. Schorsch had been called up by the military authorities four or five times and was always rejected because of his chronic rheumatoid arthritis, but this last time the doctor had simply stated: "Fit for service."

As a result, the two newly-weds had sold everything and escaped with nothing but a full rucksack each. They were arrested at the Dutch border. They could not get back to Berlin, so they came to me.

"Like a trapped bird that just flies from one wall into the next the whole time – that's what this war has brought us to," said Maria Uhla. I looked at her shyly. In fact, she was indeed looking around the room like a helpless bird.

Selma came. We drank tea and chatted some more.

We only parted company late in the night. Shortly afterwards Schorsch found a studio in the city, quite close by. He worked there every day and lived with his wife in a suburb. We often got together and argued.

At the next medical examination in Munich, my friend's conscription was put back six months. We were so delighted at this news that we went out and got stinking drunk.

11.
PORTENTS

At the time, there was already a palpable feeling of war-weariness on the streets. True, the March revolution in Russia had passed without making a major impact. But there was something in the air and in people's heads, a feeling that what was going on over in the unknown Empire of the Steppes was just the beginning. "They are still carrying on with the war, Kerensky's lot," people said, and that basically meant: "A real revolution would put an end to the warfare." But the Emperor of Austria's Sixtus letters, and then the peace moves of the government in Vienna, were made known.[36] The public paid more attention to that.

Meanwhile the great, broad masses of the lower classes dragged on in sullen apathy. The daily queues at the grocery stores got longer and longer. Emaciated faces and ragged figures with hungry eyes were to be seen in these queues. It seemed that everyone was watching everyone else, to make sure they did not get more than their share. What had once been a truly united and open movement now seemed to have crumbled. It was now each man for himself, really, each for himself.

Nobody read the yellow telegram reports from the front any more. People muttered. The whole country seemed exhausted. Nothing was working. The food demonstrations developed into peace rallies. Victory or defeat, heroic deeds, and battles, the Kaiser's words, Hindenburg and 42-centimetre mortars; overnight, such things had all become unimportant.

"Oh aye, yes, let them just get their victories until we are all up to our necks in shit!" people grumbled, and then the talk started.

"In any case! ... If they're touring around winning victories and taking booty? ... How come there's nothing to buy except rabbit meatloaf, turnip and stinking fish? ... Some victory that is! It's nothing but a swindle! Complete and utter crap!" reasoned a man on the street, and everyone nodded. People were especially furious about the poor quality of the beer, the King, and the Prussians. "The King is the biggest profiteer of the lot!" cursed a woman in the dairy. "He delivers milk from his estates to the north of Germany because he gets more money ... The moneybags are all that really matter to those fine gentlemen ... They're not mithered if we peg out."[37]

---

[36] Prince Sixtus of Bourbon Parma, brother-in-law of Kaiser Karl I of Austria, and an officer in the Belgian army, was the intermediary in an attempt to secure a separate peace with France.

[37] The King of Bavaria, Ludwig III, was mocked as the *Millibauer* (dairy farmer). His wealth came largely from his wife's estates in Austria-Hungary.

"It's his old dear who's to blame, and no one else!" said one of the others, referring to the Queen. "She's the one what wears the trousers! ... She rules the whole pigsty, the daft apeth just says aye 'n' amen. He's just a waste of space ..."

You could hear the same things every day. The rumours that went from mouth to mouth would make your hair stand on end. We heard about entire armies with VD, hidden victims of gas attacks and mangled bodies.

Hunger even penetrated to some degree into the ranks of the well-heeled. It was the talk in every beerhall; it was a spectre, unseen, but everywhere tangible. And yet in Munich a relatively large proportion of the people still had things that were now unheard of in North Germany. Everyone hoarded as much as possible. There were regular pilgrimages to the villages. Everything could be had on the black market, and deserters were no longer uncommon.

I started reading the newspapers again. I took much more of an interest in politics. News reached us of the first mutinies of the High Seas Fleet.

"Now the revolution is starting!" I said to Schorsch, full of romantic enthusiasm. Then I told him about the meetings of the radical socialists.

"The Germans will never make a revolution. There are spies everywhere," my friend thought.

"Spies, what nonsense! If everybody rises up, they don't have enough prisons to lock up all the rebels," I replied.

That evening I made my way to the meeting room at the pub that the syndicalist had told me about. On my way there I thought about my entire life since being discharged from the army. Looking back, I found nothing bright and beautiful in it. I felt excitement building up inside. Bitterness and rage gripped me and finally a single, vague passion for revenge.

"Never mind bread, peace and freedom. That's all rubbish!" flashed through my mind. Just go for it and settle accounts with everyone who has made your life a misery.

"Down with them!" I snarled, grinding my teeth and feeling the sweat breaking out all over my body. "Down with the lot of them."

I entered the pub feeling resolute. Thinking that such meetings would have to be held in secret and, if possible, under a false name, I cautiously approached the landlord, who was sitting at the table by the stove with a few guests and playing a friendly game of tarot. I was astonished when he said very loudly and without further ado: "The Independents are in the room next door. It's already started."

That already cooled my excitement a little. These revolutionaries were too open and seemed to be rather harmless.

I quickly went up to the wooden partition separating the room from the public bar. As I opened the door several heads were raised. They looked at me suspiciously. A few familiar faces nodded to me in greeting. They were syndicalists and members of the former "Tat" group, free thinkers and sundry intellectuals, a fair number of working-class women and the odd soldier or two. Everyone was sitting there calmly looking at the table in front, behind which stood a none-too-tall man with flowing grey hair and a similar beard and moustache, making a speech. He wore a pince-nez in front of his small, rolling eyes. Every now and then he underlined some sentence with a short gesture of his arm or stuck his forefinger in the smoke-filled air like a schoolteacher. He had a rather monotone and slightly squeaky voice but spoke very fluently. His clothes were untidy, and everything gave the impression of a retired school inspector or professor. Thinking about it, I remembered an illustrated history of the German revolution of 1848. It had pictures of similar figures.

"Who is the speaker?" I quietly asked my neighbour.

"Eisner," came the reply. I searched through my memory, going over all the revolutionaries and friends from my anarchist days but no, I must be mistaken. Liebknecht, Bebel, Rosa Luxemburg, Landauer, Mühsam: they all belonged to the radical socialists, but Eisner? What had I walked into?

I was already getting suspicious again. I listened carefully. No – the man sounded very revolutionary.

"Hear! Hear! Quite right!" people interjected here and there. The man raised his voice. His upper body shook: "In 1914, German social democracy failed. The proletariat was scandalously and cruelly betrayed by its leaders. The bloodbath started. Now, however, we can see the first signs of an awakening! All threats, everything that they are using to suppress any revolutionary will – martial law, incarceration, shootings and all other ordinances – will no longer be enough to check or destroy this determination of the masses! The gentlemen of the General Staff and the wise judges round the green baize table at the Reich Chancellery are making a mistake if they assume that the mutinies flaring up everywhere, the strikes and demonstrations of the proletariat are just a peace movement. This is not mere opposition, comrades, it is more – it is, we must all be clear about this, a movement that will culminate in the Revolution!"

The speaker wiped the sweat from his brow. There was resounding applause on all sides. I perked up.

"Expropriation!" yelled the syndicalist suddenly from some corner.

"Sabotage in all the factories," seconded another. "Yes!! Quite right!" rang out from all present. These strange words bothered me.

"Refuse to obey military orders! Just refuse to carry on!" I shouted out, rather hesitantly, and earned immediate applause. People looked at me in a way that inspired confidence. That made me happy.

Eisner had sat down. Chaotic chatter followed, then a bell rang calling us to order.

In the discussion, it was mostly elderly workers who spoke, and a few women. They spoke simply and bluntly. The women grew passionate and made bold demands, whereas the men were more reserved. The stock phrases they used were lost on us. We ignored them. But they spoke openly, full of rage. It warmed my blood. I felt a thrill.

From then on, I went nearly every week to the evening meetings of the USPD. Everyone in the city knew about them. I met more and more people that I knew there. I no longer thought about taking a job. I waited from day to day for the revolution and wrote poems about it. There were whole hours and days when I was in a constant state of excitement. There were more and more irksome arguments with Selma, but I now got over them more easily.

Admittedly, when I was on my own, I often felt really miserable. That's all very well and good, I told myself, they go on and on about the impending revolution, but nothing actually happens. It's always a meeting that comes to an end, everyone goes their separate ways, and everything returns to normal.

Days of depression came. I don't know if other people of my age had the same experience at the time, but one thing was clear to me: the revolution was actually something I could not fully imagine, it was in a sense a situation that the world was moving towards inexorably, but hardly anyone seemed to have a clear idea of what should happen after this irruption.

One day I had a heated discussion on this subject with Schorsch. I always raved about the need to use violence and "let loose". But he immediately confronted me with cool common sense: "Yes, but what do you imagine? ... Do you perhaps think that if there is a revolution, you will no longer need to take a job? ..."

I stalled, not knowing how to answer.

"You will have to work, just as you do now ... The struggle, for the time being, is to take political power ... By the time things have been worked through in detail, perhaps we'll already be on the scrapheap ... In the meantime, we simply have to keep agitating." That sobered me up. I considered looking for another job.

Then something unexpected happened.

One Sunday morning we were lying in bed and I said to Selma, rather fractiously: "Go back to sleep! Sleeping's the only thing worth doing! Why do we have to irritate each other every 15 minutes! That's all there is to it. When we are awake, we just annoy and disgust each other! ... Go back to sleep! ... There's nothing else to do until the revolution comes."

"It won't change a thing!" Selma reminded me, once more. Then, all of a sudden, there was a knock at the door, and someone called "Herr Graf! Graf!" At first, I did not respond. But finally, since the knocking went on and on, I quickly pulled on my trousers and opened the door. The gentleman from the Red Cross was standing there. I myself was completely dumbfounded and forced myself to smile.

"So sorry, I had to work late through the night," I said, excusing myself. The man was cheerful, came in and said, rather emotionally: "Graf! I have some good news for you. The professor has read your poems. He likes them very much. You are to receive a scholarship, which he administers, for three months."

He looked at me as if he wanted to be sure that the news had sunk in. At first, I did not know what sort of expression I should make, and stammered almost gormlessly:

"Ha, oh yes, that is really, my God, thank you! That's some kind of miracle!"

"No Graf, no. You are a great poet," the man said, encouragingly, and told me that the professor had "devoured" my poem, *The Twenty Year Old*. "It is difficult to judge a man's talent," he went on, "but the professor thinks it's drama ... You would make a good dramatist. You should give it a try."

I smiled. He smiled. I could think of nothing to say. I was to receive one hundred marks a month. I thought of our poverty and Selma, and nodded at everything the man said. It was ice cold in the flat. I stood there only in shirtsleeves and did not dare to put on more clothes. I already heard Selma in the next room. I was freezing and the gentleman got a runny nose while talking non-stop about Kleist and poetry, ethics and everything under the sun.

Now and again he came right up close to me and looked into my eyes. Again and again I mustered renewed interest in what he was saying. An hour passed. I felt utterly wretched; my stomach felt like my throat had been cut and I realized that Selma was freezing as she waited in the next room.

I stammered repeatedly: "Yes, that's very good! Very good! ... Yes of course, we'll meet up ... Yes, my God, Kleist! ... Do you know what? ... I think I really will write a play ... Absolutely. Hm, yes. Kleist, really. That could only happen in Germany – yes, hm ..."

My mind was elsewhere by now. Finally, he went. At last! I burst into the bedroom. Selma was standing there, shivering. Her clothes were in the living room and she had not dared to come out. And she did not want to stay in bed. She was crying.

"Stop crying ... ... What could I do? Did you hear, I am going to get one hundred marks per month." She nodded and coughed on and on.

"I was also freezing cold, but you should be pleased, everything's going to get better, stop crying, can't you see!" She nodded and tried to smile. I quickly lit the fire.

"Now we've got our heads above water!" I cried from time to time, while we drank tea.

"You're acting as if the hundred marks were a fortune!" she said, dampening my enthusiasm. "My God, admittedly it will help us out, but it's not that much ..."

"Yes," I said at last, care-worn and cynical: "It would have made more sense to stay in bed. You can't get worked up so long as you're still asleep."

The next day I went to the bank and cashed the cheque that the man from the Red Cross had given me. In the evening, I found a note in the letterbox saying I should come to the university the day after next, and get to know the professor after his lecture. Triumph and curiosity were both running wild. I rushed round to Schorsch and told him.

"Well, write a play then!" he said.

"Yes, but, my God, I don't have any material! ...

"It's a devil of a problem! ... Something's got to happen! ... A plot! A plot!" I exclaimed, but in the end, I added, rather more airily:

"Still, a lot can happen in three months! Something will occur to me."

On the appointed evening I met the man from the Red Cross punctually outside the professor's lecture room at the university. After a short while the students poured out, and a gentleman in modest, neat clothes came up to us. He bore a strong resemblance to Nietzsche.

"This is Herr Graf, professor," said the man from the Red Cross. I bowed my head awkwardly and held out my hand to the professor. I was overcome with the kind of shyness and excitement a child feels at confirmation. But the professor soon shooed it all away. I took an instant liking to him, as soon as he spoke. There was a kind of reassuring frankness and soundness in his face. His manner was nothing like what I had imagined in a professor. We went out on the street and talked. The professor spoke about my poems with an unfamiliar respect. This all sounded foreign to me.

"Did you know, Herr Graf, you are very creative ... People like you are very, very rare these days, and the war is robbing us of our best talent," he said, "there is an elemental force ... It all rings so true, so true ... Your poems really moved me. *The Twenty Year Old*, my dear Herr Graf, that is pure drama! ... Just as it is – pure drama! I believe, that is where your talent lies, in the dramatic ..."

It all sounded like he spoke from the heart. I felt embarrassed, but a peculiar emotion was growing inside. For the first time in my life, someone was praising me. I gained a faint feeling of self-confidence and admitted to myself, you must have some ability, if a professor says something like that, and comes to your support! I felt like a well-behaved schoolboy, receiving more praise than he really deserves from his teacher. I hardly dared to look up and was scrambling to find the right words of thanks. I talked all kinds of nonsense. I am sure it sounded awkward, as I kept repeating: "thank you", then I expressed my intention to write a play, but in such a way that it sounded like a piece of homework.

The gentleman from the Red Cross had left. We walked on a little further together.

"Herr Graf, no man can become a poet ... He simply *is* a poet," the professor said sincerely, and looked me in the eyes. "You are one; I could see that as soon as I read the first poem ... You are still so young ... You will go far ..."

I literally glowed, wanting to cry one moment and cheer out loud the next. But I managed to pull myself together with some effort and said with a faint tremor: "Yes, hopefully I will do it all to your satisfaction, Herr Professor ..."

I was pleased with myself for expressing it so nicely. But the professor smiled and countered this vigorously: "No, no, for heaven's sake! No, don't let me influence you Herr Graf! ... No, you shouldn't do that under any circumstances, it will only damage you ..."

"Er, all right then, yes, thank you, Herr Professor ... Thank you very much," I said, stammering again, and we shook hands.

I strolled carefree through the murky streets, already thick with the evening fog. I breathed freely. But it did not last long.

"My God, a play! A play?!" I muttered under my breath, and became unsettled again. I immediately bought two newspapers in the hope of reading about some tragic case among the crime reports. But I found nothing of any use. I was incredibly annoyed that so little was going on in the world.

Over the next few days I looked everywhere for subject-matter for a play and became increasingly desperate, because it was so hard to get started. I was determined to do the job well. Then, at last, I remembered the discussion evenings of the Independents. Of course, I thought, you can get something there! That's a real possibility, for sure. So this is where I focused my attention.

Sometimes, when my idiocies, awkwardness and all my confusion came to mind, I was overcome by an oppressive feeling of discontent. I wanted to be alone and untroubled, but every hour, every minute, the whole world seemed to be pressing in and tearing me to pieces. But from time to time I chanced to recall the professor's words and I repeated them to myself:

"No man can become a poet ... He simply *is* a poet! And you are a poet, Herr Graf!"

12.
A VAGUE CRISIS

I wanted some peace and quiet, to set aside the past and present, and sit down and write. I wanted to ignore the people around me, to stand aloof, you might say, not participate in anything and live my life untouched by events. Yes, I wanted to become a poet.

Somebody had said, I was a poet. If that was the case, then my actions would be judged only by the amount of effort I put into them.

Every person understands things only in ways that work in their favour. When, at that time, I grasped the meaning of the Marxist phrase, "mankind is a product of social relations", I interpreted this almost as an absolution, and at times as unrestrained freedom. And now it was precisely the same. I interpreted Stirner's irrefutable renunciation from *The Ego and His Own* in a quite specific and personal way in my own favour with regard to the enterprise on which I was embarking: "What is not supposed to be my concern! First and foremost, the good cause, then God's cause, the cause of mankind, of truth, of freedom, of humanity, of justice; further, the cause of my people, my prince, my fatherland; finally, even the cause of Mind, and a thousand other causes. Only my cause is never to be my concern."

I automatically fell into a stubborn resistance against everything. What should I care about our poverty? Or that Selma was expecting a child, and what the future held? What did I care about the war and the revolution? What had it all to do with me?

I wrote poems. At times I shut myself off entirely. And was overjoyed at a sound or a sentence.

It was just that I could not leave the flat and think of nothing. That was not an option. The moment I stepped out into the street I was overcome by a thousand things that made me restless. There was nothing I could do about it; I was entangled in it all.

It had now reached the point that I would go out when Selma came home. I attended the meetings of the USPD. They had become more animated. All sorts of people were coming together: workers, deserters, pacifist poets and impatient women, party members and instinctive rebels.

Out on the streets, the slowly rising ferment seemed to hang in the air. The insurrection could come any day. There were bread-riots outside the city hall; women screamed; it was a terrible din. The police arrived and dispersed the crowds. Abuse rained down on them. Dark clouds gathered over the housing blocks.

"Revolution! Meet terror with terror!" shouted a young man, who was arrested. The crowd charged against the police in an attempt to free him. Naked sabres flashed, and a tumultuous roar surged down the streets and side-alleys.

The revolutionaries worked feverishly and full of renewed hope. Nobody was any longer intimidated by the numerous arrests. Everybody spoke out, and everybody made the boldest demands; insurrection was written on every face. The revolution must come. It *must!*

"A general strike and revolution at home!" demanded the Independents and the Spartacists.

"Destroy all the machines! Strike! Just stop all work!" I bawled.

"Anarchist!" the crowd threw back at me. I did not listen. I repeated my call.

"Watch out, they'll nab you tomorrow!" said a Spartacist as we parted.

"Why should I care!" was my answer.

"It's bound to kick off now! It's bound to!"

Only when I got back to the flat did I calm down.

Yes, what I really wanted to do was to write and be left alone!

I often visited the professor. And then the Red Cross man. The professor was a lecturer at the university, led a conservative private life, gave his lectures on Byron, Goethe or Ibsen every evening, came from a solid bourgeois Catholic family in Franconia, impressed me as balanced in temperament and had – so it seemed – firm convictions. It was soothing to be in his company. I liked him. He was well over 50 and spoke to me in a manner that was typical in those circles. He was not actually opposed to anything. He was one of those persons who never need to say explicitly what they reject because that is already obvious. He never forced his ideas on me. But all of his utterances clearly had an educational intent. He spoke on all subjects with dignity, and of the war and the Fatherland with reverence and respect. There was nothing artificial; everything seemed to have matured with him.[38]

Every day, the man from the Red Cross sat in his warm room in the central office, and in the evening, he visited the lecture theatres and prepared for his doctoral exam. He often picked me up and took me to the lectures, because he and the professor had said: "Take advantage of our public institutions, Herr Graf." I sat next to him in a large lecture theatre, between other male and female students, and gazed in deadly seriousness at the learned man standing behind his lectern, holding forth on his views about this or that intellectual question. Whether, for instance, Goethe adhered to an ancient Germanic paganism, or if in his *Faust* he had acknowl-

---

[38] The professor in question was Roman Woerner (1863-1945), an expert on Ibsen and translator of Sophocles.

edged a profound Christian belief. I made every effort to listen, but very little penetrated my distracted mind.

Perhaps the insurrection was already breaking out on the streets, right now; I was overcome with impatience. In here, nothing is spoken about the tumult raging outside, or all the things that must be sorted out. It seemed that everyone here was well fed and led an untroubled life.

Then I pulled myself together and listened more attentively. When I first visited the University, I was shy. I only dared enter a room with the Red Cross man. Gradually though, I put this bashfulness behind me and sought out other lecture theatres.

It was the same everywhere. At most, this or that professor had a deeper or more high-pitched voice, was more or less clear in his pronunciation. Here, one of them talked for an hour about the turn of phrase in a Middle High German poem; there, another held forth about the psychological principle of Nietzsche; a third lectured on belief in God and the worship of gods in antiquity and in the present, and finally, a fourth read texts about criminal law and its foundations in the modern nation of culture. I studied the speaker and looked round at the students, male and female. It occurred to me that all their faces seemed alike. They squeezed onto the benches, sometimes had a sheet of paper or a notepad in front of them and took notes. Every now and then they stamped or shuffled with their feet like naughty schoolchildren, then they went off again with their satchels.

I looked at them more closely and then I thought about the career path of such people. So, after a couple of years, will these sorts also become professors and lecture from behind a lectern? And these ones? They will become judges and sit in judgment on us. Others will become priests, preach and hold mass; others still will enter the civil service, starting at a low level, make a good marriage and be promoted, will be given a title and high rank, and they will end up as our rulers.

The University, then, is the establishment where you listen, year in and year out.

That's how sophisticated, high society comes into being. The workers work, the peasants plough and harvest – but it is these people who say what is right and what is wrong, what is legal and illegal, moral and immoral. In a word, these people set the tone and they command.

They work on the "spirit" here. People learn how to remodel common knowledge, to make every word and term so ambiguous that ordinary people become bewildered by it and feel deference, and even more than that – yes, an indefinable fear.

And the end result? This society makes them docile.

"You know what? Give me a second-rate rag-and-bone man any day rather than all of these students, who are sent money from home every month and know next to nothing, or nothing at all, about real life!" I said to the Red Cross man. He started lecturing me.

"But Herr Graf!" he cried. "Herr Graf, you are a rationalist! Your outlook is out and out mechanistic! You must remember, the University is a Commonwealth of the Spirit! ... The University is the highest moral arbiter!" And now he became fervent: "For instance, in Luther's time it was the rallying point for the most morally enlightened from the entire German nation! ... That must be the same today, and as a rule, it is."

"Yes, but that costs a fortune ... A poor man can't get in there at all," I answered bluntly and in all bitterness, and continued: "The world will go on even without this University and all these fine phrases! ... The most morally enlightened, you say? ... It's easy for that lot inside to be good and cultured and decent and God knows what else, they are not hungry and have the best prospects."

The man literally laid into me. "But Herr Graf, you must bear in mind, man does not live by bread alone, we are a sovereign state, a nation!" he cried, before taking me back to his flat.

"State, nation? ... These are just fixations! The inventions of the ruling class! All we need is the common man!" I blustered in reply.

The man's wife now joined in. He started off about Kleist again, the moral core of the nation, the German soul. "Ah, soul!" I growled, suddenly disgruntled and contemptuous. "It's always the same story, you must have soul, you must have character ... I never learned about these two things."

"But Herr Graf, you write poetry! The poet is the most soulful of all!" The man had me cornered.

"Oh, I just want to write light fiction," I said, for the lack of a better response, and partly out of pure rage. He smiled at me and his wife shook her head, forgivingly.

"Then why do you write poetry?" the man asked.

"Oh, that's just practice," I replied in the same tone, "I can't do the other thing yet."

I wanted to clear out, but the people started lecturing me over and over again. The woman had the newspaper in her hand, opened it, read out a report about a small advance of our troops on the Western Front, and stammered: "Oh my God ... How awful, the ninth company. I wonder if anything has happened to my brother."

I glanced at the front page, I hurriedly read, in bold type:

"Revolution in Russia! Kerensky Overthrown! Petrograd and Moscow in the Hands of the Revolutionaries! Workers' and Peasants' Government in Russia!"

I was electrified. I snatched the newspaper and stared at the report, such that the pair almost backed off.

"Wow!" I shouted abruptly. "The revolution! Revolution!" I no longer noticed anything else.

"The revolution is breaking out! All over the world! Everything will change," I said, as if intoxicated. "A new era has dawned."

"In Russia!" the woman said, and her face hardened.

"You are a romantic, Graf!" said the man.

I rushed out and down the stairs, chased down the street, broke into a sweat and panted for breath.

"Revolution! Revolution!" I hummed, roared, sang, whistled, gasped as I crashed into Schorsch's studio. "Yee-hee, now it's starting ... And away with the universities and all that spiritual shit! Revolution!"

Schorsch was already in the know. We read the reports feverishly. It was quite a while before we got back on track.

"Now it has to start here, and soon, perhaps today already, or to-morrow," I exulted.

"You," said Schorsch, more subdued, as if he was afraid someone was listening. "Jung has written ... A man is coming, probably a deserter ... We should put him up."

"And?" I said, half curious, half indifferent. "Then it'll be fine, I'd better stay out of it, to make sure the informers don't become suspicious, otherwise they'll get hold of us as well as the man. Let's wait and see."

"Yes, that would be wisest," my friend said. I went.

It was all quiet on the streets. But a fire was blazing inside of me. I kept thinking of the faces in the University, how they crouched there, arrogant and oblivious at the same time. I pictured to myself all that would happen if the insurrection suddenly broke out. I thought of the professor, the Red Cross man and his wife, and all those people who talked and talked about the Fatherland and the war and Hindenburg and the Kaiser and Ludendorff, as if they were from a higher realm.

As far as I can remember, no one in our family has ever had a pro-nounced fondness for the Fatherland. Law, patriotism and war fever were all alien to us. With the exception of my older brother Max, none of my brothers or sisters has ever had any respect for bureaucracy, the military and state institutions; on the contrary, we found all this more or less ri-diculous and absurd. My mother did not hate anyone so much as the vil-lage policeman, and she instinctively lied when someone came into the house and tried to question her about our pranks. Even my father, who faithfully and honestly fought in the campaign of 1870-71, and came back with a paralysed hand, the Iron Cross, his feet swollen and loose teeth, even he, who thoroughly enjoyed telling anecdotes about the war and sol-diers' pranks, even he, who had great respect all his life for Bismarck, even he hated nothing more than militarist, disciplinarian patriotism. This aver-sion to any uniformed pomposity almost ran in his blood. It went so far with him that it extended to people such as the schoolteacher, the captain of the veterans' association, the mayor and lawyers, in short, all the people who exuded the odour of officialdom. As far as I remember, he visited the town council meeting only once and, on that occasion, he attacked the mayor with such unprecedented personal insults that the pot-bellied, red-haired farmer literally burst into tears. As far as my father was concerned, anyone who occupied an official position counted more or less as a bogus layabout, who pursues a fraudulent existence at the expense of the local community or the nation by means that are beyond the reach of the law. Nothing disgusted him more than to occupy a post of honour that commands public respect; and yet, he not only valued popularity very highly, but also sought it. He was not in the least bit curmudgeonly. Nor was he spiteful, quarrelsome or malevolent. Above all, he loved cheerful, loud and completely uninhibited sociability; he could entertain and be truly charming. But whenever he encountered any official, his cheerful disposition immediately vanished. If there were any opportunity to play a trick on anyone, he was up for it. He even looked for opportunities himself, and I know of cases in which he gave us young ones and the parish labourer, Schmalzer, a whole mark, or paid for the journeyman's beer, if we had got up to some mischief. He took a fiendish pleasure whenever we pulled off some prank.

I must admit that I inherited a great deal of this tendency; when Max started schooling me, hate became its bedfellow. A hate that could not be extinguished. And since that time I could not, with the best will in the world, imagine things such as Fatherland, militarism, soldiers, war and patriotism other than in connection with what I remembered of my brother.

Books and other sources of enlightenment, my whole mental development and the war itself, only served to clarify these vague perceptions.

I completely forgot to write the play, even though this task had gradually become a duty, a fixed idea, an obsession. I talked about it with the professor all the time, but I did not write a single line. I was immersed in the events. Coming out of the evening meetings, people said: "Well, if I am nowhere to be found tomorrow, you will know that I have been arrested." When I came home late at night, Selma woke up and moaned.

"Man alive, the revolution just has to break out any day now!" I said to console her. She writhed in pain. She found it difficult to breathe, coughed and threw up.

"When does your grant run out? You promised to write a play?" she reminded me.

"Yes! Yes, of course! I'll write it already! In no time at all!" I defended myself. I cursed the professor and the whole world. I beat my brains out, but nothing occurred to me. Two and a half months had already passed, and after the third, the money would stop. I groaned heavily.

My mind was abuzz with impressions. A complete mess.

"It all comes down to that idiotic university, everyone there is crazy about poets and plays. All year long they listen to nothing but Goethe and Faust and Schiller and Kleist and plays!" I argued under my breath. Then I flung myself into bed. I thought of Stirner again. But that got me nowhere, either.

Loud and pathetic, I suddenly shouted out in the dark: "Nothing can save us but the revolution!"

"This is the man from Jung," Schorsch said one day, entering my flat with a stranger. I promptly blocked the outer padded door, bolted the inner and drew the curtains.

The man was a little astonished at this and smiled in amusement.

"Informers! Informers!" Schorsch and I murmured.

"You're a deserter and I suppose you're looking for a hidey-hole?" I asked the stranger, who was still smiling, straight out. He nodded. Then he told me his story. He had been at the front. Both his arms had been pierced by grenade shrapnel; after he had recovered, he was considered fit for garrison duty and had served in a typing pool in some Berlin barracks or other. He had told his sergeant major three or four times: "I've had enough ... I'm doing a bunk." The sergeant major didn't believe it, and the man finally escaped to Munich with a forged furlough pass. Jung had given him our address. The night before he stayed with another acquaintance, and now he needed somewhere else to stay.

"Then we must find a bedsit or a flat," I said after we had discussed the problem at length and turned to the stranger again: "So what's your name?"

"Pegu," he replied, with an ambiguous smile.

"Of course, that's not his real name ... Actually it's Glaser, but that's not it either ... It's all the same," Schorsch broke in, and we settled on "Pegu". Eventually, we got up. Pegu put on my hat, I put on Schorsch's, and Schorsch Pegu's. We then left the house one by one. Each of us went separate ways. We agreed never to meet, except on the street.

Without telling Selma about this business, I started looking for a room or a flat over the following days. I did not go to any more discussion evenings with the Independents, to make sure the police did not watch me.

I met Pegu each day. Over time, we became friends.

"It is difficult to find anything," I said after roughly six days, losing hope, and the two of us trotted on, depressed. Then an unexpected stroke of luck helped us out. In the distance, I saw someone I had known in Munich before the war, someone I knew was in the asylum at Eglfing at the time.

"You go on," I said hurriedly to Pegu, and ran after the man.

He was called Friedrich Wunder and had been my bitterest enemy for a year and a half. When I was at Haar he had been at Eglfing as a civilian mental case, and he was allowed to go to Munich once a week. I once gave him money for cigarettes. He did not get them, spent the money, and never showed his face again. When I finally caught up with him, I gave him a good slapping. Since then it was impossible to get anywhere near him. [39]

This was because Friedrich Wunder not only had deep mental scars. He was a completely feather-brained person and an aesthete who could be flustered by the most straightforward question. He went around, no, he wandered about like a parody of a long-forgotten bohemian time. He generally muttered to himself, and when he actually got together with someone he knew, he endlessly recited poems by George and Rilke, spoke of Michelangelo, of the Pre-Raphaelites, and in times of emotional exuberance believed he was an apparition like some new Savonarola. You could already see in his face a deep-rooted hatred of the bourgeois and the hypochondriac's fear of everyone he met. His small, shrunken, dilapidated body was always wrapped in crumpled bits of clothing that were far too large. His overcoat, which must have come from a real fatso, hung pathetically around him, his trousers were too long and reminded you of an accordion, his shoes were several sizes too big and worn out, his tie sagged somewhere between the scruff of his neck and his hair, above the dirty black paper collar, and on top of it all, his hat, which was far too small, stuck to his dishevelled, greasy hair.

When war broke out, he was found out on the street early one morning half frozen and starving hungry, so they took him to an asylum. He was a semi-skilled photographer by trade, but at the time he felt compelled to make batik rugs and spent every penny on candles. It was said that he had already hoarded a huge store of wax candles, which he guarded as precious treasures.

He was also carrying a pack of them under his arm this time and was running along like a weasel.

"Hey! Wunder!" I shouted cheerily, as I finally got within four paces of him, and went right up to him.

"Ha-a-a-aha-ha, you mean old skinflint!" he gurgled, and gaped at me like a wounded calf. His watery, protruding eyes leered at me suspiciously. He just stood there.

"You know what, Wunder, that was stupid of me to hit you that time, come on, we're good," I went on with unflinching friendliness and then I asked: "Are you still at Eglfing?"

"Ha-a-a-a-ha-a-ha-ha! Yes, at Eglfing!" he laughed and nodded, pigheadedly.

"Listen, can I register you in Munich?" I asked straight out, taking no further notice of his laughter. Now he looked offended. He thought I

---

[39] What is not clear from the text is that Eglfing is a hamlet attached to the village of Haar; Graf and Friedrich Wunder were in different buildings of the same institution.

was making fun of him. I gave him a cigarette. Kindness always came a surprise to him, so now he opened up a little.

"You see, you're doing batik and might want to make a career of it one day ... I know a man who might make his flat available, see? ... No need to be suspicious ... It's quite true. If you like, I'll even register the flat in your name. What do you say?"

But he didn't believe a word and broke into frenzied laughter, smirking like a clown.

"Ha-a-a-aha-haha, you sneering knucklehead, ha-a-ha-ha-ha!" he grumbled. "Of course, Fritz Wunder has to play the clown again, ha-ha-ha, knucklehead ...!"

I now became flustered myself and it took a real effort to appear good-natured. I casually asked how old he was and got his date of birth out of him.

"Fritz! Come on Fritz!" I exclaimed when that worked, suddenly changing my manner and slapping him on the back with brutal violence, giving him a start. "Fritz, you're just incredible! ... You're amazing! ... You're much greater than Savonarola! ... You're like a living shithouse, with a poem by Rilke inside ... Fritzi, I love you!"

All this had the intended effect: namely, he now hated me even more than ever. I left him standing there and ran off.

A few days earlier I had found a bedsit to let down a side-street. So now I went in, rented it, or so I said, for a friend and filled out the registration form as follows: "Friedrich Wunder, photographer, born 24 December 1891 in Munich. Nationality, Bavarian."

"My friend will come in a day or two," I said to the concierge, and went off to find Pegu.

"Your name is Fritz Wunder, you are a photographer, a Bavarian born on the twenty-fourth of December in Munich ... Come quick, I've found your digs," I said, and he followed me, undecided, still half doubting.

On the same day we bought some sticks of furniture at junk shops, and in the evening, we sorted out Pegu's bedsit.

"It's all fine and dandy ... Just remember to grease the concierge's palm with some beer money and keep quiet ... Don't do anything to draw attention," I advised, and left him. The next day I went round to Schorsch to give my happy report.

"Let's hope it works," said Maria Uhla.

Schorsch roared with laughter when I told him about Wunder. He also knew him in the old days.

After that Pegu and I met up every day. He was a shy and sometimes even childlike person, but with a precise frame of mind. I read my poems to him. He offered an incredibly clear critique. We argued a lot and

241

he gradually threw off his depression. After a while, we even dared to go into pubs. He really didn't seem to pose any risk. Early in the evening my comrade crept into his hidey-hole, because at night-time you could be stopped. One stupid mishap and all would be lost.

At the time, the revolutionaries got a new boost and the war-weary masses became more hopeful. The Russian radio broadcast, "To All", and Wilson's Fourteen Points were echoing around the world.

The Russians declared for a general peace without annexations and for the self-determination of the peoples, and the American President proclaimed the League of Nations as a cure-all.

"Peace! Peace!" was the daily hope. "Peace! Peace!" swelled to an impatient clamour. The German delegation travelled to Brest-Litovsk.

Things obstinately refused to settle down there. Germany made claims on the border states, General Hoffman reinterpreted "without annexations" as "without forced annexations". The delegations returned home and received new instructions. The papers talked about "a broad *cordon sanitaire* as protection against bolshevism" and even the Majority SPD got upset about it.

The revolutionaries agitated tirelessly. The negotiators met again at Brest-Litovsk and now for the first time, Leon Trotsky's revolutionary speeches rang out across the eastern frontier and into Germany.

At Eisner's meeting I had heard of preparations for a strike. There was to be a general strike throughout the Reich in January. I went to Pegu.

"Nonsense!" he cried. You needn't go to Eisner and his lot.

"We have other work to do." He showed me a manuscript. It was Prince Lichnowsky's memorandum, which was being circulated at the time as a secret typed script – and only among those known within pacifist circles.[40] He gave me money and I hired a typewriter. In the following days he dictated to me Lichnowsky's *My Mission to London*.

"This must be printed and distributed among the masses before the strike, without fail ... . We need to find a printer," he said.

"That will expose you, so take care," I warned him, but he was insistent.

"The masses must find out how they have been deceived," he replied.

"Rubbish! ... Deceived? ... That's beside the point ... The lies are coming from all sides ... The pamphlet is too long for a propaganda piece. Nobody will read it ... We'll have to do it differently," I said. "Now that eve-

---

[40] Karl Max, Prince Lichnowsky (1860-1928) had been German Ambassador to London at the outbreak of the First World War. He was the only senior German diplomat to raise objections to Germany's efforts to provoke an Austro-Serbian war, arguing that Britain would intervene and tip the balance against the Central Powers.

rything is in motion, we have to spread rumours, the wildest rumours ... The masses must be roused to the extent that even the stupidest philistine becomes completely sceptical ... Then comes absolute passivity ... That's all that matters! ... Don't rise up against the war, simply refuse to support it, that's all ..."

"Tolstoy is no use now," objected my comrade.

"Tolstoy! ... He speaks for all eternity! ... But what I said is true: if nobody carries on, it's over," I insisted. He just kept shaking his head and smiled in a rather strange way.

My friend was no idle windbag. He resisted any deviation from his intentions. We soon discovered that he tried to execute his schemes systematically and with unswerving resolution. Yet something always held his resolution in check.

Everything was a problem – no matter how big, or how trivial. He could throw himself blindly into anything, even if there were thousands upon thousands of obstacles in his path. He wanted to deal with every issue directly and cleanly, grappled with it at once with his penetrating mind and then got caught up in more and more confusion because every hour and every minute threw up new challenges.

He called me a "nihilist" and took the view that such people would play no part in the actual revolution; they were just useful for a while as propagandists.

"We have to get on with it! And get the pamphlet out! It'll all kick off soon!" he said, all the time dictating, and drove me on. Finally, the manuscript was ready.

That same evening I returned to the USPD's meeting, against Pegu's advice, where Ernst Toller, who had recently fled from Heidelberg, made an inflammatory speech against the war. Highly charged, ecstatic, he screamed out his feelings with wild gesticulations and a distorted face. He trembled feverishly and foamed at the mouth.

He seemed all blackness to me. Deep, dark eyes, black, thick hair, beautiful eyebrows and a rather yellowish face.

"Your mothers!" he began – again and again – and painted the horrors of war in the fiery colours of poetical rhetoric: "Your brothers and sisters!"

He swept everyone off their feet. A few women wept or went into a wild frenzy. Everyone pitched in with:

"Down with the war! Send Ludendorff to the gallows!" We all left aroused and ready to act.

"Let everyone do whatever is in his power," Eisner had told us.

Toller travelled with me on the tram for a short stretch. He talked almost on the fly; his words simply gushed out.

"Do you also write?" he asked.

"Yes, all sorts," I replied, and then I told him about a play that was already at the press. He had a small, blond girlfriend with him, who gazed up at him continually in dumb admiration. I shook hands with the pair of them and got out.

The next day I went to the printer who had once agreed to print *Neuland*. I discussed the matter with him and handed over the manuscript. The man glanced at the title and looked at me.

"How many copies do you want?" he asked.

I did not answer immediately. The printer looked at me suspiciously. My awkwardness was making me feel uneasy inside.

"Oh, two or three thousand copies perhaps," I said, adding, "As I said, I cannot tell you the exact amount just yet ..."

"I first have to calculate the cost," the man said, and looked at the pamphlet again. "And it's really an educational text?" he asked.

"Yes ... A report," I told him.

"Good. The day after tomorrow then," the printer said, and got up. I went.

"You know ... I think, I think ... I didn't like the man at all," I told Pegu later, feeling uncomfortable. He stayed quiet and just grimaced slightly.

"Oh well, don't worry ... He won't read it," I said to calm my friend, as well as myself. We parted, uncommunicative.

Two days later Pegu came with the money to cover production costs. He was cheerful and lively. We made our way. It was a sunny day and that raised our spirits. By chance, we met Schorsch on a street corner and brought him along with us.

We left him outside the building with the printing press. We hastily passed through the two hallways and courtyards into the building at the rear and entered the office. This time the printer was sitting there almost as though he were expecting us. He had a noticeably pale face, held the manuscript in his hand and, trembling just a little, he immediately stood up as we entered, and said in a monotone: "Herr Gra-af – here is the..."

Then he stopped. A thought flashed through my mind. At that very moment a rather sturdily built man came in, and a smaller one appeared just as swiftly from behind the door to the print shop. The two demanded in unison: "Gentlemen, who are you? I am Police Commissar ..."

The owner of the printing press stared into space. His teeth chattered. We looked shell shocked. I felt the world stand still for a moment.

It was not until I noticed the printer's malicious smile that I turned quickly and looked at Pegu.

"What are your names?" the sturdy detective repeated in a more overbearing tone and sized me up.

"Graf."

"And you?" he asked Pegu.

"Graf." In case he needed it, I had given him my certificate of discharge.

"So you are brothers?" asked the detective in disbelief.

"No ... My name is Oskar Maria Graf and his is Graf-Berg," I shot back, but once again, I rued my awkwardness. Pegu was still standing there like a statue.

"Well that will soon come out in the wash ... You'll have to accompany us," said the policeman, conscious that he had us in his power, and raised his hand in warning, pointing with his index finger. "Do not try to escape or we will have to draw our weapons. Do I make myself clear ...?"

He then took the manuscript and we had to walk out singly, each with a detective at his side.

"Cheerio," the sturdy man said to the printer.

"Cheerio," returned the printer.

"Cheerio," I cried, pretending that I could not care less. No reply. But we were already outside. Out on the street we bumped into Schorsch, who had also been arrested. We exchanged glances and on we walked through streets in the January sun. People gawped. All three of us looked down at the ground, or up in the air, or straight ahead; never left or right, and each of us was lost in his own thoughts. The detectives gripped each of us by the sleeve. Suddenly, on Lenbachplatz, Pegu gave his man a determined shove, uttered a half-strangled growl, and made off like a madman. For a moment we all stood there in astonishment, and my policeman tightened his grip. From all sides there were cries of: "Stop him! Stop him!" The small detective ran, fast as he could, over the square. People scattered. We plodded on.

"So what? We'll nab the laddie soon enough," grumbled the sturdy copper by me. I pulled a disinterested face, but inside, my blood was in a boiling surge. Bolt for it! Bolt for it! Just trample everything underfoot, kill the lot of them, just make a bolt for it! The closer we got to the police station, the more overpowering the thought grew in me. My heart thumped, full of this wish. But then at once – it fairly wrenched my head around – Pegu resurfaced, at the side of the little detective. He had lost his hat, beads of sweat glistened on his high forehead, he smiled a little, panted like a horse driven to the limit, and he stared at me with strangely troubled eyes. We had to wait.

"I didn't make it!" he gasped in my direction.

"Oy you! Shut your gob!" snarled the little policeman and shoved my comrade in front. He had cuffed Pegu's arm and twisted it now and again. I clearly saw blood streaming out and flesh hanging loose.

We finally entered the police station over stone steps and through long, gloomy corridors, until we landed in a room with rack upon rack of files. It was very hot. The sturdily built detective sat down, took out a few statement forms, while the small one and a couple of others stood around us, shook us down and took everything we had in our pockets. The sturdy one looked through my papers. I threw a fleeting, meaningful glance at Pegu. He did not seem to understand and looked back, troubled. Now and then he tried to force a smile. I looked at Schorsch. He just had an uneasy expression.

"Stop making things up. What's your name?" asked the desk sergeant taking Pegu's statement. He hesitated. He seemed to be the only focus of their interest.

"Herr Gla-aser, you're from Berlin, aren't you?" Pegu still did not answer. The police clerk turned to the small policeman, who was now leaning over a paper and said with purposeful clarity:

"His name is Guttfeld and he's a salesman from Berlin. Did you know that?" the desk sergeant asked me straight out.

"Who me?" I stammered; I was annoyed at my own distress, but I pulled myself together. "Me ...? He came to me and asked if I knew of a room he could have ..."

"You were asked if you knew his name," the policeman rapped out at me.

I had won some time.

"I don't ask what a man's called. I think his name is Glaser," I replied.

"Well ... So he is called Paul Guttfeld, for your information," said the desk sergeant.

"Really, Guttfeld? ... Hm, I never bothered to ask ... I only knew him as Glaser," I answered with a naive insolence and looked boldly at the man, then I sought Pegu's eyes again.

"Don't look at one another when you are being spoken to!" the desk sergeant snapped in a fearsome tone and went on: "Right then. So Herr Glaser came to you. When was that?" He made a note.

"I don't remember exactly ... About two months ago," was my answer.

"And you never asked where he came from and what he was up to? ... Very nice, that's very nice! ... Have you known Glaser for long?" the man asked bluntly.

"I got to know him when he turned up ... Yes but we never do that, we never bother to ask what someone does or is ... When I go to Berlin, I meet all kinds of people and stay overnight with someone or other ... They couldn't care less what I'm doing either," I said, now sure of myself.

"*We?*" demanded the interrogator of me: "Who do you mean by *we*? ... Is that a club or a society of some sort?"

I smiled a little, involuntarily, and shook my head. "No, that's not it at all ... I mean among writers and artists ... If someone shows up and I don't have a room, well, I look around and see if I can find digs for him ... What he does is none of my business," I answered with some irony.

"So what you are saying is that Herr Glaser came to you and told you he needed a room? ... Was he alone?" he further inquired. Schorsch roused himself.

"Glaser came to me first and I took him to Graf," he said, instead of me. They did not forbid this intervention. The policeman made a note. "Then the gentleman came to you with him?" he asked me again.

"Yes," I nodded.

"Did he then stay the night with you?"

"No ... I am married, so he couldn't," I said.

"I see ... So did you then find a room?"

"Yes," I answered. Then all the complications that must inevitably follow flashed through my head. I racked my brains trying to think of what to say.

"Where was it?" asked the policeman.

I thought about this keenly for a few seconds, then I let loose. It makes no difference, they know a lot more than we thought, I calculated. I gave the address of Pegu's hidey-hole. The man at the desk noted it and said:

"Right-ho, number 5 Schnorrstrasse, in the garden flat," and the little policeman gave me another thorough shake-down.

"Are you done with him?" asked the small guy, and the desk sergeant nodded. They led me away. We went down a dark passageway, then we stood before a metal-plated enamelled door. The constable said to the warder who opened it: "Put him in solitary." We went down several stairs, another ten or so paces along a bare, poorly lit corridor; the warder unbolted another metal-plated door, and the constable shoved me into the cell. I heard the pair exchange a few more words outside. Their footsteps clattered along the flagstones, I heard the door being unbolted again, and then there was silence.

At that moment I was only thinking of Pegu and Schorsch. Without paying any attention to my surroundings I leaned across the cold, smooth door. I tried to imagine, what would my two comrades say? Stupid, really stupid. We should have spoken about something like this happening in detail, beforehand. To hell with it! Selma will come home, I thought, find the note, and wait. She'd be annoyed, then she would get anxious, be unable to sleep, and pace up and down. Oh God, and tomorrow I was supposed to renew the pawn tickets or else the whole lot would be forfeited ...

I grew dejected. Quite incidentally, I remembered the illustrated weeklies that we had subscribed to at home when I was a boy. They were called *Nimm mich mit* and each one had a brightly coloured picture on the

247

front page, illustrating the latest news. One such showed Father Gapon's procession during the Russian revolution of 1905, he ahead with the cross, an innumerable crowd of people behind, determined to the last ...

It was odd. Suddenly it seemed as though I heard a distant tumult, penetrating these thick walls and the barred windows, the confused sounds and the drumbeat of a thousand steps, a vast crowd storming down the streets. I listened more attentively. Now they might come up against the police, I thought, now there's a hail of cobblestones, now the fight is really on, oh, they'll be unstoppable, they'll win, they'll win! Victory is at hand!

I worked myself into a fever. My blood surged. Then I heard, once again, a door being unbolted, the buzz of voices and footsteps. I turned without thinking and pressed my eye to the peephole in the door. But I saw nothing. It seemed the hole was covered with a lid outside. I could only listen.

"Solitary," the constable's voice uttered again. A bolt slammed shut. Steps. A few words.

I felt relief. As though it was in the air, I perceived that one of my friends had been placed in a solitary cell in the same corridor. As far as I could reckon, the cell must be diagonally opposite my own.

We could not communicate by tapping. We must find some other means. I thought hard.

Yes! Now something occurred to me: I had once – for the first and only time in my life – gone to the opera, to see *Carmen* with Pegu. From then on, *Toreador en garde* was our signal.

I started to whistle quietly and shyly, then got rather louder, and there! Listen! Then it came from the cell opposite, "Toreador en garde!"

"Toreador en garde!" I whistled more animatedly.

"Toreador en garde!" came a cheerful reply, and as if coming from a deep grotto, Pegu's voice called out: "Oskar?!"

"Pegu, is that you?!" I cried jubilantly.

"Yes, yoo-hoo!" came the reply.

"Yoo-hoo, where are you then?"

"Cell five, on your corridor!"

"And I am in cell two, yoo-hoo, let them have it!" I shouted, free of inhibitions. "Where is Schorsch?"

"He must be upstairs," Pegu answered, likewise, and added: "Hey Oskar! ... They know everything."

"Shut up!" I cried hastily. "Say nothing about it!"

He fell silent. Once in a while we whistled softly to one another. I briskly walked up and down my cell. Only now did I look at it more carefully. It was rather high-ceilinged and covered in a grey-green oil paint. Embedded in the middle of the ceiling, an electric light burned away. A collapsible wooden bunk, on which there was a white woollen blanket, stood on the right-hand wall. The WC was placed at the head-end of the bunk. High above it was a tiny strip of window covered by a heavy iron grating; the window was leaning half open. Standing on the plank-bed, I could just reach it with my hands, but the wall was slippery, and the ledge was steep. I slid down; the grating bars were fixed from outside. I climbed up on the somewhat higher WC and was able to see a piece of the dark night. The air streamed damp and cold through the opening and the steam heating brought the walls into a sweat. It was not really worth walking up and down, as you could only take six paces along the cell and four across.

For a while I whistled through the window, hoping for a sign of life from Schorsch, but in vain. I postponed this until the next day, got back onto the bunk and occupied myself with my new surroundings again. Although now I had seen everything. And as generally happens if you find yourself in a new and strange environment – one that is bare and insignificant – you look for the most interesting aspect and focus your attention on it. In here – where it was extremely boring and who could know how long it would last – by far the most interesting object was the WC. I sat on its lid for a while. That was quite pleasant. Then I got up, because there was no flush mechanism to be found, I examined it, to find out how it worked. I opened the lid and shut it again. Aha! There was a gurgling sound and the water ran out. That was really lovely. This offered hours of entertainment. I raised the lid again and slammed it shut. It worked magnificently. I raised it again, faster and faster, in the end as smart as the devil. It was just tiresome that I could not see the water running.

Just as I was slamming down the lid once more, I was startled by the unexpected grinding of keys in the locks. Two warders appeared. One had a basket full of thinly sliced *schwarzbrot*, the other – who was a grubby, pot-bellied colossus – lay a single slice of the dark bread on the bunk. Without saying a word, the two locked the doors again. I heard the same everywhere outside. I sat down on the bunk, ate the bread, took a swig of the bitter coffee from time to time, and tried to order my thoughts.

I had to reckon more or less with the following: several interrogations, then a trial, sentencing and who knows how much time cut out of my life. For the time being, I had to wait things out in this hole. There was nothing you could do, nothing to occupy you, you could not even smoke; the play, the professor, the leaflets, Selma, the discussion evenings, and the coming revolution: everything was suddenly obliterated, almost as though torn from my body. And God knows for how long!

I pottered about, just for something to do. I also became a little more cheerful. Hm, I thought, you can describe all this one day, perhaps it will make a good story. Very, very good! Actually, everything is good material for a writer. I was already vaguely sketching out individual scenes and became quite content with my situation. Then all of a sudden, the light went out. Annoyed, I remained standing and grumbled under my breath. Then I cautiously groped my way along the bunk, knocking over the half-empty coffee pot. It clattered to the floor and the liquid ran over my feet. I flew into a rage and whistled out loud. Pegu answered at once.

"Oskar?" he asked across the divide.

"Yes? Pegu? ... It's enough to make you sick"

"Chin up! It doesn't matter!" he answered consolingly.

"Sleep well!" I wished him, and he wished me the same.

I crept onto the bench, took my jacket off, folded it into a pillow, wrapped myself in the blanket and tried to sleep. The hours dragged by. I froze. Now and again my eyes closed, then I lay awake again for a long stretch. When the electric light was switched back on, I felt completely knackered. There was coffee and bread again. A short time later the constable fetched me for interrogation.

14.
THE INTERROGATION

I came into the same room in which we had first arrived at the police station, and once again the sturdily built police commissar interrogated me. This time he was rather more pleasant. He even let me sit down on a chair. I had to give my particulars all over again.

"Herr Graf!" he then started, emphasizing the word "Herr" in an ironic tone. "I have looked through your wallet ... I see that you are in rather dire straits ... Most of your things are at the pawnshops, eh?"

"Yes," I said, "I wanted to talk to you about the pawn tickets ... because some of the items will be forfeited if they are not renewed ... Can a constable take me to the pawnshop, so that I can sort it out?"

The detective said no and told me that would be taken care of. Then he turned to me: "You used to be a baker? ... You are a very decent man! ... This is a nice mess you've got into with Guttfeld." He was trying it on with naive innocence. I looked into his ruddy, healthy, witless face, and since he seemed to assume that I regretted everything, his hopes rose. He continued, even more warmly: "You are married, your wife is a book-keeper, and she is expecting?" I nodded. He kept his eyes on me.

"You have also been to Eisner's meetings, Herr Graf?" he asked, harmlessly. I said yes. He nodded.

"And once you spoke during the discussion, saying that the soldiers should leave their barracks?" he asked. I hesitated, hurriedly thinking things through.

"Herr Commissar," I said in the most confiding tones I could muster, "I'm desperately hot; could I please ask you for some water?" I looked at him meekly. The man stood up in the friendliest of manners and poured me water from a bottle: "There, sup up lad." I drank a glassful in a single gulp and panted, so that he could not help but feel sympathy for me in my thirst.

"Thank you ... Thank you very much, Herr Commissar," I said submissively, and as he started up again on the meetings with Eisner, I declared willingly: "Did I speak? ... As far as I can remember, I did not speak, Herr Commissar ... No, no, I didn't speak ... That's something I am no good at, not at all, though it is possible that I was heckling ... That's quite likely ..."

"You're not a member of the Independent Social Democratic Party?" the sturdy man inquired.

"No ... I am not in no society, Herr Commissar ... I have never had owt to do with societies," I told him, speaking in a kind of rustic pub-table dialect.

"Do you think *those* people would manage things better?" he wanted to know.

"Oh my God, better? ... I really don't know. That's a matter of opinion, Herr Commissar ... I really don't know if you have ever slaved for months on end in a factory ... A bloke can get right fed up in there," I carried on with my tactic of provincial frankness and he did not interrupt me. "I doubt if there's anyone who doesn't get upset with how things are at present now and then ... A man gets grumpy and has a good old moan obviously ... Perhaps even the detective, who heard me wherever it was, has thought to himself, they're not completely wrong ... Although of course, he'll have thought, I am well paid, I have a good position, and so I'll keep quiet. Don't you agree, Herr Commissar?" That went too far for the policeman. His face reddened.

"Herr Graf!" he reprimanded me strongly. "Enough of your waffle! ... This Guttfeld, didn't he also give you money?"

I kept calm and said, quite sure of myself: "My God, I've cadged money off lots of people."

"Cadged? ... But he gave you the money to buy a typewriter ... Surely you cannot pay that back ... He probably demanded that you do him some favour or work for him in return, didn't he?" the Commissar inquired.

It was good that he asked such long questions. That made it easy to take time to reflect and dissemble. Besides, I was in no hurry to return to my cell.

"Herr Commissar, things are different among artists," I started afresh. "Somebody has money and gives it to another and then the other has money and gives it to someone else ... That's how things work with us, we don't ask to be paid back for every little trifle ... Of course, I typed for him after he had given me the typewriter."

The policeman turned around and said, impatiently, "Get to the point!", eyeing me with suspicion. "So, this Guttfeld dictated a manuscript to you ... Did you know what it was about?"

"Oh yes, of course," I replied innocently. At that instant the strong man raised his head, curious, in fact, he was astounded at my frankness.

"It was intended as a leaflet for the strike," he said, looking to convict me. I looked astonished.

"For the strike? ... What strike? ... No, no, I can't believe it ... I was producing the pamphlet for a historical study," I replied, quite unfazed, and went on: "The workers don't read stuff like that! ... That's far too long for them and much too academic ..."

"Then you say you didn't know what was the purpose of the manuscript?"

"Not at all ... I genuinely thought it was a historical study," I said, and he noted it.

"You then introduced Guttfeld to the printer. Why did you want two or three thousand copies in one go?" asked the interrogator.

"Ah well, you see, there's a minimum print run and the more you print, the cheaper it is," I answered. Herr Fuchs, as he was called, noted this down. I looked out of the window. Outside, it was a grey winter's day. Then it started snowing.

"Did you know that Guttfeld is a deserter?" Fuchs asked, abruptly.

I shook my head and said no.

"Then why did you register him under a false name?" he persisted.

"Well the fact of the matter is, I rented the room for my friend Fritz Wunder, Herr Commissar," I said, a little more uncertain of myself, and drawing on all my acuteness of mind, "Glaser could just stay there, because Wunder is still in the lunatic asylum ... When he comes out, he can take it over. He is a batik artist ..."

Fuchs surveyed me sleuth-like. But I could see that he was getting increasingly irritated.

"You can't expect me to believe that," he said more pointedly. "You found Guttfeld a flat and rented it under a false name ... That alone is a punishable offence. Nobody would do so many favours for a complete stranger ..."

I stood up and said, with conviction: "I am a Catholic, Herr Commissar! ... The first principle of the Christian faith is that you should help your neighbour ... If someone comes to me and asks for help, I don't first make inquiries ... I just do whatever I can, and that's all there is to it ..."

Fuchs leaned forward a little.

"Right!" he exclaimed, suddenly triumphant, and went on: "You are not so stupid that you wouldn't have known that Eisner, for example, and his accomplices want a revolution ... You even once said to a friend there, that people should refuse to obey the State! ... Eisner and the Independent Social Democratic Party have always said that there must be a strike to stop the war and that the current political order must be overthrown ... They even said that as a matter of principle, every deserter must be helped!" He was almost ranting. I looked at him resolutely, with no shyness. His face was one of rude health, a man who did not suffer any hardship; you could see that from his fine filled-out body, and the way he towered over me and seemed to get satisfaction from his power. That kind of thing has always annoyed me about a person.

For a few moments I teetered on the verge of screaming the whole damned truth in his face, but then I pulled myself together.

"Yes, that's what they wanted all right ... That's what they *wanted!*" said one of Fuchs' sidekicks, distorting his unshaven face into a malicious laughter.

"Wanted." I thought about that, and then I said, unflinchingly: "Herr Commissar, neither of us can change that."

The words came out with such an ironic ring to them that Fuchs turned scarlet. He looked me over as if I was a totally squalid little nobody, but I couldn't care less. I almost burst out laughing at his pompous self-importance. I thought about something entirely different, something that was never out of my mind and always uppermost at such moments.

I thought of my mother. Once upon a time, when I was a little boy, an aristocrat and a tarted-up woman came into the shop, and both complained in indignant tones because the bread bag, in which their daily rolls had been delivered, was not perfectly clean. I was standing next to my mother. The two gentlefolk talked on and on, as if the most scandalous injustice had occurred. My mother said nothing in reply, but as soon as they were outside, she stroked my round head wearily and said: "Good grief, do you now see what that lot are like! ... But when they've nothing on, they're naked just like the rest of us, and when they die, they're just a pile of dirt!"

I looked at Fuchs and grimaced imperceptibly. He read out everything that he noted in a stern tone and got me to sign it. Then the constable escorted me back to the cell, where I walked up and down, feeling strangely liberated, and suddenly broke into a bold whistle. Pegu joined in.

"They interrogated me!" I told him, when he asked. He wanted to know more.

"Keep cool, man! ... Pegu?! Keep cool! ... What can they do? ... Keep cool! ... If we are separated, always let me know your news!" I called over to him, feeling relaxed, and "Yes Oskar, I will," came his hearty reply.

Shortly afterwards, I heard them fetch him. I waited and waited for his return, but he never came. A few hours later I whistled again. There was no answer. He must have been taken away.

It was silent, and this silence made me lame.

I climbed up on the WC and whistled for Schorsch. I shouted out his name. After an hour all this effort was in vain and I jumped back down. An unbearable tedium set in. A tingling sensation and an unpleasant sense of unease permeated all my limbs. From time to time a tattered shred of an idea flashed through my mind, but it vanished in a moment and my mind was blank again.

Enraged, I suddenly jumped up to the WC, tore open the lid and slammed it down with all my strength, time and again, more fanatically, faster and faster. It was all the same to me. I just heard the water rushing.

All at once the warder outside barked abuse and threatened me. I stared stupidly at the peephole and stayed standing there. The warder walked up and down outside for some time, grumbling angrily. I collapsed onto the bunk and thought of nothing at all. There was nothing to be done except wait, though what I was waiting for was uncertain.

Towards evening on the second day, the constable unexpectedly came to get me and took me back to Fuchs. He gave me another lecture, mixed together with threats and warnings. I just said "yes" to this and "yes" to that and was released.

I breathed in a wonderfully fresh air as I left the police station. It was cold, but I did not feel it. The frozen snow scrunched under my feet, and the lanterns shone in the clear darkness.

Now I was desperate for a cigarette. I searched through my pocket for money. Yes, it was there, I had got everything back: money, keys, and my wallet. I went into a shop. "Yes, three packets of ten," I said, and lit up a cigarette. I reeled out of the shop as in a dreamlike trance, inhaling the smoke at my ease. Slowly, I remembered: yes, you live in Schraudolphstrasse, Selma is at home, yes, you can do as you like again. I had recovered my free will and my thoughts. One thing after another became real again: the tram, the people, the houses, the lights. When I got home, I smiled at Selma.

"Thank God!" she said, adding: "Now you know what you get when you are at the beck and call of others." I did not argue. I just let her talk. I did not even feel hungry. I drank tea and munched my bread and jam indifferently.

The next day I looked up Schorsch.

"Where can Pegu be?" we asked in one breath and we both shrugged our shoulders.

"You know that the general strike has collapsed ... Everyone has been arrested: Eisner, Kämpfer, the Landauer brothers, everyone ... And it's the same in Berlin! ... Now they'll really let loose the informers," Schorsch declared. "What difference does it make? ... It can't go on like this much longer!" I growled, fed up.

"My boy will never be a soldier! ... Never!" said Maria Uhla, looking down at her rounded belly. "Rather a hoodlum!"

She smiled softly and with a certain confidence.

The peace negotiations at Brest-Litovsk came to nothing. They all went home. Trotsky had declared the war to be over without signing a treaty. The German armies, in alliance with Russian counter-revolutionaries, fought on against Bolshevism and a broken country. The Soviet Foreign Minister had achieved a huge moral victory, because everyone said it was easy fighting against defenceless people who had laid down their arms.

It was reported that a definite peace had been signed with the Ukraine, which would soon be sending bread. But none came. We heard that Ludendorff had launched a new offensive on the Western Front.

Now and again a detective appeared at my place or asked the

neighbours about my comings and goings. They all looked at me askance, almost fearfully. I made discreet inquiries after Pegu, but in vain. Finally I found out that he had been transported to a military gaol in Berlin. Shortly afterwards Schorsch and I were interrogated once more by the police; we reckoned we'd be held but were released again.

"That's odd," Schorsch said pensively out on the street. "Hm ... Very odd."

"Maybe things are shakier than we think," I said as we separated. From then on, I kept my head down and the spying on me stopped, although sometimes it seemed as though they were keeping an eye on my letters.[41]

---

[41] The January Strike followed a similar action in Austria-Hungary and lasted from 25 January 1918, when workers in the Kiel torpedo works downed tools, until 1 February. It was the third major strike against the First World War in the German Reich. More than one million workers demanded better living and working conditions and an end to the war. The strike was organized by the Revolutionary Shop Stewards, the USPD and the Spartacists, but collapsed in the face of opposition by the Majority SPD and the trade union hierarchy. Many striking workers were drafted into the army and sent to the front.

15.
A PITIFUL INTERLUDE

So long as I had been caught up in the revolutionary current, so to speak, daily annoyances had been all but washed away. The widespread movement into which I had been drawn held me in perpetual tension. Every day was a sensation. I went to sleep in hope and woke in the expectation of great things to come.

Now, however, after – superficially at least – the first attempt of the discontented masses had ground to an abrupt halt, after the will to rise up had been almost extinguished by the arrest of the movement's leaders and brutal harassment, now the dark clouds of poverty were closing in on me again. Now I was again a defenceless individual, preoccupied with the question: how do you raise money, how can you rub along, how do you prevent quarrels with Selma, and how will you provide for the coming child? And then the pawn tickets; hmm, you can get cheap marmalade here, the herrings are good value there, the gas bill must be paid and so on.

And apart from that I remembered the play and all the time I had wasted. The professor was sure to have seen the news of my arrest in the papers, and obviously the consequences would make things really awkward for me. What's more, the third month of the scholarship grant was drawing to a close.

I wrote an apologetic letter to my sponsor and pretended that I had been prevented from visiting him only because I was preoccupied with zealous work on the play. I said nothing about the arrest. A card came in reply: "Don't worry, dear Herr Graf! Your work is ample apology."

So just write the play!

I started. In a bad mood. I racked my brains for inspiration. I recalled that the professor was very fond of Hanns Johst's and Unruh's style of writing. Well then, I told myself, they wrote verse, so you must also write something that is solemn, and as energetic as possible.[42]

The plot was the biggest challenge. I brooded and brooded over it, and after a few days at last the outline of a revolutionary piece floated through my head. Bit by bit, the scenes also became more tangible in my

---

[42] Hanns Johst (1890-1978) and Fritz von Unruh (1885-1970) both enjoyed early success as expressionist dramatists. Johst became an active supporter of the Nazi Party, writing his play *Schlageter* for a performance on the Führer's 44th birthday. After the war he was interned by the Allies and imprisoned for ten years, then banned from writing for ten years. He was later reduced to writing poems under a pseudonym for a supermarket chain's magazine, *Die kluge Hausfrau* (the Clever Housewife). Von Unruh, by contrast, was a dedicated anti-Nazi; in 1932 he warned of the coming *Vernichtungskrieg* (war of extermination), as a result of which his works were banned, and he was forced into exile.

thoughts. Without actually knowing how it would all end, I finally set to, churning out the verse with all my might. The hero of the drama was, of course, a man of artistic temperament and a modern universalist ethical outlook, a man, therefore, motivated by virtually nothing except idealism, who leads his people to freedom and dies in so doing. Nobody could object that a story ending in death was anything other than tragic. I searched for a striking title and solved this challenge with a word from a foreign language dictionary, namely: *The Dictator*.

"Tribune" would have also sounded good, but "Dictator" was more contemporary and, I felt, more powerful, more active. So I typed onto a blank sheet of paper, neatly centred: "The Dictator, a Tragedy in Three Acts, by Oskar Maria Graf."

Act I, a humble garret (of course). Altercation between the hero and his wife, because they are in desperate straits. The wife wants the man to find a proper job; but the hero lives in the realm of ideas and declares in spirited verse that the People can no longer bear their misery, and that he can remain silent no longer. The couple quarrel and finally the hero leaves, solemnly declaring:

I have had enough!
To bear it is too tough!
My dreams echo the People's lament!
You of no faith, I leave behind.
The path to greatness, that's my intent!

The curtain falls. A clamour is heard behind the scenes, as the exultant People greet their leader.

Now I felt more chipper. Act II must really seethe with action. First, the hero makes a long speech on a public square, then the mounted police break through, there is a clash, a struggle and screams (in iambic hexameters), dead and wounded; and at the end conspirators meet in a cellar. The loyal bring in their wounded leader on a stretcher, he gets up with all his might and, of course, makes a fiery speech to the small band of honest cadres. Suddenly the triumphant cries of the victorious People are heard from outside, and a frenzied man shouts down to the cellar the glad tidings:

Arise, downtrodden and mistreated,
Hail the dawn of freedom, the tyrant is defeated.

They all rush out, carrying the leader with them. He picks himself up, raises his outstretched arms to heaven and calls from the stage to the audience:
Bold the struggle!

Through blood and wounds
the masses have found the light!
The day of justice is now in sight!

The curtain dramatically falls to the rousing strains of the *Marseillaise*. By this time I was really enthusiastic about my powerful drama. I just wasn't really sure what should happen in Act III.

I thought about it for half the night. Selma groaned. Now and again she turned on the light, shook asthma powders into a small dish and ignited it, inhaling the fumes to help her breathing.

I did not budge; I just lay there thinking. Lying awake like that, when the stillness grows more and more intense, is dangerous. You suddenly realize that you are wasting your little stretch of life in such futilities, in such absurd pomposities. Quite slowly and torturously you come up against your utter wretchedness. The events of your life, bygone days and years, file pitifully before your eyes, everything slips away, out of reach ... The next day I awoke irritable and spiteful. I should certainly have slain the landlady's cat if I had found it sitting on the coal bunker outside the door. Selma had gone out, it was cold, the furniture looked silly and repulsive, and the morning light glared through the window.

Only after a long while did I pull myself together and start the third act. I spurred myself on with the thought that the professor would at least see that I had shown good faith. But I was no longer convinced by my grandiose *oeuvre*. Still, this is how the action ended: the insurrection is victorious, the People take everything in hand, and the idealist hero is executed by his former followers as a traitor. His wife stands in a dingy room and talks, in a long monologue, about heroism and the spirit of the crowd, about the masses and humanity. Although the whole thing was disgusting to me now, I took a deep breath and tried to convince Selma about how excited the professor would be. I sent off the manuscript at once and a few days later my sponsor called me to a discussion in the Hofgarten.

I saw him from a distance and already knew what was coming. We paced up and down. It was a lovely day.

"Herr Graf, this is no drama! ... I should never have said anything to you," he started. "No, no, you're not a dramatist ... I almost blame myself ... Poetry cannot be written to order." I shyly agreed. Now and again he looked at me through his glasses. My self-confidence ebbed away. I let him speak, nodded, and said from time to time: "Yes, you're right!" I was deeply shamed by his empathetic honesty. Then, in the very next instance I thought, panic-stricken, of the scholarship, which I probably would not get any more.

"To start with, this idiotic newspaperish title," the professor went on, "And then all these phrases! ... When I think of the maturity of all your poems, but here? ... All so clumsy! Not a single idea from start to finish! ... You must read Kleist ... But no, I would rather not give you advice ... No, no, you won't feel insulted, after all, you have a sense of humour ... But the whole thing is gibberish ... Neither fish nor fowl." I smiled in embarrassment. I did not make eye contact, just looked past him whenever he stood still.

"Yes, but that is just a first draft, Herr Professor," I uttered at last. But he rejected this immediately.

"Herr Graf, a poet must not place obligations on himself!" That sounded good.

"Everything must spring from an authentic imperative ... Otherwise better never to pick up a pen again ... You can't create anything simply by wanting to, do you get my drift?" he repeated.

"Yes," I said, "Herr Professor, let me have another go ..." I blurted it out with all the apologetic insistence that only a man who realizes his mistake and wants to put things right can feel. But the man next to me stuck to his guns.

"Herr Graf," he said with a slight touch of melancholy, "you are so young! ... What does one mistake matter? Your poems ring true with every line ... If you write everything like you did in those poems, something good will always come of it ... It is possible that you will write another play later, but that is really not important ... What matters, is simply that you stay true to yourself ... You're only just starting, my dear chap! You have your whole life in front of you ..."

I got more and more confused and ended up talking at random. As we parted, the professor gave me the manuscript. He said he would post the monthly cheque in the next few days, but for the moment he could not say if the grant would be extended for me.

I returned home and burned the play. Thank God, that was over, and I was getting the hundred marks for another month. Now all that mattered was to get provisions. I went back to *Simplicissimus*. At the artists' table they traded bread ration cards that were very scarce at the time. Meat, sausages and butter were in demand. I pricked up my ears. I remembered a man I had met at the General Post Office. You could get everyone from him. He lived very close to us. I looked him up. He acted very suspicious. I got impatient. "Hey," I said, "I have a no end of customers ... We can earn a good living."

He didn't want money, just butter. I ran around with my ears open. Selma's boss, the gravestone mason, got butter and eggs in massive quantities from his customers in the country, but he would not share any.

He preferred to let it all go rancid and smelly.

"We must get money," I said to Selma. "That man makes a living off killing. Without the war he would be a beggar. You've got to squeeze him for butter ... That's hard cash for us."

The following day she brought a pound of butter. I exchanged it for four bread ration cards and got five marks in return. This success made me industrious. I was already planning business on a large scale.

It is true that intellectuals viewed me with contempt and ran away. They all said: "That shabby little crook there," but they all wanted to buy off me. In no time at all I was the man who could get everything, because I never said "no", but always: "I'll see ... I think I can get it."

A man came to me who, it was said, owned an entire warehouse. He had previously been a cocktail waiter and – strangely – one day he came straight up to me, looked me inquiringly in the eye, and whispered: "Herr Graf, I heard that you could do with some eggs?" I nodded cautiously and hesitated for a moment. He said in a business-like tone: "Call by tomorrow."

The same evening I made discreet inquiries in *Simplicissimus* about what goods were most in demand. A dancer wanted silk stockings, a pimp wanted tinned sardines and high-quality sausage, I promised to procure the finest pre-war soap for a fat man surrounded by a swarm of ladies; I met a little Dutchman with a face like a sheep, who, it was said, was in possession of vast wealth, sat down smiling with him, and asked him what was his desire.

"Tender pig's tongue and ham," he said and asked what else I had.

I coolly listed my wares: "I can get chocolate ... eggs, fresh butter, meat, very fresh. Chop-chop, no problem."

"You know what, here's some money, bring me something tomorrow," he said, and gave me a hundred marks.

"Good," I said. "I won't let you down."

I went home and could hardly sleep for anticipation.

First thing in the morning I sought out the ex-cocktail waiter. He did not disappoint me. His large apartment, furnished in solid bourgeois style, was completely darkened, even in the living room. Thick curtains blotted out the daylight. He switched on the electric light, and it seemed as if I was standing in a fabulous grotto. Huge hams, smoked tongues in all sizes, salamis and entire sides of pork ribs hung like stalactites, neatly ordered and packed close beside each other, from long hooks fixed to the ceiling. I saw crates full of eggs, material, silk, shoes, chocolate, tubs of lard, goose fat and packs of butter. In the middle was stood a carving table, scrubbed beautifully clean, with two pairs of scales and a whole row of sparkling knives. I was overwhelmed and could barely get a word out. The man led me to another room. Bottles of wine and schnapps were arranged on shelves and numbered. There were soap and toiletries of every kind. In fact, there were incredible quantities of everything we seemed to have forgotten in those days.

With a shudder I thought of all the prevailing misery; for a moment the reckless thought occurred to me that I should rush out to the streets and scream about what I had seen. Then I pulled myself together, remembering my own misery and murmured: "Hmm, there's certainly a lot of good business to be done here."

The man was extremely pleasant and took me back to the living room. He offered me an excellent cognac and delicious ham and pastries. But my mind was elsewhere, and although my mouth watered, I ate without appetite.

"As I said, Herr Graf, if you want to earn, I will serve you well ... We have the same interests," he told me, initiating the serious business in the goods, and offering me a comprehensive typewritten price list. "Cash Only" was written at the top.

I said: "Yes, I'll have two pig's and two calve's tongues, not too heavy and very tender, then perhaps ham, but only the best quality ... Oh yes, I could also do with silk stockings and soap." I was calm and businesslike again. I gave him the hundred-mark note. We agreed that I should collect the goods in the evening. It was too risky during the day.

The Dutchman was very pleased with his supplies and placed a fresh order, immediately giving me another advance of a hundred marks. I speculated to the best of my ability with the surplus, then supplied everyone with what they wanted. It was easy, there was always money available, nothing could go wrong.

At the end of the month the professor informed me that the grant would be extended. I was almost more astonished than pleased. He sent me a very enthusiastic letter about some of my poems. I wanted to give up the racketeering and just go back to writing, but I had already gotten used to being awash with money. I was like a gambler who can see the hellish addictiveness of his passion but can't free himself from it. I earned the money too easily, and the adventurous nature of my new occupation was too beguiling; when you have spent years on end in miserable, degrading insecurity, you get an appetite. An appetite for the good life, for power, for luxuries that other people have, those who are well-fed, secure and superior. Nobody wants to be trampled on all the time, to be down on his luck day after day.

I once dined with the sheep-faced Dutchman, who was now Marietta's boyfriend. I ate the kind of dishes I had never tasted before and gulped down some blissfully delicious wines. The wine flowed and, in the end, we got very, very merry. It was like a fairy tale.

After this I really threw myself into getting rich quick. I went to *Simplicissimus*, sat down among the chattering poets and artists, and suddenly pulled a long dry sausage from one breast pocket, and ladies' stockings from the other, and the finest chocolate from my overcoat pocket.

"Need some sausage, mate? Sausage! ... That's all that matters!" was my contribution to the discussion. "And here, easy as you like, chop-chop, silk stockings! Chocolate! ... What's your fancy? ... I've got the lot!"

I said it in a vindictive and malicious tone. They looked at me enviously and forced a spiteful smile.

"What does it all matter! Humanity! Pacifism! ... Here, gentlemen, is all that matters ... Eat or be eaten!" I cried with the cunning callousness peculiar to those who will do whatever it takes to achieve recognition. The dancer whispered something into the fat man's ear and drunkenly held up the stockings, tore the chocolate from me and broke into salacious laughter. The fat man took out his wallet and paid. Everyone gawked at the money. I pocketed it casually, as though it was of no consequence. And so it went, time and again. I got drunk and no longer went home at night. I had never been good at keeping accounts. The money melted away uncontrollably, just as easily as I earned it. And of course, I chased after it more than ever.

"Don't be stupid! Money?! ... There's always money! You have enough." I snapped at Selma, when she went shopping. Our life together had developed into a bad-tempered mutual hostility. As soon as she came home, I went out in search of company.

I visited my supplier, the former cocktail waiter. He was very friendly towards his best customer. We lounged around in his living room and drank to our fraternity. He poured me one drink after another. I put the glass down and always drank the next in a single draught. Gradually, my head became clouded. I became sentimental and melancholy like an old maid, then I raged against my foul mood until it was dead and buried.

"All this filthy lucre! This dirty money!" I growled, and gurgled down the schnapps.

"Money does not smell! Business first! Business!" my new friend spurred me on. I sniffed the notes. True, they did not smell. I laughed noisily and collapsed over the chair, stinking drunk. The room went into a spin. More schnapps! Get the money in and live like there's no tomorrow!" I bawled and stood up unsteadily. "Who gives a shit! ... Corruption marches on! ... More schnapps! ... The whole world is corrupt!"

I did not return home until the early morning. I was totally plastered.

I drove about in a motorcar, made lots of new business connections, served my customers quickly and efficiently, and my circle of customers grew daily.

I became good friends with the Dutchman and was often invited to his place. Where we stuffed ourselves and acted like madmen. He was always surrounded by a crowd of sycophantic artists and others leading a precarious existence. They toadied up to him, praising everything he did to the heavens. We quaffed and guzzled for days and nights on end. As a child I had always pictured the decadent Rome of antiquity, which the priest and teachers had told me about, in this way. Now I was a Roman, and it felt good. Very good.

Over time, I got bogged down in indifference. Now and again I met the professor or the Red Cross man and lied to them about my great literary projects. I gushed hypocritically to them about the significance and seriousness of the age.

"A man will hear what he wants to hear," had become my motto.

And so the time frittered away.

"You're going downhill," Maria Uhla once said to me and, looking me directly in the eye, "You have become nothing."

I pulled an awkward expression and tried to ridicule Maria's assertions with cynical remarks about her. She was not to be deflected. "What exactly are you up to?" she asked straight out.

"Me? ... Nothing, nothing at all! ... Except eat, drink and earn a pile of money," I answered coarsely.

"You're even lying to yourself!" she cut in, not taking her eyes off me. "Everything you're doing, you're only doing because you are afraid of yourself! ... You're dealing on the black market and making money just to keep Selma quiet. You go boozing because you don't want to stop and think. You lie to your professor, because you know very well that he is a more decent man than you. You do not want to talk to anyone, and you're always making lousy jokes to cover up your utter wretchedness." She took a breath and added in another tone: "And you are the unhappiest man in the world."

"That may be," I muttered, for she had struck home, but then my tone got rougher again. "But it suits me fine! ... Who else do I owe honesty or effort ... A bloke can be called up again any day and get shot for no good reason whatsoever!"

She hesitated a while. Then she took me to task again: "Do you imagine I would change places with you? ... Schorsch and I would not live a single day like you ... And goodness knows, we're hard up enough."

I shrugged my shoulders and snorted heavily. "One day you'll pack it all in and hide yourself away," she went on.

"That may well be," I replied again.

Schorsch came back from town. We drank tea and discussed events. The courts martial had gone on a rampage after the January strike. The sentences were brutal. The prisons were crammed full of rebels. Every trace of insurrection had been eradicated. The front needed soldiers. Even the most unfit for service were re-examined and sent into the field. The spring offensive that had been launched on the Western Front raged furiously; tanks and poison gas did their terrifying work. Suddenly the attack faltered and collapsed. The newspaper reports muddied the picture. But gradually the disturbing news leaked through.

"Hopeless! Only assassinations can help us," I said. We parted, depressed.

"I am going to look for work again," I told Selma. "Yes, or write something and submit it," she said. I grumbled about something or other.

"Or get yourself an office job," she returned. I nodded again.

A few days later a girl who worked in some artisan trade had told me that the Coal Marketing Board needed typists in its distribution centre. I applied and was taken on. It was sedentary work. It was the same questions and answers all day long: "Are you a sub-tenant? Do you have your own flat? How many rooms? ... No, offices count as business premises. Yes, you are entitled to two hundredweight ..." etc.

The job only lasted four weeks. Black marketeering was now out in the open. Prices had shot up to fantastic levels, but you could get butter, lard, eggs and meat under the counter in any shop.

My supplier met me on the street, made straight for me and took me to his flat.

"Hey, what's up with you? Why don't you want my merchandise all of a sudden? Is it no good? Why are you looking at me in that way?" he inquired with a worried expression and poured me a cognac. I shook my head. His words disgusted me. He pressed me further. I grumbled about the war.

"We're not waging the war, nor are we losing it," he said. He poured me another cognac.

I raised my head and said: "You know what? ... The whole thing fills me with horror." The man was moved, stood up tall in front of me and patted me on the shoulder, as if he wanted to restore my spirits. And he exclaimed ingenuously: "Oskar! ... I want to tell you something ... You know me! I don't soft soap you ... Oskar! ... Put some money by, there are lousy times ahead! ... Money is everything! Where it comes from is all the same!"

I said nothing, gulping down one cognac after the other. He showed me his stock. He was upset with me. We lounged about for a while and got drunk again. The thought went round and round my foggy brain: what of it? What of it? It was all the same! Nothing matters! It's all pointless, all stupid! He's absolutely right! Money is everything! Money, nothing but money. I snorted like an old nag and went on drinking. I belched. My stomach was in knots.

"Come, brethren, charge your glasses! Lo-ong live the veteran!" the cocktail shaker sang hoarsely, stumbled, stared at me with glassy eyes and then repeated once more:

"Come, breth-ethren, charge your glasses! Long live the ve-veteran, who served out his time fai-aith-aithfully – Ha! Your health Oskar, cheers! Ha. Shit! ... Drink, man! Drink! ... The veteran!"[43]

I got up. "Shit, all right, I'll do it!" I said.

---

[43] The words are taken from the popular soldiers' song, *Was blinkt so freundlich in der Ferne.*

And I did so. But all my enthusiasm was gone. I became indifferent as a salesman. If a deal came off, all well and good, if not, all well and good. One day I met Hobrecker on the street with Schorsch. His fortune had melted away. He had become poor again, or, as he put it: "Things have wound down again."

We went boozing with him until late at night, and he took us to his hotel.

He ordered red wine and cold cuts. He got whatever he wanted here, as everywhere. We ate, drank and got merry.

"Oskar man! I tell you, you're a greenhorn! ... Right now I'm in a bit of a pickle, but in a few days, I'll have thousands again ... You can come then," said Hobrecker.

He talked about secret deals on paintings, of his connection to a Ukrainian oil well company, and got himself all worked up about these fantasies. He told us about his love affairs in startling and lengthy detail.

"War! What war? ... Willy Hobrecker will soon have a place among the big industrialists!" he cried, hoarse from the drink.

I looked at him closely. How he stood there, back in his worn out brown suit again, his battered patent shoes, how he pulled out a pack of pawn tickets and counted them with boisterous cheerfulness: "Dress suit, dinner jacket, two cabin trunks, gold watch chain, gold wristwatch, morning suit, paletot, Ulster coat, top hat, one dozen shirts, fourteen pairs of shoes, two golden cigarette cases, three walking sticks with ivory or silver handles." He burst out laughing: "My fortune nicely stored in mothballs!" That was staggering.

When we left him it was already a grey morning. Schorsch had taken a half-empty bottle of burgundy with him and kept saying: I'll take that to Maria ... She'll be delighted. It's good for the blood." I plodded home through the deserted streets and thought incessantly: "He's the only one who really lives ... He has it as lovely as the lilies in the field."

Selma was getting ready to go to work and looked at me reproachfully.

"I'm going back to racketeering ... You soon won't have to go to the office," I said in passing.

Two days later I happened to read in the paper that an unemployed teacher named Wilhelm Hobrecker from Remscheid had been arrested for forging paintings and cheques. He was later sentenced to several years in gaol. Since then I have completely lost sight of him and never heard from him again.

Maria Uhla had already given birth to a boy. While she was in the maternity home, Schorsch knocked together some basic sticks of furniture from plywood and one day we moved his possessions by handcart from Sendung to Schwabing, where my friend had found a studio flat. When I came home the same evening, Selma was lying on the sofa, writhing in agony.

"It has to come in the next day or two," she groaned. I ran around to the doctor, fetched the midwife and put the expectant mother in bed. I then went into the neighbouring room and kept water constantly on the boil on the gas cooker and helped the midwife when she came out of the bedroom every now and then. Finally, however, we had to send for an ambulance. Selma bore a girl in the clinic. I ran around doing deals. I didn't visit mother and child until the following day, when I awkwardly played the role of the joyful father.

"Now this. Another burden!" I thought on the way home. I decided to earn as much as possible so that I could rent a large flat. I frittered away the time pushing contraband and had no time for anything else. Selma was with me all day now. The kid screamed and kicked. I didn't dare look at it, I could hardly even bring myself to touch it for fear of hurting it. Ever since I was a child, helpless creatures made me feel helpless myself. Yes, I was almost scared of her.

"Are you going out again? Just stay here," Selma said nearly every evening.

"I have to do some business ... We have to get out of this filth," I said as an excuse. Only when I was out on the street did I breathe easily. I went in the *Dichtelei* or *Simplicissimus.*

The Red Cross man and his wife met me and congratulated me. I forced a happy smile onto my face.

I felt more at ease with the professor. With a slightly concerned expression, he told me: "An artist should not have children." But then, as if to console me, he added the bitter-sweet thought: "But of course ... There are exceptions." We walked along side by side pensively. I tried pretending to be happy with vague words.

"You know, Herr Professor, to be honest I always need frustrations; only then am I driven to create," I said. He gazed at me almost searchingly and asked, seemingly puzzled: "Frustrations? ... My dear fellow, I hear something rather peculiar in your tone ... But," he paused for a moment and sighed imperceptibly, "everyone has his demon ... And a poet more than anyone else."

I held my tongue. He also said no more, before we parted.

At around this time I got to know a young student who often sat among the artists and expressed a violent dislike of me. "Here comes that ghastly bloke again," I once heard her say. I took no notice. On the other hand, I found the girl attractive from the start. I sneakily tried to get closer to her. The craftswoman, who had told me about the temporary job at the Coal Marketing Board, was her close friend. I had known her for some time, and I gave her some of my poems and a short story.

"And, and … show them to the dark-haired girl too," I said quickly in some embarrassment, laughing a little. The craftswoman gave a knowing nod of the head, and also smiled. A few days later I met the pair of them on the street, went up to them and asked if they had liked my work.

"Very much," said the craftswoman, but I could tell from the way she said it that she had not read a word. "And," I said turning to the student with a peculiar childlike chutzpah, "and … I suppose you didn't like the stuff at all, or …" I felt an extraordinary rush of blood into my cheeks.

"Oh yes, I read it … You're not bad," she replied.

"Really?" I asked, suppressing the violent emotion I felt. "No, really … it's wonderful: *For all the unfamiliarity of our innermost being is planted in us from childhood on, and all the sweetness of the nights glides past,*" she recalled. To conceal my joy at this, I made some inane remarks and laughed coarsely, saying: "Well, yes, most black marketeers have a lyrical streak … That's because they have to creep about at night … And the darkness is very stimulating."

The craftswoman found that very witty and the student forced a smile.

And so began the thing that every poet has celebrated in song, and which really determined my future.

I visited Schorsch almost daily in his new studio. Maria Uhla was a deliriously happy mother. In spite of their poverty she retained her womanly cheerfulness. Then all of a sudden, she suffered an infection of the womb and died.

After the funeral my friend packed a rucksack and took to the mountains for a few weeks. He seemed to be a totally broken man.

And, as if we were both destined always to go through similar experiences, Selma fell ill shortly afterwards. She also gave her severe flu to the child. Both had to go into hospital. That meant I had to get hold of money, whatever it took. I purchased from my supplier on a massive scale and rushed around. The Dutchman finally came to my aid with a few hundred marks. I went to Selma.

"Have you got some money at last?" she asked.

"Yes, don't worry," I said, showing her the banknotes. She breathed a sigh of relief. "You're a good bloke," she said, tenderly. She stretched her arms towards me and gave me a kiss.

"Yes, yes, yes … But don't praise me, please … I'm only doing what's right," I said, almost pushing her away, and left feeling depressed.

The next day my brother Maurus visited. He had already been at home on a week's leave. I was genuinely delighted. We talked about books and poets. He was reconciled. Later Nanndl also came again after a long, long time and the three of us visited Selma in the hospital.

Maurus had to leave again at 11 o'clock in the evening.

"Maurus," I said, "just clobber a sergeant or an officer ... Refuse to follow orders or don't go to the front!" I told him. He laughed wearily and ironically, shaking his head.

"Yes, *you* could do that. But I can't," he replied.

"You'll see, you won't be out there more than another three months," I replied, "either peace will come or the revolution."

"Oh, you ass!" he teased, incredulously.

We ate in a pub and got a little merry. I told him about my black marketeering in arrogant tones.

"Aha ... Well, that must certainly be more profitable than writing," he exclaimed, and added pointedly: "I bet you're no mean businessman ... You're good at cheating ..."

"Oh come off it, if he's broke! ... Nobody can help him out," said Nanndl. We sauntered cheerfully down the streets under the night sky.

"Yes, you'll always do all right! ... You'll lie your way through life in supreme comfort ... Hmm," Maurus scoffed, shaking his head now and then.

We accompanied him to the railways station. He left with hundreds of others. Directly for Verdun. The most dangerous battle front.

As we parted, Nanndl looked me in the eye with a childlike fondness and said: "Oskar, I think you have a lot more trouble ahead."

I forced a laugh and pretended to be happy.

"Ah! ... Trouble! There's nothing of the sort! ... Everyone is responsible for how he feels. ... And I feel fine ... Come and see me more often," I said, and went.

17.
IT ALL KICKS OFF

While I was busy with my dirty business, spending days and nights drinking with the Dutchman, moving in artistic circles; while I was passing my time in all these trivialities, while I thought again and again about making my escape to some unknown town and while I made no effort to arrest the slow descent of our married life into utter ruin, the development of public events suddenly started to accelerate.

The parliamentarization of Germany had begun, rumours were circulating about the disasters and retreats of our troops, questions about the Kaiser flared up, the newspapers openly reported on the collapse of Austria, Magyars and Czechs were accused of cowardice, and as a terrifying signal of the approaching breakdown, the first enemy planes appeared over Munich. The alarm sounded. At first, everyone stared curiously into the sky, the trams came to a halt, and nobody was especially frightened. But the second time everyone panicked and there was general unrest.

"The mass murder must stop," demanded even the most conservative bourgeois.

"It's all the Kaiser's fault! He must go!" everyone was saying. Ludwig Thoma and Grand Admiral Tirpitz spoke at public rallies demanding national resistance to the last drop of blood. The admiral brandished warlike phrases, the poet made a poor, petty bourgeois speech. Although frankly, people only turned up to see the celebrities. No one was interested in the latest slogans.

"National resistance? It's just another swindle. It means the poor man gets his head broken and the rich man grabs even more!" Anyone could scream this in a beer hall without being contradicted. Most nodded: "He's right!" Much wilder rumours were now circulating. Decrees were ignored with scornful indifference. With parliamentarization, the press also became freer. Moreover, a new election to the Reichstag was due. There were fresh demonstrations demanding food. Leaflets and posters appeared. People carried boards bearing the words "Peace and Bread", "Bread and an Immediate Peace", and here and there more scuffles broke out with the police. The embittered masses grew much, much more daring. Gangs became a daily sight. An amnesty freed the revolutionaries, who now worked with all their might.

Every day it felt like the machinery of law and order, which was thought to be secure, was coming off the rails. When you saw the dark and compact masses streaming through the streets, it was almost as though a torrential river had broken its banks and was flooding everything in its path. There were new developments every day. I let things slide. The days rushed by, almost feverishly. I ran to every meeting with Schorsch. Only occasionally did I return to the artistic circles. They seemed unmoved. They carried on with the same old debates about expressionism, van Gogh and Cezanne, night after night. I interrupted, brazenly and caustically: "Art will be the very first thing we deal with! It must be eradicated!" Nobody objected. At most, one or two smiled ironically.

Eisner spoke in the Schwabing Brewery as a candidate for the Independent Social Democrats and savagely attacked his opponent, the Majority Social Democrat Erhard Auer. He squared up to his opponents hoarsely and caustically with a fanatical élan. He was surrounded by a tightly packed crowd. He stood on the podium amid the crouching multitude and gesticulated wildly now and then. His long hair flowed down almost to his shoulders and his beard was more ragged than ever. Other than the fact he wore glasses, he looked like an apostle. "You see me just as when I was released from Stadelheim!" he called out; there was a note of vanity in his words. He was greeted with tumultuous applause. "The revolution, my dear friends, will sweep away this election. Other powers will arise and show the way forward to the downtrodden masses!" he shouted with powerful emotion. "And he who gives his vote to those who approved war credits, those criminals who conjured up all the misery of this bloodiest of mass slaughters! – He who votes for this Auer, he declares that this crime is somehow justified!"

"Down with the traitors!" they screamed from every corner. "Put Auer under lock and key!"

And finally: "Long live the USPD!" After a warning not to form a procession, the crowd left the hall. A few days later the Democrats held a meeting in the Wagner Hall. The famous professor Max Weber held forth on "the new political order in Germany". For unity of the Reich, the abdication of the Kaiser, and a complete reorientation of foreign policy. "The cry doing the rounds so dangerously in Bavaria, 'Separation from Prussia', is a crime and an idiocy," he declared. Tall, gruff, dressed in a frock coat, solidly and respectably democratic like a true Badener, he replied skilfully and manfully to the heckling.

"The question, will there be national resistance or not, is one that the men at the front must answer!" He spoke sharply against militarism and demanded a taxation on wealth to cover the war debts.

"It is madness, it is a crime, it is impossible, that bourgeois society should be transformed into a future society based on socialist foundations," he declared coldly amid the cries of "Oho" from the audience. "We would have the enemy in our midst, followed by reaction in the worst form!" he replied. The revolutionaries, who had turned up in large numbers, burst out laughing. There were heated exchanges and during the discussion I saw Erich Mühsam again for the first time. He shouted wildly:

"Just ask the men at the front what their position is on peace!" and called upon women to take part in more and more peace demonstrations. My whole body trembled as I stood on the high, half-domed platform and shouted cloddishly: "The revolution is coming! It is coming! I call upon soldiers to refuse to obey orders and leave the barracks!"

A flood of abuse, and at the same time, a torrent of applause came from below. I stopped abruptly and quickly ran down the stairs. Another took my place, a man who, when he had been sent a commission, refused to accept it. He shouted even louder: "Yes!! Destroy your rifles! Just put an end to the great swindle!"

"Shabby deserters!" people barked and hissed from here and there. And the next day the newspapers called us the same. "It'll all kick off in three days! Long live the world revolution!" an unseen man in the gallery bawled down to the people looking up. Most of them laughed.

"Yes, peace is coming ... Army headquarters has demanded it ... But it won't happen overnight," I heard a fat, comfortable bourgeois say. That appalled me. So calm, such trust in the "leadership"; he spoke as though they would put everything to rights. And how extraordinary it sounded: "Army headquarters has demanded it." Funny, I thought, previously they were demanding a million fresh soldiers or cannons, now they were demanding peace! I was curious to know if Army HQ would also demand the revolution.

The next day – it was there in bold newspaper headlines – there suddenly came the news of the Kiel sailors' insurrection. For the first time, it was there in black and white: "After a few hours red flags fluttered on all the warships. The Admiralty has submitted to the decrees of the Soldiers' Council. The advancing troops went over to the mutineers."

Schorsch ran towards me, waving the paper from afar. We stood for a good half an hour in his studio reading the news over and over again. "In Germany. Amazing. I would never have believed it possible in Germany," cried Schorsch again and again.

"Now do you believe that the revolution is coming!" I said.

"Yes, soon ... I am intrigued," he admitted. To be honest, we were more surprised by the news than enraptured.

The same evening the USPD had called a meeting in the small hall at the Hacker beer cellar. As we were arriving, the masses had gathered on the Theresienwiese. "You know what?" Schorsch said in a strange tone, "it's finally kicking off today." Dripping in sweat, we reached the Bavaria monument, and heard Eisner shouting in the dark to a dense crowd: "Munich will rise up in the next days, I would bet my life on it!" He swore this, solemnly. A shiver ran up my spine. "Kiel! Let's do what they did in Kiel!" shouted several in the crowd and made efforts in that direction.

"Agents provocateurs! Don't be provoked!" warned one man with a stentorian voice.

"Wait and see!" we heard from here and there. And finally the crowd dispersed. Most of them grumbled. One said, coarsely: "The cowardly dog! He's always saying: it's coming, but he never acts ... All he cares about is winning followers!" I was disappointed, too. The word *Kiel* chimed encouragement in everyone's ears. Yet nobody could explain why we were not starting the revolution here, now, immediately. That made people suspicious.

The next day's newspaper reports about this gathering in the dark were rather ironic.

"You see, that's what they do when nothing happens ... it's all made to look ridiculous and people become alienated again," I moaned at Schorsch, boiling with rage. There was nothing left but individual acts of terrorism, I said. In those days I felt like I was shut up in a barrel and being constantly flung this way and that. I went about my day-to-day business soberly and mechanically. I visited Selma and talked to her indifferently. I had hardly left her before I forgot it all again. The girl had taken an office job. I met her in the evenings and talked to her just as absently. I spoke with the professor about everything under the sun, but my mind was elsewhere. I did some deals, drank with the Dutchman, ran around. I could find no rest. I could not think straight. From time to time my ears pricked up, like a dog hot on the scent.

"Why should I care a damn about anything!" I would grumble bitterly, as if to hold my hopes in check. But that was so utterly false, so stupid! Everything was my concern, everything that was happening! But what did I really want?

Ask a man who is mad with rage what he wants when he hurls himself at his enemy! Ask a prisoner what he wants when he hears insurgents in neighbouring cells overpowering the warders, running into the corridors and escaping!

Movement, excitement, anything to avoid a standstill. Perhaps that is what I wanted.

In the end, perhaps Pegu had been right, when he said: "You are a nihilist! Such people are not revolutionaries!"

Unusual events had driven me off the usual rails. It was kicking off! It was – to express it in poetical terms – as if you were on the ocean and waiting for a mighty wave to lift you up high and carry you far away to another place.

What then happened was of little importance. At least for me.

I read the *Bolshevik Programme*, read Landauer's *Aufruf zum Sozialismus* again, and the revolutionary leaflets and pamphlets. But they endlessly repeated the same old phrases, no more. What did that matter to me? Just get on with it! And that, for me, was the beginning and end of it.

18.
COMING APART AT THE SEAMS

Very early in the morning, the bell rang. I stretched out sleepily in bed, grumbling. I did not want to answer. But someone was now banging loudly on the door to our flat. Finally I got up and opened it. Selma's father was standing there. I had only seen him fleetingly once or twice before. He was a widowed master locksmith. His children had left him, apart from his eldest son, who was his foreman. But he cared nothing for the others, living for himself. For some time the old man had belonged to a pious sect of Bible-bashers and believed in somnambulism.

"*Him?* ... You want to marry him?! ... He has the mind of a villain! ... You'll soon see how long the Good Lord stands for it ... You're going to damnation!" he had said to Selma at the time, when she told him about our intentions to marry. He did not show his face again until the child was born. He said little, just growled some text from the Bible now and again, usually something that sounded menacing. Most of the time he cast furtive, almost contemptuous glances at me and smiled in a curious way. He now looked at me with the same smile, nodded shakily with his large, shaggy, grey head, and said: "Yes, yes, it's coming now ... She didn't believe me." He fixed his baggy, watery eyes on me.

"What?" I asked crabbily.

"Yes, yes: He shall deliver six afflictions upon you; and yea, in seven there shall no evil touch thee," he babbled, standing there, a bent old man.

"She's in the hospital," I said and stared at him angrily, because he was grinning so maliciously.

"I've already inquired. I know already," he admitted, and did not let me out of his gaze. "Shall we go and see her?" I asked.

He nodded and said something about the seven angels and the seven plagues. He seemed to be entirely absent. I left him standing there, went into the next room and got dressed.

"Don't you believe in the Lord God?" he asked me directly, as I came out of the bedroom.

"Oh yes," I replied indifferently, keen to leave.

"Then why did you marry her?" he persisted.

I could not help laughing a little, and said: "What on Earth has that got to do with the Lord God ...?"

He looked at me with a dull and bleak expression, and nodded a few times: "True, very true ..." Then he monotonously babbled out some texts learned by heart: "But the Spirit saith expressly, that in later times some shall fall away from the faith, giving heed to tempting spirits and doctrines of devils ..." He paused, then spoke as if he was only addressing himself: "It is the lunar cycle ... The same woman from Ingolstadt spat out thirty-seven nails and shards of glass ... So there – that's what's known as witchcraft, isn't it? ... Isn't it? ... But you'll see soon enough ..." I remembered the story of the woman possessed by devils, who was made to spit out broken glass and nails. He generally told the story mixed up with sayings from the Bible.

"Oh for goodness sake! ... Let's go," I said, annoyed, and flung the door open. He followed, grumbling under his breath.

In the hospital, by Selma's bed, he hardly bothered asking how she was. He launched straight into Bible texts, spoke of the coming dawn of the thousand-year Reich, interweaving bizarre observations.

"How are you then?" asked Selma.

"Who, me? ... You can see for yourself! ... I have nothing to fear," he exclaimed, and regarded us rather like a person for whom heaven is open, and who takes pleasure in seeing people around him who are damned to hell.

We let him talk.

"How's your revolution coming on?" Selma asked me in the meantime.

"Yes, it won't be long now," I said indifferently. The old man laughed and leered at us. He pointed at me with an outstretched index finger and suddenly said: "Him? ... He'll desert you! ... Just you see! ... You never believed me ..."

Selma smiled. I looked distressed.

"You're talking rubbish," Selma said to the old man, crossly. But he wasn't listening. He sat there and stared vacantly into space. He had folded his gnarled hands idly on his bony knees. He really seemed to be on another planet. His dirty, tattered clothes hung from his body, his wrinkled, bearded face was impassive, his eyes were dull. The patients around us looked at him with something like fear. Once again, he recited in a monotone: "By common confession, the mystery of godliness is great: He appeared in the flesh, was vindicated by the Spirit, was seen by angels, was proclaimed among the nations, was believed in throughout the world, was taken up in glory."

I left with him.

Out on the streets I saw large yellow posters with bold lettering, warning against riots. They were government orders banning the expected demonstrations. Social Democrats and Independents had called upon the masses to appear on the Theresienwiese at three in the afternoon.

"Well, I must go now," I said to the old man and let him get into the tram. I hurried off to find Schorsch.

"Today could be decisive," my friend thought, as we made our way. We met people we knew. A female worker ripped down the government's ordinance. Now and again she shouted: "Long live the revolution!" There were no police to be seen. The closer we came to the Theresienwiese, the larger the crowds. Everyone hurried. Before the Bavaria statue, the dense crowd grew by the minute. Men were speaking from the slopes and the steps of the monument. Here and there a red flag was raised. "Up with (whatever)!" the crowd shouted, then "Down with (whatever)!" The crowd surged restlessly; it became a scrum. We found Eisner at last, who was speaking from a side slope at the top of his voice. When he paused for breath for a moment, we heard the voices of the other speakers. More and more people came. The crowds stretched further than the eye could see, swarming in like a vast column of ants.

"My God, all of Munich is here ... Now there's a chance to act! Hopefully today they won't just go back home and do nothing," I said to Schorsch. A bearded giant in army uniform heard this, smiled thoughtfully and said, brilliantly: "Give over cock, nobody's goin' 'ome ... We've got other ideas ... It's all kickin' off."

"Long live peace!" people shouted around me at this very instant. "Peace!" the cry went up and echoed through the crowd. And they all roared thunderously: "Long live Eisner! Long live the world revolution!" Then it was still for a minute or so. Applause rang out from the Bavaria and beyond. We forced our way up the slope. Suddenly Felix Fechenbach,[44] dressed in field grey, barked out to the surging throng, almost like a military command: "Comrades! Our leader Kurt Eisner has spoken. There is no point wasting more words! Whoever supports the revolution, follow us! Follow me! March!" And all at once the yelling masses surged forwards. The black wave of thousands upon thousands of excited people rolled up the slope to the street; the procession continued past locked houses and drawn blinds and headed straight for the barracks. We marched, wedged in by a storming throng, almost at the front, barely five steps from Eisner, whom I watched assiduously. He was pale and looked ahead in deathly earnest; he spoke no more. It almost looked as though he too had been taken unawares by the sudden turn of events. Now and again he stared straight ahead, half anxious and half bewildered. He walked arm in arm with the broad-shouldered, blind peasant leader, Gandorfer,[45] who

---

[44] Felix Fechenbach (1894-1933) was a poet and political activist. He was gaoled in 1922 for his role in the Eisner government. Later, he was active in the *Poale Zion* Marxist-Zionist movement, travelling to Palestine in 1926. In August 1933 he was shot by the SS while being transported to the Dachau concentration camp.

[45] Ludwig Gandorfer (1880-1918) was a leading voice of the Bavarian rural working classes in the USPD. He took care of Karl Liebknecht's son Helmi when the later co-founder of the Communist Party of Germany was imprisoned in 1916.

strode along purposefully. This figure moved far more freely, stepping out massively and solidly, the way Bavarian peasants do. The two men were closely guarded by trusted paramilitaries.

The march, once started, was unstoppable. It met no resistance. The police seemed to have disappeared. Inquisitive faces gazed down upon us from the many open windows in the houses. At every point fresh troops joined us, including some that were armed. Yet most people laughed and chattered as though they were off to a party. Now and then I turned around and looked backwards. The whole city seemed to be on the march. We also learned that sailors had stormed the royal palace.

"Over there, over there! Move it! It's breaking out over there!" somebody shouted from behind us, and everyone started running. There was a wild struggle. We stormed through the open door of the Guldein School.[46] All of a sudden, we wedged into a dark corridor.

"Halt!" someone roared. "Haa-alt!" echoed the command, now fragile, and died away.

"There, you dog!" came the call from ahead, and there was a tremendous commotion. I resisted with both my elbows, wanting to go further. But those at the front shoved us back and forced us onto the street. A shot rang out sharply, causing a momentary silence, which was swallowed up again in the howls and the trampling of feet. As if on a signal, the hordes stormed into the corridor, and I now also saw armed men. There was confused chatter, screams, and then suddenly someone up above flung open a window, waved a red flag, and shouted: "The soldiers have declared for the revolution! They've all come over! March on, march on! Onwards!"

"Bravo! Hurrah! Long live the revolution," everyone was yelling in the street, and soldiers emerged from the Guldein School, with or without rifles, red handkerchiefs tied to their barrels. The demonstration now headed through the city at the double. Here and there platoons of armed soldiers broke off and vanished inside a house. As we crossed the Donnersberg Bridge for the first time an army paymaster, in uniform, entered the crowd, a few of whom ripped off his epaulettes and jostled him. The man began to cry and raised his hands pleadingly. The giant wanted to attack him, but I pushed everyone aside and held him off.

"Let him go! It's not his fault," I bellowed at the top of my voice. The giant stared in astonishment and took a menacing stance towards me. Others took his side.

"Make yourself scarce!" I shouted at the terrified paymaster. But he

---

[46] The Guldein School was converted into a barracks and munitions store during the First World War.

278

was so confused, he just froze.

"Laddie!" snarled the giant, grabbing me by the arm. His eyes sparkled. Then someone nearby shouted: "Stop scrapping! That's Graf! Move on!" And when I turned around there was a syndicalist between me and the giant, swearing like a trooper, and the scuffle was over.

"What it is, right, I thought you were one of theirs," the giant chuckled, and gave me a slap on the back: "Nah, yer sound, our kid. The little'n can leg it! Nah buvver, comrade!" We linked arms good-humouredly and marched on. The paymaster had disappeared.

"What it is, right, I can't stand blokes like that, me!" my companion said occasionally.

Most of the barracks gave in without a struggle. There was already a system behind these conquests: a delegation stormed inside, while the masses waited; a few minutes later a red flag hung from one of the windows and huge cheers rang through the air when the delegation came out again.

Now the march divided, some of the crowd going this way, others going that way. "They want to fire on the Max-II barracks," was whispered from ear to ear. That spurred us on even more.

But it turned out otherwise. The sentry threw his rifle away at once and joined us. We ran through the gate, directly into the courtyard. Incredible. There stood an elderly officer drilling a company of soldiers who were standing in rank. He never even turned around. Someone hit him with all his force on the head, driving his helmet right down over his ears. He fell without a sound, and already in the next seconds the soldiers flung their rifles crashing down to the ground, as though they were responding to an order. They came over to us, laughing. "It's over! Revolution! March!" I heard in all the commotion. A boy from the Alps whooped as if he were dancing the *schuhplattler*. To one side, a man was giving a speech to a group of people, calling for the formation of a Soldiers' Council. The procession marched into the open towards the military prison. It was all locked up and quiet. Ladders and tow-bars were fetched, stones were flung against the barred windows, threatening yells echoed, a few soldiers pounded against the locked door with axes and rifle-butts; everybody was ready to make an assault. Then the door was flung open and we all rushed in. I was literally swept along and only came to my senses upstairs in the cold, dank-smelling, noisy corridors. To this day I can still see the cell doors opening and the prisoners coming out. One gazed at us wide-eyed and in amazement, convulsed and started sobbing heartbreakingly. And then he fell feebly onto the chest of a small man and clung to him. He sobbed, over and over again:

"Tha-ank you! Thank you! ... God bless you!"

"Revenge!" the crowd yelled and again: "Revenge against the

screws!" Then they looked for the warders and prison officers. We heard a din coming from below and the pounding of clubs and rifle butts. Then someone shouted: "Take it easy! Take it easy!"

Someone was being lynched, it seemed. I couldn't see anything. But people near me said: "It's all up for them!"

Then a voice was heard above all the racket: "Everyone out! The troops are coming!" Losing their heads, everyone rushed out, and only when they got downstairs did they realize that it was a false alarm. There were clusters of people here and there, each listening to a speaker appealing for the immediate formation of Soldiers' Councils. Finally, they turned towards the city. The streets seemed too narrow as every man and woman joined the flood of people. From time to time an officer came into the crowd; he was shoved around, his epaulettes and imperial cockade torn off. Nobody came to their defence. Most of them were distraught and deathly pale. Some actually joined the procession straight away.

At Isartorplatz I ran into the hair salon, to Nanndl. "Revolution! Revolution! We have won!" I shouted to Nanndl triumphantly. She at once dropped her curling tongs and beamed. I was gone in a flash.

Around eight in the evening we ended up in the Franziskaner beer cellar, on the other side of the Isar. There we learned that the Majority SPD, led by Auer, had marched through the city in an orderly manner, accompanied by music, and had dispersed at the Max Monument. Uproarious, ribald laughter greeted this news. "Shitheads! Schoolboys!" everyone jeered.

"That's the army of reaction," someone shouted, and "Too right! Too right!" was the answer on all sides. The congested mass of people stood there, unsure what to do. We heard that Eisner would speak in the hall. The revolution had won. Everything had fallen into the hands of the workers: the post and telegraph office, the railway station, the royal palace, the parliament and ministry.

I was hungry.

"Let's go to the bar and get something to eat and drink," I said to Schorsch. We pushed our way through and entered the smoke-filled pub. Stolid and disinterested customers, with real Munich faces, were sitting there. It was as though nothing had happened. "Wally! A pork knuckle over here!" a stout, round-faced man called to the waitress. One man was eating at a table, another was playing tarot, the usual scene. Nobody took any notice of us.

"Wow! I'll be damned!" was all I could stammer, I was so dumbfounded. We ordered beer and sausages and knocked it all back in a hurry. I listened carefully to see if anyone uttered a single word about what was going on. Nothing, not a dicky-bird.

"Wally, a pork knuckle!" That was the only thing going on here.

When we left the pub, the masses had dispersed. We hurried into town. There, we found out that the Workers' and Soldiers' Council was being elected in the Mathäser Brewery. The streets were teeming with activity. Troops and clusters of people were here and there. Rumours were circulating. There were no trams running.

Lots of people were strolling up and down in front of the palace. Now and again someone shouted threats up to the darkened windows. The red flag was already waving over the sentry-post. I parted from my friend and fetched the girl.

"Revolution and peace!" I gasped, and we went back to the palace, where we met the Dutchman and Marietta. They were curious to see what was going on.

"All this splendid grandeur is over," I said with thinly veiled *schadenfreude*. My words were directed at the rich man. He did not catch my meaning.

"Yes, fabulous," Marietta simply said, again and again. We didn't start off for home until deep into the night. After the girl had gone, I went off with the Dutchman. We spent the whole night drinking at his place. When I staggered home at dawn, the streets of Schwabing were quiet and empty. Now and again a shot was fired in the distance. The city slept. The revolution, it seemed, was taking a break. The broad, grey sky stretched peacefully over the houses. "Action! Bang! Bang! Bang! A-ac-action!" I barked mindlessly in the silence; I reeled, belched, and carried on. When I got back to the flat, I sat down and wrote to Selma: "I don't care for you any more! I never cared for you! It was nothing but false pity! Leave me alone! We must all go our own way!" Everything was broken, everything had changed, and now life must change for me!

I suddenly started in alarm at this mad idea and ripped up the letter. Feeling depressed, I flung myself into bed.

The next day the advertising pillars were plastered with decrees from the new government. The city was quiet. Lorries full of armed men drove about and machine gun emplacements stood in front of public buildings; there were military patrols to be seen. There were even red flags flying from the towers of the Frauenkirche.

There were long queues at the bakeries. Everyone was panic-buying bread. People ran off, clutching the hot, steaming rolls, almost like thieves.

In the Bavarian parliament, the Workers' and Soldiers' council held its first session under Eisner's leadership, and elected the provisional government of the Free State of Bavaria. The lead story in the evening edition of the *Münchner Neueste Nachrichten* was a report on the abdication of the German Kaiser and the Crown Prince's renunciation of the succession. I read, underneath, that this came from "The Reich Chancellor, Max, Prince of Baden".

A rumour was going around that the King of Bavaria had been taken prisoner in Leutstetten, and someone said: "They will shoot him soon!" Just a few hours later I found out that Ludwig III and his family had moved to Schloss Wildenwart by car and had abdicated.

An old man read the newspaper on the street, turned pale and wailed loudly: "Sickening! Sickening – We'll be annihilated!" He was reeling, as if about to faint.

"What's up?" asked people who were standing around. He handed the paper to a younger man standing nearby, who read out the terms of the armistice. Everyone was struck dumb and there was general consternation.

One worker in a ragged army uniform, his face pinched with hunger, suddenly shouted to everyone: "That's their revenge for Brest Litovsk!" He went on. Nobody said anything against him.

The Saturday streets were buzzing with people, joyful and eager for news.

19.
CONFUSED

The days flew past like splintered minutes. I had been to the hospital. Selma was in a really bad way. She lay there emaciated and pale as death, with restless eyes. Her breast went up and down as she gasped for breath. All the other patients looked at her as though she was about to die.

"Look, last night I wrote a lot of notes, because I thought I was dying ... At four in the morning they wanted to take me to the room where they all go to die ... Just read, it was horrible," she said, gasping for breath.

I leafed through the notes; they were written in pencil. One of them said: "Dear Oskar, don't worry if I die. Marry the girl." I felt as though I had been stabbed. Another note said: "All happiness is short-lived; see that the child grows up a free woman."

I pulled myself together and stared ahead. Selma smiled and held my hand. "Ah, nonsense! You'll get better," I said. There was a pause. I had no idea what to say. My head was in a whirl.

"The child is as sound as a bell, the nurse says. We should take it away soon," Selma said in turn. I tore myself away from my thoughts.

"Yes, of course ... I must take her home ... That's for the best," I blurted out mechanically.

I went home and wrote a long letter to my sister Theres, telling her about the child. I praised Selma and presented our marriage as something quite special. As I wrote down the sentences, I kept thinking, that's not true, that's just a lie, but I did not want anyone to say, "I told you so". They should not exult in their previous warnings. Better any exaggerated phrases rather than admit my unhappiness, least of all to my brothers and sisters. It made me shudder at the thought of what the future held, but I sent the letter. Then I sought out the professor. I burned with curiosity, what did he think about the revolution?

"What do you say now, professor?" I asked. "Nobody thought it was possible." He shrugged his shoulders and seemed a little embarrassed. We were walking through the bare, deserted English Garden.

"Perhaps I am just too old, my dear fellow," he said pensively, "but it's quite a good thing that the eternal parliamentary chatter has come to an end ... What have they done? Jabbered ... Nothing but jabber ... This business with the councils is obvious to me ... I mean, representation of the lower classes ... That's better, no doubt, because it comes directly from the people ... It's just that, I wonder if they will find the right men."

For the first time it seemed to me that this man, usually so sure of himself, was having doubts. I was secretly tempted to trot out a bunch of revolutionary slogans, all at once. But I held back, without knowing why. I spoke no more about the events and said, probingly: "I am also turning over a new leaf, professor ... I think you will disapprove of it all and won't understand ... You see, I think I have been on entirely the wrong track until now ..." I wanted to talk to him about my bungled marriage, I had a huge desire to know what he would say if I suddenly left Selma. But strangely, I did not dare mention it. "Aha ... So, what is going to happen?" he asked, half smiling.

"Oh well, yes, I cannot really tell you anything," I said evasively, and he did not trouble me further. I was annoyed at my cowardice.

At other times you are the most bloodthirsty revolutionary; this man is human just like you, he eats same as you, goes on the bog same as you, will die one day same as you, so why this stupid anxiety in his company? At times I hated him, yet I feared him; I loved him, yet I was a stranger to him, an utter stranger. Every time we met, I resolved to express my opinion clearly, but every time I lied to him and to myself.

But the good man was neither a fascinating personality nor a rabid partisan who refuted all my ideas mercilessly. Intellectual freedom seemed to be more precious to him than anything; he really did not care about anything else I got up to. He did not attach any conditions to my scholarship, in fact, he disliked it when I expressed gratitude. All his sympathy was reserved for my poems.

So why did I always act like a hypocritical schoolboy in his presence? He was practically giving me money as a present, and I had known since childhood that you only get wages in exchange for solid labour. I could not understand good deeds that demand nothing in return. A few verses were a pretty questionable exchange. Who would serve up a roast dinner with all the trimmings just to honour a stranger? I couldn't make head nor tail of it.

And the same applied to everything else.

I had married and was duty-bound to provide for my wife. I couldn't simply run away from this. It was expected, and that was all there was to it. On the other hand in these few weeks I had fallen in love with the girl and, without exaggerating, terribly in love. At times, that left me totally confused. I forgot everything. We walked together for hours every day and talked incessantly. Whenever conversation dried up, my heart thumped. I turned really giddy, my mind and body turned to mush. I felt my companion's arm, lightly caressed her hips. My blood ran hot and cold; I wanted to jump on her like a wild animal but held myself in check. I thought of Selma in dull despair and hastily returned to the conversation. Now and then I burst into foolish laughter. My teeth chattered. "Are you getting cold?" the girl asked. "No, no, I'm always like that ... I've been under such pressure lately," I lied.

I was no longer able to sleep. I wandered around all night long, racked my brains and finally went back to the whores. They revolted me but how else was I to shake off my restlessness, I thought. But it remained. One whore was so fat that I ran away from her in total disgust. I staggered out onto the street. It crossed my mind that I belonged in the lunatic asylum after all. I left the whores. I ran through the revolution, through day and night, like a crazed bull, in a manner of speaking.

I became more and more confused. From time to time I went to church, in secret, and attempted to pray. Like a brainless child. But that didn't help either, not at all. Terrible. I tried with all my power to come to a proper decision, but everything went to pieces again. I started to sulk, totally at a loss.

Schorsch came and said: "The business with the police is over. Let's go and fetch our papers and tell that informer Fuchs what for." And so we went. Suddenly, I said: "You know what, this is complete rubbish! It doesn't matter a bit!" We roamed through the bustling city.

"This revolution amounts to nothing," I grumbled. "They made a rumpus for one single day and that was it! What are they doing now? ... Now they're just clearing things up again. But there's nothing worth clearing up!"

"Idiot!" snapped my friend.

"Well, have you noticed any change as a result of the revolution?" I asked bluntly.

"No, not yet ... But it takes time," was his answer.

"Nor have I ... We're sitting in the same shit as ever," I moaned. I ran off, all of a sudden, fetched the girl and the two of us visited Selma. We collected the baby and took it to my folks in Berg. Things were the same as ever in the village. Everyone worked, the government decrees were drenched in rain outside the village hall, nobody saw them. Nobody here cared about the events. Nobody uttered a word about them.

My mother greeted us with a laugh as we stepped into the low-ceilinged kitchen; my brother Maurus, who had just returned from the front, was chopping wood in the yard and Theres was sewing in the living room. We drank coffee and they all looked at the screaming kid.

"There! That's what you get for marrying, Mr. Husband," mocked Theres. My mother asked about Selma.

"Is there much going on in the city?" Maurus asked casually.

I wanted to tell him about it. He smiled ironically: "The main thing is that the war is over. This new lot won't make things better."

"But now we are in power!" I blustered, stupidly.

He looked at me derisively and exclaimed: "You? ... You'll make a fine mess of it! ... Nobody around here cares what's going on in the city." And because I stayed quiet, he started up again: "They are all asses! ... They don't have the foggiest idea about the country ... And they are totally naive! Every farmer now has his army rifle at home ... They'll be in for a brawl if they come after anything here, you see! ... Just let them carry on!" He shook his head. "Such asses! ... Such a bunch of jokers!"

We left. Beyond the village we went across the frozen stubble-fields. A startled hare ran down a plough-furrow. Crows flew screeching in the air, the mail coach drove along the road, and children ran out of my old school in the village of Aufkirchen.

"My God, that's doing me good," I said, stopping to take a deep breath, "the city fills me with horror."

I felt a touch of melancholy.

"They make wars and revolutions there, rush about and fight, get themselves killed for their obsessions, make laws and prohibitions, and arrest people. And outside, all around, life carries on as ever: the farmer ploughs, the corn grows, winter comes and then summer, people are born and die, everything is beautiful and peaceful ... What use is all the hulla-balloo?" I persisted, turning to the girl. My brain became clear and calm. A sudden wishful impulse seized me. I wanted to take the girl in my arms. But then I said hastily: "But you know, if I was out here alone, I would die of boredom ... Constant agitation is no bad thing ... The revolution must be permanent!"

The girl smiled and said: "You don't even know yourself what you want."

We walked on and I spoke in a softer tone. The journey back to Munich went too fast for my liking.

The city was in uproar again. Eisner had refused to work with the Foreign Office in Berlin and was threatening to sue for a separate Bavarian peace settlement.

The north German press worked itself into a fury over this in the next days. Pegu wrote to me. He had been sprung from the military prison by the revolutionaries on 9 November and was in the thick of the fiercest movement in Berlin. Events were more radical there. Street fighting was taking place.

This wild confusion was almost comical: after much back and forth the bitterest enemies – the Majority SPD and the Independent SPD – had taken over the provisional government and, after a conference with the governments of the federal states decided to hold elections for a national assembly. Every day the newspapers were full of muddled decrees, which nobody bothered reading any more. These proclamations all sounded the same:

"Calm and order! Peace! No bloodletting! No fratricide! Never again war!" Everyone was an out-and-out pacifist, from left to right, but they all attacked each other by every means available; they shot at each other as in the war. Each party preached reconciliation but struggled for undivided power.

On the one side stood Ebert, Scheidemann, Landsberg, Barth, Haase and Dittmann together with the troops led by von Wels and other old officers; on the other stood the Spartacus League with Liebknecht, Rosa Luxemburg, Ledebour and the masses. "Down with the national assembly! Abstain in the federal elections! All Power to the Councils!" were the slogans of thousands and tens of thousands of rebels. The Spartacus League had established its headquarters in Berlin and spread the movement to all of Germany's states, provinces and cities.

In Munich, too, the new parties were forming and began their election campaigning. Here too, the masses packed into halls. One day they heard Eisner and Toller, the next the Majority Social Democrats Auer, Schneppenhorst and Timm. But the Spartacists, Mühsam, Levien and Leviné attracted more and more support. They openly called for struggle against the governments. They demanded the seizure of power by the proletariat.

The streets heaved with the discontented who flocked to them in droves. They refused to keep quiet, scurrying here and there and waiting for the things they desperately needed: food, shoes, clothing, shelter and revenge for the terrible injustices suffered. Whole families joined in: fathers, mothers, daughters, sons and school children.

Then the police or the Republican Guard turned up in lorries. They directed machine guns menacingly against the wavering demonstration, fired a volley into the air, everyone screamed, surged forward again, and then, when the second volley followed, they ran screaming and cursing in all directions.

"Bloodhounds! Mass murderers! Traitors!" rang out on all sides. "Down with them! Down with them!" roared a thousand voices on the streets. Trust in Eisner slowly evaporated; bitterness grew. The newspapers lied and baited. Censorship was abolished. They could say what they liked. The craziest rumours did the rounds, increasing the unrest.

One night, a crowd ran through the streets and occupied various newspaper presses. In the courtyard of the *Münchner Tageblatt* Mühsam made a speech about the immediate steps that had to be taken and how the press was therefore to be socialized. The old editors were thrown out, and the revolutionaries wanted to start work on a new organ. The print workers were won over, because they had been promised a share of the net profits. But then all of a sudden Eisner turned up with the Police President at the time, Staimer, and a company of the Security Police. It could have been a bloodbath. Eisner disappeared into the building and when he reappeared it transpired that he had secretly gone into the print room and sent all the print workers home. Everyone looked at each other aghast. Then the air was filled with curses and cries of derision. Eisner and Staimer drove off, the company of soldiers withdrew, and the crowd dispersed angrily. The following day there was a single sheet of newsprint, then the usual newspapers appeared every day. They carried on with their lies, undaunted.

"There you are! That's Eisner's revolution for you," I snarled when I met up with Schorsch. "That's the German revolution! As soon as you want to take action, along come our lords and masters with soldiers, and if you do not obey, you are shot! Nice, isn't it!?" I damned the lot of them. I was saddened and bitter. This Munich revolution was a delight to its opponents. It was boring, harmless, intolerable. It was a joke, and a bad one at that. The King had abdicated, yes! All the shops were removing the coat of arms that proclaimed, "By Royal Appointment". People made great speeches at meetings, marched down the street shouting and waving flags, like a blustering Veterans' Association. "Down with this," and "Long live that," they shouted, though they hardly knew why. The rich continued to live in luxury and enjoy themselves; they had hoarded supplies, sat in the best hotels and restaurants, and nobody so much as harmed a hair on their heads. Posters threatening punitive measures against black marketeers were stuck up everywhere, but they were just laughed at, scornfully. The bourgeoisie was already kicking up a fuss and the counter-revolutionary parties engaged in brazen rabble-rousing, the papers scoffed at Eisner, students conspired, and workers were arrested or shot when they came forward with demands.

And now the artists and intellectuals made their move. The so-called Artists' Council held a large gathering in the *Deutsches Theater*. They intended to debate reform of the Academy and the School of High Arts, and the reorganization of teaching the arts. Eisner appeared and spoke brilliantly for a whole hour. He had barely finished before total confusion broke out. The participants abused one another and stopped anyone from speaking. One man was told he could not call himself an artist; it was suggested to another that he would be better off attending church fetes. There was indiscriminate clamour against all and sundry. Everyone shouted and gesticulated, everyone stood on his table and spoke. It was a complete farce. The painter Stanislaus Stückgold finally made himself heard and, despite all the ferocious threats hissing around him, stepped up onto the stage, placed a chair on the speaker's table, lay back comfortably in it, and rocked it slowly to and fro, so that Eisner, who was holding onto one chair leg, see-sawed up and down.

"You're not even a painter! You don't even know how to hold a paintbrush!" somebody shouted. "Decorative kitsch!" yelled a red-bearded man from one corner, shaking his fist.

"De-corative?!" Stückgold shouted assertively. "Yes, very true, very true! I am a decorative painter! ... What's wrong with that then, gentlemen?

288

... What's all the fuss about? ... What is an aaartist? ... A proletaaarian, that's what!" And he put his finger to his head, and then to his stomach: "That's yer brain, and here's yer stomach and guts – that's an aaartist! A Proletaaarian!" He was shouted down. The screams rose to a tumult, a veritable hurricane of abuse. Finally, everyone dispersed.

There was a conference at the home of the Minister of Finance at the time, Jaffé. The aim was to set up an "Intellectual Workers' Council". I went. They considered educational work through the press, school reform, and intellectuals' participation in other cultural issues.

The narrow-faced Katzenstein ran around self-importantly, and there sat Karl Wolfskehl; Rilke was modestly leaning in a corner; I also noticed the face of the lyric poet Alfred Wolfenstein, in his black horned spectacles. They were all cultured and elegant people; you could immediately detect that they had never had anything to do with ordinary people. That made me angry again. A rather short, squat man dressed as a priest, with a broad face, red beard and wrinkled brow stepped forth. He snorted loudly and seemed highly charged. He viewed all these people very critically.

"Leaflets must be written and distributed to enlighten and calm people down," Katzenstein said.

"It is absolutely necessary to calm the masses," a literary gent repeated in a mincing voice. The masses, so they said, were ill-disciplined, the country folk felt agitated, and starvation threatened the city. At the sound of the words "country folk" I jumped up and rudely interrupted the shocked meeting with some nonsensical comments.

"Nobody in the country gives a damn about the revolution! And if any of the gentlemen here took the trouble to go out there, they'd laugh in his face," I bellowed bitterly, and then, sliding into more confusion: "First and foremost, we must stand up to the reactionary bourgeoisie ... The Republican Guard is nothing but a student army baiting the workers ... That's not on! No worker understands any more what's actually needed because you all talk like intellectuals!"

Most of those present stood up and argued with me. Only the man with the full beard looked at me approvingly.

"For God's sake, Graf, we mustn't make provocative speeches or else there will be a bloodbath!" Katzenstein and Wolfenstein blurted out. "Incendiary speeches are extremely dangerous!" They all tried to calm me down.

"But it's true! This is nothing but empty chatter, it's no revolution," I blustered from pure disgust at these people: "You're nothing but literary types!"

"Hans Ludwig Held!" called the chairman, and that squat man now rose to his feet and made a powerful speech condemning intellectualism.

"The previous speaker was right!" he declared. "What he says about country people is true! You, gentlemen, should not show your faces in the countryside!" Indignant mutterings ensued here and there.

"It is up to us, gentlemen! Revolution is not the product of the brain, it depends on human material!" he went on, and described the new era in fantastical terms, then turned to religious matters with rambling quotes from mystics. I slunk off, unnoticed. At home I found a letter from Pegu. He also used the expression: "It depends on human material."

I could not stand it, being so alone. I wanted to visit the girl, but it was already very late. I ran around to the Dutchman's and drank a great deal, astonishing everyone around the table. This boozing always followed the same course: at first, we sat together comfortably and became more and more cheerful, then we grew boisterous, and at some point, we became inexplicably irritable. Not infrequently, it all ended in wild arguments and ranting.

For some trivial provocation Marietta suddenly leapt up and gave the Dutchman a good slapping; the two fought, then Marietta started to smash everything up and finally ran off with two painters. The Dutchman and I were left alone. For a time we sat in the smoking room, facing each other in silence. The wealthy man was deeply depressed; he kept on tugging and twisting the thin hair at his temples, sometimes screwing up his face in exasperation. I was not yet drunk and got the clear impression that the man wanted to talk to me. But what business was it of mine? I wanted to leave. He held me back.

I sat down again.

"Hmm, it's all very absurd," I muttered presently. He said nothing.

"You are a wealthy man; I am a prole up from the country ... We are oceans apart ... In fact, we are enemies but, you see, at the same time, we're quite similar ... You're in the shit, and I'm in the shit," I said, pensively.

"Oh come on, wealthy man! Prole! Come off it!" parried the Dutchman.

"Well, it doesn't matter any more!" I said and casually spoke about Marietta: "She'll be back soon enough ... She'll come back with some cock-and-bull story to deflect your attention." I immediately regretted all this frankness, but I was happy that the Dutchman said nothing in reply.

From the next month on, the professor told me, a returning student would get my scholarship, and I had to go back to dealing in contraband. But there was no business to be had. On top of this, Selma was due to come out of hospital in ten days. So once again I was just a low dog who had to knuckle under. Knuckle under and get by as well as I could through everything that was repellent to me. Once again, the grey reality of poverty was creeping up on me from behind. It would have suited me best to sit with the Dutchman drinking night after night, forever drinking and thinking of nothing at all. So I could not really explain why I was feeling so cheerful.

Suddenly the bell rang and in walked Marietta. And indeed, she did tell us that someone had fired a shot just around the corner. We two men gave each other a knowing glance. I got up. The Dutchman took me to the door and said, shaking my hand: "Come back soon."

Every day I went to the hospital in the late afternoon. Finally Selma said: "I'm being discharged tomorrow."

I ran home, bought food, tidied up the flat, put clean sheets on Selma's bed and worked like crazy. Now and again I simply stood there, reflected, and said, as though everything was now in order: "Yes! ... Hmm, that will have to do."

First thing in the morning I rushed round to Schorsch, borrowed some money and bought flowers. I stood one vase in the bedroom and another on the living room table. I went to the hospital and fetched Selma. We barely spoke the whole way. She could tell I was upset.

When we got back home, I told her that I could not stay with her any longer. There now followed an indescribably dreadful time. Tears, pleading and hatred, each in their turn. She howled through entire nights, screamed through entire days. I became utterly helpless in my pity and revulsion, so for the most part I kept my distance.

I finally went to an estate agent to inquire about a flat. The present tenant, a sculptor, had only given notice two hours earlier. She was startled when I arrived.

"It's my flat now," I said abruptly to all her objections.

"But I still have a pile of firewood and coal here," she protested.

"Wood and coal belong to the property, not to the occupant ... I myself worked at the Coal Marketing Board, so I know the law," I said, as though I were some kind of authority.

"Yes, okay, then you can move in tomorrow but not until the afternoon, please," the sculptor asked pleadingly. "So I have to leave the wood and coal behind ... Hopefully I will get just as much in my new flat."

"Sure you will," I said, and we finally agreed that I could bring my furniture that same day. I wandered around the city for a while and finally borrowed a handcart from the coalman. Selma sat slumped on a sofa and seemed to be mentally disturbed. I talked to her very gently for a long time, and she grew calmer and more composed. I hauled a table, a chair, my typewriter, my clothes and books and a sofa down to the street, loaded it all up, and when I got to the sculptor's place she had already moved out. She had pinned a note to the wall, which said: "I have cleared out already, I wish you all the best."

I sat down on the chair and let my thoughts wander. The split had affected me quite badly. I was feeling tired, ground down. I left everything standing just as I had put it in my haste, took the cart back and went into town. I did not want to see any of my friends. In a state of restless depression, I walked up and down the streets. I wanted to go into the parliament house, but the sentry stopped me. I bumped into a radical worker that I had got to know previously. I walked with him for a while and discussed things.

"This revolution is worse than the monarchy," I said. He agreed.

"But in time, we will take power ... First, we have to get weapons," he said.

"Yes, but aren't you a pacifist?" I asked.

"Well, sort of ... But we will have to fight a proletarian struggle against the counter-revolution ... And that means you can't be a pacifist," he returned.

"So ... well, I've always said, pacifism is rejection of any war and all use of force ... Perhaps the militarists were right all along," I replied.

He looked at me and did not know what to say.

Then, after a while, he said: "Yes, once we have taken power, there will be no war." He asked: "What do you think?"

"General strike! Quite simply, a radical general strike. The rich and the bourgeoisie have not felt any impact of the revolution yet ... When there is no more water, light, bread, absolutely nothing more, the counter-revolution is finished ... Then we won't need to shoot, just don't do a stroke of work," I answered morosely.

"Yes, yes, that's all very well, but nobody's going to do that," he said, "unless everyone joins in, it's completely useless ... The Majority Social Democrats will sabotage everything again ... That's why it's better to look for weapons."

"And then, with the shooting, will everyone join in?" I asked, at once mischievously and sadly.

"Oh yes, for sure."

"Then we are all lost ... The revolution and all of us," I answered, and went.

AN IDIOT STEPS UP

The popular myth of the "lucky fool" seemed to be true in my case. As time went on, I became known in the most diverse circles. Virtually every revolutionary knew me at least by name, the Schwabing poets and artists envied me for my friendship with the rich Dutchman, people in other aesthetic circles had heard of me, a good deal of my work had appeared in magazines, as had, a few weeks earlier, a slim volume of poetry, which the professor warmly promoted everywhere, as did the Red Cross man and the girl. What's more, at the time there was a curious wave of enthusiasm among sections of the upper classes with artistic and literary tastes for talent rising from the people.

It was not unusual for the salons to show off a renowned proletarian. Why, was not entirely clear; perhaps an unacknowledged anxiety, or else a disavowed cunning.

Bit by bit I made my flat more comfortable. The Dutchman donated a few sticks of furniture and oriental drapes. I was his daily guest. Since every prospect of getting hold of money was closed for the time being, I schooled myself in the role of the rich man's hanger-on. I undoubtedly developed a great skill in this respect, because I soon became the most popular person in that stormy household. With a well-practised naivety, which never failed in its effect, and with an incontestable callousness I dealt with the frequent moods of irritation that preceded trouble and strife, and calmed things down with a few words. "Oh yes, let's have another quarrel! ... Let's profit from a scandal! There's not enough going on in the world!" – I generally said this on such occasions to Marietta and the Dutchman and – whether they wanted to or not – they burst out laughing. Everyone was back in good humour. As a result, I was always more than welcome. I nursed some faint hopes, which can be guessed at.

What's more, I was in luck elsewhere. A little while earlier I had been invited to visit a lady, to whom the professor had recommended me. She was known as a patron of poets and artists, was very wealthy, lived alone with a maidservant in an extraordinarily large apartment furnished in the best possible taste, and she hosted a kind of salon for cultured minds. She felt a certain humanitarian sympathy towards the revolution, even if everything about it was alien to her. She had a strong preference for modern art and possessed much sought-after paintings by contemporary artists. Apart from that she wrote poetry and had published several books.

We got on well together and I turned up often. The lady inquired about my private life and took a keen interest. She seemed to be very well informed about my unhappy relationships and before long, quite unexpectedly, she gave me a monthly allowance of two hundred marks. I could now provide for Selma and the baby.

It was curious, but I felt no shyness towards this patron and was quite frank about many things. This brought us closer together. She even took in the baby one day until my mother came and fetched it, taking it back to live permanently in the country.

Now I could move more freely again. I wrote and moved in revolutionary circles. Something had to happen, much more! I was literally gasping for it.

"Jung has written ... It's kicking off in Berlin! Liebknecht can't stomach the fraud any longer," Schorsch said to me one day. "Spartacist uprisings are coming."

"Oh, that's rubbish," I ranted and started off again with my idea about a general strike. "General strike until the bourgeoisie and the counter-revolutionaries are forced to grovel ... Then we can have a fresh start ... Terror makes no sense."

"But that is also terror, you idiot," roared Schorsch.

"Yes, but without shedding blood," I countered. It was odd, until now I had just run around, in the thick of things, but only as an outsider. Now I really wanted to pitch in. Although I had not thought through any programme yet, fixed ideas were swirling through my head daily.

I wrote highfalutin manifestos and wanted to publish them as the programme of the "individuals".

The Intellectual Workers' Council had already been established. There was a meeting at the home of Baron von Bernus, where Paul Ernst, who had been elected to the Executive Committee, gave a speech. People sat inside and listened to his address, while outside in the darkened hall a few wandered around talking about all kinds of things. Katzenstein asked if I could write leaflets. I agreed and wanted to know what I should write. "Don't worry, I'll come back to you," Katzenstein said, and the next moment he was talking to others. He flitted about self-importantly. Several days later I got a letter from the publishing house Georg Müller, inviting me to become editor of a journal they were founding. I swelled with pride. You see, I told myself, how famous you are, and went. A Herr Neuhöfer and a Baron von Gemmingen greeted me. The former did the talking. His intention was to defend the concerns of southern Germany. Sharp words had to be found to attack Prussianism. He thought that Kurt Eisner had done the right thing when he rejected any cooperation with the Reich Ministry of Foreign Affairs.

"So, a magazine to kick up a racket?" I asked.

"No, no; politically serious. But cutting, don't you see, cutting! Not boring," said Herr Neuhöfer.

"Then why don't you just buy *Simplicissimus*. It's in dire straits," I said, "buy it and turn it into the opposite ... It has been glorifying war all this time and once we get hold of it, we must turn it in the opposite direction ... It must be pacifist, Spartacist, Bavarian and all the other things we want ... That would be a brilliant joke."

The gentleman now seemed to be sufficiently informed of my incompetence and said he would let me know. I left.

But this business had made me think. I went to see the Dutchman. We drank manfully, and in the course of conversation I blurted out: "You know what? We should found a really radical-satirical newspaper, one that makes fun of everything, one that will force the revolutionary bigwigs into finally leading a real revolution ... Right now, all this idiotic back and forth makes easy targets for such a magazine ... It would have to be something like a new *Simplicissimus*. Do you see what I mean?"

"Good," said the Dutchman at once, greatly to my surprise, "Good! It's not such a stupid idea ... I know a bookseller in Frankfurt, a good friend of mine ... He can let us know ... We'll travel up to Frankfurt tomorrow, and if it's a workable scheme, I'll hand over the cash immediately ..."

For a moment I was so astonished I was unable to speak, then I agreed immediately.

"That will be nothing but a booze-fest," Marietta said sarcastically, but we stuck to our plan.

I went home, couldn't sleep a wink all night, packed a few things in my tattered suitcase, and the next day we travelled to Frankfurt. We put up at the *Frankfurter Hof*, where I had one luxurious room and the Dutchman another, with a shared bathroom in between. I was positively intoxicated by such a new beginning. I already saw myself as the all-powerful editor in a palatial newspaper office. It was almost like a dream. I was wearing a shabby green suit and inlaid patent leather shoes, which pinched like crazy. The Dutchman, as usual, was dressed in the latest fashion.

I would sit at a desk smoking fat cigars, with a fantastic number of bell-buttons at hand; sub-editors, poets, reporters, lift boys and servants would carry out my orders in an instant. I would be feared by the upper classes, loved by the common people – what lay ahead was beyond my imagination. I did not take a nap and rest a little, as the Dutchman had advised. I brushed my suit again and again, polished my shoes with a piece of sackcloth, combed my hair and readied myself. That evening we were to dine with acquaintances and then talk business over select wines. The Dutchman knocked. I rushed to the door. "Ready?" he asked.

"Yeah, let's go."

I hurried out, and we went to the sumptuous, well-lit dining room. Even if I summoned every drop of self-assurance and tried to ignore the agonizing pressure of my shoes, even if I mustered up an air of casual cool

– I could not fail to notice how condescendingly every waiter regarded me.

The table at which we sat down was laid for several people. There was a mass of large and small plates. Cutlery of all sizes was lined up side-by-side, sparkling clean. Although I was already accustomed to all kinds of meals with the Dutchman, I was at a loss to imagine what was the purpose all this clobber. I couldn't work it out. It puzzled me. But, I told myself, you just need to pay attention!

"It's really lovely here," I murmured casually: "Really lovely."

The Dutchman wasn't listening. The wine list was commanding his full attention. He muttered the name of some wine or other now and again with a tone of satisfaction: "Hmm-m-hm, Deidesheimer Hassert, 1914 ... Hm-hm, oh look! ... Schiersteiner Hölle, Groroder Hof growth ... M-hm-hm, Wachenheimer Riesling 1915 ... Wehlener Abtei, Ehses-Koppelkamm growth. Hm-hm ... Excellent, very agreeable! ... Very agreeable wines!"

Then our guests arrived. The bookseller Tiedemann with a curvaceous blond, the tall, dark-haired painter Starcke with his wife and the painter Rudolph Lewy with his red face, which seemed incapable of being impressed. The Dutchman introduced me. They all looked at me wryly. Wine was ordered, reverently tasted, and deemed to be good. The waiter brought a fabulous hors d'oeuvre. Oysters, among other things. Unobserved, I looked around quickly to see how they were consumed, picked up the shellfish and gulped the slime down just like all the others. They made me feel sick, but I forced them down.

The main course was brought. We drank and grew livelier. I laughed and my face broke into a sweat. I wiped it with a serviette. They all looked at me with curious smiles.

After we had stuffed ourselves the waiter brought crystal bowls of water, which puzzled me greatly. I hesitated and waited cautiously. What idiots, I thought, after all this they're going to drink water; I was already grasping my bowl when I saw the Dutchman dip his fingers in the water and wipe them on a napkin. I quickly copied him.

Everything went off without incident. I breathed easily.

Well-fed and in good spirits and excited about new projects, we got up and went to the bar. Starcke told endless anecdotes about the playwright Carl Sternheim, Lewy made jokes, and finally the Dutchman broached the subject of the magazine with his friend Tiedemann.

"Uh, hmm," muttered Tiedemann, casting me a sidelong glance. I tried to present the project in glowing terms but was strangely lacking in confidence and it all faded away. Nobody was interested. We drank and drank until long after closing time. Finally, we all lounged in the hotel's darkened reception hall, every one of us inebriated and speaking with a slur.

"Man, I'm pissed!" Tiedemann droned. Every now and then his

head sank to his chest. Fed up and dejected, I carried on knocking back the oily whisky and cursed the whole lot of them. Marietta had been right. What was I doing here, in fact?

The next day, after we returned to the hotel from a stroll, the waiter gave me a telegram from Berlin.

"Come at once! It's starting! Important!" Schorsch informed me. I was both shocked and delighted, borrowed money off the Dutchman and rushed off to Berlin.

Pegu met me at the Anhalt Station. We literally fell into one another's arms.

"What's going on?" I asked, showing him the telegram. He smiled. "Oh. nothing at all."

I started swearing so dreadfully that people turned and stared at us. We went to visit Jung. In fact, Berlin looked the same as usual. The trams were running, and the people ran around in a hurry; you could just see lorries with armed soldiers here and there as well as barbed wire in front of houses. Jung told us about Liebknecht's meetings and said there would be action in the coming days. We sat in his flat, played gramophone records, discussed articles in *Die Rote Fahne* and drank schnapps.[47] That evening, we attended a meeting of the syndicalists. Some spoke in favour of working with Liebknecht, others against. Someone rushed into the hall and said that there had been a pogrom a few houses along. A Jew had been murdered in the most outrageous fashion. And we really did hear gunfire. We grew agitated in the hall. I leapt onto the platform and said something about a general strike and human rights. Here and there people spoke in agreement, but the hall was already emptying. There were groups milling about on the dark streets. The usual rumours were being whispered. Here and there, people bellowed, "Down with Ebert-Scheidemann". Strong military patrols then appeared and dispersed the crowds.

The next day there was to be a tremendous demonstration by the Spartacists. Schorsch spoke of the secret recruitment of armed bands. Riding around the streets, you could see clusters gathering here and there. A man called for the dictatorship of the proletariat and, speaking like a persuasive salesman, drummed up recruits to join him in the Red Combat League. Most of those present cracked jokes, listened half-heartedly, and then went away. Others came. In the evening we went to a meeting where Liebknecht was to speak. But people turned up in such numbers that we were turned away on the wide outer steps.

---

[47] The newspaper *Die Rote Fahne* (The Red Flag) was founded by Rosa Luxemburg, Karl Liebknecht and Paul Frölich during the November revolution as the central organ of the Spartacist movement, later the Communist Party of Germany.

"What's going on?" I asked a Spartacist.

"A fight to the death! The dictatorship will come any day now!" he said.

"And then?"

"Liebknecht and Rosa will swing it," the man answered.

I went off to Pegu, moodily.

"It's all rubbish! All this shooting. They ought to manage it differently. Starting now!" I said to Pegu.

"Hmm," he muttered.

I went back to Munich. A few days after my return I went to see my patron and set out an ambitious plan. My rather meagre idea was to prevent a reign of terror. Something had to be done to unite the entire people in a definitive republic. Until there was peace in all strata of society, the statesmen could do nothing; ultimately, there was the risk of an unspeakable bloodbath.

"And, what do you want to do now?" asked the lady.

"Quite simple!" I said. "I will summon a great meeting and speak to that effect. Then we have to work on all the intellectuals so that they are all working in the same direction, especially the university professors ... We must get all layers of society to agree to this new era and then it will be possible to move forwards ... For the time being a meeting must be held and a kind of union of free people must be founded ... I shall need money for that."

This made sense to the lady. She did not hesitate and gave me 2,000 marks for the project. This left me utterly bewildered. Now I had committed to an enterprise and was compelled to do something. I wrote leaflets and had 10,000 of them printed in one go. I ran to an advertising printer and had a giant poster made, with the following words:

People of All Classes! A Great Public Meeting! Against Terror and for Humanity! Speaker: Oskar Maria Graf, Munich.

Men and Women! Workers, Soldiers, Citizens, Artists, Scientists, Students! Members of all Parties! All Social Classes! A senseless massacre has gone on for four years.

For four years, the rule of violence suffocated all reason and humanity! After four years of horror, bloodshed and death the Revolution has emerged triumphant and brought peace, opening the door to a new life. While the governments are concerned to restore law and order, while each of us goes to work, agitators and crooks go about spreading unrest and trying to incite the people into new acts of violence, armed uprisings, etc.

People! After four years of murder, is there no end to it?

People! Come together! Say no! Everyone who has not forgotten humanity, come! Not to found a party that only represents its own interests. But with the interests of the People in view.

The fellowship for the foundation of the League of
"Free People"

The next day I stuck up my posters. I covertly positioned myself by the advertising pillars and gazed with immense admiration. I tingled with a blissfully satisfied vanity. I had never yet seen my name printed so large. I telegraphed Pegu. He came the next day.

"A new organization. The League of Free People! Money is there! It's all sorted!" I said. His jaw dropped as he read the poster.

"You're the purest counter-revolutionary, man," he cried.

"Ah! ... On the contrary! We must work in an anarchist direction again! With individuals. There can be no revolution without the right quality of people!" I explained to him. He shook his head again and again.

I was in a whirl. I got some students I knew to distribute the leaflets. The girl, Pegu and I stuck them in every letterbox. It would be a crush at the meeting, I thought, like a pompous twerp.

The day of the meeting was approaching fast.

"Have you already written your speech?" asked the lady.

"Yes of course," I replied. I hadn't written a word.

The girl and Pegu asked the same. I just rushed around. The words would come, I thought; the main thing was to fill the hall.

The 2,000 marks melted away in no time. Secretly, all this mad rush terrified me. Finally, the great event arrived.

The Mathäser hall was packed to the gunwales; nobody could get through, and outside, rows and rows thronged in half the garden. I stepped up to the speaker's platform. A student chaired the meeting.

He rang the bell and spoke a few words. Then me. The girl sat on my right and took shorthand.

"Assembled people! Rebels! Citizens!" I shouted and paused to think. But I could hardly think of another word.

People lolled about at the tables.

"I have called you together here to raise my voice against terror! Terror is war! None of us want war and another bloodbath! I was in Berlin and heard Liebknecht and saw pogroms! Nothing but confusion everywhere!" Then the heckling started. I lost the thread and had no idea how to continue. The chairman could not ring his bell for long enough, as far as I was concerned.

"Knock him down!" some shouted, and at the back a worker shouted threats and a small scuffle broke out. To my right, the Communists were bawling at me. I shouted with all my might: "I am against all terror! Wherever it comes from!" The atmosphere became even stormier, and in the end Joseph Sontheimer, a man who had formerly founded the Free-thinker movement and was now a radical Spartacist, stepped up to the podium and seized the leadership of the assembly.

"We know him already! He is a harmless Tolstoian, and totally muddle-headed!" he started, and since there was nothing left to do, I shouted out at once: "Enough! This meeting is closed!" The chairman did likewise. And now things turned ugly. I just stood there staring at the uproar like an idiot, while Sontheimer spoke. The discussions got confused and when, after a long while, people dispersed, the cry went up on all sides: "This scally stirs up half Munich then says bugger all! He wants a good hiding!"

We scurried through the scrum and hurried back to Schwabing with our tails between our legs. The next day all the newspapers were raging against the swindle. My only thought was: how can you settle things with the lady? The money is nearly all gone, and nothing has come of it. I would have to present an account, even if none had been demanded.

I therefore hastily established a "League of Free People". Me, Schorsch, Pegu, the girl, one other female student and one worker. And that was it. I went to the lady as one who is not put off by failure and told her she was an honorary member of the League. She was not bothered, but neither had she any interest in the League, she just half-heartedly said yes to everything. I announced that she would soon receive an account of our expenditure and a report on her work. But she protested that this was not necessary, and I left her with a sigh of relief.

"We must draw up a programme," I said to Pegu. We sat down and thought about it. Our main aim was to establish settlements on a purely socialist basis. "Settlements created by purchasing uneconomic farms, managing them collectively and sharing the common good collectively," so ran the relevant passage.

We met in my flat now and again, without ever knowing quite why. Over time I grew more and more uncomfortable that I could present no genuine "activities" to our patron. Finally Pegu produced two Free Germans who had become radical socialists – Koch and Kurella, who wanted to join a settlement. I saw at once that they were serious, which pleased me. For their part, they imagined that we had a pile of money or rather thought we could get hold of it through our contacts. They set out their plans.[48]

---

[48] Alfred Kurella (1895-1975) met Lenin in 1919, became a member of the Communist Party of the Soviet Union, and worked as an author and translator. His younger brother Heinrich was shot in the Great Purge of 1937. Kurella returned to Germany in 1954 and became the leader of the Cultural Commission of the Politburo of the DDR. The life of Hans Koch (1897-1995) was no less interesting. After the suppression of the Munich Soviet Republic in May 1919, the authorities alleged that the Blankenburg commune had sheltered Max Levien, and the com-

"Good," I said. "Yes, that is excellent. We can arrange it ... We see our task as materially supporting every socialist project, that's all ... Everything runs through us." I then mentioned the lady and shortly afterwards the two of them received from her and some others a considerable sum of money. They did indeed buy a large farmstead in Blankenburg, settled it with several students and female artisans, and worked on purely socialist lines. Unfortunately, not one of them had the first idea about farming. The settlement became a refuge for persecuted revolutionaries, and in the end, it had to be abandoned. I never saw it and took no further interest in it.

A little earlier the student had moved in with the lady. She occupied a room rent free and reported all kinds of things that we were supposed to keep to ourselves. The lady became suspicious and asked me to visit. She was ill and received me in her bedroom. I now had to explain how the money had been used, which was very painful for me. I also had to listen to the lady telling me she was by no means happy about my attitude towards her. I was cornered by the unanswered questions and forced to admit time and again that I had carelessly squandered the 2,000 marks handed over to me and my comrades. Finally, I said: "You know what, I have always hated people who have property and money! ... I hate money itself! We are really enemies ... I can't reproach myself!"

The lady thought that very honest and was satisfied. Her allowance continued. I went home and summarized: the magazine came to nothing, the meeting was a fiasco, the "League of Free People" was a revolting nonsense.[49]

I swore to myself that I would never start another project and re-

---

munards were held on remand for a few days. In court, Hans Koch defended himself so impressively that the prosecutor asked if his daughter could join the commune. The penalties imposed were relatively lenient, not least because of Koch's speech. Koch went on to found further communal enterprises with more success, including an asparagus farm in Harxbüttel, Brunswick. Here, he invented a mechanical hoe, patented in 1924. It became the model for many later hoes, right up to the present day. In 1930 Koch founded the company DiMoHa, "The Motorized Hand". After the Second World War Koch founded the company HaKo. In 2018 the Hako Group, headquartered in Bad Oldesloe near Hamburg, employed more than 2,000 people worldwide and generated sales of approximately € 440 million. Koch died at the age of 97.

[49] The "lady" was Hertha Koenig (1884-1975), born into an aristocratic family at Gut Böckel, an elegant stately home in Rödinghausen, north Germany. Between 1910 and 1913 she had been married to "the professor" Roman Woerner. From 1905 to 1921 she lived temporarily in Munich, where she published her own poems and hosted a literary salon. She acquired paintings by Picasso, Hodler, Nolde and Klee, among others, and struggled to hold on to these during the Third Reich. Her estate is today in the German Literature Archive, Marbach. In 1994 the Hertha Koenig Society was founded, dedicated to the care of the author's work and estate and in 2004, on the occasion of the writer's 120th birthday, the Hertha Koenig Literary Prize, for authors writing in the German language, was awarded for the first time.

turned to writing. I wanted to show people what I was capable of and invited all manner of people to a reading in my flat. Rilke, the Dutchman and Marietta, Karl Wolfskehl, the lady, accompanied by a friend, and a crowd of elegant people came. But the stove smoked so horribly that after a short while the gentlefolk fled, all at once. I was upset about this, and now I wanted to withdraw into my shell for ever. I lost all confidence in myself and hated every idea of fresh efforts.

"You blockhead! You utter idiot! Idiot!" I cried at the slightest provocation.

I started binge drinking with the Dutchman again and played the hanger-on. The man was building a villa in Nymphenburg. It was nearly finished. He meant to move into it a few weeks later.

Useless, I thought, useless. There goes your last cushy drinking den around here.

21.
STORMS ON ALL SIDES

Christmas was approaching. Nearly all soldiers had returned from the front and there were homecoming celebrations in their honour. They were strange: usually the first to speak praised the heroic deeds of our undefeated troops with flowery patriotic phrases, then came another speaker, who welcomed the men in field grey as soldiers of the revolution. At the National Theatre Gustav Landauer addressed the soldiers with these words: "You, who have been forced to sacrifice your lives in a senseless massacre of the nations for four long years! The hour of freedom has struck – now fight for yourselves!"

Thousands thronged the streets every day, had no work, waited, grumbled and did not know what to do or where to go.

The whole of Germany was having convulsions. Disturbances had broken out in the Ruhr.

I met workers in town who laughed at me from afar. "Aha, the disgraced Simple Simon of the Mathäser!" they mocked and told me that they had had to stop work for ten days because none of the works had received deliveries of coal. "And we get our wages in full, because the government has decreed it," they said, beaming with joy. "There's time for politics now."

The electoral struggle for regional and national assemblies had flared up. All the heavyweights of the parliamentary parties gave agitational speeches. Stormy meetings followed one after the other.

The streets were flooded with leaflets, livid posters screamed from walls and advertising pillars. The Spartacists tenaciously carried forward their opposition movement, fanatically proclaimed abstentionism in the elections, and held demonstrations.

Every corner of Germany was in ferment. In Berlin, the bombardment of the People's Marine Division by government troops had ignited the great Spartacist struggles. Once again newspaper offices were occupied and there were massive demonstrations in support of the Marines and against the Council of People's Deputies in all cities; after a short crisis the three Independents, Barth, Haase and Dittmann, resigned. Noske, Wisse and Löbe joined Ebert, Scheidemann and Landsberg.

There was a conspiratorial atmosphere in Munich. More and more fugitive Spartacists arrived from Berlin and appeared before the masses with Mühsam, Levien and Leviné, loudly cursing their enemies in the packed, suffocating halls. A proclamation, signed by nearly all of the Bavarian ministers at the time, called for the formation of a Citizens' Guard. Eisner's name had been added without his consent. There was a tremendous uproar in the provisional National Assembly, but the Citizens' Guard was created almost overnight. It gathered together all of the elements hostile to the republic and the revolution: in particular students and unemployed army officers. The Majority SPD ministers, Auer and Timm, proved to be its chief promoters. An unknown gunman shot at Mühsam five times from the cover of darkness. The first antisemitic leaflets surfaced. They mostly appeared in small dairy and grocery shops but were also secretly pasted on walls. Myths were spread like street ballads about Eisner's origins and his supposed wealth.

At the beginning of January we heard about the insurrections in Bremen. Johann Knief, a man of great energy, true grit and comprehensive knowledge, who had been arrested in January 1918 at the same time as us in Munich, was their leader.[50] In Berlin, open warfare raged. We heard gruesome reports: cannons thundered on the streets, flame throwers did their work and machine guns rattled. Noske had declared a state of siege, deposed Eichhorn, the Chief of Police, recaptured the newspaper offices, arrested Ledebour and Meyer, and issued warrants and rewards for the apprehension of Liebknecht and Rosa Luxemburg.

Now Munich flared up. Every day the cry rang out: "Down with the bloodthirsty government of Ebert-Scheidemann-Noske!" Ernst Toller sent a telegram to the Berlin government: "Scheidemann, Ebert, Noske, Members of the Berlin Government. You must recognize that you are guilty for every drop of blood that is yet to be shed. Though the German people have not called even Ludendorff to account, you will appear before a People's Court, and you will find not one conscious worker who will not declare you guilty. We have long since known that you are no socialists. But we no longer know if you were born of women." The demonstrations thronging the streets grew fiercer and fiercer. On one occasion I was crossing the Lenbachplatz and saw a dense crowd rushing noisily into the Promenadenplatz.

"What's up?" I asked as I joined them.

"Eisner has had Mühsam, Levien and another ten comrades locked up in Stadelheim," I heard. We were already before the Ministry. The crowd surged this way and that. Machine gunners stood behind the locked gate, ready to fire, it seemed. We discussed the situation for several minutes. Suddenly, a sailor climbed up the lamppost onto the balcony, vaulted over it and disappeared through the door to loud applause.[51]

---

[50] Johann Knief (1880-1919) founded the International Communists of Germany (IKD) as an anti-war breakaway from social democracy. They later merged with the Spartacists in the Communist Party of Germany. The original text mistakenly refers to Jakob Knief.

[51] The sailor was Rudolf Egelhofer, who later commanded the Red Army.

Shortly afterwards he appeared with Eisner who, panic-stricken, shouted down: "Fetch them then, for God's sake! They have been released!" He vehemently forbade any dictatorial pressure from the street and threatened us with an outstretched index finger, like some enraged schoolteacher. If he had not vowed to prevent the events in Berlin repeating themselves in Munich, he would have taken stronger measures, and next time he would shoot, he declared. Toller stood behind him, ashenfaced and distraught, his arms shaking. A deafening roar of abuse went up, a lorry thundered past, and we withdrew at the double. I went as far as Marienplatz and the crowd went on to Stadelheim to fetch out the prisoners. I met Schorsch. He had turned off down the Promenadenstrasse on his way home. There had been shots from the *Hypotheken und Wechsel Bank*. A sudden burst of machine gun fire.

Nobody knew why. A worker with an agitated expression came up to us.

"They have reinforced the barracks. And set up a machine-gun post at the train station," he hurriedly told us. "We don't know what's going on! ... It seems as though Eisner is also a counter-revolutionary ..."

It was already evening when we reached Stachus. Heaps of people were streaming down the Prielmayerstrasse and Schützenstrasse to the station. A sudden burst of fire rang out from that direction and those in the front ranks started back, screaming, and now the whole square was packed full of bodies that spoke confusedly with each other, swore, shouted and wailed. They had fired into the crowd. Six dead and 15 wounded were left lying on the ground.

"Forwards! Do not run away! Storm the station!" cried a sailor, which checked the retreating human tide. But trucks full of soldiers were already rattling through the Karlstor and from the Promenadenplatz. Everyone raised their heads in helpless surprise, and the converging flood of people fled in disorder. It was only at the Sendlinger Gate that the demonstrators regrouped before marching down Müllerstrasse. I had lost Schorsch, ran here and there, up and down, finally arriving back at my flat ready to drop from tiredness. The following day, around noon, Schorsch came to me with news of the Bavarian elections.

"There will be a coup today. They are going to storm the parliament," he said.

"Fifty-two Majority Social Democrats, 38 Democrats, 31 Centre and just four Independents," I read in the newspaper, adding gloomily: "Terrible! ... Now everything is lost ... A coup will result in nothing but corpses ... We won't win." There was a knock. Pegu came in. We stood there in silence for a while.

"It's all going to hell," Pegu said after a while.

I shook my head, incredulously. Schorsch nodded.

"I just don't know what to think," he growled, fed up: "I don't want to hear or see any more ... It's enough to drive me to despair ... The death knell should toll across the whole city ..." We drank tea and then parted, disconsolate. I did not leave the flat again. I just wanted to hide myself away, at all costs.

That was a true martyrdom. The clock seemed to stay still. I was tormented by restlessness and curiosity. Then again, when I thought about everything, I was seized by anger, and I considered ridiculous plans of assassination. Early in the morning Schorsch knocked at the door, waking up me and the girl. He brought news of the murder of Liebknecht and Rosa Luxemburg.

"Yes, and now it will be Eisner, Mühsam, Gandorfer, Levien, Toller and Leviné, and so it will go on ... Just watch out! ... And then they'll start with the small fry. It's fantastic, how these people work ... They know exactly what they're after," I argued sardonically, "but it never occurs to us to do the same and clear out the lot of them. Because we have character! We have morals! We are such respectable people."

"You idiot, you yourself always railed against terror!" Schorsch threw back in my face. "Yes, but that was then! Now it's totally different! ... None of us are born revolutionaries! Some catch on faster than others," I argued in my defence.

The girl laughed at our confused and heated arguments. I picked up the papers and glanced the headlines.

"Idiots!" I shouted, reading the outraged articles about Liebknecht's and Rosa Luxemburg's murders. "They howl about pack hounds and murderers! ... But Noske is systematic! The Spartacists are forever preaching the seizure of power through armed struggle, but when anyone fights against them and defeats them, they call it a crime! If you want to fight, you cannot complain if your opponent fights back!"

"You ass! Noske and Ebert still claim to be socialists, and shoot down their own people ... Don't you understand the difference? That is why they are such swine," ranted Schorsch. I got the point in a flash and said no more.

"There seems to be no logic here in Bavaria," sneered the girl.

Pegu now arrived with a refugee from Berlin. The man blustered rather noisily and talked even more confusedly. He hobbled about on a club foot. He had nowhere to stay, so I offered him my small room upstairs.

After a long argument Pegu said to me with a smile: "Just write your verses ... Revolution is not your style."

"Oh well," I said peevishly, "the best thing would be for me to return to a bourgeois lifestyle." And I did so, to some extent. I pushed all current events aside, as it were. I was falling more and more in love with the girl. Day after day we talked, got closer and closer to each other, and were very happy. Every now and then I roamed the city utterly aloof, dropping into various pubs. At the *Soller* I met the giant who had marched at my side on the 7th of November again. He recognized me at once and sat down with me.

"Hey, what are you up to these days?" I asked him.

"Me? ... I'm looking after Number One," he replied with a quirky smile. "The revolution is also nowt but a swindle. Only the bosses benefit ... Cheerio, proles."

"Looking after Number One? How?" He bent over closer to my ear and whispered: "Poaching".

"I see ... How does that work?" I wanted to know, and he told me about his new occupation in a low voice while peering around cautiously.

He had bought a carbine and ammunition, a bike and a rucksack. "I go out every night ... Shame that cycling ain't possible now ... It's a long way out," he said, still keeping his voice down. He shot game in Freimann and the surrounding forests, gutted his quarry on the spot, packed it in his rucksack and sold it in town.

"So far I haven't run into a single gamekeeper and if I did – he'd soon be out of the way ... A right fool I'd be to go hungry, when there's game about ... The gentry in that parliament have seized the State, but what I say is ... Roebuck, you're all mine, and *basta*." Which was fair enough, I thought at once.

"I trust you mate, you're all right ... Want to join?" I nodded and promised to come some time. The life of a robber thrilled me something rotten. My mind turned back to my entire youth. And I pictured romantic adventures. How easy it is, I kept telling myself on my way home, how easy it is to make a living. Beautiful. Wonderfully beautiful! Hundreds up-on thousands were starving on the streets: I wanted to give them this great tip, right on the spot. That was definitely a practical socialist act. And I was able to explain it so convincingly to a few workers that they actually started poaching.

Everywhere I went, they called me "the Anarchist". "Self-help" was my new gospel. I was so enthusiastic that I started working on a pro-gramme again, which I wanted to duplicate and covertly spread among the unemployed. Oddly enough, I did not mention my plan to any of my friends.

I surprised myself with my ingenuity in devising catchphrases: "The revolution has not ended your poverty, comrade, so follow these short and really practical tips from a well-wisher," my intended leaflet started, and then in the course of a few nights I sketched the outline of my programme as follows: organization of bands of poachers, control of the sale of the booty through comradely cooperation between all trades, digging of fox-holes in the forests as hiding places for poachers, secret sign language among the "Self-help Organizations" and finally sale of deerskins.

I wanted to get in touch with the giant.

He was to be leader of the organizations, and I wanted to be its theoretician. But in the meantime events derailed me once again. A thousand things were happening. Eisner came back from the Socialist Conference in Bern and gave one of his best speeches, then he moved at the head of a powerful demonstration through the city to protest against the lies that appeared in the press about his actions at the Conference. The elections were over, the National Assembly had met in Weimar, Germany's provisional constitution had been passed, and Ebert elected the first President of the German Republic.

My lodger, Pegu, Schorsch and a worker we knew turned up in great excitement. The worker told me that word had gone around all the large factories in Munich, putting workers on alert that counter-revolutionary sailors were on their way from Berlin and planned a putsch, with the violent deposition of Eisner. Their leader was the sailor Lotter, elected to the Bavarian National Assembly, but Auer and the Majority SPD were behind it. I was seething again. It drove me back onto the streets. In the city, it felt like the troubled calm before the storm, which put everyone's nerves on edge. We ran around mindlessly, wanted to find Mühsam, wanted to put the Spartacists on their guard. In the city, leaflets were being handed out, proclaiming: "Governor, Your Time Is Up!" A huge crowd stood talking confusedly before the union headquarters. It was being said that the Munich garrison had declared for Eisner and was ready to defeat all attacks. Others said that the Household Guards and the Engineers were on the side of the putschists. "To arms! To arms!" some were shouting. All of a sudden, a group of Spartacists came running Pezzalozzistrasse, waving their arms wildly.

"The station and the telegraph office are already occupied by the counter-revolutionaries," one of them exclaimed breathlessly. There was a gunfight at the parliament building, another said. "Auer is the traitor," shouted a Spartacist dramatically and shook his fist, screaming louder than ever: "To arms! The revolution is under threat!"

"What's to do? Where?" asked agitated people here and there. The crowd surged in a confused mass, then we led a demonstration to the Sendlinger Gate, where we met other Spartacists, who told us that it was all over.

Once again there were wild and confused questions; we all stopped and listened.

"The guards at the parliament building shot at the putschists, who all ran off!" one of them exclaimed, and a hundred voices roared in reply: "Bravo! Hurrah!"

"The guards have already retaken the station and the telegraph office!" they now announced.

"Bravo! Hurrah! Down with the counter-revolution!" echoed on all sides.

"Be prepared!" roared the speaker, and the demonstration slowly dispersed.[52]

I was angry and swore at my comrades because they had dragged me away from my work again and again for no good reason.

And as I was now on my way, I called in on the Dutchman again. His flat had already been cleared out. Removal men and maids stood in the bare rooms. Marietta came over and said: "Look, if you could use the curtains and carpets, just take them." I rummaged through the pile to see what there was and hauled three large packages home with me.

"Come and see us soon, we're in Nymphenburg now," Marietta said as she got into the car. "Yes," I said absent-mindedly, thinking only of my new possessions. Gorgeous curtains and carpets, all genuine Turkish! The thought flashed through my brain, man, you could furnish a mosque! Then I would shut myself up behind iron doors, never to go out again.

There was something seriously weird about me. I was constantly wavering between two extremes: either I buried myself away from the world – because at times I was actually afraid of it – or I let myself be carried along at random. Everything that happened – whether it was the giant's poaching, the idea for a poem, the emerging reaction, the botched revolution or the carpets – immediately seized me, so my efforts to assimilate it reached almost comical proportions. I started making plans at once, developed them, speculated idiotically, and sketched out programmes. That was me, from childhood on. Even at home I was already thinking how I could destroy the people I hated; I worked out quite detailed plans to murder my brother Max, the postman or one farmer or another. Later these elaborate schemes were directed against the boss or some political figure. My logic was that if the bearer of ill-intent was out of the way, the cause of my misery would also be out of the way. If I killed Max, there would be no more beatings; if I disposed of the postman, nobody would spread tales about me; if there were no more farmers, I could do what I wanted in their fields and gardens; if the boss snuffed it, there'd be no more slave-driving; finally, if I shot Ludendorff, the war would come to an end and if I picked off the reactionaries one by one there would be no more reaction. Nothing could be easier.

---

[52] The events described, the Lotter Putsch, took place on Wednesday, 19 February 1919. Conrad Lotter (1889-1978) was a First Mate with the Imperial Navy in Wilhelmshaven. A few days earlier he had met Auer, who wanted to recruit a counter-revolutionary force to overthrow and arrest Eisner. Six hundred sailors were sent and one person died in the putsch. Lotter was interned until May but went unpunished.

I could plunge myself so fervently into these fantasies that some-times I genuinely thought I was in the process of making them reality. Eve-ry obstacle seemed ridiculous and I did not occupy myself with any of the consequences of such an action. I indulged in such bizarre reflections for hours, if not days or weeks on end. But then something else shoved its way into my laboured thought processes, an impression perhaps, or a book I had read, an experience, an irritation, and my latest resolutions would crumble into nothingness with puzzling rapidity, so that whole business would start over from scratch. I literally appeared in my mind like the blessed Tartarin de Tarascon.[53] I was perpetually living in an adventurous contemplation of the ebb and flow of events; the tiniest molehill became a vast and mysterious mountain, exciting, romantic and powerful, but at the very next moment once again ridiculous and pointless, stupid and boring: yes, a mosque! Bury yourself away in a mosque! A fabulous refuge in a dingy flat! That was my latest craze. I forgot all about the self-help organi-zations. I rearranged my flat with the zeal of a fanatic. Nothing else inter-ested me. Nothing at all.

Except, a storm was brewing outside.

---

[53] The name of an 1872 novel by Alphonse Daudet, adapted for film in 1908. Daudet described Tartarin as Don Quixote and Sancho Panza rolled into one, torn between a thirst for adven-ture and a fretful desire for comfort.

22.
THE INSURGENCY

That's to say, one morning – I was just going out to buy wire nails – word spread like wildfire to the remotest corner of the city, already whipped to a fury. "Kurt Eisner murdered! Minister Auer wounded, Centre Party MP Osel dead, Major Jareis fired on! A shoot-out and panic in the parliament!"

It was 21 February. The day set for the opening of the Bavarian parliament. It was icy cold. I ran on, as I was, without hat or coat. I was in complete turmoil.

The bells started ringing from all the city's towers, the trams all ground to a halt, here and there someone hung a red flag with a black mourning ribbon from the window, and an uneasy silence fell over the city. Everybody was heading into the city, looking distraught. The further I got, the greater the vague sense of urgency. A black swarm of people was clustered around the parliament, among them soldiers and armed civilians. I rushed on further down Promenadenstrasse to the scene of the crime. Hundreds had formed a circle around Eisner's pool of blood, now covered over by sawdust. Virtually no one uttered a word; women sobbed faintly, as did men. Several soldiers stepped into the middle and stood their rifles up in a pyramid. Huge tears were streaming down the swarthy cheeks of one of the soldiers. "Our Eisner! Our one and only!" wailed a woman and now the sobbing got louder. Many laid flowers in the square, more and more and more. Suddenly, in front of Promenadenplatz, a fully occupied truck, thick with flags and machine guns, passed by, with loud shouts of: "Vengeance for Eisner!" The words rang out like a terrible storm alert, and a furious roar came back from the hundreds, like a piercing cry of despair: "Vengeance! Vengeance for Eisner!" A cold shiver ran down my back. I went on.

The Promenadenplatz was densely packed with people; lorry after lorry roared past, and the first leaflets rained down:

> Workers and soldiers! The counter-revolution has struck its first great blow, shooting down its most hated leader of the socialist revolution! The Citizens' Guard, the White Guard, Wednesday's coup, these are steps taken to strangle the socialist revolution! It found its expression in the slanderous agitation of a venal press, which, hypocritically preaching peace and order, has created the atmosphere for assassination.
>
> Workers and soldiers! They want to bend you under the old yoke of militarism and capitalism! Now is the time to act and save the revolution! The General Strike! Out of the factories! Down with

the bourgeoisie and their criminal accomplices! Long live the socialist revolution!

Independent Social Democratic Party
Schröder, Kämpfer, Weiss, Paula Mayer, Fechenbach.

We read the leaflets, almost voraciously. I saw people trembling, white
with rage or thirsting for blood. The screams of vengeance echoed from all
sides. The teeming masses stirred and streamed through the city. This time
it was different, quite different from 7 November. If anyone had stood up
and called out: "Slaughter the bourgeoisie! Burn down the city! Destroy
everything!" it would have happened. Thousands of small squalls had
united and a single, gloomy, dark, incalculable tempest was brewing. I felt
it most clearly in myself: never before had I felt the impulse of the masses
like this, never before was I so much at one with the thousands.

The demonstration swept to the Theresienwiese. Many made
speeches under the Bavaria; Toller recited a poem. The women were
moved by it; the men cried out for weapons. Then someone shouted out
that there were weapons in the city arsenal. A huge crowd marched off in
that direction, and I went with them back into the city. Soldiers and sailors
were in the vanguard, as though in an assault. The red flags waved. The
locked doors of the German Theatre were smashed in, glass shattered into
shards, there was a crack, and everyone surged into the hall.

"From today the Workers' and Soldiers' Council is in permanent
session," roared a sailor. At first there was an indescribably confused
trampling and screaming; commands were shouted, then gradually order
was asserted. The councillors had come together, the people sat down, at
the back there was standing room only, and the galleries filled up to the
point that they threatened to break down at any moment. I was so wedged
in between bodies that I saw nothing but backs, necks and hair, caps and
hats. Now and again I heard someone speaking, then cries of applause,
then a dull movement around me. I forced my way out. "Down with the
newspapers!" I called out to a few people, and they also made their way
outdoors.

"Hey, Strobel!" I shouted as I looked around at the troop following
me. It was the comrade from the League of Free People!

"They're talking again and doing nothing," he grumbled. We
walked along the Bayerstrasse and saw from afar pillars of smoke and
flames flaring up.

"The squalid den of iniquity is finally burning," said a worker beside me. Strobel had disappeared again into the crush. Moving along, we
saw a wall of fire on the street and a mass of screaming people literally
dancing around it. They had dragged out the entire next edition of the
Münchner Zeitung and set it ablaze. The Republican Guard was already

posted in front of the entrance. In Paul-Heyse-Strasse a large placard had been posted above the entrance to the *München-Augsburger-Abendzeitung*: "Occupied by the Workers' Council." I went past the sentries.

"Wait, what do you want? Get out sir!" a soldier said, pulling me back.

"Come off it comrade, you don't have to call me 'sir' ... I have to go in, I need to see Ehrhardt!" I shouted. He let me in without further ado. I didn't want anything; I was just taking delight in the dismantling of this newspaper. I went up the steps into the outer editorial office. There was no receptionist there, as there had been when I delivered my book reviews. On the Chief Editor's office door was written: "Committee Room of the Workers' and Soldiers' Council. No Entry." A former editor came and greeted me quite pleasantly.

"Ah, Herr Graf, were you looking for the Workers' Council?"

"No, no," I smirked maliciously, "I am just pleased that all this now belongs to us."

The man made an embarrassed expression and tried to smile: "Hmmm ... You know, we were just employees ..."

"Yes, paid to lie," I snapped at him spitefully, and went to the Workers' Council. Several comrades were present. Some were writing, others hurried in and out carrying sheets of paper.

"Hello, Graf," said Ehrhardt, and I returned his greeting.

"Do you need me? ... I can write for you," I said.

"No need for the present ... They are just printing leaflets to send outside the city," Ehrhardt told me. I gave him my address and left.

"Comrade," I said to the sentry, "don't let others through ... In my case, you've done nothing wrong, but watch out, otherwise anyone could slip in." The man scowled at me and growled something.

The streets were busy. The factories had shut down, the general strike had started. Aeroplanes buzzed above the houses, making bold loops and plunges and announcing a state of siege. The streets were to be cleared by seven in the evening. I hurried into the city At Stachus I found a crowd, in the middle of which a speaker said that the Council Republic had been proclaimed in the German Theatre. "Anyone who robs, steals or plunders or undertakes anything against the new government will be shot," warned a poster. Another one forbade all drunken revelry and proclaimed a national day of mourning.

People ran around restlessly, constantly gathering in crowds, and there was always a new rumour doing the rounds.

Members of the Central Workers' Council occupied the offices of the *Münchner Neueste Nachrichten*, the *Bayrischer Kurier*, the *Münchner Tageblatt*, the *Bayrische Staatszeitung* and the Majority SPD *Post*, none of which were published. Only the Independent SPD's *Neue Zeitung* appeared. Copies were literally snatched from the hands of the sellers. Eisner's corpse, it was said, was already laid out at the Ostfriedhof cemetery. Almost every hall in the city was packed with meetings to honour the murder victim. When I returned to Promenadenstrasse, a portrait of Eisner framed in mourning crape leaned against the rifle-pyramid, and a mountain of flowers and wreaths lay around it. It was cold and getting dark. I was hungry, thirsty and tired. When I arrived home, I met my lodger, who gravely informed me that hostages had been taken. He hobbled up and down, highly agitated, and said over and over again: "We've got to hold out now! ... Only in Munich is there anything left of the revolutionary movement. The White Guards are outside, and counter-revolutionaries are plotting in our midst.

"Unless all proletarians are armed at once, we're stuffed ... The students at the university all yelled 'bravo' at the news of Eisner's murder ...

"That's the state of the revolution! ... Oh well, the shithole is closed now ... They're all trapped together. Guillotines will have to be put to work immediately."

He talked on as if he were the highest authority in the State. While he hobbled around, I took stock of him, unobserved.

The thought spontaneously went through my mind: the whole German revolution is like him. It is also limping along on a club foot. I suddenly had to laugh out loud, exclaiming: "Hey, you're a symbol! You're a real symbol!" He turned his chubby head sharply towards me, paused for a moment, then he said curtly: "Don't talk rubbish, man! This is no time for jokes!"

He had come back from the parliament, where at his suggestion it had been decided to form a Revolutionary Artists' Council.

"I suppose they'll design the new guillotines?" I asked mischievously He wasn't listening and shouted even more loudly: "You really must join! We are taking control of the press, theatre, the cinemas, the universities, the churches and academies."

"Who is actually governing?" I wanted to know.

"The Central Council! All that about the government is just sugar coating ... An eleven-man committee is exercising power ... Our Artists' Council is subject to nobody. We can do as we like," he explained to me. He then started making a speech about the true dictatorship, and I grew irritated at all this waffle.

"Show me your hands, man!" I said at once, threateningly, and grabbed hold of his fleshy, stubby fingers. "You have never held a shovel, never worked in a factory! ... Did the workers send for you? ... Can't they manage without you? ... Aren't the guillotines for people like you!?"

He was visibly upset and started to rage, calling me a counter-revolutionary. But then he threatened jokingly: "If you weren't a great poet, I'd denounce you on the spot ... Watch out that I don't have you stood against the wall!"

"You?!" I burst out laughing contemptuously. "You?! Oh dear, oh dear!" And then I became spiteful again: "Yes, yes, that's also the easiest job of all, denouncing someone and getting them stood up against the wall."

"No, joking apart, there's important work to be done. And a lot of it," the club-footed man continued at last. "I am organizing the workers' celebrations in the German Theatre ... And then a recital of Spartacist literature ... I want to read something of yours." I nodded indifferently, and the man finally hobbled out of the door.

Left alone, I wondered for a long time about how I could be of use to the revolution, but nothing halfway decent occurred to me. My stomach started rumbling. The pubs were shut, and I had no food in the house. And no money at all. I thought of the Dutchman. Despite the curfew, I made my way to Nymphenburg.

On my way I thought on and on about what I could do for the revolution. Quite involuntarily, the meeting at the Mathäser came back to my mind. "Come on, you'll only make a fool of yourself again," I muttered to myself, and my enthusiasm faded.

The streets were empty. Here and there I ran into a patrol.

"Where are you off to?"

"To Nymphenburg, comrades! I was kept late," I said casually, and they allowed me to pass. I was amazed at this blind faith. Once again, I began to have doubts about the whole revolution.

The further I went out of the city, the darker and quieter it became. I never saw as much as a lighted window. The wind swept cold around the corners and hit me.

I felt an uncomfortable rootlessness.

Marietta and the Dutchman received me with the utmost friendliness. The over-elegant painter Davringhausen had been living with them for some time and was, it seemed, a close friend. We drank several glasses of schnapps and I was shown the rooms. Every one of them was like a veritable jewel box. Like an unreal and disturbing dream, all of these select luxuries appearing after such a day.

We sat down in a comfortable, wood-panelled dining room at an exquisitely covered table. Old models of Viking ships hung from the ceiling. A solemn servant waited on us in silence. We ate and drank. I talked and talked. We left the dining room and went into a spacious smoking-room, which extended to a kind of winter garden, a glass-roofed conservatory with Chinese vases and exotic plants. We lolled comfortably in plush armchairs, and each blew his cigarette smoke into the air. The servant brought champagne, the Dutchman popped the corks and poured the sparkling liquid into tall, slender glasses.

"It will perhaps come to the point that private wealth is confiscated," I said casually.

The Dutchman looked uneasy for a moment. Davringhausen laughed out loud and said it was all nonsense. He made snobby wisecracks.

"Oh come on, we are foreigners!" exclaimed Marietta. She told her story, for the umpteenth time, about her arrest under suspicion of espionage and launched into reminiscing about her bohemian life in Paris. We all knew every word by heart. It was boring. Nevertheless Davringhausen went on laughing as though charmed and I would not be outdone. A man must show gratitude for such abundant hospitality.

The Dutchman lounged there with outstretched legs, simply smiling wryly now and then.

I grew increasingly bored with this toadying until it finally became an absolute torment. I was overstrung, depressed, distracted and nervous. My eyes were burning with the thirst for sleep, my thoughts seemed exhausted, the day's events were still buzzing through my corroded brain. Each time I needed to yawn I took a drink, again and again, hoping to feel more at home in my present environment and most of all to share in the merriment. If I could do this, all else would follow. It was impossible to sleep and rest here. There were already pauses in the conversation; there might be an explosion at any moment, as Marietta was really speaking into a void. If she detected our lack of interest, that would be it. In despair, I grasped for my champagne glass, drank, drank, boozed.

We heard, somewhere out in the darkness, the long drawn-out crack of cannon-fire. Its effect was almost soothing. We all four raised our heads and listened. "What was that?" the Dutchman asked hastily.

"Shooting! ... A little shot! ... A teeny-weeny little shot!" quipped Davringhausen, imitating Max Pallenberg, and hitched up his exquisitely creased trousers.[54]

"You know what? ... They are all idiots! ... Only the French know how to carry out a revolution," Marietta said gormlessly. I was still listening. All was silent again.

"Well, that should not prevent us from looking forward to the future in confidence," said Davringhausen with forced irony, and he raised his champagne glass. He also seemed determined to create a cheerful atmosphere. He toasted Marietta and smiled again. Then he sprang elastically to his feet, went to the gramophone, put on a record, took Marietta by the hand and exclaimed: "Madam, may I have the honour? ... Just a little

---

[54] The Austrian singer and comedian Max Pallenberg (1877-1934) was a star of the stage and silent film.

dance. A dancette ..." Soon the two were whirling around.

My God, my God, how infantile, how boring, how stupid wealth makes people, I kept thinking. The Dutchman yawned and looked listless.

"They have fired on the Soviet Republic in the city," I said to him. "Hmm, yes, that scoundrel Arco," he grumbled.[55] I could see that he was irritated; he was probably conscious that his way of life and comforts were becoming unsettled in some vague way. A consoling thought struck me like lightning.

"You know what? ... It's all very simple!" I loudly exclaimed to him at once. "You're a foreigner, so declare your villa and garden a neutral Soviet Republic ... Then nobody will bother you again!"

Davringhausen had heard this and burst out laughing: "Fabulous, hahaha, brilliant!" My remark did not fail in its effect and everyone became merry in an instant. The Dutchman leapt to his feet and whooped: "Splendid! Excellent! Kids, we must celebrate!" He rang for the servant.

"What are we celebrating?" asked Marietta "The Soviet Republic of Marietta!" I replied.

The Dutchman explained.

"Delightful," seconded Davringhausen. The servant came and more sekt was ordered. Our host went to the cellar in person and brought back a new bottle of whisky.

Now in the best of spirits, we sat down and started drinking again.

"Graf, you must stay with us. What does all that fuss matter to you!" declared Marietta, after a brief silence. I nodded. I was gradually getting back into my role as the household's jester.

"Yes, yes! We yield, we bow to your will," I loudly toasted our hostess. "Long live all the crap!" Davringhausen put the gramophone back on and danced with Marietta again. Things got noisier and noisier. In the end all four of us were whooping it up around the room like Red Indians gone wild and made a terrible spectacle of ourselves: glasses crashed to the floor, each of us grabbed something, waved it around and threw it at the wall or against the brass-topped smoking table. I put the full sekt bottle to my lips and gulped noisily, swung it in the air and reeled around in circles like a great hulking bear. "We're going to booze bra-andy, we're going to get ra-andy, we're going to swap wi-ives, we're leading free li-ives!" we all roared, completely sloshed. Everything went blurry, I felt suffocated, clutched myself, rushed through the door, fell upon the toilet and threw

---

[55] Anton Graf von Arco auf Valley (1897-1945) was Eisner's assassin. He was tried and sentenced to death, but a judge reduced this to five years. He was imprisoned in Landsberg gaol and released from his cell to make way for Adolf Hitler. He said, "Eisner is a Bolshevist, a Jew; he isn't German, he doesn't feel German, he subverts all patriotic thoughts and feelings. He is a traitor to this land."

up. It was as though I had spewed up my entire guts and stomach. I leaned against the wall and held my hot head in my hands. Through the door I saw the other three still fluttering about. They laughed, prodded me now and then and shouted confusedly. Finally they took me between them, dragged me back to the devastated smoking-room and dropped me into a chair.

"A-a-a-gh!" I snorted like a horse. "A-a-a-gh! ... Yes, that's better now. Get me some whisky! Let's hit the bottle! Come on! ... Man, life's a sick-bucket. Come on! ... A-ah!" I drank. "Let's go! Bang! Carry on!" Suddenly I got giddy again, I heard a tremendous noise, it stopped, and I swayed and fell down lengthwise.

It was only the next day that I came to, half-undressed, with a sticky face, wrapped in silken quilts and lying on a sofa in Marietta's room in the turret. My head throbbed and my mouth stank like a cesspit. I stood up quickly, found my soiled clothes, put them on, gave myself a cursory wash in the lavatory, then went down to breakfast. The three of them, already seated there, received me with tumultuous laughter. "My God, that was some session last night, fantastic," I blabbered, provoking further amusement. Even though I could not explain why, this flattered my vanity. And, I thought, people are wonderfully easy to amuse, you can get your feet under the table here.

I sat down, thoroughly enjoyed drinking the strong coffee, wolfed down the soft eggs, tender ham and buttered rolls with the most voracious appetite. Slowly, I recovered myself. I did not get back to the city until midday. I went out to the Dutchman's villa more and more often and ended up living there entirely.

Eisner's funeral, a few days later, was a moving affair. A demonstration, stretching further than you could see, set off from the Theresienwiese. People had come from every district in Bavaria. The Penzberg and Hausham miners were at the head of the march, in black costumes, and behind them followed thousands upon thousands. It was not only the numerous deputations that brought wreaths; I saw sobbing female workers and scowling proletarians carrying a solitary last flower for the dead man. Every counter-revolutionary in Munich gawped in amazement. The lower classes were marching in unison; vast, immense masses appeared. I had not seen such a gigantic procession since 7 November.

Spectators sat close together on the wooden casing that covered the fountain in the square by the Sendlinger Gate. Suddenly the wooden casing broke and collapsed under the weight; they all fell screaming terribly into the icy cold water and had trouble to pull themselves out, grappling and punching. "Let them all drown, the reactionary dogs!" snarled a worker. This made everyone laugh at the catastrophe.

The Ostfriedhof cemetery was so full that there was nothing to be seen but heads and flags. Gustav Landauer gave the memorial oration, but nobody heard him, there were too many mourners. When the last "Long live the revolution" rang out, it seemed as though the Earth itself were crying.

23

THROUGH STORM AND SWAMP

One day the girl travelled to Berlin to visit her parents. It was wretched; now I did not have anyone I could speak to now and again about what was on my mind. Pegu had been in Blankenburg for some time and only surfaced occasionally. My club-footed lodger had been joined by a girlfriend from Berlin, who was living with him in the small box-room. The man spent the whole day somewhere in the parliament building or in the city and his lover went with him. Schorsch was constantly surrounded with the weirdest people. I never met him alone. A half-finished oil painting stood on his easel in the studio; he had left the work uncompleted. The nature apostle Gusto Gräser was staying with him.[56] He had arrived and never gone away again. He spent most of the time loafing about on the sofa, moaned that he was ill, and when he got up, he started quoting all kinds of passages from Chinese philosophers, Nietzsche's Zarathustra or his own texts, as though giving a sermon. He was a full-blooded vegetarian with a flowing Jesus hairstyle and full beard to match, wore a kind of toga made of sackcloth that was held together with little wooden pegs, a broad leather belt over it and short trousers underneath. On his feet he wore leather soles fastened with string. He ate only fruit, vegetables and bread, and he drank only water. He was so gentle that he did not even kill the lice and fleas that lived on him; he had moved so close to nature that he stank like a goat. Gräser claimed that he only washed in natural spring-water, and since there were no springs in the city, he never washed at all. He, of course, preached a complete renunciation of civilization; he carried brown, square sheets of paper in his leather pouch, on which his ideas were printed in aphoristic form, and from time to time he sold these or handed them out.

One day I visited Schorsch and was really shocked by the devastation in his studio. I stared at Gräser in silent hostility. My friend got dressed in order to go out with me. He buttoned up his waistcoat.

"Buttons ... They are ... a-ah ... absurd ... totally absurd," muttered the prophet.

"Let's go," Schorsch said, and left with me.

"Hey, what kind of vermin have you got living with you?" I asked on the stairs.

"I can't get rid of him," came the answer. "What? ... Just chuck him

---

[56] The Transylvanian Saxon Gustav "Gusto" Arthur Gräser (1879-1958) has a strong claim to being the first hippy. He co-founded the Monte Verità settlement and influenced literary figures such as Hermann Hesse. Because of his obsessive vegetarianism, he was later named the *Kohlrabi-Apostel* ("Turnip Apostle").

out!" I exclaimed.

"He is holding a meeting this evening. We are all going along," my friend told me instead of answering. I exploded. We met another acquaintance of Schorsch's, very elegant, with horn-rimmed spectacles and an exceptionally large gob when he smiled. He was an unemployed, eccentric, literary aristocrat from Berlin, who also "went in for the revolution". He was exceedingly sprightly and walked in a coquettish manner.

Schorsch introduced him to me as "Ado von Achenbach".[57]

We shook hands. The little man immediately started arguing. I remembered having seen him once at *Simplicissimus* and at the Dutchman's old apartment. He told us that a few days earlier a detachment of police had been at the Congress of Councils and had arrested Mühsam and Levien, but they were released again after a few hours.

"In any case – it's really come to a head now ... Either a Council Republic or reaction ... The trade unionists and Majority Social Democrats are getting in the way again ... It's still the dictatorship of the proletariat, but nobody knows what is going on," he continued, handing us newspapers from elsewhere in Germany. They contained the most disgusting lies. *Vorwärts* reported on a civil war in Munich, a murderous bloodbath between the Munich Independents and Spartacists and the leaders of the Bavarian Social Democrats. The *Vossische Zeitung* declared that Arco, the murderer of Eisner, was not of sound mind. Other papers claimed that no law-abiding citizen's life was any longer safe in Munich. The *Berliner Tageblatt* already spoke of a Bavarian Soviet Republic.[58]

The rump government was still there and cooperating with the Central Council. Everything was uncertain. House searches for hoarded food were made, a decree from Toller had recommended the inspection of large hotels and the transfer of confiscated supplies to inns in the working-class districts, and citizens had been called upon to provide arms, but that was all. Kress von Kressenstein,[59] the German nationalist publisher Lehmann, senior officers, students and other right-wing personalities were hostages in the *Hotel Bayerischer Hof*.

---

[57] The communist and animal lover (Baron) Adolf von Achenbach (1896-1956) fled from the Gestapo in 1936 to Yugoslavia, taking nothing but a baby crocodile, which he smuggled under his shirt. He was returned to Germany and held in a concentration camp, where he was treated with respect as an aristocrat. The story was told in the novel, *A Crocodile for Zagreb* (2017) by his daughter Marina, well known in Germany as war correspondent in Yugoslavia.

[58] *Vorwärts* was the newspaper of the Majority Social Democrats; the *Vossische Zeitung* was a semi-official "newspaper of record"; the *Berliner Tageblatt* was a liberal daily, closed down by the Nazis in 1939.

[59] Baron Otto Kress von Kressenstein (1850-1929) was a Bavarian Colonel General and Minister for War from 1912 to 1916.

"Colonel Epp is sitting in Coburg and recruiting volunteers for the White Guard ... In Württemberg and Baden, Noske has recruiting stations everywhere ... All of the students from out of town are being enrolled ... The Munich garrison is very shaky," Achenbach reported pessimistically.[60]

Aeroplanes were circling overhead. "What are they doing?" I asked.

"They are dropping propaganda leaflets in the country," I was told.

"And what is the situation out there?" I asked again.

"So long as Gandorfer is with us it's tolerable, but for the most part the peasants have been incited against us and won't deliver any more," said Achenbach.

"And there's division here," I grumbled. I was horrified.

"All right mate!" said a pale, haggard young man with a thin face, joining our party.

"Ah, Tautz! All right!" Schorsch and Achenbach replied and asked after the latest news.

"They say the general strike has been called off for the time being ... Arming the people is under discussion; Landauer and Marut are members of the Educational Council," he said.[61] Then we spoke about Gräser's meeting and we became more light-hearted. "That will be a laugh," exclaimed Tautz. "Yes, then let's all go to Schorsch and hound the blighter out," I proposed.

"By the way, why do you hardly ever turn up to the Artists' Council, you skivers?" argued Tautz.

"I am a private person ... And anyway, I don't trust all those artists ... What's the point of making a distinction between artists and workers anyhow? ... Either you stand shoulder to shoulder with the workers or you keep out ... And if that's the case, we don't need any Artists' Council," I interjected.

"But we are proletarians," said Tautz and demanded again that I appear at the parliament building. I nodded casually.

We dispersed and met again in the evening at the Gräser meeting, all at the same table: my lodger and his girlfriend, Tautz, Achenbach, Schorsch and me. The hall was relatively full. Smoking was not allowed. We smoked. It was noisy, already. In front of us sat ecstatic girls with plaited hair, old maids, *Wandervögel*, idealistic cranks and such like. There

---

[60] Franz Xaver Ritter von Epp (1868-1947) was the commanding officer of the counter-revolutionary Freikorps Epp, appointed by the SPD Minister of Defence, Gustav Noske. He later joined the Nazi Party and was the *Reichsstatthalter* (Imperial Lieutenant) of Bavaria from 1933 to 1945.

[61] Ret Marut (1882-1969) was later known as B. Traven, author of *The Treasure of the Sierra Madre* and many other novels.

were also some upright beer drinkers present, party members, typical Spartacists and various other folk.[62]

"What's all this rubbish about? ... We should smoke him out!" raged my lodger. "These herbivores just confuse things!"

"Sh, sh, sh! ... Shhh!" the tables at the front admonished us and gave us dirty looks.

Gusto Gräser came marching in and climbed to the podium.

"Billy goat!" someone yelled. Everyone laughed. But others were indignant. Gräser made a sign as though he were blessing the audience and then began his monotone sermon. He spewed an incomprehensible smorgasbord of quotes and cranky opinions over those present, accompanied by applause, laughter, yells of derision, and clapping.

The prophet started to speak about the spirit of non-violence.

"Spirit, yes! We need schnapps!" I shouted loutishly.

Our table started laughing. The noise level rose. Gusto Gräser carried on talking regardless.

"Eating grass and loafing about is nonsense!" I taunted.

"Yes!! Dictatorship of the proletariat!" seconded several others at the table.

The Spartacists present joined in. The *Wandervögel* cooed angrily, the old maids and young girls hissed waspishly.

"Down with nature! Long live science!" my lodger shouted. "Spartacus is on the march."

"We are no longer human –" cried Gräser. The rest of his sentence was lost.

"No, you critter!" I yelled in the uproar.

"The great day cometh!" preached the windbag further.

"On the bog!" shouted Tautz. No more could be heard except a confused, angry din of voices. Everyone trumpeted their own views. It was comical: Gräser standing up there, powerless, shaking his head now and then. A fanatical Spartacist jumped up onto the table and made the usual propaganda speech: "Proletarians! World revolution is on the march! Close ranks around Spartacus! Down with the bourgeoisie and the traitorous rabble of Majority Socialists!! Power can only be won by force! For Liebknecht! For Rosa Luxemburg and Lenin!"

Everybody applauded and then departed amidst laughter. "Very entertaining! Brilliant!" we heard on all sides. We went with Schorsch to his studio and waited for Gräser.

"He's got to go!" we all agreed.

---

[62] The *Wandervögel* (Birds of Passage) were a back-to-nature youth movement founded in the late nineteenth century.

323

Gräser came and we started to tease him; our jibes were coarse, mean and intended to wound him. But he just mumbled a gentle word now and then.

"Very well. Nature! Nature, good neighbour! Please move your quarters to the English garden, tomorrow!" I said at last in an almost threatening tone, and we finally left. It took a further two days for Gusto Gräser to clear off. He was to be seen wandering around the city, constantly followed by a pack of children. We heard that he had settled in a goat-shed.

There were tons of such freaks around at the time. One of them had a long ponytail and a straw hat, very tight, chequered trousers and matching jacket. He sought out the crowds, then whispered in everyone's ear: "We are Christ! Be calm, beloved children! Do not hammer your own cross!" Then he disappeared as quickly as he appeared. Another – dressed in mangy clothes, with a pinched, ratty face – spent most of his time sitting in cafés and doing sums. He calculated in tables on long, white pages. If anyone spoke to him, he said, panting, if we all ate just ninety grams of rye bread and ten grams of meat a day, there would be no more poverty. The sight of cakes would send him into a rage. Standing before a shop window, he would break into noisy abuse: "There, look at that, neighbour! ... Can't you see! ... This luxury is our ruin ... Confectioners are the biggest crooks! We must take action against them ..."

Christians preached to gatherings, nudists promoted their rallies, individualists and Bible-bashers proclaimed the dawn of the millennial kingdom, old codgers advocated polygamy, then there were oddball Darwinists and racial theorists, theosophists, and spiritualists. There was every species of crank disseminating harmless theories. But one night I was crossing Stachus. A gaunt man rushed over to me, hurriedly thrust a leaflet in my hand and ran quickly into the foggy darkness. I stepped under a lamp and looked at the scrap of paper. All that was written was: "The Jew intervenes! Germans, reflect!"

The ferment in the masses was growing more and more intense. The bourgeois press was appearing again but was edited by the Council of Censors. The socialist parties struggled incessantly, generating a lot of heat. A proletarian meeting was permanently in session at the Hotel Wagner. Spartacists and Independents held forth continuously, denouncing the Majority SPD. Resolutions were drawn up, and delegations assembled, which always sent their demands immediately to the Central Council at the parliament building. There was perpetual movement in and out, here and there.

On one occasion I attended such a standing assembly with Schorsch. We stood on the gallery. An energetic sailor was speaking. Suddenly the crowd below was divided, the speaker broke off at once, and police officers marched through the frightened mass of people, went up to the rostrum, mounted it, and took up their position. A drummer beat his drum and the soldiers aimed their rifles at the hall, ready to shoot. Panicked, people ran into each other, each trying to cover himself behind the man in front. The sailor waved madly and shouted. A soldier shoved him aside and shot in the air. Our lives were now at risk. There was a terrible crush. Screams, stampedes, howls and cries of distress. The wild tangle of people pushed toward the exits. Whoever did not go with them was trampled underfoot. The runaways trod on those left lying on the ground who thrashed about wildly. Up on the gallery we galloped, terrified, to the emergency exits and windows, battered them open, and suddenly saw more police on the street, rushing towards us. We were all seized by an indescribable terror and rushed back in again, ran down the stairs and fell in a confused heap upon the mad scrum of people underneath.

"Watch out! I am dead!" someone moaned below us.

"Help! I am being trampled to death" came a scream from under my feet. I stretched out my elbows with all my strength, pressed my head to my chest, closed my eyes and knocked people out of the way, barging harder and harder, pushed again, bent down and hauled up a girl who, splattered with blood, clutched hold of me by the neck and shrieked. I stormed forwards, hearing and seeing nothing more. Several people had grabbed hold of my arms and threatened to pull me and my charge down to the ground; I let my arms sink and pushed on. The girl held on to me and deafened me with her shrieks; her cheeks were pressed hard against mine and her warm blood streamed down my neck. I made it to the exit, where there was a small avenue of the paramilitary police, who were only letting people out singly. They stopped and searched each person for weapons, then shoved him out. I was on the receiving end of such a shove, falling down in the mud with the girl. Others rushing out dragged us along for a few seconds. Finally I stood up again, and the girl was gone. Everyone glared and gawped. I wiped myself down and breathed in. All around me people were pointing and shouting at the paramilitaries.

"Idiots! Brutes! What the hell are you up to?"

"We are revolutionaries! Why are you firing on us?!" roared others.

"Go home! Swine! Idiots!" clamoured another.

"Who sent you? ... Staimer?! ... The traitor! Don't let them misuse you! Go home! Withdraw! ... You'd be better off shooting counter-revolutionaries!" resounded all around. And – it was almost comical – all at once the police squad relaxed, lowered their rifles and spoke with those in front. "Yes, no, we're not counter-revolutionaries! ... We were told there was a putsch being hatched. We're going soon, you'll see," I heard, and the soldiers marched off in unison.

We marched behind them in close formation to Stachus. "To the

Luise School to get weapons!" one cried. "All out on strike!" another roared. "To the Central Council," shouted others. A tram whirred towards us. It was stopped. Someone clambered onto the roof and tore the contact bar from the cable. The car stood still and so did the next one. "Strike! Go home! Get out of the tram!" roared one after the other. The tram drivers ripped out their control levers, stepped down from their vehicles, and went home. "It's all the same to us, we're on strike already," they hummed. We moved on, with one group going to the parliament house, and another to the Luise School.

"Halt! Halt!" shouted the sentry at the parliament house, pointing his rifle at us again. We hesitated. Many turned away. "Don't shoot! Deputation to the Central Council!" shouted a sailor.

"Makes no difference! Disperse! No one may enter the parliament building!" the sentry shouted back. More and more people broke away.

For a few minutes we stared dumbly down the menacing barrels.

"Nothing we can do!" whispered the two sailors who were leading us: "Let's go to the Luise School!" We turned around. I left, turned down Briennerstrasse and went to parliament house gate on my own.

"I'm going to the Revolutionary Artists' Council ... Graf is my name," I told the guard. He let me through. After some searching and questioning, I found the assembly room and went in. There were just a few people there: Tautz, Achenbach, Stückgold, the sculptor Pillartz and my lodger. They were sitting around idly as though they were enjoying an evening's entertainment.

"Hey! Are you still there?" Tautz called out to me with a malicious grimace.

"Who is that?" asked Stückgold, pointing.

"Graf! ... Dear little Oskar Maria," clarified my lodger.

"Also a revolutionary? ... What does he do? ... Aha, a writer! ... Yes, we can use him," Stückgold now said.

"You're lounging around in here while out there it's all blood and thunder," I snarled, and reported the events. They all listened with interest. They did not seem to have anything whatever to do. When I had finished my story, they started arguing, most of them swearing against the Majority Socialists; my lodger demanded the immediate dismissal of Staimer. It became even more unclear to me what they were doing here.

"So, what are you up to here exactly?" I asked.

"Tomorrow's session is to discuss our new measures," jabbered Stückgold, leaning over the table and giving the others a sly wink. "I like the young comrade ... He has very dashing eyes ..." They all started laughing. My lodger went into the neighbouring room. I heard the clatter of a typewriter, then the man came out and gave me a typed identity paper stating that I was an artist and a member of the revolutionary council, should be admitted everywhere, unrestricted by any police curfew. I glanced at the scrap of paper, folded it up, put it away and said: "Well, that's something! ... If you really need me, let me know ... I'm off."

"Boozing again in Nymphenburg?" asked Tautz with a slightly irritating, satirical tone.

"Yes, perhaps, it depends ... What can I do here? ... I'm only spoiling things for you," I replied.

"Come more often ... There's work to be done!" a few of them shouted after me, as I went out the door.

Yes, I went back to Nymphenburg. And why not? I liked it, and it did nobody any harm. Besides, to be honest, I felt like I was surplus to requirements in the revolutionary movement. I had no confidence in anything or anybody and least of all did I expect anything of myself.

When it was, "Down with the war! No more militarism!" I was fully behind it; it was all about me, it was what I understood, because I hated militarism from my youth. But I could not really grasp the later slogans and catchwords.

I was one of the millions who only take action when their own interests are at stake, who struggle when they are forced to defend those interests, and who only intervene when they feel that there is a tangible meaning behind the cause, in line with their desires. When I thought about this more carefully, it seemed to me that most of the leaders regarded ordinary people in very abstract terms and spoke of things for which people would never risk their lives unless forced to do so. And for this reason I was profoundly sceptical about the success of the revolutionary movement, and more than this, I was sceptical about the movement itself. True, I was enthusiastic when something stirred that came from people like me; I was carried along by the masses, but never by the leaders. And although in the end I did a lot of things, it was in fact always the same: I ran with the masses when things started, I shouted when everyone else was shouting, I went on the attack when they went on the attack, but I did little else.

So I started to become a drunkard. Life in the Dutchman's villa was perfect for this purpose. The days proceeded as follows: the breakfast was a kind of fortifying preparation, so many cups of strong coffee and enough lining of the stomach to wake you up and get you moving again. It was usually already eleven o'clock and the boring morning served for a drive into the city by car to buy replacements for the things that had been smashed during the night, such as antique mirrors, Chinese vases, decorated jugs, porcelain miniatures, lamps and the like. Marietta also visited various fashion boutiques, buying everything possible, and when the shopping was done, we visited *Böttner*, a posh breakfast restaurant in the Theatinerstrasse, where we took a hearty brunch, which always lasted quite a while. Our spirits revived; we drove back to Nymphenburg for lunch. The food was the most refined and exquisitely prepared. Gradually, the drinking started. I have never since encountered such a knowledgeable keeper and drinker of wine as our host. He was a real genius for it, he performed miracles. We sampled wines on a graded succession, with each one enhancing the mood. First came light wines, then sparkling wines, which were strangely exhilarating, and finally the full-bodied wines, and then again, those that dissolved all inhibitions. It was wonderful to observe how each of us was affected by this carefully planned mixture of drinks. We slipped from a pleasant cosiness into sentimentality and the desire to sing; melancholy alternated with a violent urge to display our brilliant cynicism; we then passed into a kind of limbo, but our brains were intensely active, ideas followed one after the other, driving, as it were, towards an ever-bolder clarity; everyone became droll, then quick-witted and bubbly, we rattled off smutty jokes, the air was thick with coarse but clever turns of phrase, the conversation became razor sharp, hot-tempered passions fought a constant battle for supremacy with smirking superiority, everything commonplace and everything profound was brought to the surface – it seemed as though we were swimming in lukewarm, tingling water, raised up by high waves and then brought crashing down, again and again.

Some afternoons were also monotonous. No one knew how to fill the time; we loafed around for hours on the sofa and read indifferently, waiting spinelessly for new alcoholic sensations; we drank coffee in Marietta's turret-room, she read poems, someone or other visited, and we argued, or the Dutchman tinkled a little on the piano, Davringhausen tried to paint a picture, and I entertained the hostess.

Occasionally we drove around the district in the car, but in reality, we were always just waiting to go on the next bender. Nothing destroys will-power quite so completely as a constantly full stomach, not having a care in the world, and the kind of wealth that can fulfil every whim on the spot. I suffered wretched hangovers and yet never made a decision to change my ways. Sometimes I went into town on my own and visited my flat. It seemed alien to me, like a spent memory. It was dusty and smelt of airless mould. I moved on. Pegu and Tautz met me on the street. Laughing, I stepped between them and wrapped my arms around their necks.

"Drunk again?" asked Tautz, with an acid laugh.

"No, no, just being sociable, awfully sociable!" I bellowed expansively, and with a theatrical vulgarity.

"I am so depraved, sooo depraved, you know! ... But it is beautiful, sooo beautiful, all this shit! ... Beautiful! ... Tremendous!" On I babbled, on and on, whinnying and shaking now and then. The two of them could only laugh.

"*Mariechen*, you're just a useless drip! ... Don't mess about with your

328

bohemian airs! ... You're an absolute petty bourgeois, a shabby, down-at-heel bourgeois, nothing more," Tautz interjected with a humorous earnestness, and Pegu growled, "Damn right!" But they could not get a rise out me, because constant drinking had brought me to the point that I took nothing seriously any more, absolutely nothing. I just trumpeted boldly, mockingly: "Yes, yes, I have always said it! ... Yes, yes, I am the complete petty bourgeois, a contemptible bourgeois! ... Yes, of course! ... With drunkard and comedian as side-lines! ... Quite right. Quite right!" And impervious to insult, callous, wickedly vicious, I chuntered on: "Yes, yes, man is something grand, so terribly grand! ... Troughs on meat and vegetables, swills water, beer and wine, begets children, and then snuffs it, yes! ... That, that is unique, unparalleled! ... Yes, and then he suddenly hits on an idea and gets angry about it! ... Extraordinary, isn't it? ... Yes, extraordinary! ... And these angry people call themselves revolutionaries! ... Lovely! Wonderful!" I ranted and ranted, and we parted, laughing.

I was never completely sober, never completely drunk, constantly steaming in an entirely indifferent intermediate state, and breathed a sigh of relief whenever I sat down to dinner in the Dutch villa. After that we could start quaffing again. It made me happy, and I had the opportunity to crack my sleazy, clownish jokes.

It all started in the dining room; the binge then continued in the smoking room or in the winter garden, and on particularly merry occasions, downstairs in the Gothic wine cellar. It was a cool, round space with a high vaulted ceiling. The walls on all sides were covered with shelves, filled with ancient wine bottles, somewhat mouldy, containing the oldest and best vintages. In the middle stood a small, old oak table, surrounded by empty barrels that we perched on. To one side a thin stream of water splashed incessantly into a small stone basin. We splattered each other with water and ended up flooding the cellar, threw the wine bottles at the door and attacked each other with barrels. Soaking wet, we finally went off to bed in the early hours.

There were frequent brawls. Out of sheer irritation, or because a word that annoyed her slipped out, Marietta gave the Dutchman a slap, spat at him and bawled us out. The man hit back, and soon we were in the middle of a nice little scuffle. I made wisecracks about it all, and sometimes the storm dissolved into laughter, but that was increasingly seldom. As a rule, Davringhausen and I sat by and watched the combatants unmoved, encouraging them now and then. "Yes!! Go for it! Tear him to shreds! Crash! Bang! Action! Aaaaction! Wallop! Cra-ash!" I drunkenly yelled, reeling and staggering around, I swung my arms and shouted above the din. The smoking table clattered to the floor, the glasses rattled, smash! That did it, and the mirror or the windowpanes crashed into shards and splinters, chairs flew, the tattered door panel broke in, and the heavy curtain sagged. In the end we left everything in total devastation and the ker-fuffle came to an end. We guests went off to sleep, not unusually Marietta called for the car and drove off to visit painters in Schwabing, and the Dutchman lay down on his bed. The next day the lady of the house came back, either on her own or with others; sometimes the Dutchman fetched her home. Then we ate breakfast as usual, made jokes about last night's tempest and laughed at our clawed and scratched faces and the wrecked furniture. And life started over again.

One day my brother Maurus came to the Dutchman and offered to deliver the best quality patisserie. We looked at each other like hounds snuffling out truffles and spoke a few indifferent words to each other.

I thought: just demand ludicrously high prices and fleece the rich brute for all you're worth!

The corners of his mouth trembled slightly, with a mocking impression. His thoughts were like mine: be a shark, man! A real shark! Get your feet under the table here and stuff yourself! This is the ideal place for a shark! Though we mistrusted each other, we understood each other perfectly. Maurus delivered the finest cakes and pastries. And the Dutchman's custom was highly profitable.

As time went on, I got completely used to this way of life. I mastered every situation and was the indispensable, invigorating element in company and conversation; I was as at home here as the dog in his kennel or the wine on the table.

Sometimes we went into town in the evening and supped at the *Bonbonniere* or *Simplicissimus*, joined by a pack of good-time girls and men, painters, poets and artists; Marietta endlessly recited poems by Lichtenstein and van Hoddis, and basked in admiration. After the curfew hour a whole column of cars drove back to the villa. The drinking carried on, sometimes a game of poker, a scandal broke out and the guests stood around with embarrassed faces or fled hurriedly from the hospitable residence. I laughed at it all uproariously.

Events, the present and future, politics, the masses, the revolution: all were wiped from my memory, all that mattered was living for the moment. As I drove drowsily through the city, everything that occurred in the past surfaced in my memory like something disposable and shoved aside to a corner of brain, only to return as the inspiration for a joke or juicy obscenity. It all seemed to be the same: nobody knew who was in charge, the socialists' slogans changed from day to day, life swung eternally this way and that, meetings, crowds, shootings, rumours of putsches collided with one another.

And me? I was just a private individual and a drunkard, nothing more. The swamp had swallowed me up.

March was gone, and April brought the first warm days.

24.
IMPERFECT WORK

"Graf! Graffff!" Marietta's voice screamed from below, in a clipped tone. I opened my eyes with a start.

"Yes!" I replied and sprang quickly out of bed.

Repulsive, being dragged from your sleep like that! I drowsily pulled on my trousers.

"Oskar Maria!" shouted Davringhausen sarcastically, and I heard heavy, rapid steps on the carpets. The door was flung open and the curtains drawn.

"Now then, little piggy! Now then!? ... Quick, quick! Come on! ... Herr Tautz wants to speak with you! Telephone!" said Davringhausen; and off he went again. "Come quick, we're having breakfast already. There'll be nothing left!"

"Yes, all right, all right! ... Just coming!" I exclaimed, still half asleep, and hastily buttoned my vest, threw my jacket over my head, and ran down to the telephone. "Graf speaking! ... What's up then?" I spoke into the receiver, rather grumpily.

"*Mariechen*! Is that you, you drunken zombie? ... Listen, come to the Artists' Council at the parliament house, right now! ... There's work to be done, you lazy pig!" said Tautz.

"Yes, yes, I'm coming already! ... Ciao!" I answered, hung up and went to breakfast.

"So, what's going on in politics? ... Are you being made a Minister?" asked Davringhausen, laughing, and shoving a slice of bread and butter in his mouth. They all looked at me with a sneering curiosity.

"There look! ... Another public holiday!" said the Dutchman, pushing the *Münchner Neueste Nachrichten* in my direction.

"It's the Soviet Republic," Marietta said curtly, and I glanced at the front page. It contained a huge proclamation in bold type: "To the People of Bavaria!"

"Hey! Hey?! It's going wild! I have to go at once!" I blurted out and hurriedly read on: "The decisive moment has arrived. Bavaria is a Soviet Republic. Working people are in control of their destiny." So it went on. Today, Palm Monday, 7 April, was declared a public holiday and the whole proclamation was signed by the revolutionary Central Council.[63]

"Arseholes!" grunted the Dutchman. He was annoyed. I was secret-

---

[63] A pedant writes: there appears to be a small confusion here, as Palm Sunday – and the Palm Sunday putsch – took place the following weekend.

ly delighted and thought, it's all up for you, my boy. I gulped down the rest of my coffee and got up.

"I'll go with you," Davringhausen decided, and we left. I was in a great hurry. I ran over the frozen meadows so fast that my companion could hardly keep up. The sky was the exquisite blue of spring, the first starlings were singing, planes glittered in the sun and the trams were not running. We reached the city drenched in sweat. The parliament house was buzzing with nervous energy. Soldiers and civilians were piling up ammunition in front of the machine gun posts in the vaulted gateway. It looked like they were bracing for expected attacks. Nobody paid us any attention, they were all flitting back and forth; words such as "White Guards! Munich encircled! Noske troops are on the march!" flew from ear to ear.

People ran up and down corridors, disappeared into the meeting rooms and came out again. We went into the room housing the Artists' Council, which was almost full this time. I saw familiar and unfamiliar faces: Schorsch, Achenbach, Tautz, my lodger, Wolfenstein, Georg Kaiser, Schwabing painters and writers. Stückgold's voice penetrated out of some group or other. There was non-stop coming and going. Everyone sized up the elegant Davringhausen suspiciously. [64]

"Jackass in pressed trousers," I heard someone say.

"Graf, you must come with me! I am the censor at the *Bayrischer Kurier!*" said Achenbach and after a few words I went with him inside.

"You are exactly the right man for these Bavarian clerics ... They are always trying it on with passive resistance," said Achenbach on the street, half hesitant, half swaggering. "No problem, I'll manage," I grunted, indifferently.

The editorial offices were empty when we arrived. Achenbach hung his hat and coat on the wall, took a long manuscript out of his breast pocket and went to the table, where the galley proofs were laid out. I had not taken off my things and sat down, uninterested.

"That has to go in today's paper," said Achenbach. "Very well," I grunted again. A typesetter came through the door and greeted us casually.

He walked up to the editorial table matter-of-factly, took the galleys and asked: "Ready to go?"

"Yes, we're putting that in as the lead article in today's edition," an-

---

[64] Stanislaus Stückgold (1868-1933) was a German-Polish-French painter. He fled from Poland to Paris in 1907, having been persecuted for his participation in the socialist and anti-Russian movement, and studied under Henri Matisse, before moving to Munich in 1913. He opened an art school in Munich, which he led until 1921, before moving to Paris, where he also taught art. He painted still-life, portraits and landscapes in bright, often garish colours.

swered Achenbach. "Good," said the typesetter, and went. We were alone again and, it seemed, there was no more work to do.

Achenbach strutted up and down nervously and said from time to time: "Of course, this all has to be strictly organized."

I stood around dumbly for a while, then, feeling bored, I sat down and tried to work out what purpose I was serving here exactly.

I was about to ask this question when the door opened and a man of my size, with a short-cropped grey moustache and stubble, a straight face and casual clothes, walked in. One pace behind him there followed a stout, red-faced, and agitated cleric. The two of them went up to Achenbach resolutely and started arguing at once. "Herr von Achenbach, you have given the printers an article ... Look, we'd like to state at once, it's not on ... As Catholic citizens, we cannot tolerate it ... No, not at all."

The priest started gesticulating wildly, and the other man promptly backed him up: "No sir, our faith forbids it. You have your own convictions, do you not?"

"That is neither here nor there, this has been mandated by the Central Council, and you must submit to it ... I take full responsibility ... The article is merely a critical analysis," interjected Achenbach.

"No! Absolutely not ... I have been Editor-in-Chief here for ten years already and cannot ... The article does not only attack Catholics, our faith – it attacks all faiths, Protestant, Jewish, Muslim ... It does serious injury to religious freedom ... You cannot expect us to preach atheism in a Catholic journal ... Even your Herr Landauer can't have expected that," shouted the priest once again and protested, again and again: "No, no-no-no."

"I have already said, you do not have to take responsibility. And in any case, if we publish an article attacking the various religions as dogmatic, that doesn't mean we are doing injury to religious freedom. We are addressing intelligent readers, the proletariat ... They can all decide for themselves," began Achenbach in his conciliatory, pontificating manner, and seemed to be taking the greatest pleasure in conversing with the gentlemen. He read, as far as I knew, Kierkegaard and the mystics and was a real nit-picker.

But the editors were not to be moved.

"Decide for themselves? ... No, no, as Catholics we have our God and our faith ... That won't do, we decided for ourselves long ago, Herr Achenbach ... We don't want to waste our time discussing the matter ... Please take us to Herr Landauer ... We would rather hand the paper over to you altogether. We would rather give the whole thing up," insisted the priest.

"Our conviction ... You can nail us to the cross like our Lord Jesus ... We Catholics have always been persecuted ... No, no, we cannot reconcile that with our conscience before God ... We are also lowly workers, we have nothing against the government, but we cannot tolerate ... The article is a sin against religion," the other one started up again. Achenbach could not get a word in edgeways.

He waved his arms about, smiled, toyed with his Browning; he had become unsettled, he did not want to hurt them, but he wanted to impress upon them that he was a fearsome man.

"Yes, but for God's sake ... I have been commissioned! ... The article must appear! Those are the orders ..." he clearly stated. Then, probably because he could see how little he intimidated them, he threatened, though in a very courteous tone: "I can have you stood up against the wall ... Bear in mind ... that you are resisting the current authorities! I am the authorized representative of the government!"

But the men were not alarmed; on the contrary, I even saw how the priest smiled a little pityingly and said right off: "Yes, you can do that ... We expect that with all our faith ... But we will not deny our religion ... No, no. Please take us to Landauer. If we cannot reach an understanding, we will resign and hand everything over to you ... But no, we won't do that. We would rather die in the arms of Jesus. Please take us to Landauer."

Achenbach smiled and was already wavering. All of a sudden, I jumped up and confronted the pair, boiling with rage.

"What?! What's that?! Yes, our Lord God in Heaven, by His Sacrament and Crucifix, what do you imagine!" I screamed at maximum volume, and the two gentlemen jerked back and turned to Achenbach for help. But I was going for it.

"What?! In the war you had to print all the lies that Ludendorff ordered you to, in the war you preached that men must be massacred, for God's sake! During the war you printed every lie and were part of the whole swindle! And now you come to us with your faith? You call yourself Catholics?

"Well, so am I. But I have never heard so much deceit and corruption! You are the worst of Pharisees! ... We're having none of it! The article will be printed, and you won't see Landauer! There is nothing to negotiate! The government is the government! ... Every washerwoman in Munich would like to see Landauer! ... There's nothing to add, nothing at all. We're going nowhere!"

I blustered, already foaming at the mouth.

"For Heaven's sake, Herr von Achenbach, such blasphemy, such language! No, no!" wailed the pair of them. They were quite consternated. Again and again they demanded a meeting with Landauer.

Achenbach was helpless and was about to start arguing again.

"Don't talk rubbish! ... We are here, and we have a mandate. And that's that!" I bawled and then yelled again at the two men: "Where was your faith in the war? That was all Christian and proper! You prayed, swindled and haggled to get us all sent to a miserable death for those criminals around the Kaiser! Now you are unemployed, get out! There's nothing more to discuss. And that's all there is to it. You can go!" I snapped again, and turned to my comrade: "So, we needn't trouble Landauer! Put your Browning away! It's only making them laugh! ... They know perfectly well that you won't use it! I wanted to sit down, but the priest and his sidekick kept on about Landauer, they wanted to go on their own and made ready to do so.

"No! Go if you will. We will issue an order for your immediate arrest!" I snarled and said to Achenbach: "Ring up and order their arrest! Don't show them any more respect than they showed us." But my comrade did not do so.

A short while passed in hostile silence. I sat down and gazed out of the window. The two men then started negotiating with Achenbach again and after a long and stubborn back and forth, in which I did not participate, my comrade declared himself ready to go to Landauer.

"And with that, my commission is over," I said, stood up and went with them. The two marched ahead; we followed. Out on the street I hastily whispered in Achenbach's ear: "You're the world's biggest sucker! Cheerio." and I left him. He looked at me a little dumbfounded and then joined the two men. Later I heard from Pegu that Landauer really had respected the gentlemen's convictions and ordered the article to be withdrawn.

"Aha ... Yes, of course, freedom first, even if that means freedom to destroy the revolution," I jeered. "Ludendorff would have had them shot on the spot, as would Noske, but we, yes we, are humane."

"This Soviet Republic is useless, too," said my friend, "It will soon go to pieces ... The Communists have rejected it."

A noisy demonstration, flags waving, streamed down the Sendlingerstrasse with Max Levien, sporting riding boots and spurs, at its head.

At the Schiller memorial Levien mounted the plinth and made a speech. It was a curious spectacle, the man with the Napoleonic strut, and behind it the calm figure of a poet.

He demanded the immediate confiscation of bank funds, the opening of safes, the death penalty for opponents of the revolutionary cause and more of the same. I could not help but laugh. I went on my way. On the Türkenstrasse I bumped into a wizened old man who regarded the crowds that had gathered closely and sneeringly.

"Oh, beg your pardon!" I exclaimed rather stiffly and stood there in front of him. He looked deep into my eyes and said with a smile: "No harm done, bonnie lad! ... A've been trodden on the fyeut see often!" He smiled even more and pointed to all the people with an outstretched walking stick. "Them? ... They'll aaal coin intee canny Catholics, yet! ... Yee wait an' see."

"Why's that then?" I asked, astonished. The man lowered his stick and blinked at me again with cunning eyes. "Nar na ah divvint sa owt! Nar na! Nar na! ... Ah divvint sa a thin!" he hastily added in his thick Swabian accent and trotted on hurriedly. I heard him chuckle at himself. For a moment I wondered if I should follow him and ask for an explanation, but I let it go. He was one of those cranks, I thought, and was satisfied. Ahead, the crowd was now surging away from the square towards the parliament house, with Levien.

I went back to my flat, sat down at my typewriter, and wrote a long letter to the girl. Time and again as I typed out sentence upon sentence, it occurred to me that it would perhaps not be delivered, writing is pointless, but I carried on regardless. I was spurred on by a strange yearning, a world-weary feeling of oppression.

"I do not know what I am or where I belong," I wrote, "but sometimes it seems to me that others are not so very different. It's odd. When I read the north German newspapers, I secretly want to travel up north and shoot the scribblers, first those that the publishers pay, then the publishers themselves. 'Civil War in Munich' they write and 'Unscrupulous rabble-rousers are establishing an unprecedented reign of terror with a fanatical minority'; in reality we are all eternally desperate for peace. What a disgusting, slimy, hellish instrument it is, this press!

"They lied in the war, and when the revolution came, didn't they all say we had to tell lies, yes, we had to do it, yes, we were compelled to do it? And now? Now they are lying just as much. I would just like to know what kind of excuse they will come up with when they are called to account.

"There is no civil war here, and most of the leaders actually live in fear. They have two reasons to be afraid: first they are afraid of the masses and talk themselves into an ever-greater radicalism, and then they are afraid that their own courage will fail them. Nothing has happened to anyone here, on the contrary, whenever someone feels threatened, he goes to the highest authorities and negotiates; he always gets what he wants.

"Under the old regime everyone from the lance corporal, from counter clerks up to the Minister himself would snap at you. Most of the time you would not get through to him at all; today it is quite different.

"It all looks a little like Schilda – the citizens get upset and puff out their cheeks and run to the highest authority.[65] And who is he? He is the

---

[65] The citizens of the fictional town of Schilda are the protagonists of a whole series of short stories written by various authors from around 1597. Alongside the tales of Till Eulenspiegel, they are among the best-known German stories in the picaresque tradition.

one who does everything to oblige, asking: 'Yes, what seems to be the trouble? Then I will set things to rights at once, gentlemen!' It is comical, but it is human. It is so human that all humans have lost their respect for it. And that is what will destroy this revolution, because the NCOs cannot be eradicated in Germany. They want order, and they will emerge victorious.

"Did I write that I do not know where I belong? I think I know now, and now I am content ..."

There was already a dusky air in the streets as I wandered back to Nymphenburg. On the footpath leading across the meadows to the Dutchman's villa, I suddenly heard footsteps. I turned around. A figure was coming towards me, a man's. I slowed down; it always unnerved me when someone walked in my wake. The man caught up. I looked at him, and he at me, and we were both somewhat stunned. It was the grey man from the *Bayrischer Kurier*. "Good evening, neighbour," I said. He recognized me perfectly.

"Good evening," he replied, in the same tone. I could not help but chuckle. His face was not in the least unfriendly.

"Hm, that is funny ... I did kick up a row at your place today," I said, in turn.

"Yes, well, that's not so bad ... Just differences of opinion ... A matter of temperament," the man answered good naturedly. That did me good.

"Yes, sometimes I'm a bit hot-headed," I said, also good naturedly.

"Are you in the government?" my companion wanted to know.

"No, not at all, I just help out a bit now and then," I replied, harmlessly.

"Aha ... Well, there's plenty of work to be done. Do you live around here?" he enquired.

"Yes, well no, actually, I just visit over there now and then."

"Oh you mean with the Dutch gentleman ... Then we are almost neighbours. Indeed," the grey man said, turning off towards his nearby house "I live here ... Good night ..."

"Good night," I called amiably, and thought, oh no, if Noske's troops emerge victorious, you've had it. He will denounce you at once.[66]

Davringhausen was already in the villa. The Dutchman looked like he was in a good mood, and Marietta asked cheerfully: "So, how's the

---

[66] The grey man's name was Josef Osterhuber (1876-1965). In fact, he proved to be a committed opponent of burgeoning National Socialism. After their seizure of power, the *Kurier* was confiscated on 10 June 1933. Twelve days later the editorial offices were searched and Osterhuber was briefly put in protective custody. Finally, the Bavarian Interior Minister Adolf Wagner enforced his dismissal without notice and banned him from the profession of journalism. In 1945 Osterhuber was elected Director of the Association of Professional Journalists in Bavaria and was from 1948 to 1951 press officer for the Bavarian Farmers' Association.

Minister?" All three laughed sarcastically.

"Who, me? ... I'll stay on as your court jester," I said to the Dutchman, and recounted what had happened. Davringhausen reported that he had left straight away after seeing the Artists' Council.

We spent the night in the usual manner. But I was not in the mood this time and went back into town the next day.

It had a warlike appearance now. There were armed civilians everywhere. The Communists had occupied the clubhouse of the Catholic Associations – Leohaus – and were provisionally using it to print *Die Rote Fahne*. Huge bales of paper were rolled up into a sort of barricade in front of the entrance, a machine gun stood in the doorway, and a party man was patrolling on guard duty, marching up and down. I went up to him. He recognized me and let me through. Downstairs there were guardrooms; weapons of all sorts were lying around. I saw familiar and unfamiliar faces and heard self-important chat followed by the cracking of jokes. Upstairs in one of the rooms I met a gigantic girl with a *coiffure à la Titus*, who went by the name of Hilde.[67] Some Spartacists asked me if I knew a printer who could be relied upon, but I did not, and we discussed it without reaching a conclusion. I moved on. In the anteroom of the Artists' Council chamber I met my lodger, who was supervising the receipt of news reports and issuing the official statements for the press.

"You are just in time! Come here! You can type, can't you?" he asked me, and when I nodded, he ordered me to sit at the typewriter. I did so. He dictated. "The Hungarian Soviet Republic sends revolutionary greetings to its Bavarian brothers," he said, looking absent-mindedly at the typed sheets lying around the table. The telephone rang. He picked up the receiver.

"Central Council News Department! ... Hallo! ... Yes, Titus is that you?" he said and took a sheet. "Hang on ... What's that? The Augsburg Works Council has gone to Bamberg to negotiate with Hoffmann ... That's scandalous! Who gave the order? ... What? ... No! Speak softly! The Soviet Government is standing firm! ... Yes, I know ... Schneppenhorst is in Nuremberg, the bastard. Graf is here, yes ... Hallo! Can you hear me? Yes, Noske wants to wipe us out, I know ... We'll plug him full of lead!"[68]

---

[67] *Coiffure à la Titus* was a short-cropped curly hairstyle popular during the First French Empire. It sounds rather more brutal in German: *Tituskopf*. Hilde Kramer, who was barely 19 at the time, was the KPD's stenographer at the Second World Congress of the Third International in 1920. In 1937 she fled with her son to England, where she died in 1974. Her autobiography, *Rebellin in München, Moskau und Berlin: Autobiographisches Fragment 1900 - 1924*, was republished in 2011.

[68] The deposed Bavarian Government, a coalition of the SPD and bourgeois parties, moved to Bamberg. It was headed by Johannes Hoffmann. Ernst Schneppenhorst was Minister of Defence.

He put the receiver back in the cradle and turned to me again: "Hey, the Majority Socialists have joined in X times and every time they have betrayed us ... I was there myself. Schneppenhorst agreed to the proclamation of the Soviet Republic and now he is sitting there in Nuremberg spying on us ... As for the Independents, it's enough to make you puke! They always prattle on about unity, and then they fall in together with those traitors ... Spartacus stands alone ... Nothing will happen until the Communists take full control ...

"No one else has a clue!"

I waited for him to dictate and said nothing. He no longer seemed to be in a hurry, lit a cigarette, and wanted to chat with me some more.

"Are you still boozing?" he asked.

"Yes, of course," I replied and stood up.

"Are you going out again?"

"What else is there to do? Tell Pegu I am at my flat and he should come," I curtly replied and did not rise to his jibes,

On the street I met Schorsch.

"Hey! Hey! Graf! Schorsch! Come with us!" someone shouted from a car that was hurtling past but pulled up briefly. It was the Nymphenburg set. We got in and went for lunch with them at *Böttner*. My friend was ravenous and jaded. He wolfed everything down greedily and quaffed. We got up and went to the gents.

"Stuff your face! Eat and drink all you can! Our heads are already in the noose!" I whispered to Schorsch, who nodded with glassy eyes. He drove back to the villa with us. On the road we also picked up Achenbach. It became a wild binge. We romped like wild animals. All of a sudden, Schorsch burst out crying.

"Ma-a-aria! Ma-a-aria!" he howled, totally in bits, and ran like a madman through the front door into the starlit night. He stumbled and fell in a freshly dug ditch. He lay there, crestfallen and contrite, wailing: "Ma-a-aria! Ma-a-aria!" He threw up and flailed about helplessly in vomit.

Achenbach and I ran over to him and hauled him out. We carried him up to bed. He dropped onto it and fell into a deep sleep, with a rattle in his throat like a dying beast.

"He cannot bear to be alone! He is pining for his Maria!" I muttered to Achenbach.

"Yes, we all suffer from that complex. None of us can bear to be alone," said the know-it-all.

The binge drinking had come to an abrupt halt, broken by a mood of disgust. Marietta was annoyed and swore at us all, the Dutchman grumbled bad-temperedly, and we all went to bed, barely exchanging a word. The next day at breakfast our friend was back to normal. He had torn his trousers and put on a fresh pair from the Dutchman. After lunch the three of us wandered into town.

"There! Listen! Listen!" I shouted, startled, as we left the Dutchman's garden. All three of us pricked up our ears. Tagggdaragg-daggg! came the distant rumble.

"Something's happening!" exclaimed Schorsch, and we started running.

"A putsch! Barricades!" panted Achenbach. We heard shots from the direction of the railway station, then volleys of machine-gun fire and finally the thunder of cannons. We ran as fast as we could down Nymphenburgerstrasse and to the Stiglmairplatz. Before the Löwenbräu beer cellar there were scuffles and screams. The gunfire was now quite close by and unusually heavy. More and more people were storming down the Dachauerstrasse.

"What's up? ... What? A putsch?" I asked a worker running past.

"Yes! The Hoffmann regime and the Majority Socialists!" he shouted back breathlessly. Then he was gone. Aeroplanes rattled through the air, spewing white clouds of leaflets. Groups of people were running this way and that; they snatched at the falling leaflets, clustered around them, read them and started effing and blinding.

Red Guards and soldiers took aim and fired at the aeroplanes and fired again. An ear-splitting racket.

"Schneppenhorst lies! Majority Socialist treason!" I heard, "On we go! Into struggle! To the railway station!" At last I got hold of a man who had a leaflet, and I read in haste: "To the working people of Munich! Workers and soldiers!" I just managed to glance the words, "the Central Council is declared deposed" and "outside agitators, pursuing their own political interests", when the man ripped up the leaflet. "The scabs! The scoundrels!" he snarled. I whistled, but there was no response. The gunfire and banging, the general tumult drowned everything else out. Over our heads, up in the air, small sparks flashed continuously from gun barrels and vanished in clouds of smoke. I shoved forwards with all my strength, elbowed people out of the way, ran on a few steps and managed to reach the perimeter of the station square.

It looked like a constant ebb and flow of bodies. Advancing from Prielmayerstrasse, Schützenstrasse, Schillerstrasse and Bayerstrasse, armed masses constantly attacked the Central Railway Station, out of which spewed gunfire; then they retreated, bellowing and shrieking, before turning and attacking again, with renewed fury.

"Down with them! Down with them! Down with them!" boomed the crowd; the machine guns rattled, the attackers advanced again, shooting at will. Sontheimer emerged from the cloud of smoke, brandishing his rifle, and shouted back: "Forwards! Attack! Attack!" He had two more rifles hanging from his body and two pairs of binoculars; he was wearing a broad red sash, into which he had stuck a huge revolver. Bullets whistled around him. "Forwards! Up! Attack!" he yelled again, and everyone rushed behind him. More cannon fire, windows shattered, the wounded fell, houses and the ground shook, the crowd into which I was wedged surged onwards with the attackers and into the station to the sound of crashing masonry, and with a terrible clamour.

Unarmed! Sitting ducks, to be shot like lumps of flesh was the thought that raged in my confused head, and with clenched fists and my teeth clamped tight I allowed myself to be carried forward. I suddenly shouted with all fury at those wedged around me: "Yes, for the love of God, but what's going on here? Who are we attacking?!" I roared so loud that the bodies pressed against me started to tremble in shock. I was close to grabbing hold of someone and tearing him to pieces, just from the angry, blind passion not to be shot down for no purpose whatsoever. And all the time I was thinking: Idiocy! Complete idiocy! You always get mixed up in the crush without knowing what's going on.

Since then I have always understood how a coward can be transformed into a hero.

"Against the Bambergers! Against Hoffmann, you idiot!" came the reply, and I felt a sense of relief. "All right then! That's good to know! Let's go for it! Just go for it!" I answered. Nobody heard.

The gunfire had pretty much stopped, and the cry resounded around the lofty halls: "Victory! Victory! Long live the Soviet Republic!" The station had been stormed and occupied by the Communists. Laughing faces beamed at me. Our crowd had forced its way into the hall from Arnulfstrasse and I came out with it again into Bayerstrasse. The packed throng diffused like mush from a meatgrinder, ran across the square and into the side-streets. Everyone breathed a collective sigh of relief. Only then did I find out what had happened. A handful of Majority Socialists had secretly won over a number of barracks councils to the Hoffmann government on the previous night and had distributed a poster, claiming to be on behalf of the entire Munich garrison, attacking the Soviet Republic. They proclaimed martial law, occupied the most important buildings, declared the Central Council to be deposed, arrested Mühsam, Wadler, and various other councillors, and deported them to Lower Bavaria.

At this, the Central Council demanded a general strike; Communists assumed the leadership of armed factory councils and the masses, the putschists were beaten back, disarmed and driven out. A new Central Council was in government, the Communists seized power, the so-called second Soviet Republic came into being, and almost overnight the Red Army, already set up but sloppily organized, was established.

25.
THE COLLAPSE

For a whole fortnight the working masses of Munich gathered and made ready to resist Noske's advancing task force, as well as the lurking threat of revolt by the enemy within. For a whole fortnight the best known of the new rulers – Leviné-Nissen, Levien, Egelhofer, Landauer, Toller and Axelrod – together with an army of haphazard, fickle supporters and unreliable helpers, tried to construct a communist Soviet Republic. For a whole fortnight the property-owning classes felt uncomfortable and seemed to have crept away somewhere.

"Everyone will receive a minimum allowance," I said to the Dutchman, "for example, you as a musician! ... You will receive 20 marks or so from the State, and I will too." The man's brow puckered for a moment, then when I laughed, he laughed frostily. Our villa was still an undisturbed island. Life went on as before; events did not interfere one iota. One day I went to visit my patroness in the city. She was rather unsettled.

"What will happen, Herr Graf? ... They want to rent out my apartment ... You know, I have nothing against it, so long as my furniture and pictures are taken care of ... What do you advise?" she asked. I shrugged my shoulders. I couldn't think of what to say.

"Give your paintings to the care of the State for safe keeping," I then advised, "there is sure to be heavy fighting." She nodded, thought about it for a while, and then said more cheerfully: "We are all human ... The workers are right, for sure ... I can understand it ... All I want for myself is to live in peace."

"People who want to live in peace will be left in peace ... No doubt about it," I said and promised to stand by her whatever might happen. Those exercising supreme power were doing the same. Her friends and acquaintances, no matter how rich they were, only had to mention her name and they would have protection.

The professor grumbled timidly, then laughed nervously and told me about house searches in his neighbourhood. They had given the Reds schnapps and been friendly, and the Reds went off again. There was a hint of scorn in his words.

"Yes, my dear thing, there are hard times ahead ... Quite terrible times," he said with something of a sigh, and stared into space. "I think there will be a terrible bloodbath, professor," I said, agreeing with him, "but I think it can be avoided ...

"If the most respected professors and citizens of the city would send an open letter to the Hoffmann Government, saying that nobody has been plundered, robbed or terrorized in Munich ... I mean, if the people of truly high standing here would speak out against the appalling lies that are being spread outside the city, and offered to mediate," I said.

"But that's out of the question ... We cannot do that. It might be misinterpreted as a counter-revolutionary act," he shouted giving an ironic emphasis to the word *misinterpreted*.

"Well then, there's nothing for it ... To the best of my knowledge, people are genuinely grateful, if you want to help," I repeated.

"Yes! Yes! But Graf, you are on their side ... And in this, I can't join you," he concluded.

I went to my flat. I heard the creak of a lock in my neighbour's room, then a knock at my door.

"For God's sake, Herr Graf, Herr Graf, help me ... I was arrested as a hostage! ... They released me again, but tomorrow I have to report to the police headquarters and will be interned again," whimpered my neighbour, a chubby painter. He was trembling; almost crying.

"But will you go? Why should you? ... Just sit down ... It's all nonsense! It's sure to be a mistake," I exclaimed, and let him in. He told me that his neighbour, a hysterical painter, had denounced him to the Communists as a counter-revolutionary spy.

"You know them! Come with me! Help me out. I will never forget it, never!" he begged.

"I know hardly anyone who is in the police, but let's go, we'll see," I consoled him, and we went together to the headquarters. We had no trouble getting past the sentries. Every one of these seemingly ferocious men loosened up as soon as we spoke to them in good Bavarian. We got through and went upstairs to the very room in which I had been interrogated in January. The enormous woman Hilde was there, and a few others sat on the tables, men with rifles lounged about and casually smoked cigarettes, some more stood behind the racks and looked through the files.

"Hey, Graf! So what do you want?" Hilde asked me boyishly. They all gathered around us.

"It's complete and utter madness arresting this man! He's been my neighbour for a year and a day! I will vouch for him any time! What's he being charged with?" I blustered, good-humouredly.

"Well, he has been listed as ... A counter-revolutionary! ... But if you vouch for him," a man said, and then called out to Hilde: "Write a note to say there is nothing against him." The gigantic girl went into a neighbouring room, I heard the clatter of a typewriter and chatted casually with the others. Hilde brought a note certifying that my neighbour was under the protection of the Soviet Government. We left. The rescued man would have liked, most of all, to hug me and made all kinds of promises and kept shaking my hand.

I met Pegu in front of my flat. He was taciturn, tired out.

"I can't be in several places at once ... I am so tired," he said, and stretched out on my sofa. I knew all too well that he needed rest. He worked behind the scenes on every action, he put together the newspapers that appeared in other people's name, he slaved through entire nights and did all the uncelebrated minutiae for the revolution; he was tireless, showing up and doing everything asked of him and then going off to do more elsewhere. "There, you have a key to my flat! ... You can live here ... In any case, I am living out in Nymphenburg," I said. He nodded. I let him sleep and went off.

Workers' battalions with shouldered rifles kept moving through the streets. Everyone looked serious, almost sad. They tramped along behind laden lorries, through the cheering crowds, with a melancholy tread. Old, broken down and bearded workers were there and young kids with dashing eyes. They did not seem all that enthusiastic. The young faces were saying, more or less: sorry, but we cannot put on a show for you! Their brows were furrowed under the weight of silent responsibility. Almost as happened in the last war years of 1917 and 1918, this army rolled on to its posts, with a stoical courage, hard and bitter, because there was no other way.

I reddened with shame. "Good luck, comrade! Here are some cigarettes," I said to an old man, and gave him my packet. My heart was in my throat. He laughed a little, popped his eyelids up and down, and murmured: "Thank you!"

The girl sent me letters; she seemed worried. I noticed that one or two of my letters had been lost in the post and I could gauge what kind of lies the Berlin newspapers must be writing about the Soviet Republic.

Our drinking binges became more subdued; they were no longer fun. Through the night I could hear the cannons thundering in the distance, the windowpanes rattled slightly, the walls trembled a little. The flavours of the wine had lost their appeal. The slaughterhouse, the slaughterhouse, was my constant, gloomy thought; gruesome the picture I painted of how they would be butchered, the thousands and thousands of workers. They were no match for the professional NCOs, who knew nothing but war and slaughter. "A-a-a-gh, fill me up! Fill my glass, man! Let's drown our sorrows!" I groaned and drank with a snort. One night the dog started barking and did not stop. The bell rang and rang. There was a sound of shouting outside the gate.

"Who is there?" we three men shouted as one through the open front door, and saw two figures under the lantern. "Schorsch! Achenbach!" came the answer. They had gone to Dachau as paramedics, but they had been sent back again. We were relieved. We let them in. Then the bell rang again. Tautz, my lodger and Pegu came in.

This gathering released the old merriment once again.

We boozed until daybreak. We argued passionately from time to time. The Dutchman sat at the piano, Pegu composed a song, we found a tune and finally sang fervently:

Brothers, we're struggling for our freedom!
Brothers, the final clash is now!
Should we win, our victory is total!
Stay united, and victory is ours!

"This revolution has no song! That's what's wrong," I said. The others laughed.

"You old romantic! It's weapons that the revolution needs," said Tautz.

"The French Revolution won at Jemappes with the *Marseillaise*," I retorted.

"On the other hand, all of France was revolutionary, and not just a single city," the Dutchman pointed out, with a bit of a sneer.

"Yes! Yes! That's true," Davringhausen laughed snobbishly. "Gentlemen, we'd better put on our black ribbons."

"We shall win," shouted Achenbach and my lodger, unconvincingly.

"We shall lose," I said emotionally. "But they will never be able to kill off the revolution."

"Hear, hear," Schorsch agreed, as though he were at a meeting. The next day the first and last parade of the Red Army took place in Ludwigstrasse. The ranks marched past the Ministry of War, red flags waved, and shouts of "Hurrah" echoed. Dense crowds of spectators thronged the pavements. Egelhofer, the Red Army Commander, spoke from an open window. Determined and unadorned in his sailor's uniform he stood there, sometimes raising his fist. Whoever heard him must have faith in him.[69]

The three socialist parties were making preparations for May Day.

The Majority Socialists wanted the usual procession and meetings, the Independents wanted much the same and the Communists wanted war to the last drop of blood. The schools and public buildings were turned into barracks, as they had been in the war years. People went in and came out. Troops and deputations came, and lorries left fully loaded for the front at Dachau.

---

[69] Rudi Egelhofer, born in Schwabing in 1896, was a leader of the Kiel sailors' mutiny that initiated the German revolution. He arrived with 600 other sailors in his home city of Munich in February 1919 and organized the Red Army. In the original Graf mis-spelt his name as Engelhofer.

In the *Hotel Vier Jahreszeiten* members of an antisemitic, counter-revolutionary organization were arrested. They were in secret communication with the government troops and working against the Soviet Republic; using forged official seals, the newspapers reported that they were being held as hostages in the Luitpold Grammar School.

The Red Army yielded to superior force. The men under arms streamed back into the city, bringing with them the grisliest news. Throughout the surrounding area the government troops had fired without mercy: in Rosenheim, in Starnberg, in Puchheim, in Schleissheim and Perlach. They even shot wounded Red Guardsmen, medics and innocent bystanders.

The leaders of the Independents called for weapons to be surrendered and, for the umpteenth time, for a general strike. Many of them handed over their rifles and ammunition, went home, and did not come back. The workers' army crumbled. Only a fraction held together, powerless and demoralized. These few, mostly Communists, took refuge in buildings, fortifying them as best they could.

Aeroplanes appeared in the sky again. They rained down leaflets from the Hoffmann Government. They contained the usual stuff about mindless rabble rousers, self-serving agitators, and alien fantasists. They claimed that the troops were not coming as "White Guards" but merely to restore peace and order, so that the socialist state could be reconstructed and the councilist ideal could be realized peacefully. They threatened strict justice for the ringleaders of the misguided working masses, but compassion would be shown to those who had been seduced, because "Comrade Hoffmann was not a reactionary or counter-revolutionary, but a radical champion of the socialist movement" – and there were food trains for Munich standing ready in Augsburg.

The troops and Noske and Schneppenshorst's volunteer brigades pushed into the outer suburbs, pushed on, and reached the city centre. The workers put up a defence with unparalleled courage. All Munich wept; all Munich trembled. Shrapnel whizzed, cannons thundered, machine guns rattled, armoured cars spewed fire, houses crashed in, people dashed into the streets, wailing, cursing and shrieking; Munich was a warzone, pure and simple.

"The hostages in the Luitpold Grammar School have been murdered!" was being yelled from mouth to mouth. The workers had shot those prisoners and two captured government soldiers.

"Sontheimer is dead! Egelhofer shot! Landauer murdered!" was the immediate response and now the soldiers started a driven hunt for civilian suspects. Terrible denunciations took place. Nobody was safe. Whoever had an enemy could send him to his death with just a few words. The bourgeois had come out from under their stones and were now rushing around busily after the troops, with rifles slung over their shoulders and wearing the blue-and-white armbands of the Citizens' Guard. They looked around with their greedy eyes, pointed here and there, ran after a man, beat him up, spat at him, stomped on him like savages and dragged him off, beaten half to death, to the soldiers. Or it went even faster: the unsuspecting victim stood numb, the pack rushed at him surrounded him, a shot rang out and that was that. Satisfied, they ran off laughing.

Making a long detour with Davringhausen, I reached a friend in the city. There I learned that Schorsch, Achenbach and many of our circle had been arrested. The Citizens' Guard had awarded itself the task of searching all the flats in Schwabing with soldiers sent to assist. They arrested whoever they found. I left Davringhausen with my friend and went on my way. "Make yourself scarce boy," a worker who knew me whispered in a doorway and hurriedly told me that my flat had been searched. The comrades who were living there had left a short while earlier. One of them had been shot in the street. Ducking down and bounding across streets with mighty steps, I made it to the junction of Dachauerstrasse and Augustenstrasse. I forced my way onwards between people anxiously pressed up against house walls, because there was particularly fierce fighting at the railway station. An armoured car thundered down from Stiglmairplatz, firing incessantly. We all braced ourselves against the locked front doors looking for escape; we chased headlong into the vaulted gate of the Apollo theatre. The armoured car passed. We hauled ourselves back into the street and saw the murderous bombardment of the police station, which was occupied by the workers. It crashed and smoked, the walls crumbled in a cloud of dust, windows rattled and splinters flew. The besieged stubbornly returned fire, but gradually this subsided, with fewer and fewer shots being fired from the house. A detachment of government soldiers advanced from Marsstrasse, ready to fire with their rifles, and broke down the door. No further gunfire came from within.

"They are all dead," said a man standing with us. The shooting had stopped, and the armoured car was already in front of the station. We wanted to move on. An old woman was hobbling along the street. Ahead, a government soldier at the street corner took aim. There was a crack of gunfire and the woman fell and, after a few spasms, lay still.

"Oh no! For God's sake! For God's sake!" shrieked a young girl, wringing her hands.

"Don't shoot! "Don't shoot!" we all yelled. A small boy had broken away from us unnoticed. He ran over to the corpse with a fluttering red handkerchief. Another shot rang out. The lad gave a piercing shriek, tumbled once or twice, then lay still.

"Murderers! Rogues!" we all shouted, powerless and in utter despair. We shook our fists. Many cried. "Clear off! Move on!" roared a voice in front. The soldier took aim again. We ran like mad into the rear court-yard and waited, cowering together. We all shuddered; we all had faces white with rage. Nobody uttered a word. We stood there like animals herded together in a breaking thunderstorm. "They're not human!" an old man muttered after a long time and rubbed his eyes. "They are beasts! They are butchers!" howled a girl. Only after several hours did calm return. I moved on.

Everywhere you looked battered and bloodied workers, their arms held high, moved in files. Soldiers marched ahead, behind and at their side, bellowed whenever an exhausted arm dropped, and jabbed the pris-oners in the ribs, or beat their quivering victims with their bare fists. I wanted to scream out loud but clenched my teeth firmly together and swallowed. Behind my eyes, I was crying inside. I caught glances from the prisoners and nearly broke down, pulled myself together and looked an-other in the eye.

They are all my brothers, I thought contritely; they were born into the world to be beaten with the rod, flung out to fend for themselves, they were taken in by a master and the abuse went on, they were exploited as journeymen and finally they became soldiers and fought for those who beat them. And now? Now they all live a dog's life, as I have; they have had to obey orders and humiliate themselves, and now, because they wanted to bite back, they are killed.

We are prisoners!

Wide-eyed with consternation, the people of the working-class dis-tricts stared at the columns of prisoners and pressed their lips together in silence.

After walking this way and that I arrived on the Ludwigstrasse. There, the shooting was over. The gentle folk were frolicking once more here and in the fashionable cafés of the Hofgarten. Well-dressed, well-fed members of the Citizen Guard and monocled playboys chatted with sol-diers and officers; elegant ladies distributed cigarettes, cigars and choco-late, flirting and joking around with lieutenants in tightly fitting uniforms.

A column of prisoners came along. Everybody ran up to them at once, screaming and jeering, swearing and menacing. Elegant ladies heroi-cally slapped the prisoners, old-fashioned officers' wives glowered at them in disgust and swung their bleached parasols; Citizens' Guards thumped them on the sly and the playboys smiled their approval. Nobody held them back.

For days afterwards we heard of nothing but arrests and executions. Twenty-one members of a Catholic journeyman's association, who were innocently holding a meeting in an adjoining room, were arrested, dragged into a cellar and literally butchered to death.

So ended the Soviet Republic. The revolution was defeated. The summary court martial set about its work with great diligence. The former worker, and now Social Democratic Party Reichsminister Gustav Noske sent the following telegram to Generals Oven and Möhl:

"For the prudent and successful management of the operations in Munich, I express my full appreciation and cordially thank the troops for their efforts."

Every evening the military bands of the government regiments played patriotic songs in the large beer gardens and were greeted with thunderous applause. I was now expecting nothing other than my arrest. I wanted it.

I finally knew where I belonged, and with whom.

26.

THE CURTAIN FALLS

Strange. They searched my flat but then the bloodhounds abandoned the hunt. It was even stranger that the gentleman from the *Bayrischer Kurier* lived over there and only had to inform on me; many of my enemies knew where I was, but nothing happened. Strangest of all, one day six soldiers and an officer showed up at the Dutchman's villa, because, as the officer said, champagne parties were given there. It was easy to see from his bearing and his questions that he expected to find hidden revolutionaries.

"And what about him?" the officer asked the master of the house and Marietta, pointing to me.

"My name is Graf and I live here ... Here is some identification," I replied, "I only have this employment card ... I'm no longer a baker, I am an author." The officer glanced through my papers casually and gave them back.

"The gentleman is a poet ... He is a friend of ours," Marietta said, firmly. The officer asked them to show him the room in which I usually slept and kept my manuscripts. He looked at a few sheaves on the table, said nothing more, and withdrew with the soldiers. Apparently, the luxurious villa had been too much for him.

"They can't touch you," said Marietta, "you're a permanent guest here ... And we are foreigners."

"And if they do ... It's all the same to me now," I growled.

"Thickie!" she interjected, clearly offended. I said no more. My days passed as a long, oppressive wait. Various revolutionaries turned up. I persuaded the Dutchman to give money to the fugitives.

I went to my flat one day. It was locked as usual. But the books had been ripped out and the drawers, which had been ransacked, stood open. I waited a while to see if my neighbour showed up. All was silent. The man must have gone away or gone on a journey. I would have liked to ask him what had happened. I knocked at his door without any result. Later I saw him in the Citizens' Guard.

As I went through the two dirty courtyards, a few residents saw me. Their expressions clearly said, you're another of those Red dogs. But they let me go.

Out on the street, the thought kept going through my head: now you'll be arrested. There! – Yes, that soldier is coming for you.

I was simultaneously on edge and indifferent. When the man had gone by, the same thought started over again. Nevertheless, going back to Nymphenburg did not occur to me. I could not keep still; I found no rest.

The city had a hostile face. Machine-gun posts stood at the entrance to official buildings, barbed wire was rolled out, or so-called *chevaux de frise* wooden barricades were in place. Two heavily armed sentries marched up and down. The military ruled. Soldiers roamed around singly or in groups, decorated officers walked along the pavements or drove past in cars; Citizens Guards made busy. The persecution of the Soviet supporters continued, more or less underground. They were keenly searching for Toller, Leviné, Levien, Axelrod and the other leaders. Again and again prisoners appeared in ranks, some small, some large, and again and again everyone ran after them and the usual yapping started up. A few workers appeared here and there: fearful, looking as though they had just taken a thrashing. We exchanged glances and went on our way in silence. Everyone knew whose side he was on.

The prisons were full to overflowing, and the shootings continued. "Those savages! Those Hottentots!" snarled a gentleman in the Marienplatz and spoke of the Communists' destruction in the police offices. Shortly before the troops marched into the city, they had thrown most of the police files into the courtyard and burnt them. In the Isartorplatz they told me that most of those who had been shot were lying in the Ostfriedhof cemetery. I had wanted to go to the hairdresser's salon to speak with my sister Nanndl. They mentioned a gruesome number. I did not believe it, but I did not go to Nanndl. I did not want to see the corpses. Nevertheless, something impelled me to go and visit the Ostfriedhof.

In the mortuary the fallen government soldiers lay covered with flowers and laden with many wreathes, adorned with blue and white ribbons. Everyone filed past, nobody looked in. Nor did I. To the left and right, through the wooden gates that lead to the courtyards and gardens of the cemetery, the many workers' wives, the crestfallen men, girls and tormented schoolchildren staggered toward the refuse rooms where old wreaths and withered flowers are thrown. With these mourners and searchers I came to a long shed, musty like a cellar, with side windows. The dead workers lay on the filthy cobblestones. Flung down, straight, bent, on their backs or on their sides. Only their feet had been set in a straight line. There was a putrid stink of blood and death. The mourners shuffled over the reddened wood shavings, from man to man. All around me, people were whispering, crying, moaning and whimpering, now and then leaning down over the dead, upon whom small cardboard labels or parcel addresses had been attached. On these were written either a name or a number. I could breathe no more, I wanted to run away, but there were many others standing around me, in front or behind me, who pushed me gently forwards. I stared at the wall for a few seconds, then again at the lifeless bodies. My heart, stomach and guts were churning in me. I violently clenched my hands and pulled myself together. I tried to count – twenty, forty, and on, seventy, and more, ninety, one hundred, on and on. I lost count. I could not go on. My eyes were streaming. I felt cold, I shivered. Most of the dead men were mangled: one lay in a bloodied shirt, a piece of artery hung from another's funnel-shaped neck wound, another was missing his lower jaw, this one his nose, two, three or more bullets had wiped out another, over there a man lay with a covered head, next to him a man with half a head and his brain running out, just a small fragment of bone at the back of his skull. One had the label tied to his toe, because all else was torn to bloodied shreds. The weeping and wailing grew louder. The looks of those seeking their loved ones, the haunted, were terrible to behold.

When I got out it seemed as though the whole city smelt of death.

In Nymphenburg I found a telegram from the girl: "ARRIVE MORNING 9. MEET." A visit. I gulped down my food, drank, even talked, but it seemed as though someone else was doing it. All through the night, in my sleep, I counted on and on and saw nothing but the stinking, gruesome cellar. I got up very early and spent a good hour washing myself; then at last I dressed and went into town. I bought a bouquet of flowers. Even they smelt like the surrounding stench. Just in front of the platform barrier someone suddenly called out my name from behind me. I turned around quickly. A soldier grabbed me by the sleeve and said abruptly:

"You are Herr Graf, aren't you?" and led me to the station guardroom. I almost breathed a sigh of relief. The officer examined my papers, casually again. The soldiers lounging around eyed me spitefully.

"Take him to the police," said the officer. I did not want to say anything, but blurted out: "Call Nymphenburg, please, number —."

"Get moving," the soldier cut me off, and took me to the police station. All the way I carried the bouquet in front of me, calmly, almost mockingly, as though I was about to present them at any moment.

I was not interrogated but led straight to the prison antechamber. In it was a long table. Apathetic, the warder took everything off me. He even noted receipt of the bouquet. The soldier left. Another warder led me to Cell 13. It was a room with about nine wooden bunks. All of them were occupied. So too was every square inch of the floor. You could not walk up and down; you could barely push past each other and occasionally catch a breath of air at the two small, open lattice windows. I was surrounded by an odd bunch; mostly workers, a few waiters and black marketeers, a gentleman in a light sports jacket and an editor in spectacles.

"Hullo, are you innocent too?" asked a cheeky worker ironically, and everyone laughed. Me too.

"A pusher?" asked a waiter.

The air was thick with smoke, sweat and body odour. An old worker with a full beard sat at the back on the WC, grunting, straining and moaning about his haemorrhoids giving him gyp. A few were crouched on a bunk in a small, crowded circle, playing a noisy game of tarot. Many whistled, sang, chatted, and there were others who simply stared ahead vacantly and in silence. Once I had grasped the situation somewhat, I felt more at ease. At least I was not in solitary, at least I was with a crowd and there would be small distractions all the time, I thought calmly. I made friends quickly. I asked around and virtually always heard the same story. "Because of Red activities," they all calmly replied. No one cared. Nobody thought about the morrow, everyone made the best of the whole situation. From time to time the door opened and a new prisoner was flung in.

"My God, there's no room left as it is," most of us grumbled.

"It will soon be emptier," said the warder, closing the door again. "Yes, when a dozen more are shot!" most of us shouted back sardonically. And then the newcomer stood like a doused poodle, and we all laughed with gallows humour: "Hullo, you innocent too?" He then tried to protest his innocence, which only made the laughter even louder. Well-intentioned joshing followed: "Yes, we're all innocent, comrade! But you don't have to say a thing. It's simple enough. Whether you've done anything or not, they'll shoot you anyhow. The smartest thing is just to say straight out that you blasted away twenty Whites with a shotgun."

"Dead good!" came from the card school, and "That were 'angin! Heaaaarts! It's ours!" seconded another player.

Within a few minutes, the new arrival found his feet and was one of us. The cell was already full, and got fuller. We were packed in like sardines. It got hotter and hotter and there were lice, fleas, bugs and Russian ticks. I jostled back and forth, pulling myself up against the bars of the window and looking down at the police station. I saw rifle pyramids and companies of soldiers standing around, machine guns and baggage-wagons. I also saw outstretched heads at the cell windows opposite; we shouted and waved to one another. Suddenly a soldier below picked up a rifle and shouted up to us: "Oy you! Get back, you dogs!" And then the window remained empty again for a short time. And so the hours passed by. It got darker, a light in the ceiling was turned on, two warders brought us a thin soup and army bread.

"So how are you supposed to sleep in here?" I asked. "Sleep?" laughed a comrade. "Yes, that's easy, if you still have two healthy feet ... Well then ... You stand on one, then the other, and now and then if you are lucky, you'll get a turn on the bunk."

And then it was time to sleep. All the space on or under the bunks was occupied. The rest of us tried to sleep by leaning on the wall or against each other. But it never lasted long. We started to fidget. Everyone who was standing slumped sideways, woke up again with a start and shifted drowsily this way and that. We cursed, we mumbled, we started chatting then broke off again, exhausted. The hours of darkness dragged by at a snail's pace. Our eyes hurt, our bodies itched, we scraped and pawed the man next to us, who growled and snorted heavily. A man suffering from tuberculosis lay groaning in the corner; he had been brought in that afternoon and gasped and coughed as though vomiting, and spat. Another shouted and hit out as he dreamt. Those next to him and on top of him woke up, grabbed him, and looked for somewhere else to lie. A few fought over the toilet, the water flushed noisily, and someone complained, demanding silence. Finally, finally, the dawn slowly broke and light fell over the desolate mountain of sleeping bodies, which gradually came back to life. They brought us a tin can of black coffee and army bread, and some of us were allowed to troop down to the wash booths.

The girl had come and asked after me with the police. She was not allowed in though. The warder handed me a tin of jam, some bread and a few cigarettes through the square hole in the door. I shared it out, as everyone here did. We smoked the cigarettes communally down to the last stub, then someone flicked off the glowing tip and chewed what was left.

"Schuster!" bawled the warder outside again. The man who had been called got up and went through the door. He was placed between two soldiers who led him up the stone staircase.

"Phew! They're finally starting the hearings," said a stunted worker. I found out that some had been here for five to eight days without being interrogated. Sometimes the man who had been called came back, sometimes not. Some speculated that he had been shot, others thought he had been taken to another gaol. "Hardly anyone here will be shot ... Yes, perhaps in the first days ... But no longer ... Lucky for us that they caught us so late," said an old worker, and told us about the executions at the city abattoir and cattle sheds, and at the Hofbräuhaus beer cellar. Many innocent civilians, who had been denounced and randomly arrested as Red Guards, had been stood up against the wall and summarily shot without trial, he told us. It was all true. Later, even the police report and that of the SPD's Action Committee admitted this.

I told them what I had seen in the Ostfriedhof. "Yes, they are the ones that were summarily executed," said another comrade. "Did you see any women among the dead?"

"No."

"That's because they cleared them away, so as not to look so cowardly," he said. We kept quiet for a while. "And that's the kind of treatment we risked our necks for in the war," someone growled.

The door opened. A new prisoner came in. It was a battered looking worker, aged about forty. He remained standing and gazed at us as if he would have liked to eat us up. As we tried to comfort him, he suddenly screamed terribly, ran to the door and tried to tear it down, screaming and screaming: "My wife is dying! My wife! Let me out!" The warder came and swore at us, then went away again. The man began to wail horribly, ran around like a lunatic, found the toilet, and kicked it with his heavy boots. We overpowered him and calmed him down, as far as this was possible. He lay on the bunk, shivering, stared at the ceiling, then he roared again, terribly: "My wife! The dogs! The butchers! A-a-a-agh!" And cried and cried.

They pushed in another prisoner, and in a flash the crying man was at the door, but it slammed shut again. In his fury he tore at it once more, and fell pale, foaming with rage and flailing about for some time. We lay him down on the bunk again. Someone dipped his handkerchief in the flushing toilet water and lay it on the screaming man's forehead. He started sobbing again, and the man with TB joined in, constantly breaking into bouts of coughing.

The new man talked about Leviné-Nissen's arrest.

"They'll shoot him like a dog!" someone said.

"But of course!

"No matter how much he is in the right, they'll kill him!" another replied.

"He must be here, at the police headquarters," the new man said. Those sitting next to him raised their heads and stared at him.

"Yes, here ... He must be in one of the solitary cells." Everyone crowded around the new arrival at once and started questioning him. The indifference was suddenly dispelled and every face revived.

"Here? ... Quite sure? ... Really ... Here, in the police station?" The newcomer said yes again. Now we all knew; each of us looked for a second into the eyes of the others. A stagnant silence set in, broken only by the sobs, and at once several in the middle of the room shouted:

"Long live Leviné! Long live Leviné!" And everyone took up the cry as a sudden signal of courage.

"Don't shout that, it will make things worse for us," said the sports jacket.

"Coward!" someone bawled at him menacingly, and as though we all took it as a cue, the entire cell shouted: "Long live Leviné-Nissen! Hurrah! Hurrah!"

And now it reverberated from all cell windows on all sides, from top to bottom, from left to right, criss-cross, the whole house screamed: "Long live Leviné-Nissen!" Down in the courtyard, a shot rang out. We all crowded at the window. Orders were barked up from below.

"Shut your gobs! Get back from the window! Back! Stop the racket up there! Back, back!" yelled the soldiers, and suddenly they fired shots upwards, forcing those at the window to fall back into the cell. It remained still for a few seconds, then curses were hurled from every cell: "Swine! Scummy bastards! You can kiss our arses!"

"I, I told you, I told you, now it will be all the worse for us!" wailed the sports jacket, but nobody listened to him. Again and again furious men ran to the window and swore at those below. We were all overcome with a bitter courage; even the black marketeers and the timid editor ranted.

And because this was so fine I, with a few others around me, started singing the *Marseillaise*. More and more joined in; our cell sang, then the whole building sang. It was just a pity that most of us only knew one verse.

"Silence! Silence, you mob!" screeched the soldiers in the yard again. We struck up *The Internationale*.

"Shut up! Put a sock in it up there!"

"None of your business. Stick it up yours and take a photo!" someone jeered, and the cells echoed with laughter.

"And now we will sing the lovely song: *Oil the Guillotine!*" I blurted out, and as nobody knew the words, I recited the verses keenly, going from one to the other, and taught everyone in the cell.[70]

"Now then! Now then, let's go!" I shouted and waved my arms to beat time. "Oil the Guillotine! Oil the Guillotine!" Everyone sang along. It boomed out. Suddenly we all broke off. The men at the window warned: "They are on their way!"

"For God's sake, we're lost," whimpered the sports jacket and leaned against the wall, white as a sheet. We hustled one another as usual and talked indifferently.

"Yes, yes, they're coming! Listen! Listen!" called someone at the door. We listened. Below, we heard a din and beating on cell doors. Then the tread of heavy boots coming up the stone steps.

"Nobody sang!" someone cried under his breath. "Whoever lets on is done for!" Everyone understood. The door opened and a lieutenant clutching a revolver and a dog-whip marched in with three soldiers.

"Who was singing? It came from here! Answer!" he asked sharply. No reply. We all looked at him dumbly. He brandished his whip, plainly desperate to hit out.

"It came from here! Who was singing?!"

We stayed silent.

"Do I get an answer or not?" he threatened.

"No one was singing here ... There are two crying back there," a gigantic worker with remarkably broad shoulders finally answered, and you could clearly hear most of us breathing a sigh of relief. The officer stood

---

[70] *Schmiert die Guillotine mit Tyrannenblut* (Oil the Guillotine with the Blood of Tyrants) is a line from the *Heckerlied*, a song written and sung during the democratic revolution of 1848-9 in Baden.

still for a few moments in this sullen silence, turned around sharply, looked back once more and shouted with a rasp: "Just you wait, you buggers! We'll put the lot of you up against the wall!" But it had no effect. He left the cell with his men, clattering his spurs. For a while we waited in silence; everyone had an indifferent expression.

At last the editor said: "I'll remember that." Then we started talking again.

At first, it was actually quite entertaining in there, though I wish I could have been elsewhere at night, and when I looked up through the barred windows to the beautiful, blue sky during the day, I became morose and impatient. For four or five days it was just a long wait, but gradually time started to drag out unbearably. There were hours when everyone was unapproachable and became grumpy.

Relatives were allowed to bring food and hand it through the hole in the door. The girl came nearly every day, we exchanged a few words hastily, and she was gone again. One day my wife also appeared and whined at me. I could not say anything in reply and was pleased that the warder only put up with it for a few minutes.

After a week I was interrogated. My personal details were written down by an interrogator in a room where each prisoner had to make a statement. The small, fat police inspector then asked: "Have you any statement to make?"

"I wanted to ask you the same," I asked, impertinently.

"What?" the policeman asked sharply.

"Yes, I wanted to ask you what statement you have to make against me," I repeated with suppressed anger.

"So you have no statement to make?"

"No."

The man now asked: "Have you witnesses for your defence?"

"Yes," I said, and then, having reflected a little, "if there is no charge against me, why would I need witnesses to speak for me?"

"Then you have absolutely no statement to make?" asked the inspector, who was getting short-tempered and grouchy.

"No."

He wrote. I had to sign his report.

When I got back to the cell there were new inmates. All workers. One was permanently stood sadly below the window, gazing in front of him. When questioned, he answered: "They want to ruin me ... I was in the Luitpold School to collect my wages. Now they say I murdered hostages."

He said no more. He was quiet and depressed. After four days, his hair had turned grey. Later he was sentenced to fifteen years in prison.

A medium-sized, chubby baker had been brought in with him. He was always in good spirits and freely admitted that he had seen the shooting; someone had given him his rifle, and he had held it while the man went out. He was later sentenced to death and shot. His name was Pürzer. He was always ready to give others a helping hand, made crude jokes and had something of a good-natured pet about him.

Once the warder shouted through the door-hole: "Kastenberger!" The worker who in the first days had missed his wife so passionately jumped up from his bunk and ran over to the door.

"Your wife is dead!" the warder shouted, quite indifferently, and went. Kastenberger stood stock still for a few moments, staring straight ahead. Everyone standing around him braced himself for a new fit of rage, but the man only staggered a little, snorted and crept back to his berth. He turned to face the wall and did not utter a single word. Suddenly, in the night, there was a shriek in his corner, and we heard dull thuds and we heard gasps, almost like a death rattle. Kastenberger was banging his head constantly against the wall with all his might, and when a couple of us overpowered him, he almost bit one of our fingers off. There was a terrifying uproar. We raised the alarm and called the warder. He went away. Things only settled down after nearly an hour. The next day Kastenberger lay on his back with severe head injuries, his back covered in blood. He did not stir when spoken to; he let us cover him in the dirty, soaking sackcloth, and wipe him down. He just snorted heavily now and then. It was only after two days that he was taken away.

The next day the girl shouted through the door: "The lawyer says they'll probably place you under protective custody."

The following day, I told her: "They are going to place me under protective custody."

"You? ... Who says so?"

"No one, but I am going into protective custody," I replied again. The girl looked sad and anxious and ran off. I held my head in my hands. I realized that I was getting dopey. I was no longer capable of thinking straight. I leaned against the wall and closed my eyes. There was a constant, unchanging hum around me. Yes, well then, yes-yes, yes-yes, I was in gaol, yes, oh yes, that was just the chatter of my comrades, yes-yes, hmm, hmm, outside sunny sky, yes-yes, hmm, in the police station, yes-yes. Then I recovered again.

This strange condition recurred time and again, time and again. Limp, broken and unspeakably tired, I dozed off into uncertainty. I finally managed to wangle a place on a bunk and in an instant, I had sunk into a completely empty, black darkness. I slept like the dead.

"Graf! Graf! Up! Get up! Out!" a comrade shook me awake. Barely conscious I stumbled forward in a pack of men, then we stood down in the courtyard by a police lorry and only then, as the fresh air blew over me, did my brain begin to clear.

We were driven to the old military gaol in Cornelisustrasse. There, I and two other comrades were put in a small cell with a bunk.

"Thank God, now we can breathe and get some rest," said the oldest among us. "Each of us will get a night on the bunk in our turn," we agreed. Footsteps outside, the lock creaked. A soldier appeared and called my name.

"Get out," he said, and I followed. "You are discharged," he told me in the gaol house door, "and there's someone waiting for you outside."

My blood froze for a moment, and I stared at the man in astonishment. He shoved me out into the open.

The girl was standing in the street. We embraced each other as though just saved from drowning. "Never, never forget!" I stammered. We went on our way.

EPILOGUE

I was ten years old when someone entered my life who had been trained by soldiers – NCOs and officers – and took my education in hand. I was ten years old, when that someone started to shout at me, beat me, and beat me again.

I was ten years old, when I first learned, what compulsion is, and began to hate it, with a blind hatred. I was ten years old and in the fifth class at primary school, when we made our first confession in preparation for our first communion. The priest who instructed us told us about the vast change that we should undergo by receiving the body of Christ. He described, with many examples, the torments suffered by those who received it unworthily, those who "cheated Christ".

There were sudden lightning strikes out of the blue for such sinners, lifelong unhappiness, sickness, restlessness, paralysis. The nagging conscience suffered by these cheats drove them into the world to commit crimes. They typically ended in prison and after they died, they were met by the everlasting torments of hell.

But the penitent and the pure could look forward to peace and happiness, miracles and transfiguration.

I listened keenly. I learned. I was on my guard against any sin, living in perpetual fear of having to experience something that would damage my soul. I often lay awake until deep in the night and whispered endless prayers. I spoke simple-mindedly to God. I rinsed my mouth out after every meal and cleaned my teeth like a fanatic. For Christ should not only enter into a pure soul but also into a pure stomach.

I often forgot everything and was beaten by teachers and at home. I was in terror, terror, terror!

When I was alone, I was seized by a mad ecstasy, a senseless joy, as I imagined that the Lord had entered my soul.

Then I no longer felt the beatings; everything around me was extinguished. I had the feeling that I was surrounded by a wafting unreality.

But then the terror returned, the terrifying fear of sudden sin, followed at once by a stabbing mistrust, a dread of all humanity.

My mother was very pious. She had received the Lord again and again and had remained unchanged. My brothers and sisters were gossips; they had received the Host many times onto their loose tongues, but it seemed not to have had any effect. The villagers were all either pious or sinful, but they had all swallowed the body of Christ again and again, and this did not seem to have changed them.

My father often swore so much that the whole house shook, he drank, and went every year to a famous place of pilgrimage and received the body of Christ after confession – afterwards, he got drunk in some pub and swore just the same way as he had sworn the day before, blaspheming God. Nothing had changed. Everyone received the Lord over and over again, and no one was transfigured, no one had changed. They all stayed the same. Exactly the same!

I was confused.

What did that mean? *That! That,* the fact that after receiving the sacrament, everyone stayed exactly the same, there was nothing new to see?

That, the fact that God left no mark on those who shared his body?

I looked at my father, my mother, my brothers, my sisters, the villagers, all of them.

Suddenly I was overcome with horror. They were all cheating God! The Devil lurked in every single one of them. Hell waited on them all. They must all burn, suffer, burn, suffer for ever and ever!

I often cried until deep in the night. I had anxiety dreams. I hid in the hay when my father swore, and my heart often suddenly stopped still, because at any moment, a bolt of lightning might – no must – strike him down. Could, no must, strike him forever dead. Could! Must!

I hid myself away, let them call me and call me and did not reply. I stopped eating. I hardly slept. I suddenly screamed out loud in the night and only felt protected during religious instruction at school.

Then the sacred ceremony took place.

I no longer remember how I behaved. I felt a wafer on my tongue and swallowed it down. And tore open my eyes. Now I must see the light! Now I must start to feel an inner warmth!

We stepped back to the pews. My limbs moved just as they had always done. I was not floating on air. I saw everything, felt everything, just as I had always seen and felt it.

Nothing had changed! Nothing, nothing at all!

The priest had lied! Lied!

There was no God, no sacrament. Nothing! It was all lies! Lies! Lies! Lies!

There was no bolt of lightning from heaven, there was no hell! My fear, my prayers, my tears – all, all for nothing!

There was no God, no peace, no miracle, no transfiguration! There was nothing! Nothing whatsoever!

*

No one is lonelier than the adolescent whose heart is unprepared. No one waits on miracles and love as much as he.

I was barely seventeen. I had read Shakespeare and Schopenhauer, Tolstoy and Stirner, Heine and Strindberg, Nietzsche and Maupassant, Balzac and Wedekind, Ibsen, Zola and Flaubert, Schiller and Grabbe, Bakunin and Herzen – book upon book.

I knew long passages by heart, quoted them often, loved them, was moved to tears by them and intoxicated by their beauty. And uttered the words almost like a consoling prayer, even when I did not understand them.

I wandered through the city streets full of restless uncertainty. Over and over again, this one dull, tormenting feeling penetrated my confused thoughts: you belong to no one and no one belongs to you! You are alone and dispensable.

Disgust and despondency came and became so great, so destructive, so terrible, that I literally tried to flee from my own miserable condition. From time to time I gazed almost imploringly at the people passing by, was suddenly startled, looked away hastily, like someone who is afraid to betray what is hidden deep within, walked faster, aimlessly, all the way down one street and back again, around a residential district and back again, repeated the entire process from the start and in the end hardly knew where I was, where I stood, why I was walking, or even why I was in the world at all.

"Come with me!" a prostitute suddenly said to me. For the first time in my life.

I stared at her, my heart stood still, then the blood boiled in my limbs.

She gave me a knowing smile, nodded, and I went with her. We arrived in her room. She turned on the light. I staggered, fell upon her, clasped her wildly, wanted to kiss her and love her as only a young person loves for the first time.

"Ouch! Get off! You'll tear my blouse! ... Slow down! ... Not so wild!" she said, beating me off and demanding money. I let her go. My arms, my whole body went lame. I stood there stupidly and stiffly and let her do with me as she liked. She took the money from my wallet herself, undressed routinely, and lay down. Everything grew hazy, seemed to be sinking. I fell like hot coals on her cold body. I heard nothing other than her hoarse, ugly giggles.

Slowly, very slowly, everything returned. The green wallpaper, the yellow light, the sofa and her broad, fleshy face. I pulled myself up and sat next to her, sad as death. I wanted to smile but my face seemed frozen, I wanted to speak but only stammered. I threw my hot head into her breasts and gulped down my sobs. I started telling her my life story, babbled, broke off and clung to her body more helplessly than ever. I broke into floods of tears.

"Take the lot! Do what you want with me! You! You! I love you so much! You! You! I want to marry you I must have you! You! You! I'll work, do everything. You! You! I can't help myself! You! You! You'll have what you want! You! You!" I wailed into her breast, moaned, sobbed.

It was as though I were slowly dissolving.

She shuddered in shock, broke away hastily and stood up. Angry and alarmed, she looked at me, grumbling and griping. She quickly got into her clothes, pulled me up, helped me on with my jacket and hustled me out onto the street.

"Keep quiet, you wretch! Keep quiet I said! Hush! ... There, that way! Just go! Away with you! Go on!" were her last words and she ran off in disgust.

All around was gloom. The massive houses had a threatening aspect in the dark sky. I tramped on. Ever deeper into the grisly loneliness. From which there was no escape.

*

Miracles were dead. Faith and love had crumbled to dust. All hope seemed absurd.

My loneliness was compounded by mistrust of any inner emotion, hostility to the world, and fearful hatred towards all men. Cunning and deceit seemed to be the only weapons to defend myself against all on-slaughts. My world shrank to minute proportions. A world that was simp-ly called: I.

Quite bluntly, I.

Windbags and fanatics tried to change me. I pretended to be a con-vert, feigned friendship, exploited their most convincing turns of phrase and mental tricks and yet I remained my old self.

Ideas and events pressed around me. I did not hide away from them, oh no! I found them entertaining and in my innermost soul I smiled at them incredulously. In the end it always came to the same thing: Protect yourself! Protect yourself or you will be trampled underfoot! Eat or be eat-en!

The war came and was for me nothing but complete idiocy. That meant getting out of it as quickly as possible. It was for someone else's benefit and I only wanted to live for my own benefit.

*

It was 1917. I had freed myself from the military with persistent cunning. I was back in the city. My life was back on track. Nothing had changed. Fac-tory work, workers, the master, my landlady, hypocrisy, toadying, cant, suspicion of everybody, and calculating what was to my own best advantage, it was all the same. And me?

Was I free?

No! A thousand times no!

Had I gained anything, at any rate? Had my actions benefited anyone? Had I set any kind of example?

No! A thousand times no!

Nothing but emptiness then. Nothing but this stupid "I". Self-loathing took hold of me. An ever-increasing loathing of myself and all the life around me.

I numbly paced the streets. Someone laughed. I suddenly got the urge: jump to it! Strike someone down, kill him! Kill lots and lots of people, throttle them! And then get yourself locked up again, in the madhouse or in prison. Who cares where! Just to be alone, quite alone! Desperate, restless, I walked up and down in my room. Up and down. The whole night.

"What am I?"

"What do I want?"

"Who do I help?"

Endlessly, endlessly. And just as often: "Nothing! Nothing! No one!"

And suddenly: "But *I am! I want!* Help, help, help, help! But who? Who!?"

That "who" stood there, overpowering me.

Day broke, grey, through the window. I packed my suitcase, wrote a letter to the master baker, and tried to escape. But for what, where to, and who from?

I tore up the letter, got ready and went back to work. Everything was submerged under the everlasting sameness of survival.

I kept reading books, tried my luck with women, married, mixed with all manner of people, romped and drank with them day and night; I was considered one of a kind and encouraged this view of myself through hushed vanity and shrewd instinct – but I felt no less alone. I started to write. "Man," I once wrote, "has always been, since the beginning of time, the stupidest and most boorish thing of all. Every animal, every plant, even every raindrop is more sensible, happier and freer. Because all of these are just what they are, and that's enough. But we imagine we are capable of more, and that's our whole tragedy."

I wanted to live, just live! I wanted to be, just be, nothing else.

*

It was shortly after Leviné had been shot. I was walking in the English Garden. A worker, who had been with me in Cell 13, met me. We looked each other in the eyes, cautiously, almost suspiciously.

He nodded a short greeting and wanted to go on.

"Comrade, we know each other," I said. He hesitated, eyed me timidly again, and smiled mournfully. And now he seemed to remember everything.

"Jesus, yes," he said and went with me. We walked along, taciturn, through the strolling crowds, turned down a dark, lonely path and sat down for a while on a park bench. At first, he made small talk and kept glancing around, searching, as if he feared invisible eavesdroppers. It became more and more silent. The park seemed empty; here and there a sleeping bird shook itself, and occasionally the hum of a tram penetrated from the distant city. He breathed in, leaned closer to me, and gripped my arm. The moonlight fell on his haunted face.

"Do you remember? Kastenberger?" he whispered to me.

I nodded and asked: "Yes, what became of him?"

"He started ranting again in the prison transport ... They murdered him," he told me.

"Oh," I murmured, shaking my head, and my blood ran cold.

"They shot my father in the Hofbräuhaus cellar ... My wife gave birth prematurely and isn't well any more," he gasped and then began to stammer a little: "I was in the field for four years ... Wounded three times ... I never wanted anything to do with the revolution ... I have plenty of long references ... Everyone in the factory was issued a rifle ... On the 30th of April I gave it back again ... The next day they fetched me from my bed ... And they worked me over all the way to the police station ... There ain't no God in heaven!" Tears welled up in his eyes, he swallowed, came to a stop. He broke down and leaned against me. I held him upright. He sobbed as though crushed.

"Leviné was right ... There are too many of us for them ... We are just dead men on leave, it's true ... I wish they had shot me," he stammered on.

There was nothing I could say; I let him lean on me and did not move. His head dropped and he wiped his eyes. His hat fell to the ground. He left it there. I stayed silent but stroked him on the head a few times. Gradually he became quieter.

We squatted there, leaning against one another, in the darkness, like two relics in a wasteland.

"You needn't feel so dejected, comrade ... Nothing has been in vain," I managed to say, after a long while, and standing up: "Come on, let's go ..."

He breathed heavily and stood up as well. We went. I became faintly aware that he was gradually stepping out more confidently and holding his body more erect. Suddenly, he stood still and raised his fist, it was quite strange, quite unexpected.

"If it all kicks off again, I will fight ... I will fight until my last breath

... Then at least I will know, I was fighting for *us!*" he cried with sullen rage. And then he added, with a peculiar solemnity: "The hour will come!"

A shiver ran up my spine. I did not let him out of my sight. He turned to me again and shook my hand. He went off into the darkness, silently, urgently. I remained standing and reflected. I wanted to call after him, wanted to follow him, but turned for home. My heart was burning more and more intensely. All the scenes stamped on my memory flashed through my head: the masses on the streets, the workers' army, the grim lines of prisoners, the corpses of those who had been shot, and this one comrade. And everything became even sharper and even more indelible. This man with his clenched fist became legion. "The hour will come!" I shouted, in spite of myself.

"It was not all in vain!" I repeated, deeply moved.

My tiny world fissured and burst. I was no longer just "I" alone. An immense happiness ran through me.

*

After all the convulsions I had gained fresh insights, partial or complete. The horrors lay in the distant past.

One day, as a wandering journeyman, I was walking on the sandhills on the coast. It was night. It suddenly started to rain, followed by thunder and lightning. The nearby sea roared. There was not a tree, not a light. Just darkness, nothing but darkness and rain, rain, rain, howling wind, thunder and lightning. More and more terrible, more cruel. Raging storm. Lashing rain.

Rain that cast me down like a helpless leaf. It pressed me deep into the mud and battered down on my shivering body with a violence such as I never experienced again. Rain that buried me without mercy. Alive, utterly desperate, utterly alone. And the trembling earth, the roaring heavens, the burning air, the raging wind! And the sea boiled and shrieked, towered aloft and came smashing down. I screamed, roared, sobbed. All around me crashed, quaked, roared, hissed and lashed. I stretched out helplessly and clasped my hands together with no will of my own and screamed, screamed again in prayer:

"God!"

Then I lost consciousness.

When I woke up, all was still. The air around me wafted like delicate crepe. I worked my way out of the muck and gazed into the radiant light.

And fell on my knees.

Totally exhausted, after a long march I reached a small town. I had a few marks left. I found a small inn where I stayed overnight. When I entered the room and saw a pen and ink, I felt a sudden urge to write to someone. Almost unconsciously, I took a last few scraps of writing paper from my breast pocket. All tiredness was gone.

The pen flew. The sentences were hashed, irregular, slung down.

When I finished, I scanned the sheets, read once – twice – three times, and began to cry.

Exasperated by fatigue, I lay down on the bed without undressing, tried to sleep, closing my eyes tightly, almost violently.

But I could not.

I shivered, I shuddered, I thrashed about.

I got up again, switched the light on, took up the pen and started writing. All of a sudden, something became uncannily clear. I was over-come with a strange calm. My limbs ached. My eyes burned. I wrote.

The end collapsed behind me.
Morning freshness opened the gates.
The earth below my feet rings clear
and my steps are firm with hope.
Once again I crave to view the past,
and watch my brothers through the fog approach,
on the same path, bent by the same burden.
The daily grind and distress of our age
have stamped their foreheads with a bright "And Yet!"
We simply gaze at each other
and march on, man for man.
For that Eternal, which God chastises, in his unbounded love,
has remained deep in our blood,
and shines forth like the light of grace.

*

Smiling constantly, I sent the girl this greeting: "I love you! I love you un-utterably! I will come back to you as soon as I can. Miracles and salvation, faith and hope have burst upon me. I love you! I love you unutterably ..."

POSTSCRIPT

Graf's friends: Schrimpf, Jung, Oehring, Pegu, "the Dutchman", Marietta and "the girl"

When I first read *Wir sind Gefangene*, I had no idea what an extraordinary cast of characters Oskar Maria Graf counted among his friends, people of such diverse talents who went on to lead fascinating lives despite the disappointments of the failed revolution and other personal and political setbacks. For the most part he made their acquaintance in Munich's bohemian quarter of Schwabing, and in particular, at the *Café Simplicissimus* on Türkenstrasse, or the *Alter Simpl* as it was known.

Georg "Schorsch" Schrimpf (1889-1938) became a leading artist of the *Neue Sachlichkeit* (literally "new objectivity" but the German word *sachlich* can also be interpreted as "matter of fact" or "no-nonsense") school, and counted as a classicist within this movement alongside Alexander Kanoldt and Carlo Mense, and another painter who appears in the text, Heinrich Maria Davringhausen (1894-1970). *Neue Sachlichkeit* ultimately took its name from an exhibition at the Mannheim *Kunsthalle* (art gallery) in 1925.

Olaf Peters wrote in a catalogue in 2012: "Schrimpf's figurative process, which he began to develop during the First World War, represents a synthesis of Jugendstil, Expressionism and Henri Rousseau's naive monumentality. The individual, harmoniously embedded in nature while simultaneously neutralized by it, appears as the main focus of the image."

In 1995 *Deutsche Bundespost* honoured Schrimpf with the issue of special stamp featuring his 1923 painting *Still Life with Cat*.

After being thrown out of home by his stepfather, Schorsch apprenticed, like Graf, as a baker and led the life of an itinerant worker until he discovered his talent as an artist in the anarchist colony of Monte Verità. Schrimpf's woodcut was the cover picture for Graf's first poetry collection, *The Revolutionaries*, in 1917.

Also like Graf, Schorsch was a working-class autodidact; he learned by copying the Old Masters. The two were strongly influenced by the philosopher Max Stirner and developed their respective talents largely as a "union of egoists", criticizing and correcting one another, and occasionally falling out. The closeness of their friendship is revealed in Graf's short story *Ein barockes Malerportrait*, which appeared in the volume *Mitmenschen* (1948), in which the artist is characterized according to the identical formulation of Georg Schrimpf: "For many a year Max Stirner's *The Ego and His Own* was his true gospel." Based on his experiences in revolutionary Munich, Schrimpf joined the Communist Party of Germany in 1919.

In 1917 Schrimpf married the successful artist and designer Maria Uhden (called Maria Uhla in the text). They had one son, shortly after whose birth Maria died. From 1927 he took a professorships at art schools first in Munich and then in Berlin. In 1937 Schrimpf was dismissed from his post and several of his works were confiscated as "degenerate". He died a year later.

Franz Jung (1888-1963), born the son of a clockmaker, met Graf while he was writing his dissertation ("The Consequences of Production Tax on the Matchstick Industry") at LMU. When he arrived in 1911, he was unimpressed by bohemian Munich. He considered the veteran anarchist Erich Mühsam a "fossil". His first book, *Das Trottelbuch*, appeared in 1912. In it, the decay of bourgeois identities, gender roles and the liberation of sexuality, the onset of modernity in the psychological constitution are reflected in the eponymous "idiot", who appears weak-willed, demonic and vicious, and remains deeply lonely. Jung's work clearly had a massive influence on Graf, as did his outlook on life, but the relationship, Graf later wrote, was ambivalent, a *Feindfreundschaft* (a friendship of enemies) and a "coarse manly comradeship without the slightest erotic undertone", wholly shaped by binge drinking. But Jung provided a bridge to the expressionist milieu in Berlin and significantly broadened Graf's horizons, while Graf provided a distraction for Jung's first wife, a dancer named Margot from Breslau.

In Berlin, Jung worked on a number of political and cultural projects in the underground in collaboration with the publisher of *Die Aktion*, Franz Pfemfert. He edited the magazine *Die Neue Jugend*, the first dadaist journal in German and from 1918 he was co-editor of the *Club Dada*. During this time, Jung made the acquaintance of Helmut Herzfeld (whose pseudonym, John Heartfield, Jung probably invented). When the revolution broke out on 9 November 1918, Jung led revolutionary soldiers to Potsdamer Platz and occupied Wolff's telegraph office in the Leipzigerstrasse, from where he was soon expelled by troops loyal to the government.

In 1919, Jung took part in the revolutionary struggles on the side of the Communist Party of Germany (KPD) and was arrested but managed to escape to Breslau. In 1920 he was expelled from the KPD and was a co-founder of the Communist Workers' Party of Germany (KAPD). As a member of the KAPD's delegation the the Third International, he and Jan

Appel captured the trawler *Senator Schröder* and sailed to Murmansk. The talks with Lenin, Bukharin and Karl Radek at the Third International were however unsuccessful. The KAPD became increasingly critical of Moscow and the leadership of the KPD.

Back in Germany Jung served time in prison for hijacking on the high seas, writing several books that were published by Malik Verlag. Shortly after his release under caution in 1921 he took part in the March insurrection along with Karl Plättner and Max Hoelz. He subsequently attempted flight to Great Britain, but was arrested and detained in the Netherlands, from where he managed to escape to the Soviet Union.

He returned to Germany under a false name and continued to write, earning a living as a business journalist. From 1933 he was active with the *Rote Kämpfer*, an underground resistance group organized by former members of the KAPD, in which connection he was arrested in 1936. On release in 1937 he fled to Prague, beginning a long period in exile. In 1945 he was arrested while travelling between Austria and Italy and interned in the Bolzano transit camp, Nazi Germany's largest concentration camp on Italian soil. That same year he was deeply traumatized by the death of his daughter Dagny in mysterious circumstances in a Vienna clinic, inspiring him to write the novel *Das Jahr ohne Gnade* (The Year without Mercy), which has been republished, along with many of Jung's other works, by Nautilus press.

After the war he worked in Italy before moving to the USA, gaining American citizenship in 1955, and finally returning to Germany towards the end of his life.

Paul "Pegu" Guttfeld (1893-1991) – who, in contrast to Graf, appears in *We Are Prisoners* as the indefatigable but unsung hero of the revolution – was the son of a Berlin knitwear manufacturer, whose business was dissolved in 1936. He volunteered for service in the First World War and after being severely wounded was assigned to desk duty. In 1915 he joined the pacifist *Bund Neues Vaterland* and acted as its liaison with revolutionary working-class youth, bringing him into contact with militants such as Karl Becker and Karl Plättner. In November 1917 Guttfeld was living in a Berlin commune and conducting Spartacist anti-war propaganda, as a result of which the premises were searched by the police and Guttfeld was prosecuted. As recounted by Graf, he made his way to Munich, but was arrested and sent to a military gaol in Berlin.

During the Munich Bavarian Republic he edited the government newspaper.

After the failure of the German revolution, Guttfeld was involved in various "alternative" communes and settlements up and down Germany (as "a substitute for the now limited political-revolutionary action", he later wrote). In 1925 Guttfeld married his cousin Eva (later Chava) Jenny Herrmann, who gave birth to their son Michael in 1928 and daughter Hanna-Liv in 1935.

From 1931 Guttfeld worked with Franz Jung and Harro Schulze-Boysen on the magazine *Der Gegner* (The Opponent). He occasionally managed the business of the Folkwang-Auriga publishing house and was involved in the setting up an "Ernst Fuhrmann Institute for Biological Research", named after the *Neue Sachlichkeit* photographer and pioneer of organic farming, forerunner of the modern "green" movement.

In 1936 the family emigrated to Palestine and settled in the town of Kirjat Bialik, founded in 1934 by German immigrants, near Haifa. Guttfeld worked there as an agricultural engineer. Michael was killed, as a soldier, in 1948.

In 1962, Paul Guttfeld wrote about his job in a letter to Franz Jung: "I have promoted the need for organic fertilizers for 26 years and although I have propagandized as little as possible against the chemicals on which contemporary agriculture is based, I am considered a fanatic, which does not take into account the scientific results. Now I'm tired of the compromise and refuse to engage in farms that use concentrated chemicals. As a result, I have dissolved all my links with agricultural organizations, including the one I worked with and set up."

He lived to the age of 98.

Richard Oehring (1891-1940) had a successful career as a writer, economist and political activist. His brother Fritz was an early victim of the First World War. Richard Oehring was stationed in Brussels during the war, where he undertook medical work. Falling ill, he returned home to Berlin, but was re-assessed and declared fit for military service. He was re-conscripted and deserted, eventually achieving his dismissal by refusing to accept either food or wages. His friendship with Franz Jung ended when his wife, Cläre Otto, also a communist activist, deserted him for Jung. After the war he worked in Moscow and Berlin as a trade representative. In 1933 he fled Nazi Germany, relocating to the Netherlands, where he worked again for the Soviet trade organization. He committed suicide shortly after the Netherlands capitulated to Germany in 1940.

Anthony van Hoboken (1887-1983), the "rich Dutchman" was a musical collector, bibliographer, and musicologist, especially well known for his scholarship on the music of Joseph Haydn and the creation of the Hoboken catalogue, which remains the standard scholarly catalogue of Haydn's works.

He was born into a bourgeois Rotterdam family, initially studied engineering before switching to music, and moved to Munich in 1917, where he entered into his relationship with Marietta di Monaco, and built his own villa two years later. He used his great wealth to collect urtexts of the great composers and worked on a project for the Austrian National Library with his former teacher, Heinrich Schencker. After the Anschluss he moved to Switzerland, dying in Zürich at the age of 96.

Marietta di Monaco (born Kirndorfer, 1893-1981), cabaret artist and *diseuse*, was one of the co-founders of the Cabaret Voltaire in Zürich and is credited with being the first to use the term "Dada" in one of her recitations at the *Simpl,* where people called her the "muse of Schwabylon". She modelled for the *Neue Sachlichkeit* school of artists and was the subject of a novel published in 1920, *Marietta. Ein Liebesroman aus Schwabing* (Marietta. A Love Story from Schwabing) by the novelist Klabund.

Mirjam Sachs (1890-1959, "the dark girl" or simply "the girl"), eventually married Graf in 1944 after he succeeded in divorcing Selma (real name: Karoline Bretting, 1889-1947). She came from Berlin, but at the time they met she was studying in Munich. She was also a friend of the poet Rainer Maria Rilke. For many years after they fled Germany, Mirjam was the main breadwinner, working as a secretary. She was the sister of Manfred Georg Cohn, who emigrated to America in 1939, where he edited *Aufbau,* a periodical published in German, which he transformed into an important weekly newspaper, especially during World War II and the postwar era, when it became an important source of information for Jews trying to establish new lives. Graf was a frequent contributor. Mirjam's cousin, Nelly Sachs, won the Nobel Prize for Literature in 1965.

Graf never got to know the daughter from his first marriage, Annemarie (13 June 1918-2008), called Annamirl, until 1958, on his first return to Germany since 1933. She had been brought up by her mother, and later became (as was usual for a girl her age) a supporter of the Nazi regime.

Of one of the most colourful characters in the novel, Wilhelm Hobrecker, I, like Oskar Maria Graf himself, can find no trace.

The fate of the Bavarian Soviet Republic & its opponents

Several insurrections took place between 1918 and 1923 in Germany, but it was only in Munich that a communist government proclaimed the dictatorship of the proletariat.

At least 606 people were killed in the suppression of the Bavarian Soviet Republic, of whom 335 were civilians. Between 1,000 and 1,200 of its actual or assumed supporters were executed in the days that followed.

Gustav Landauer was tortured and shot at Stadelheim prison. His killer was later sentenced to five weeks in prison for "dangerous assault" and stealing Landauer's watch; his abuser, Baron von Gagern, was fined 500 marks.

The commandant of the Red Army, the sailor and native of Schwabing Rudi Egelhofer, was tortured and summarily executed at the Hofbräuhaus on 3 May 1919. His final resting place was discovered and honoured in 2016.

The businessman, freethinker and anarchist Josef Sontheimer was arrested by a detachment of the *Oberland Freikorps* consisting of Thule Society combatants and murdered behind the scenes in the Franziskaner beer cellar, after they had hypocritically given him the opportunity to escape.

Eugen Leviné at least had his day in court, where he famously pronounced: "We Communists are all dead men on leave. Of this I am fully aware. I do not know if you will extend my leave or whether I shall have to join Karl Liebknecht and Rosa Luxemburg." He was sentenced to death and shot at Stadelheim on 4 June 1919.

Erich Mühsam, sentenced to 15 years' imprisonment, eventually died in Oranienburg concentration camp in 1934. Max Levien escaped to the Soviet Union, only to be executed in Stalin's anti-German purge of 1936.

The playwright Ernst Toller and the novelist Ret Marut (B. Traven) escaped.

The hostages executed by the Red Guards at the Luitpold Gymnasium were members of the antisemitic, anti-communist Thule Society. According to the Hitler biographer Ian Kershaw, the Thule Society's "membership list ... reads like a *Who's Who* of early Nazi sympathizers and leading figures in Munich".

The German Robin Hood
The Extraordinary Life of Max Hoelz

He was dubbed "the German Robin Hood" in England; to his enemies in Germany he was better known as "the Dictator of the Vogtland". Max Hoelz was a worker, engineer, soldier – and an irresistible womanizer – who became one of the most fascinating and charismatic figures during the working-class insurrections in Germany that followed the First World War. *From the 'White Cross' to the Red Flag* was the title of his autobiography, which appeared in 1929. It follows Hoelz's progress from simple farmhand through Germany to London, his efforts to educate himself, and the breathtaking action and horrors he experienced as a cavalry messenger and front-line soldier. He returns from the fighting to lead his local unemployed workers' committee, before taking up the armed struggle and a life on the run from the authorities. As leader of the Red Army in Central Germany during the Kapp Putsch of 1920 and again during the March Action a year later, Hoelz robs from the rich to give to the poor – but runs afoul of the Communist Party bureaucracy in the process. Framed for a murder he did not commit, Hoelz is sentenced to life imprisonment and begins a new struggle against the cruel regimes of Münster, Gross-Strehlitz and Sonnenburg prisons.

This book also includes Hoelz's *Indictment against Bourgeois Society*, his speech to the Moabit Special Court in Berlin on 22 June 1922, and an introduction by the translator, Ed Walker.

ALSO FROM REDLINES PRESS

Eros in Prison
Karl Plättner

Like Max Hoelz, Karl Plättner (1893-1945) led an armed band during the Central German insurrection of March 1921. For months afterwards he led the life of a bandit, robbing banks, mining companies and post offices. After a lengthy trial he was sentenced to a long prison term. Unlike Max Hoelz, Plättner had already spent years in the working-class movement and had written in favour of a proletarian dictatorship based on workers' councils. He was a founder member of the Communist Workers' Party of Germany (KAPD). *Eros im Zuchthaus* deals with the torments of enforced sexual abstinence suffered by prisoners. It won the attention and approval of the leading sexual scientist of the time, Dr. Magnus Hirschfeld, who contributed a foreword to the book. Karl Plättner also provided the inspiration for the 1928 movie, *Geschlecht in Fesseln* (Sex in Chains) while writing *Eros im Zuchthaus*. It dealt with taboo subjects such as homoeroticism that would have made such a film impossible in Hollywood. The film starred Swedish actress Mary Johnson and director Wilhelm Dieterle.

The book is translated, introduced and annotated by Ed Walker.

Printed in Great Britain
by Amazon